Special Interest Tourism

Concepts, Contexts and Cases

Edited by

Sheela Agar
University of Plymouth, UK

Graham Bus
University of Plymouth, UK

and

Rong Huang
University of Plymouth, UK

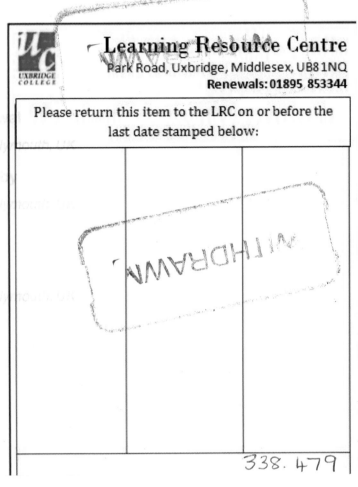

CABI

CABI is a trading name of CAB International

CABI	CABI
Nosworthy Way	745 Atlantic Avenue
Wallingford	8th Floor
Oxfordshire OX10 8DE	Boston, MA 02111
UK	USA

Tel: +44 (0)1491 832111
Fax: +44 (0)1491 833508
E-mail: info@cabi.org
Website: www.cabi.org

Tel: +1 (617)682 9015
E-mail: cabi-nao@cabi.org

A catalogue record for this book is available from the British Library, London, UK.

Library of Congress Cataloging-in-Publication Data

Names: Agarwal, Sheela, 1970- editor. | Busby, Graham, editor. | Huang, Rong (Associate professor), editor.
Title: Special interest tourism : concepts, contexts and cases / edited by Sheela Agarwal, Graham Busby, Rong Huang.
Description: Wallingford, Oxfordshire, UK ; Boston, MA : CABI, 2017. | Includes bibliographical references and index.
Identifiers: LCCN 2017035455 (print) | LCCN 2017049726 (ebook) | ISBN 9781780645674 (pdf) | ISBN 9781786394323 (ePub) | ISBN 9781780645667 (pbk. : alk. paper)
Subjects: LCSH: Tourism--Management.
Classification: LCC G155.A1 (ebook) | LCC G155.A1 S6219 2017 (print) | DDC 910.68--dc23
LC record available at https://lccn.loc.gov/2017035455

ISBN-13: 9781780645667 (pbk)
          9781780645674 (PDF)
          9781786394323 (ePub)

Commissioning editor: Claire Parfitt
Associate editor: Alexandra Lainsbury
Production editor: Tim Kapp

Typeset by SPi, Pondicherry, India
Printed and bound in the UK by CPI Group (UK) Ltd, Croydon, CR0 4YY

Contents

Contributors

Sheela Agarwal, School of Tourism and Hospitality, University of Plymouth Business School, Plymouth, PL4 8AA, UK. Email: S.Agarwal@plymouth.ac.uk

Nazia Ali, University of East London, College of Professional Services, Institute of Hospitality and Tourism, University Way, London, E16 2RD, UK. Email: naz.ali@uel.ac.uk

Richard Benfield, Department of Geography – Tourism, Central Connecticut State University, 1615 Stanley Street, New Britain, CT 06050, USA. Email: benfieldr@ccsu.edu

Ralf Buckley, International Chair in Ecotourism Research, Griffith University, Gold Coast 4222, Australia. Email: r.buckley@griffith.edu.au

Graham Busby, School of Tourism and Hospitality, University of Plymouth Business School, Plymouth, PL4 8AA, UK. Email: g.busby@plymouth.ac.uk

Alison Caffyn, Tourism consultant, Ludlow, UK and PhD researcher at Department of Geography and Planning, Cardiff University, Wales, UK. Email: alison.caffyn@gmail.com

Harry Cameron, Cardiff Metropolitan University, Llandaff Campus, Western Avenue, Cardiff, CF5 2YB, UK. Email: hcameron@cardiffmet.ac.uk

W. Glen Croy, Department of Management, Monash Business School, Monash University, Australia, and Oxford School of Hospitality Management, Oxford Brookes University, UK. Email: glen.croy@monash.edu

Violet Cuffy, Senior Lecturer, Tourism & Events Management, University of Bedfordshire, International Business, Marketing and Tourism, Luton, LU1 3JU, UK. Email: violet.cuffy@beds.ac.uk

Rong Huang, School of Tourism and Hospitality, University of Plymouth, Plymouth, PL4 8AA, UK. Email: Rong.huang@plymouth.ac.uk

Claire Humphreys, University of Westminster, 35 Marylebone Road, London, NW1 5LS, UK. Email: c.humphreys@westminster.ac.uk

Lynn Minnaert, Jonathan M. Tisch Center for Hospitality and Tourism, New York University, 7 East 12th Street, New York 10003, USA. Email: l.minnaert@nyu.edu

Ade Oriade, University of Wolverhampton Business School, Wolverhampton, WV1 1LY, UK. Email: ade.oriade@wlv.ac.uk

Derek Robbins, Senior Lecturer, Faculty of Management, Bournemouth University, BH12 5BB, UK. Email: drobbins@bournemouth.ac.uk

Carol Southall, Senior Lecturer in Tourism and Event Management, Staffordshire University Business School, School of Business, Leadership and Economics, Staffordshire University, Leek Road, Stoke-on-Trent, ST4 2DF, UK. Email: c.southall@staffs.ac.uk

Dallen J. Timothy, School of Community Resources and Development, Arizona State University, 411 N. Central Avenue, Suite 550 (MC 4020), Phoenix, AZ 85004, USA. Email: dtimothy@asu.edu

Allan Watson, Department of Geography, Loughborough University, LE11 3TU, UK. Email: A.Watson3@lboro.ac.uk

Preface

This book will provide a refreshing, engaging and integrated approach to the conceptualisation of special interest tourism from both supply- and demand-side perspectives. In essence the structure of the book will allow for the triangulation of tourism supply, demand and marketing, with each of the context chapters further dividing an increasingly fragmented tourism market into a multiplication of heterogeneous market segments. From the outset the book will examine special interest tourism concepts, policies and practices from a predominantly marketing and management perspective for students studying for a degree, diploma or single module in the subject or for tourism practitioners.

It is expected that this text will appeal to undergraduate students in the second and final years of their studies, in addition to postgraduate students. It is targeted at students studying core modules in contemporary tourism issues, special interest tourism, tourist destination management and marketing modules, and as a pre-requisite to a range of complementary tourism development and destination management modules. Additionally, it will appeal to academics, researchers and practitioners working in tourism and destination management. A key feature of this book is the inclusion of chapters contributed by leading, established academics, emerging researchers and industry practitioners.

Acknowledgements

The vision and origin of the idea for this textbook lies with Paul Williams, Head of the Business School within the Faculty of Business, Education and Law at Staffordshire University, UK. Enormous gratitude is extended to all of this book's authors for their contributions and patience.

1 Special Interest Tourism: An Introduction

SHEELA AGARWAL, GRAHAM BUSBY AND RONG HUANG

Learning Objectives

- To provide an overview of the origins and evolution of special interest tourism
- To examine the complexities of defining special interest tourism in the 21st century
- To discuss several different approaches to conceptualising and understanding special interest tourism
- To consider the marketing and types of special interest tourists

Introduction

Special interest tourism (SIT) has rapidly grown in volume and value across both the developed and developing worlds since the 1980s, fuelled on the one hand by the increasing diversity of leisure interests which characterise contemporary society (Douglas *et al.*, 2001; Trauer, 2006), and on the other by a more sophisticated and heterogeneous travel market. As a counter-point to mass tourism (Robinson and Novelli, 2005) the consequence of these drivers is the demand for more focused activity or interest-based tourism experiences (Ali-Knight, 2011) that invoke an emotional response, which require involvement and engagement, and which are intimate and personalised (Opaschowski, 2001).

The development potential of SIT is vast as it encompasses diversity, differentiation and individualism, characteristics that are becoming increasingly scarce in a globalising world accentuated by sameness (Robinson and Novelli, 2005). Indeed, Brotherton and Himmetoğlu (1997, p. 11) contend that 'the next frontier in the tourism development process lies beyond the highly packaged destination-based tourism product in the realms of SIT'. This view is reinforced by Varley and Crowther (1998, p. 318) who state that 'successfully providing the creative space for the consumer's aesthetic personal projects to unfold is surely the challenge facing the late-

modern entrepreneur'. However, what exactly is SIT? How may SIT be defined and conceptualised? How may special interest tourist experiences best be understood? And what are the characteristics of special interest tourists?

This book represents a small, individual collection of papers which together consider a range of selected forms of SIT in an attempt to provide a greater depth of understanding of its complexities. It begins with this introductory chapter, the purpose of which is to provide an overview of the key concepts and theoretical approaches to the study of SIT. Thus, the first part of this chapter details the origins and evolution of SIT, after which its meaning and nature are considered. Then several approaches to conceptualising SIT are detailed including those that incorporate product-, interactive- and service-led dimensions. Recognising that, as part of an experience-hungry society, special interest tourists seek real, authentic experiences, this chapter then discusses the nature of the SIT experience before moving on to demonstrate how an understanding of consumer behaviour, motivations, typologies and the adoption of a segmentation-based approach is useful in designing, engineering and delivering the SIT experience. Following this, a brief summary of the book's structure is provided, with particular attention being given to detailing the focus of subsequent chapters, ending with some concluding remarks.

Origins and Evolution of SIT

The term SIT was coined in the 1980s (Hall and Weiler, 1992) to describe the emergence of a phenomenon which marked a shift away from demand for mainstream tourism offerings that were standardised and rigidly packaged in nature, to forms of tourism that were more specialised and unique. The changing nature of such tourism demand has been more generally linked to the alleged shift from Fordism, characterised by mass production and economies of scale, to post-Fordism. The latter, in contrast, is consumption-led, and is based on economies of scope as consumers drive the production process so that their demand for more customised, tailor-made and differentiated products, may be catered for (Urry, 1992; Pretes, 1995).

Within tourism, a variety of different forms of tourism were created to encompass this demand, including for example alternative tourism, green tourism, sustainable tourism and responsible tourism (Ali-Knight, 2011). By implication these products were qualitatively different, and were the antithesis of mass tourism which had widely been credited with negative environmental, socio-cultural and economic impacts (Morgan and Pritchard, 1999). Combined with the influence of the growth of a more sophisticated and experienced consumer, global economic restructuring, the evolution of tourist buying behaviour, and the search for individuality, mass packaged holidays became less fashionable as tourists began seeking alternative, more personalised modes of delivery. Consequently, for many, mass tourism was no longer seen as the dominant paradigm, and the special interest tourism segment became the 'new' tourism (Poon, 1993) of the 1980s and 1990s. For Poon (1989, p. 98) 'the economics of the 'new tourism' are very different from the old – profitability no longer rests solely on economies of scale and the exploitation of mass undifferentiated markets'. Thus, types of tourism products typically associated with these earlier notions of SIT include ecotourism, adventure tourism and cultural tourism (Ali-Knight, 2011), and they focused on relatively small, homogeneous groups of consumers that were similar to what Stebbins (1982) termed specialised, serious leisure consumers.

As SIT has evolved over time, the nature of this form of tourism has become ever more complex. This is in part because in order to tap latent demand and attract a larger market segment of the 'soft' or 'novice' (Trauer, 2006, p. 184) special interest tourist, individual operators capitalised on their own expertise of a special interest and developed more diversified offerings. Stebbins (1997, p. 18) labels such markets 'casual' consumers who are motivated by a desire to pursue a 'relatively short-lived pleasurable activity requiring little or no special training to enjoy it'. In addition, contemporary tourist demands before, during and after visitation, incorporating experiences which evoked an emotional response and which are involving and engaging, became more central. This is because, as Hall and Weiler (1992) suggest, the growth of SIT is reflective of the diversity of interests of contemporary society that encompass increasing concerns for environmental conservation and for society more generally, and the desire for self-improvement and self-fulfilment. Thus, according to Opaschowski (2001), tourists want to personally experience the immaterial qualities, seeking ambiance, aesthetics and atmosphere. Such a transition from what was essentially specialist product-based demand to a demand for experience or service encounters has been linked more broadly to the rise of the 'experience economy' (Pine and Gilmore, 1999), whereby memories, sensations, engagement, fantasy, involvement and emotions have value, and are packaged, commoditised and sold to create unforgettable, highly satisfying experiences.

Over the course of the last thirty years, it is clear to see that SIT has evolved from the creation of a fairly narrow set of highly specialised products, designed to cater for relatively small numbers of tourists, to one that appeals to a much larger and more mainstream audience, and which enables a more meaningful set of experiences to be created. Robinson and Novelli (2005, p. 26) argue that this change is reflective of contemporary tourism since it involves 'a series of subjective emotional experiences'. As a consequence, SIT has become a highly attractive business that enables destinations in pursuit of economic development to tap into, and exploit a vast range of markets, based on forms of tourism that at least on the surface appear to be qualitatively different (Morgan and Pritchard, 1999) from traditional notions of mass tourism. It is in this respect however, that there has been a blurring of boundaries between mass tourism and SIT, particularly since the latter was originally based on the notion that it was small-scale and primarily involved non-commercialised forms of travel as opposed to mass tourism.

In addressing such ambiguity, the issue of context and scale become important here. Clearly there are numerous local examples of companies which offer types of small-scale SIT in a range of destinations. Many belong to the Association of Independent Tour Operators (AITO), and offer small escorted group tours, for example to Iceland's Snaefellsnes peninsula to watch orcas, or small guided tours of the scenic spring wild flower drives in South Africa's west coast, Cederberg and Namaqualand (AITO,

2017). Others, however, such as safari holidays in Kenya, although initially starting out on a small-scale basis, appealing predominantly to wildlife enthusiasts, have evolved over time. Consequently, despite being cleverly packaged and marketed so as to appear to be more personalised in nature, this form of SIT is now offered on a mass scale by large multinational companies including TUI and First Choice.

This contention is reinforced by Ali-Knight (2011, p. 10) who cites 'its use by a large number of tourists and large multinational companies (e.g. a packaged summer cultural tour of Florence including queuing at the Uffizi Museum) offering fairly standardised and homogenised products. At the other end of the spectrum, smaller community-based and locally owned enterprises occur offering highly individualised experiences (e.g. a locally run winery tour in Tuscany)'. Furthermore, it is a view emphasised by Novelli (2005) who recognised the existence of a niche tourism continuum with macro-niches at one end occupying relatively large market shares (e.g. ecotourism) and further segmented micro-niches at the other end of the spectrum (wildlife tourism).

Thus, it may be argued that it is more appropriate to view many forms of SIT tourism as a 'wolf in sheep's clothing'. The structure of the SIT is reflective of an increase in production flexibility that has occurred across the tourism industry, resulting in what Ioannides and Debbage (1997, p. 119) describe as 'a complex and inchoate polyglot of [co-existing] production forms'. In light of the co-existence of a variety of forms of SIT, it is a deceptively complex term to define.

Meaning and Nature of SIT

Hall and Weiler (1992, p. 5) provided one of the first definitions, proposing that it occurs when 'travellers' motivations and decision-making are primarily determined by a particular special interest'. Other academics have elaborated upon this understanding by identifying key characteristics that may be associated with SIT (Brotherton and Himmetoğlu, 1997; Derrett, 2001; Douglas *et al.*, 2001; Swarbrooke and Horner, 2004). These include:

- SIT is motivated by a desire to engage in new or existing interests in a novel or familiar location;
- SIT is the opposite of mass tourism;
- SIT is undertaken for a specific or distinct purpose;

- SIT emanates from the desire to deliver a more sustainable form of tourism; and
- SIT involves flexible delivery, market segmentation and advances in technology.

In short, SIT is a term that can be used to describe products that have been tailored to meet the needs of a particular audience and/or market segment. Special interest tourists therefore have specific interest-based motivations for travel, and are distinctive from what Brotherton and Himmetoğlu (1997) describe as general interest tourists, whose motivation for travel is stimulated by the general destination and its characteristics. According to Ali-Knight (2011, p. 23) it relates to 'the super-segmentation of larger homogeneous markets such as cultural tourism, heritage tourism or event tourism, into small, more focused markets that better reflect the activities that tourists engage in'.

However, the notion of SIT being associated with super-segmentation of the market based on tourist motivation and purpose has compounded some of the ambiguities surrounding the term. On the one hand, McKercher and Chan (2005) challenge the idea that SIT should not be viewed as a distinctive form of tourism. They argue that although secondary to their reason to travel, tourists participate in a wide variety of activities and interests at a destination. Furthermore, Stebbins (1997, p. 19) argues that the majority of special-interest tourists are no different from what he terms casual leisure participants who unconsciously 'often dabble in or play around at an activity pursued as serious leisure by others'. Indeed Eagles (1996) and Craik (1997) support this notion in the context of ecotourism and cultural tourism.

On the other hand, SIT is often confused with niche tourism and both terms are used interchangeably. This is because the latter term is generally understood to refer to how a specific product can be tailored to meet the needs of a particular audience or market segment, resulting in the creation of niche tourism products which appeal and are targeted at niche tourism markets (Novelli, 2005). Clearly, there are overlaps between SIT and niche tourism. In truth there is little that separates them, other than the latter is perhaps more production-centred whilst the former is driven by the consumer's specific interest-based motivations. Given these definitional difficulties, it is not surprising that a number of approaches have been proposed to conceptualise SIT.

Towards a conceptualisation of SIT

Product-supply approach

Traditional ways of conceptualising SIT adopt a tourism product-supply approach. This is tourism-centric in nature, and focuses on a range of products that may be developed around a variety of tourism activities undertaken in cultural, environmental, rural, urban and other settings (see Fig. 1.1). According to Ali-Knight (2011), the development of specific tailored products at a destination level is a means of attracting high-end, high-yield tourists through the provision of an individualised service. Added-value related activities may also be offered which increases visitation and expenditure. Destinations therefore can develop a SIT portfolio which enables them to differentiate themselves from their competitors and to compete more successfully in a highly cluttered tourism environment (Sharpley and Telfer, 2002).

While the product-supply approach is useful in highlighting the diversity of SIT products that may be undertaken in a range of environments, given the growth, evolution and super-segmentation of SIT, clearly such an approach is less than satisfactory in elucidating understanding of contemporary developments. Thus, in order to understand how SIT products help to market, promote, develop and differentiate a tourist destination, an understanding of the motivations and needs of tourists who seek these products and services is essential (Ali-Knight, 2011). A market-led approach can therefore be valuable in conceptualising SIT.

Market-led approach

In contrast to attention being focused on the characteristics of a destination, as is the case for the product-supply perspective, it is the characteristics of special interest tourists – their motivations, behaviour and their consumption of products that have been tailored to meet the needs of a particular audience and/or market segment – that are the key concern

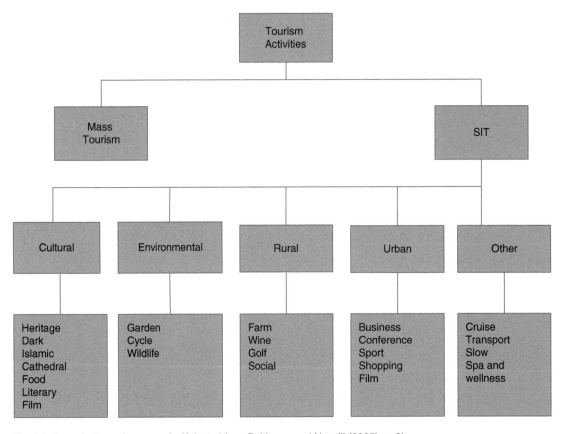

Fig. 1.1. A product supply approach. (Adapted from Robinson and Novelli (2005), p. 9)

S. Agarwal, G. Busby and R. Huang

of a market-led approach to SIT (Brotherton and Himmetoğlu, 1997). Motivation is generally understood to reflect a state of arousal of a drive or need, which induces a pursuit of goals; to date, in the context of tourism, numerous classifications of motivational factors have been posited (e.g. Plog, 1974; Crompton, 1979; Gray, 1979; Dann, 1981; Pearce, 1988). Some are general in nature and based on the motivations of a person who chooses to travel, whilst others are based on the motivations which lead a person to choose a particular form of tourism to engage with (Swarbrooke and Horner, 2004). Since special interest tourists have specific interest-based motivations for travel, the latter is arguably the most useful to furthering understanding of SIT. It consists of *psychological* motivations such as the desire for relaxation, exercise and health; *emotional* motivations which might include nostalgia, romance, adventure, escape, fantasy, and spiritual needs; *personal development* motivations including raising the level of knowledge or learning a new skill; and *cultural* motivations, for example sightseeing or the experience of other cultures.

Given that SIT may be understood as the desire for particular products, then it is possible to identify a SIT spectrum, underpinned by a set of motivations which are driving demand and participation (see Fig. 1.2). Of course, it is important to note that several motivations may be driving an individual to participate in a particular form of SIT, and consequently, such categories should not be viewed as being mutually exclusive or self-contained. A good illustration of this point is the example of film tourism. A number of authors have identified that the motivations of film tourists include the desire for emotion engagement and involvement (Carl *et al.*,

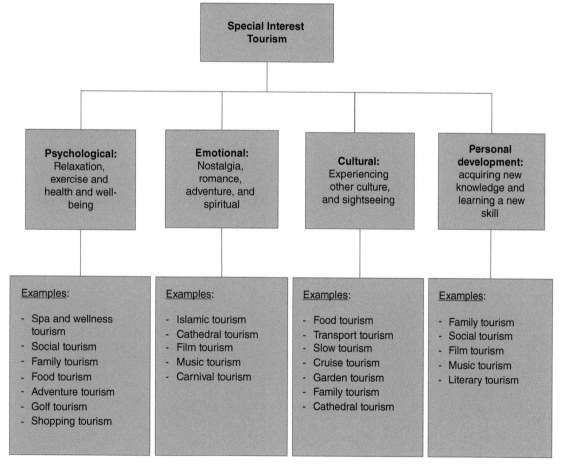

Fig. 1.2. Special Interest Tourism spectrum.

2007; Kim, 2010; Buchmann *et al.*, 2010), but also the desire to experience the cultural landscape (Connell, 2012), and for status and prestige (Macionis and Sparks, 2009).

Thus, forms of SIT may appear to be underpinned by more than one motivational driver. Trauer (2006) also makes this point by demonstrating how various special interest segments can merge with other SIT categories. To illustrate this she provides the examples of sport, rural, event and adventure tourism which all may be considered to be separate forms of tourism with their own distinctive characteristics until, that is, a mountain bike event held in a mountainous region is introduced, thereby transversing all four SIT segments. What is clear here is that the types of products that fall within the special interest tourism spectrum are highly specialised, and are tailored around the needs, demands, and anticipated and expected experiences of particular audiences. SIT is thus a product spawned from demand and supply; it is the demand and the creation of products that appeal to these distinctive market segments which enable destinations to differentiate themselves

in a fiercely competitive market-place. As such then, perhaps it is more appropriate to view SIT as an interactive system.

An interactive systems approach

So far, the approaches to conceptualising SIT have concentrated on supply, as in the case of the product-supply perspective, or on demand, which is the primary focus of a market-led viewpoint. In many respects demand and supply are inter-related and thus, an alternative approach to conceptualising SIT is to instead view it as part of 'an interdisciplinary system' (Trauer, 2006, p. 185). This consists of an amalgamation of the 'overall environment, the tourist demand system, the tourism industry supply system, with the media being conceptualised as a major influencer on tourism in the 21st century' (Trauer, 2006, p. 185; see Fig. 1.3). This interactive system encompasses the political, economic, ecological, technological, socio-economic and socio-cultural environments at local to global levels. The tourism industry supply system comprises elements

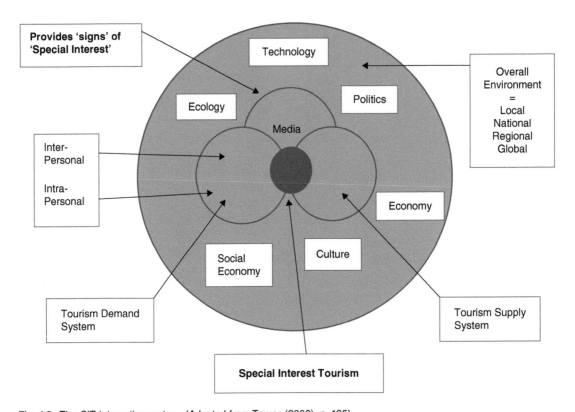

Fig. 1.3. The SIT interactive system. (Adapted from Trauer (2006), p. 185)

S. Agarwal, G. Busby and R. Huang

such as tourist destinations, tour operators and travel agents, accommodation units, transport providers, and SIT amenities and infrastructure. Meanwhile, the tourist demand system encompasses intrinsic and extrinsic characteristics relating to the individual tourist such as their financial situation, their ability to access and participate in SIT, and their motivations (e.g. desires and needs, level of involvement or personal development).

At the core of the SIT interactive system sits the influence of the media as it is the latter that shapes the representation of SIT products by suppliers and which helps give the tourist meaning to their experience prior to, during and after, their participation in SIT. This is because the media including tourism brochures, magazines, books, films, television and the internet generate images and convey stories which induce and fuel desires, wants and needs. They create the anticipation before a trip by providing a medium for tourists to envisage themselves in place and in action (Kim and Richardson, 2003). Moreover, according to Trauer (2006, p. 186) 'It generates positive cognitive and affective response – knowledge of and familiarity with the activity and places within which it occurs, and an emotive response to those activities'.

The media is thus instrumental in the formation of tourists' pre-conceived ideas about the destination they are visiting and the experiences they have been 'promised', and often it is these narratives that the tourists try to relive and mirror during their holiday. The media is often used as a source of information by tourists during a holiday or experience, thereby serving to further embed pre-conceived perceptions and expectations, and is used after the event as tourists often share their experiences with other tourists. The media therefore helps to shape the information and image of destinations (Butler, 1990) and plays a fundamental role in raising awareness of a destination, destination image formation and intention to visit (Gartner, 1993; Govers et al., 2007; Harrill and Peterson, 2012).

Consequently, given the media influence on the demand and supply of SIT, it perhaps isn't surprising that Trauer (2006) places it at the heart of her SIT interactive system. However, what this conceptualisation more importantly highlights is the centrality of the interaction between tourists and producers/suppliers, which goes beyond the simple act of demand and supply, in shaping the experiences of special interest tourists. Such interaction is facilitated by engagement platforms, primarily social media, which allow ongoing collaboration and communication amongst firms, customers and other stakeholders (Vargo and Lusch, 2016). The emergence of this new relationship between consumers and producers has been more recently captured within theorisations provided by co-creation and service-dominant logic (S-DL).

Co-creation and service-dominant logic approaches

In light of the increasing demand for more participative and interactive experiences previously described, the term co-creation coined by Prahalad and Ramaswamy (2004) outlines this shift from passive to active consumers. Co-creation is generated by 'The joint creation of value by the company and the customer; allowing the customer to co-construct the service experience to suit their context' (Prahalad and Ramaswamy, 2004, p. 8; see Fig. 1.4). Many consumers, it is argued, are co-creators and co-producers of value through service experiences and relationships (Vargo and Lusch, 2004), with such experiences, based on engaging customers by providing a memorable and personal product, appealing to their sensations.

The ideas underpinning co-creation led Vargo and Lusch (2004) to propose the Service-Dominant Logic (S-DL) which places customers also as the co-creators of value (Lusch and Vargo, 2006; Payne et al., 2008). It highlights the customer–supplier relationship through interaction and dialogue (Shaw et al., 2011) in which customers are viewed as operant resources. They apply their skills, knowledge and expertise to create the service which is the essence of the exchange (Vargo and Lusch, 2008). Thus, through constructive customer participation, they are actively involved in the co-production of service creation and delivery (Auh et al., 2007), and as a result, are integrally involved in the design and development of new products and services (Shaw et al., 2011). Of particular importance here is the recognition that the characteristics of the consumers are unique and therefore, each affect the process in different ways (Pralahad and Ramaswamy, 2004).

Co-creation and S-DL are highly relevant to tourism generally and to SIT specifically as both are intrinsically involved in the selling of personalised and memorable experiences (Holbrooke, 2006; Volo, 2009; Kim, 2010). Tourists are no longer

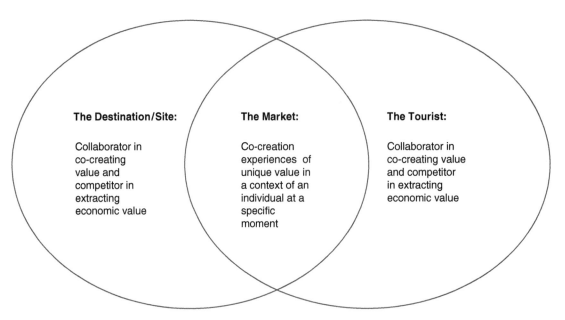

Fig. 1.4. SIT and co-creation.

buying and the suppliers of tourism products do not charge for goods and services (Richards, 2014). In fact according to Neuhofer *et al.* (2013, p. 3) 'Co-creation postulates that companies merely facilitate 'experience environments' for tourists (the beneficiaries), who use their resources for unique value to be extracted'. Instead, tourists are co-creators of their experiences (Prebensen *et al.*, 2013; Tan *et al.*, 2013; Campos *et al.*, 2015) and of value (Rihova *et al.*, 2014) through the meanings they derive from the experience that they have created, directed, produced and consumed. As a result, such experiences should be made as real, memorable, stimulating, compelling, personal and satisfying as possible (Pine and Gilmore, 1999; Andrades and Dimanche, 2014). Clearly the service dimension entailed with SIT is critically important to not only conceptualising SIT but also shedding light on the SIT experience, and it is to this issue that this chapter next turns its attention.

Understanding the SIT Experience

So far this chapter has discussed a number of approaches to conceptualising SIT. In doing so, the motivational factor, the need for involvement and engagement, is highlighted as being a key characteristic of SIT, as it creates the foundations for the co-creation and co-production of tailored and individual experiences. Indeed, there are many studies within the SIT arena which highlight the importance of involvement and engagement in co-creating the tourist experience. For example, in the context of film tourism, Couldry (2007) suggested that becoming a film tourist required a considerable amount of emotional investment. Such a view is reinforced by the investigation by Carl *et al.* (2007) of on-site experiences of film tourists visiting 'Hobbiton' (Matamata and Wellington), two main locations for the *Lord of the Rings* films in New Zealand, and by the work of Reijnders (2011) who found

S. Agarwal, G. Busby and R. Huang

that some tourists attempting to connect with Stoker's novel *Dracula* (1897) and its screen adaptations wished to gain an emotional experience which he terms the 'lieux d'imagination' (p.15).

Involvement itself is a multi-dimensional construct, partly because it may be applied in many different ways and can result in different responses. For instance, involvement may be induced by an advert, a product or during a purchase decision, and may result in greater product knowledge, greater commitment to a brand, or to an extended search for related products and/or experiences. Within the field of consumer behaviour, drawing on the work of Rothschild (1984) and Havitz and Dimanche (1997), Andrades and Dimanche (2014, p. 97) define it as 'an unobservable state of motivation, arousal or interest toward a recreational activity or associated product'. Additionally, it is generally understood that levels of involvement may be affected by different situations, people and physical characteristics of the product (Houston and Rothschild, 1978; Bloch and Richins, 1983), and reflects the relevance of a product or activity to an individual. In the context of tourism, according to Trauer (2006, p. 191) involvement 'has been interpreted as a process of psychological identification resulting in varying degrees of behavioural, cognitive, and affective investment in an activity, product or situation'. Several scales have been proposed in a bid to measure its influence on behaviour such as The Personal Involvement Inventory (Zaichkowsky, 1985) and the Consumer Involvement Profile (Laurent and Kapferer, 1985).

It is thus a complex construct, consisting of multiple antecedents and dimensions (see Table 1.1), some of which are enduring whilst others are more situational (Richins *et al.*, 1992). With regards to the latter, although these are of personal relevance to an individual, they relate more to the context of place and time, and are dynamic components or stimuli such as place promotion and marketing which may influence an individual's level of involvement. In contrast, the former relates to the level of importance an individual attaches to a product and/or activity, is dependent on their personal values and is more stable and constant since it is derived from intrinsic motivations (Andrades and Dimanche, 2014). The *affective/personal, identity affirmation/expression* and *centrality* dimensions are all aspects of enduring involvement that are situated within the broader context of a tourist's life, thereby generating a continuum of level of involvement from low to high.

Certainly the view that involvement comprises enduring and situational components is widely supported (Cohen, 1972; Pearce, 1988; Sharpley, 1999) though most research to date within tourism has focused on the enduring aspects (Andrades and Dimanche, 2014). Nevertheless, given that involvement

Table 1.1. The antecedents and dimensions of involvement. Compiled from Havitz and Dimanche (1999); Iwasaki and Havitz (1998); Kyle and Chick (2004); Laurent and Kapferer (1985); McIntyre (1990); McIntyre and Pigram (1992) and Trauer (2006).

Antecedents of involvement	Dimensions of involvement
Individual mediating facets	*Affective/Personal*
Values or beliefs, attitudes, motivation, needs or goals, skills and competence, prior experiences of pleasure experienced	Degree of interest, attraction, importance, and enjoyment and pleasure associated with a product or activity
Individual moderating facets	*Identity affirmation/expression*
Intrapersonal constraints including personal finances, health, access, and anticipation of personal benefits	Symbolic value or statement made to self or to others regarding the product or activity; degree to which driven by social ties
Social-situational moderating facets	*Centrality*
Support from others, incentives, cultural norms, intrapersonal constraints, anticipation of benefits and rewards	Importance of product or activity to an individual sometimes reflected in life-style choices
	Risk probability
	Perceived potential of making a wrong or poor purchase
	Risk consequence
	Perceived importance of negative consequences of wrong or poor purchase

may vary in intensity at any one time, combined with the existence of a multiplicity of motivations, there is an obvious need to embrace a theoretical framework which is capable of capturing the complex and dynamic interplay of micro- and macro-factors together with the multi-phasic nature of SIT, in which to conceptualise tourist behaviour and experiences. It is in this context, based on the multi-dimensional and cyclic concept of involvement, that Trauer (2006, p. 194) proposes her model of the SIT Experience.

The SIT experience

The SIT experience provides a framework for exploring the influence of possible enduring involvement in the leisure (home) context and situational involvement within tourism, with a potential for a career path in SIT (see Figure 1.5). It consists of a four cell matrix, organised around a horizontal and a vertical axis. The horizontal axis represents a continuum of multi-dimensional involvement that ranges from low, in the case of an individual being attracted to a SIT activity or setting for instance, to high, characterised by centrality and commitment. The vertical axis is also representative of a continuum, in this case, participation (Trauer, 2006) which ranges from one-off experiences to more enduring involvement reflected in repeat purchasing or participation, the acquisition

of behaviour, cognitive, social and psychological skills and engagement in more risky challenges.

The four-cell matrix itself is comprised of types of special interest tourists (expert/specialist, collector and novice), and four related zones (risk, high challenge, exploration and comfort). The 'SIT Expert/Specialist', is highly involved in terms of interest and experience in travel, and chooses SIT products and experiences that are fundamental to their way of life. 'The Novice' meanwhile is characterised by low experience, lack of familiarity with the activity and limited exposure to it but who in their desire for self-expression and for change, seeks fashionable and/or popular products or experiences. This type of tourist is similar to what Brotherton and Himmetoğlu (1997) term 'dabblers' who will select suitable products and experiences depending on their perceptions and attitudes towards risk. Thus, according to Trauer (2006, p. 194), the 'Novice' is pursuing a special interest 'of high importance and centrality to the 'Expert/Specialist Interest Tourist' as well as the 'Travelling Recreation Expert/Specialist' while being a novice at travel'. As a consequence of exploring travel as a new interest, the novice strays into the realms of the 'SIT Collector's expertise of travel (Trauer, 2006). In contrast, the 'SIT Collector' participates in, and essentially collects, a variety of SIT experiences/products, while the 'The Travelling Special Interest Expert' consists of individuals who

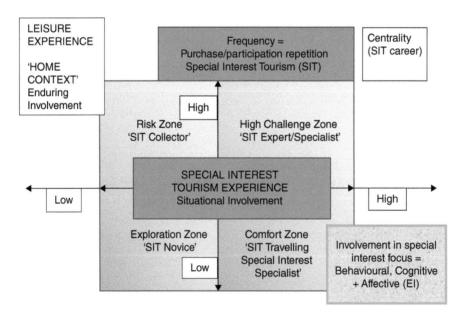

Fig. 1.5. The SIT experience. (Adapted from Trauer (2006), p. 194)

                                                       S. Agarwal, G. Busby and R. Huang

are highly involved from a leisure perspective, but are infrequent travellers and therefore remain in the comfort zone.

Although this model has not been empirically tested, it does however appear to be applicable to a number of different types of special interest tourism, including for example adventure tourism and dive tourism. Indeed, based on Ewert and Hollenhorst's (1989) adventure recreation framework, Trauer (2006) illustrates the applicability of the SIT Experience model to adventure tourism and presents a refined version adapted to this context. Garrod (2008) also notes the model's fit in the context of dive tourism. In particular, he highlights its value in incorporating the spectrum of divers' involvement ranging from hard-core enthusiasts to casual divers, which appear also to mirror contemporary trends in scuba-diving participation. Moreover, Garrod (2008) also draws attention to the model's utility since it also encompasses notions of complexity and challenge which have become increasingly important motivational factors as divers become more experienced.

When taken together, these studies serve to highlight the importance of examining the characteristics and attributes of the product alongside the nature and level of a tourist's involvement. This is arguably a key consideration given the complexity of SIT. Such an approach is captured in Trauer's (2006) SIT Product Experience framework. This conceptualisation brings together SIT product dimensions consisting of their individual characteristics and setting attributes, with those attributes associated with any individual who might participate in SIT which may influence their decision-making, experience and satisfaction (see Table 1.2). Such an approach is useful in informing its planning, development, management and marketing and may be applied to any form of SIT in any context and circumstance. In summarising a range of individual attributes associated with special interest tourists, it also highlights the diversity of demand which exists for SIT. Consequently a thorough understanding of the nature of SIT markets and types of tourists are required if a complete examination of SIT is to be achieved. It is this very issue that this chapter next considers.

The SIT Market: Typologies and Behaviour

Consideration of the nature and meaning of SIT in addition to approaches to its conceptualisation have inevitably touched upon aspects of the SIT market, particularly regarding the types of tourists with specific motivations who engage in this form of tourism. Indeed, if we accept the notion that SIT is distinct from mass tourism since it emanates

Table 1.2. The SIT product experience. (Adapted from Trauer (2006))

Product attributes	Individual attributes
Product specific	*Behavioural*
Perceived and real risk (soft to adrenalin-induced adventure tourism)	Frequency of participation (measures prior experience with activity, familiarity of setting)
Competition (play/social to pure sport or serious orientation in sport tourism)	
Formality (informal to formal in education, cultural or heritage tourism or ecotourism)	
Depth of interest (shallow to deep in heritage, cultural and ecotourism)	
Social orientation	*Cognitive*
Individual, family, friends, peers, teams, courses	Skills, knowledge, setting attributes – low to high
	Locus of control/autonomy (perceived to real competence)
Environmental/physical orientation	*Affective*
Natural/unstructured to developed/structured	Importance/enjoyment (attraction)
	Self-expression
	Centrality
Local to global	*Risk probability*
Familiarity/proximity to novel/exotic	Choosing one activity/product over other options
Access	*Risk consequences*
Cost, time, equity, low to high	Making poor choices

from a specific desire to pursue a special interest, by implication, its participants are imbued with particular characteristics and motivations from which a unique special interest tourist typology may be discerned. Research of tourist typologies has traditionally neglected to consider in any real depth the particularities of special interest tourists and that which does relate to SIT, has generally been undertaken in relation to a specific interest. For example, Fogelman (1992) proposed a golfing tourist typology for this specific type of SIT. More recent examples include typologies that have emerged from studies of cultural tourism (e.g. Richards, 1996; McKercher, 2002), film tourism (Macionis, 2004), heritage tourism (Peterson, 1994; Kerstetter *et al.*, 1998; Prentice *et al.*, 1998), educational tourism (Arsenault, 1998, 2001), bicycle tourism (Morpeth, 2001) and wine tourism (Charters and Ali-Knight, 2002; Marzo-Navarro and Pedraja-Iglesias, 2010).

Thus, typologies of special interest tourists are rare. One exception was proposed by Culligan (1992) who, in suggesting a travel career path for general interest tourist holiday-makers linked to increased travel experience, greater confidence and increased affluence over time (see Fig. 1.6), identified a grouping of tourists - 'Total Immersers', who desired more adventurous, more risky, novel and authentic experiences; such characteristics and motivations reflect contemporary desires of special interest tourists and are those that have been identified to lie at the heart of Trauer's (2006) SIT experience. Culligan's (1992) notion that tourists may 'trade up' over time was of course not new, having been previously aired by Smith (1979), Wynne (1990) and Brown (1992). It was later developed further by Brotherton and Himmetoğlu (1997) who, based on Culligan's framework, proposed their 'Tourism Interest Continuum', consisting of general interest tourists, mixed interest tourists and special interest tourists.

This conceptualisation suggested that tourists opt for more adventurous forms of tourism as their travel experience increases and as they mature or pass through the life-cycle. Thus, the focus of the decision-making process of general interest tourists would be 'where would I like to go?', with 'where do I want to go and what activities can I pursue there?' for the mixed interest tourists, and 'what interest/activity do I want to pursue, and where can I do it?' for the special interest tourist (p.17). Based on this transitional platform, Brotherton and Himmetoğlu (1997) then went on to focus on special interest tourists and proposed four distinct types each with their own set of salient characteristics: Dabblers, Enthusiasts, Experts and Fanatics (see Table 1.3).

Despite the lack of specific special interest typologies, the wealth of those which share particular

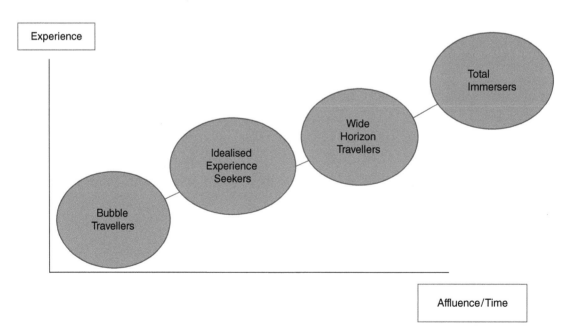

Fig. 1.6. Travel career path for general interest tourists. (Adapted from Culligan (1992))

S. Agarwal, G. Busby and R. Huang

Table 1.3. Special interest tourist typology. (Adapted from Brotherton and Himmetoğlu (1997), p. 19)

The Dabbler	The Enthusiast	The Expert	The Fanatic
Desires a change from the boredom of previous travel experiences	Interests are clearly defined and like to choose one activity to pursue rather than many	Has a high level of skill and/or extensive knowledge of chosen special interest	Entirely devoted to the pursuit of their chosen special interest and thrives on fear and adrenalin
Requires familiarity with their everyday lives and will select the novel or different	More aware of needs and capabilities and of the interests/experiences which will satisfy them	Strongly committed to a specific activity or experience	Highly committed to the pursuit of their chosen activity or experience, which almost represents a form of addiction
Concerned with symbolic value and social status, so activity likely to be fashionable	A level of commitment is discernible, as there is a wish to develop skills, expertise and knowledge	The activity or experience is central to their home (leisure) life	Generates intense motivation which may result in the pursuit of the activity beyond reasonable limits
Their skill or expertise in chosen activity will be low and safety is an important consideration	Possesses a positive self-image, confident and self-assured	Desire to experience the activity/experience with other like-minded and skilled individuals	Highly skilled individuals with a wide range of experiences in practising chosen activity/interest
Requires a considerable amount of information on the activity/experience choice available to them	Demands a higher level of challenge than the Dabbler and desires a range of new but not overly demanding opportunities to practise their interest	Desire to undertake activity/experience in risky, challenging environments and to have the opportunity of obtaining further qualifications and skills	Likely to be independent travellers, as standard packages are unlikely to meet their needs. Moreover opportunities for the gaining of advanced qualifications will not be highly valued
Upwardly mobile and socially aspirational	The activity pursued represents a life-style enhancement	Their chosen experience reaffirms their identity	Pursuit of activity is dominant motivating factor
Need to be persuaded that the change is good for them	Provision of creature comforts is important as is the social aspect	Demands tailor-made packages or engages in independent travel	Desire for 'off the beaten track' destinations for a customised and individual experience

pursuits, interests and/or activities, heralded a shift in studies of SIT away from a dominant concern with the destination and its amenities, and towards the activities that tourists might like to pursue whilst on holiday. Such a focus enables the planning, development, management and marketing to be more targeted. From a marketing perspective, niche marketing has emerged to describe a process of 'concentrating marketing resources and efforts on one particular market segment' (Huh and Singh, 2007, p. 213). Thus, there is likely to be a high degree of product specialisation, as marketing activities are likely to focus on a smaller segment of the market, be customer centric, and involve product differentiation and relationship marketing (Dalgic and Leeuw, 1994).

According to Dalgic and Leeuw (1994, p. 43), niche markets are 'steadily eating up parts of the formerly traditional mass markets' resulting in a myriad of fractured markets in contrast to one mass market' (Dalgic and Leeuw, 1994, p. 43). Companies are realising that they have to tailor their products and services to customer needs and tastes. Thus, according to Ali-Knight (2011), the focus has shifted away from the pursuit of the mass market and towards particular market segments. Niche marketing therefore adopts a customer-centric approach, because as Dalgic and Leeuw state (1994, p. 46), 'if you can involve your customer in the design of your product you are half-way there'. Such involvement in co-creation and co-production is even more pertinent with the growth of e-marketing and the prevalence of online social networks (Ali-Knight, 2011), combined with increasing demands for interactive, real and authentic experiences. The extent to which SIT experiences are authentic and indeed whether special interest tourists are capable of distinguishing between authentic and inauthentic experiences is an over-arching issue which commanded much interest alongside examinations of the characteristics and motivations of special interest tourists. It is this very issue that the final section of this introductory chapter explores.

SIT and the Contested Concept of Authenticity

Authenticity is an extremely complex and contestable term that has been used in a variety of different ways within the tourism literature. Cohen (1988) for example explains that it has not only been used to describe something that is real or genuine but has also become a socially constructed concept based on individual subjective perceptions which varies according to the tourist and their point of view (Cohen, 1988). Alternatively, Selwyn (1996) uses 'hot authenticity' and 'cool authenticity' to distinguish between tourism which is based on fiction and myths as in the case of 'hot authenticity' and that which relates to the aspects and products of society that are verified as being authentic by science-based investigations. Meanwhile, Wang (1999) proposes a classification of three different and discrete types of authenticity: (i) object, (ii) constructive and (iii) existential. Object authenticity refers to the originality of an object such as a site or a specific event which can be measured with pre-determined criteria. Constructive refers to the heterogeneous ways that tourists perceive authenticity, whilst existential authenticity relates more to the tourist rather than the object in question and equates more to an emotional experience in which contemporary tourists make meaning from their travel experiences (Reisinger and Steiner, 2006).

Based on these understandings, at one level, SIT is perhaps arguably no more or no less authentic than mass tourism. This is because although SIT destination images may also be based to varying degrees on truths and myths, on metaphors and similes, on the authentic and the inauthentic, in an attempt to entertain and provide spectacles for special interest tourists, clearly, it is a negotiated process. It is unique to each individual tourist, and thus its meaning and importance can only be assessed alongside an understanding of the various manifestations of special interest tourist experiences (Li, 2000; Reisinger and Steiner, 2006; Wang, 2007). Related to this contention is a parallel issue which revolves around the ability of special interests to identify an inauthentic experience. Again, this ability is unique to the individual and very much depends on their needs and motivations, their level of interest, expertise and knowledge of their particular interest, and their experience of travel. It is at this juncture that the arguments rehearsed in this chapter come full circle, as deeply embedded in contemporary understandings of SIT are its meaning, the conceptualisation approaches that may be adopted to explore it, and resulting experiences and the motivations, behaviour and types of special interest tourists. These issues amongst others are explored with reference to selected examples of SIT, within the remaining chapters of this textbook.

Book Structure and Conclusion

The structure of the book consists of a total of seventeen chapters, including this introduction and the conclusion, with each focusing on a specific 'interest' or tourism theme, organised into five distinct sections. Each of the chapters will cover a variety of aspects and present a contextualised overview of contemporary academic research, concepts and principles, and industry-based practice insights, linking theoretical frameworks to practice, and underpinned by current international examples and case studies. Part One, entitled 'family and faith' covers social tourism (Dr Lynn Minnaert, New York University, USA), family tourism (Carol Southall, Staffordshire University, UK), cathedral tourism (Dr Ade Oriade, University of Wolverhampton, UK), and Islamic tourism (Dr Nazia Ali). Part Two deals with the 'performing arts', and topics of interest here are literary tourism (Dr Graham Busby, Plymouth University, UK), music tourism (Dr Allan Watson, Staffordshire University, UK), film tourism (Dr Glen Croy, Monash University, Australia), and carnival tourism (Dr Violet Cuffy, University of Bedfordshire, UK). Meanwhile, Part Three relates to 'active' forms of special interest tourism and encompasses golf tourism (Dr Claire Humphreys, Westminster University, UK) and adventure tourism (Professor Ralph Buckley, Griffith University, Australia).

Part Four focuses on aspects of special interest tourism that involve 'therapeutic leisure', and the specific chapters in this section relate to 'shopping tourism' (Professor Dallen Timothy, Arizona State University, USA), 'food tourism' (Dr Rong Huang, University of Plymouth, UK), and 'garden tourism'

(Dr Richard Benfield, Central Connecticut State University, USA). The final section of this book, Part Five, is structured along the theme of 'travelling along', and consequently the forms of tourism that are discussed include 'transport tourism' (Mr Derek Robbins, Bournemouth University, UK), and 'slow tourism' (Ms Alison Caffyn, Tourism Practitioner and Consultant, UK). The textbook ends with a conclusion, in which a summary and some further insights are provided for each chapter and in which the future of SIT is considered in light of the emergence of ethical consumerism.

References

Ali-Knight, J.M. (2011) The Role of Niche Tourism Products in Destination Development. PhD Thesis, Napier University, Edinburgh, UK.

Andrades, L. and Dimanche, F. (2014) Co-creation of experience value: a tourist behaviour approach. In: Prebensen, N., Chen, J. and Uysal, M. (eds) *Creating Experience Value in Tourism*. CAB International, Wallingford, UK, pp. 95–112.

Arsenault, N. (1998) A Study of Educational Travel and Older Adult Learners, Participant Types and Program Choices. PhD Thesis. McGill University, Quebec, Canada.

Arsenault, N. (2001) *Canadian Ed-Ventures, Learning Vacations in Canada: An Overview*. Canadian Tourism Commission, Ottawa, Canada.

Association of Independent Tour Operators (AITO) (2017) *AITO: A World of Quality Holidays*. Available at: https://www.aito.com/ (accessed 26 January 2017).

Auh, S., Bell, S.J., McLeod, C.S. and Shih, E. (2007) Co-production and customer loyalty in financial services. *Journal of Retailing* 83(3), 359–370.

Bloch, P. and Richens, M.L. (1983) Shopping without purchase. An investigation of consumer browsing behaviour. *Advances in Consumer Research*, 10, 389–393.

Brotherton, B. and Himmetoğlu, B. (1997) Beyond destinations – special interest tourism. *Anatolia: An International Journal in Tourism and Hospitality Research* 8(3), 11–30.

Brown, G. (1992) Tourism and symbolic consumption. In: Johnson, P. and Thomas, B. (eds) *Choice and Demand in Tourism*. Mansell, London, pp. 57–71.

Buchmann, A., Moore, K. and Fisher, D. (2010) Experiencing film tourism. Authenticity and fellowship. *Annals of Tourism Research* 37(1), 229–248.

Butler, R.W. (1990) The influence of the media in shaping international tourist patterns. *Journal of Tourism Recreation Research* 15(2), 46–53.

Campos, A., Mendes, J., Oom do Valle, P. and Scott, N. (2015) Co-creation of tourist experiences: a literature review. *Current Issues in Tourism*, 1–32.

Carl, D., Kindon, S. and Smith, K. (2007) Tourist's experience of film locations: New Zealand as Middle-Earth. *Tourism Geographies* 9(1), 46–63.

Charters, S. and Ali-Knight, J. (2002) Who is the wine tourist? *Tourism Management* 23(2), 311–319.

Cohen, E. (1972) Towards a sociology of international tourism. *Social Research* 39(2), 164–182.

Cohen, E. (1988) Authenticity and commoditization in tourism. *Annals of Tourism Research* 15(3), 371–386.

Connell, J. (2012) Film tourism – evolution, progress and prospects. *Tourism Management* 33(5), 1007–1029.

Couldry, N. (2007) Pilgrimage in mediaspace: continuities and transformations. *Etnofoor* 20, 63–74.

Craik, J. (1997) The culture of tourism. In: Rojek, C. and Urry, J. (eds) *Touring Cultures: Transformation of Travel and Theory*. Routledge, London, UK. pp. 113–136.

Crompton, J. (1979) Motivations of pleasure vacations. *Annals of Tourism Research* 6(4), 408–424.

Culligan, K. (1992) Developing a model of holiday-taking behaviour. *Leisure and Tourism Futures Conference Proceedings*. The Henley Centre for Forecasting, London.

Dalgic, T. and Leeuw, M. (1994) Niche marketing revisited: concept, applications and some European cases. *European Journal of Marketing* 28(4), 39–55.

Dann, G. (1981) Tourist motivation – an appraisal. *Annals of Tourism Research* 8(2), 187–219.

Derrett, R. (2001) Special interest tourism: starting with the individual. In: Douglas, N., Douglas, N. and Derrett, R. (eds) *Special Interest Tourism*. Wiley, Brisbane, Australia. pp. 1–28.

Douglas, N., Douglas, N. and Derrett, R. (2001) *Special Interest Tourism*. Wiley, Brisbane, Australia.

Eagles, P.F. (1996) Issues in tourism management in parks: the experience in Australia. *Australian Leisure* 7(2), 29–36.

Ewert, A. and Hollenhorst, S. (1989) Testing the avenue model: empirical support for a model of risk recreation participation. *Journal of Leisure Research* 21, 124–139.

Fogelman, B. (1992) Opportunities and strategies. In: Brent-Ritchie, J.R. and Hawkings, D.E. (eds) *The World Travel and Tourism Review*. CAB International, Oxfordshire, UK, 21, 129–134.

Garrod, B. (2008) Market segmentation and tourist typologies for diving tourism. In: Garrod, B. and Gossling, S. (eds) *New Frontiers in Marine Tourism, Diving Experiences, Sustainability, Management*. Elsevier, Oxford, UK, pp. 32–48.

Gartner, W. (1993) Image formation process. In: Uysal, M. and Fesenmaier, D. (eds) *Communication and Channel Systems in Tourism Marketing*. Haworth Press, New York, USA. pp. 191–215.

Govers, R., Go, F. and Kumar, K. (2007) Promoting tourism destination image. *Journal of Travel Research* 46(1), 15–23.

Gray, H.P. (1979) *International Travel: International Trade.* Heath Lexington Books, Lexington, MA, USA.

Hall, M. and Weiler, B. (1992) Introduction. What's special about special interest tourism? In: Weiler, B. and Hall, C.M. (eds) *Special Interest Tourism*. Belhaven Press, London, UK. pp. 1–14.

Harrill, R. and Peterson, R.R. (2012) Tourism, conventional wisdom, and the news media. *Tourism Analysis* 17(6), 813–817.

Havitz, M.E. and Dimanche, F. (1997) Leisure involvement revisited: conceptual conundrums and measurement advances. *Journal of Leisure Research* 3, 1–18.

Havitz, M.E. and Dimanche, F. (1999) Leisure involvement revisited: drive properties and paradoxes. *Journal of Leisure Research* 31, 122–149.

Holbrooke, M.B. (2006) Consumption experience, customer value, and subjective personal introspection: an illustrative photographic essay. *Journal of Business Research* 59, 714–725.

Houston, M.J. and Rothschild, M.L. (1978) Conceptual and methodological perspectives on involvement. In: Hunt, H.K. (ed.) *Advances in Consumer Research*. Association for Consumer Research, Ann Arbor MI, 5, pp. 184–187.

Huh, C. and Singh, A.J. (2007) Families traveling with a disabled member: analyzing the potential of an emerging niche market. *Tourism and Hospitality Research* 7(3/4), 212–229.

Ioannides, D. and Debbage, K. (1997) Post Fordism and flexibility: the travel industry polyglot. *Tourism Management* 18(4), 229–241.

Iwasaki, Y. and Havitz, M.E. (1998) A path analytic model of the relationships between involvement, psychological commitment and loyalty. *Journal of Leisure Research* 30(2), 256–280.

Kerstetter, D., Confer, J. and Bricker, J. (1998) Industrial heritage attractions: types and tourists. *Journal of Travel and Tourism Marketing* 7(2), 91–104.

Kim, J.-H. (2010) Determining the factors affecting the memorable nature of travel experiences. *Journal of Travel and Tourism Marketing* 27(8), 780–796.

Kim, J.-H. and Richardson, S.L. (2003) Motion picture impacts on destination image. *Annals of Tourism Research* 30(1), 216–237.

Kyle, G. and Chick, G. (2004) Enduring leisure involvement: the importance of personal relationships. *Leisure Studies* 23(3), 243–266.

Laurent, G. and Kapferer, J. (1985) Consumer involvement profiles: a new practical approach to consumer involvement. *Journal of Advertising Research* 25(6), 48–56.

Li, Y. (2000) Geographical consciousness and tourism experience. *Annals of Tourism Research* 27(4), 863–883.

Lusch, R.F. and Vargo, S.L. (2006) Service-Dominant Logic as a foundation for building a general theory. In: Lusch, R.F. and Vargo, S.L. (eds) *The Service-Dominant Logic of Marketing: Dialog, Debate and Directions*. Armonk, New York, USA. pp. 406–420.

Macionis, N. (2004) Understanding the film-induced tourist. In: Frost, W., Croy, W.G. and Beeton, S. (eds) *Proceedings of the International Tourism and Media Conference*. Tourism Research Unit, Monash University, Melbourne, Australia, pp. 86–97.

Macionis, N. and Sparks, B. (2009) Film-induced tourism: an incidental experience. *Tourism Review International* 13(2), 93–101.

Marzo-Navarro, M. and Pedraja-Iglesias, M. (2010) Are there different profiles of wine tourists? An initial approach. *International Journal of Wine Business Research* 22(4), 349–361.

McIntyre, N. (1990) Recreation involvement, the personal meaning of participation. PhD Thesis, University of New England, Armidale, USA.

McIntyre, N. and Pigram, J. (1992) Recreation specialisation re-examined: the case of vehicle-based campers. *Leisure Sciences* 14, 3–15.

McKercher, B. (2002) Towards a classification of cultural tourists. *International Journal of Tourism Research* 4, 29–38.

McKercher, B. and Chan, A. (2005) How special is special interest tourism? *Journal of Travel Research* 44(1), 21–31.

Morgan, N. and Pritchard, A. (1999) Building destination brands: the cases of Wales & Australia. *Journal of Brand Management* 7(2), 102–119.

Morpeth, N. (2001) The renaissance of cycle tourism. In: Douglas, N., Douglas, N. and Derrett, R. (eds) *Special Interest Tourism*. Wiley, Melbourne, Australia, pp. 212–229.

Neuhofer, B., Buhalis, D. and Ladkin, A. (2013) A typology of technology enhanced experiences. *International Journal of Tourism Research* 16, 340–350.

Novelli, M. (2005) *Niche Tourism: Contemporary Issues, Trends and Cases*. Butterworth-Heinemann, Oxford, UK.

Opaschowski, H.W. (2001) *Tourismum im 21. Jahrhundert, das gekaufte paradies*. BAT Freizeit-Forschungsinstitut GmbH, Hamburg.

Payne, A.F., Storbacka, K. and Frow, P. (2008) Managing the co-creation of value. *Journal of the Academy of Marketing Science* 36(1), 83–96.

Pearce, P.L. (1988) *The Ulysses Factor: Evaluating Visitors in Tourist Settings*. Springer, New York, USA.

Peterson, K. (1994) The heritage resource as seen by the tourist: the heritage connection. In: Van Harssel, J. (ed.) *Tourism: An Exploration*. Prentice Hall, Englewood Cliffs, NJ, USA.

Pine, J.B. and Gilmore, J.H. (1999) *The Experience Economy: Work is Theatre and Every Business a Stage*. Harvard Business School Press, Boston, USA.

Plog, S. (1974) Why destination areas rise and fall in popularity. *Cornell Hotel Restaurant and Administration Quarterly*, 14(4), 55–58.

S. Agarwal, G. Busby and R. Huang

Poon, A. (1989) Competitive strategies for a 'New Tourism'. In: Cooper, C. (ed.) *Progress in Tourism Recreation and Hospitality Management*. Belhaven Press, London, UK, 1, 91–102.

Poon, A. (1993) *Tourism, Technology and Competitive Strategies*. CAB International, Wallingford, UK.

Prahalad, C.K. and Ramaswamy, V. (2004) *The Future of Competition: Co-creating Unique Value with Customers.* Harvard Business School, Boston, USA.

Prebensen, N.K., Vittersø, J. and Dahl, T.I. (2013) Value co-creation significance of tourist resources. *Annals of Tourism Research* 42, 240–261.

Prentice, R., Witt, S. and Hamer, C. (1998) Tourism as experience: the case of Heritage Parks. *Annals of Tourism Research* 25(1), 1–24.

Pretes, M. (1995) Postmodern tourism: the Santa Claus industry. *Annals of Tourism Research* 22(1), 1–15.

Read, S.E. (1980) A prime force in the expansion of tourism in the next decade: special interest travel. In: Hawkins, D.E., Shafor, E.L. and Rovelstad, J.M. (eds) *Tourism Marketing and Management Issues*. George Washington Press, Washington, DC, USA, pp. 193–202.

Reijnders, S. (2011) Stalking the count. Dracula, fandom and tourism. *Annals of Tourism Research* 38(1), 231–248.

Reisinger, Y. and Steiner, C. (2006) Reconceptualizing object authenticity. *Annals of Tourism Research* 33(1), 65–86.

Richards, G. (1996) Production and consumption of European cultural tourism. *Annals of Tourism Research* 23(2), 261–283.

Richards, G. (2014) Tourism Trends: The Convergence of Culture and Tourism. Available at: www.academia.edu/9491857/Tourism_trends_The_convergence_of_culture_and_tourism (accessed 26 July 2015).

Richins, M.L. and Bloch, P. (1986) After the new wears off: the temporal context of product involvement. *Journal of Consumer Research* I, 12.

Richins, M.L., Bloch, P.H. and Mc Quarrie, E. (1992) How enduring and situational involvement combine to create involvement responses. *Journal of Consumer Psychology* 1, 143–153.

Rihova, I., Buhalis, D., Moital, M. and Gouthro, M.B. (2014) Conceptualising customer-to-customer value co-creation in tourism. *International Journal of Tourism Research* 17(4), 356–363.

Robinson, M. and Novelli, M. (2005) Niche tourism: an introduction. In: Novelli, M. (ed.) *Niche Tourism*. Elsevier, Oxford, UK, pp. 1–11.

Rothschild, M. (1984) Perspectives on involvement: current problems and future directions. *Advances in Consumer Research* 11, 216–217.

Selwyn, T. (1996) *The Tourist Image: Myths and Myth Making in Tourism*. Wiley, Chichester, UK.

Sharpley, R. (1999) *Tourism, Tourists and Society*. Elm Publications, Cambridge, UK.

Sharpley, R. and Telfer, D.J. (2002) *Tourism and Development: Concepts and Issues*. Channel View, Clevedon, Buffalo, USA.

Shaw, G., Bailey, A. and Williams, A.M. (2011) Service dominant logic and its implications for tourism management: the co-production of innovation in the hotel industry. *Tourism Management* 32(2), 207–214.

Smith, V. (1979) Introduction. In: Smith, V. (ed.) *Hosts and Guests: The Anthropology of Tourism*. University of Pennsylvania Press, Philadelphia, USA, pp. 1–14.

Stebbins, R.A. (1982) Serious leisure: A conceptual statement. *Pacific Sociological Review* 25, 251–272.

Stebbins, R.A. (1997) Serious leisure and well-being. In: Haworth, J.T. (ed.) *Work, Leisure and Well-Being*. Routledge, London, UK, pp. 117–130.

Swarbrooke, J. and Horner, S. (2004) *Consumer Behaviour in Tourism*, 2nd edn. Routledge, London, UK.

Tan, S.-K., Kung, S.-F. and Luh, D.-B. (2013) A model of 'creative experience' in creative tourism. *Annals of Tourism Research* 41, 153–174.

Trauer, B. (2006) Conceptualising special interest tourism – frameworks for analysis. *Tourism Management* 27(2), 183–200.

Urry, J. (1992) The tourist gaze and the environment. *Theory, Culture and Society* 9, 1–26.

Vargo, S.L. and Lusch, R.F. (2004) Evolving to a new dominant logic for marketing. *Journal of Marketing* 68(1), 1–17.

Vargo, S.L. and Lusch, R.L. (2008) Service-dominant logic: continuing the evolution. *Journal of the Academy of Marketing Science* 36(1), 1–10.

Vargo, S.L. and Lusch, R.F. (2016) Institutions and axioms: an extension and update of Service-Dominant Logic. *Journal of the Academy of Marketing Science* 44(1), 5–23.

Varley, P. and Crowther, G. (1998) Performance and the service encounter: an exploration of narrative expectations and relationship management in the outdoor leisure market. *Market Intelligence and Planning* 16(5), 311–318.

Volo, S. (2009) Conceptualizing experience: a tourist based approach. *Journal of Hospitality Marketing & Management* 18(2–3), 111–126.

Wang, N. (1999) Rethinking authenticity in tourism experience. *Annals of Tourism Research* 26(2), 349–370.

Wang, Y. (2007) Customised authenticity begins at home. *Annals of Tourism Research* 34(3), 789–804.

Wynne, D. (1990) Leisure, lifestyle and the construction of social position. *Leisure Studies* 9, 21–34.

Zaichkowsky, J. (1985) Measuring the involvement construct. *Journal of Consumer Research* 12, 341–353.

2 Social Tourism

LYNN MINNAERT

Learning Objectives

- To understand the characteristics and historical development of social tourism
- To learn why in some countries governments are involved in social tourism provision, whereas in other countries this role is performed by voluntary organizations
- To discover the potential impacts of participation in social tourism
- To explore different social tourism models that are in operation

Social tourism is not a well known concept in tourism studies, or across large sections of the tourism industry. The term is often misunderstood, and sometimes mistakenly used as a synonym for responsible tourism, accessible tourism or community-based tourism. Even within the social tourism community, the term is debated and often maligned, as it can appear old-fashioned and pejorative. However, social tourism initiatives are in operation in many countries, either as part of public policy, or provided by the voluntary sector. This chapter will define the concept, provide a brief overview of its history and development, review different social tourism systems, and discuss the potential impacts of social tourism on participants.

Key Concepts

The earliest definition of social tourism by Hunzicker defines social tourism as "the relationships and phenomena in the field of tourism resulting from participation in travel by economically weak or otherwise disadvantaged elements in society" (Hunzicker, 1951, p. 1). Social tourism thus refers to initiatives that encourage participation in travel and tourism activities by groups in society who would otherwise be unlikely to do so. The two groups that are most commonly addressed in social tourism are low-income groups and persons with disabilities.

The tourism sector has changed drastically since this early definition was developed. From the 1970s, the development of mass tourism resulted in a democratisation of tourism, with ever increasing numbers in society having the ability to travel. Many groups, such as manual labourers, who were unable to travel before, could now afford foreign travel due to lower prices. The Hunzicker definition focuses on the inclusion of non-participating groups into tourism – and despite the growth in tourist numbers, this is still a primary purpose of social tourism. Tourism participation levels (also referred to as 'travel propensity') vary strongly between countries, and can usually be correlated with the strength of the countries' economies. In Europe, Eurostat monitors travel propensity in a yearly report. In 2014, according to this report, the proportion of EU residents aged 15 and over that did not participate in any trips of at least four overnight stays in 2012 was 60.0%, an increase of 12.4 percentage points on 2007 (Eurostat, 2016). More than half of the Europeans who did not participate in tourism reported financial reasons as one of the main reasons. One in five non-tourists mentioned health problems, while no motivation to travel was mentioned by 18% as one of the main reasons for not taking holidays. Work or study commitments were mentioned by 18% of the European non-tourists for not participating in tourism, while 14% mentioned family commitments. This indicates that a lack of disposable income is still an important factor in non-participation in tourism. In Portugal 73.5% of the respondents who did not travel indicated this was because of financial reasons; in Greece this was 72.1%. In contrast, in Finland only 16.4% of non-travellers reported this financial barrier (Eurostat, 2016).

The rapid growth of the tourism sector since the 1970s also led to the emergence of the many negative social effects of mass tourism – it soon became apparent that a higher participation in tourism did not automatically result in a more equitable society.

Initially, 'many considered the tourism industry to be a virtually costless generator of employment and well-being, offering seemingly limitless opportunities for "real" economic development to countless communities away from the centres of global industry and financial power' (Deakin *et al.*, 1995, p. 1). It soon became clear however that this view was wildly optimistic: tourism revenues did not always reach local populations because of large-scale foreign ownership and leakages, and tourism could be detrimental to local cultures and environments. This had implications for (social) tourism practitioners and policy makers: the development of mass tourism drew attention to the fact that communities could be excluded from the benefits of tourism in two different ways – either by lacking the opportunity to participate, or by not receiving an equitable share of the economic benefits of tourism.

More recent definitions of social tourism have often been extended to include these new developments. ISTO (the International Social Tourism Organisation) for example defines social tourism as 'the effects and phenomena resulting from the participation in tourism, more specifically the participation of low-income groups. This participation is made possible or is facilitated by initiatives of a well defined social nature' (ISTO Statutes, 2003). The participation of low-income groups in this case can refer to both the supply and the demand side of tourism: ISTO aims to encourage the access to tourism for all layers of society, and to develop models of tourism that are more beneficial to the host community (Bélanger and Jolin, 2011). Minnaert *et al.* (2009) take a similar approach by focusing on the moral stance of social tourism, defining it as 'tourism with an added moral value, of which the primary aim is to benefit either the host or the visitor in the tourism exchange'.

By extending the reach of the social tourism concept to host communities, social tourism starts to show similarities with the concepts of community-based and sustainable tourism: one could even argue the different concepts start to overlap. Therefore, this chapter will define social tourism as ***tourism initiatives aimed to increase the participation in travel of groups in society who, because of financial or health reasons, are prevented from taking holidays.*** Two main target populations are thus considered. On the one hand there are tourism initiatives that are aimed at travellers with disabilities, which strive for equal opportunities for this group to enjoy a holiday in the commercial tourism

sector. On the other hand there are the initiatives for low-income groups, for people who cannot afford a holiday. This is in line with the point of view of the European Union: 'social tourism is organised in some countries by associations, cooperatives and trade unions and is designed to make travel accessible to the highest number of people, particularly the most underprivileged sectors of the population' (European Economic and Social Committee, 2006, p. 3). In practice, social tourism usually refers to budget-friendly holidays in their own country, either individual or as part of a group, or in some cases day trips to theme parks, museums and attractions, that are funded or made available at highly reduced rates, by charities, trade unions or agencies in the public sector.

Major Factors

In this section the major factors influencing the interpretation and implementation of social tourism will be discussed. To fully comprehend the concept's position in the policy sphere today, a brief historical overview of its origins and development is necessary.

The origins of social tourism in Europe can be dated back to the emergent industrialised societies at the end of the 19th century. The rapid process of industrialisation, leading to overcrowded and unhealthy conditions in cities, prompted a significant increase in interest for the health and social conditions of workers and their families at this time. Tourism was beginning to develop as a commercial sector in response to increased mobility through the introduction of the rail networks. Holidays now became accessible for the highest earners in the working class: 'Although poverty was widespread in the rapidly expanding industrial cities, some working people were able for the first time to accumulate savings to pay for holidays' (Sharpley, 1999, p. 47). Social tourism started to emerge alongside commercial tourism, and targeted lower-income workers. It expanded strongly in countries with a well developed social system, in particular in France, Belgium, Germany and Italy. Introduced by unions and other social welfare and health structures, these initiatives aimed to provide access to holidays for all. Other initiatives concentrated on inner-city children or workers who were taken to the countryside or the seaside by charities or labour unions, which was seen as beneficial to health (CESR, 1999). In the UK, 'following the impoverishment of the British aristocracy, a series of well kept properties surrounded by big parks was put on the market at very low prices, representing only a small percentage of their former value. In this way several organisations, especially the "Co-operative Holiday Association" and the trade unions have acquired properties that were later turned into family holiday homes' (Lanquar and Raynouard, 1986, p. 14).

Following these early beginnings, social tourism became a policy issue in some countries. A pivotal point in the development of popular tourism was the 1936 Holiday with Pay Convention, formulated by the International Labour Organisation in Geneva. Article 2.1 of this convention states that 'every person to whom this convention applies shall be entitled after one year of continuous service to an annual holiday with pay of at least six working days' (International Labour Organisation). The Second World War slowed down the implementation process, but holiday with pay legislation was introduced for most workers across Europe after the war ended. This is also when some governments started subsidising the social tourism sector in their social policies (Chauvin, 2002).

The years following the Second World War were the heyday for social tourism in Europe. The period between 1950 and 1980 is described in French as the 'trente glorieuses', the glorious thirty. Traditional social tourism was based around the holiday centre in mainland Europe. The holiday centres on the mainland (e.g. in France, Belgium and Italy) created a product that was new, desirable and affordable and helped towards a democratisation of holiday-making. Traditionally they offered a stay in full board with all entertainment and activities included. In many cases, the activities had an educational, even political, component. The organised activities on holiday were often inspired by the ideals of the popular educational movements, and sometimes had a strong militant character (Jolin, 2003). The holidaymakers stayed in basic accommodation at low rates, and often helped with the daily chores. Over time, many holiday centres switched from full board to half board formulas, the visitors had more freedom when choosing their activities, and help with the chores was no longer required (Chauvin, 2002, p. 67). It is no coincidence that these changes occurred when commercial tourism became more accessible to people from weaker economic backgrounds.

The USSR also developed an extensive social tourism network. After decades of relative neglect by the Soviet state, leisure and tourism provision in the USSR underwent a period of rapid growth and institutionalisation between 1962 and 1990, including initiatives focused on children and youth tourism, wellness tourism, sport tourism, and even tourism retreats for military staff (Assipova and Minnaert, 2014).

From the 1980s, social tourism went through a period of transformation and reorientation. This was partly due to changes affecting the traditional target group for social tourism, manual workers: they were increasingly able to take holidays in the commercial sector, because of the low prices mass tourism could offer. In many cases, it transpired that traditional social tourism establishments found it hard to match the low price offered abroad. Manual workers were now no longer by definition excluded from commercial tourism, and other groups became the focus for social tourism initiatives: for example the unemployed, one-parent families, young families on low incomes, and persons with disabilities.

Another factor that contributed to the re-orientation of social tourism was the changing political climate, and the deepening influence of neoliberalism in many countries. The neoliberal ideology proposes the free market system as the best model for society, and argues government control should be dismantled, via reductions in taxation, reductions in industry protection and welfare spending, and privatisation of state assets (Veal, 2010). From Thatcher and Reagan to the responses to the economic downturn of 2007, the welfare state and the role of public interventions that aim to redistribute wealth have come under increased pressure: there has been a trend towards elimination of public aid programmes, 'on grounds that their recipients must be snatched from their culpable torpor by the sting of necessity' (Wacquant, 2009, p. 51). 'The American state is the prototype of the "residual welfare state" to the extent that it offers support only in response to the cumulative failures of the labour market and the family, by intervening on a case-by-case basis through programmes strictly reserved for vulnerable categories that are deemed "worthy": ex-workers temporarily pushed out of the wage-labour market, the handicapped and severely disabled, and, subject to varying restrictive conditions, destitute mothers of young children' (Wacquant, 2009, p. 46).

This increased influence of neoliberalism in the political sphere has also extended into the discourse about social tourism. Proponents of social tourism sometimes refer to the practice as the exertion of a 'right to travel'. Haukeland for example defines social tourism as follows: '[…] the concept of "social tourism" means that everybody, regardless of economic or social situation, should have the opportunity to go on vacation. Seen in this light, holiday travel is treated like any other human right whose social loss should be compensated by the welfare state' (Haukeland, 1990, p. 178). The European Economic and Social Committee (2006, p. 68), in its 'Opinion of Social Tourism' also define social tourism as a right: 'Everyone has the right to rest on a daily, weekly and yearly basis, and the right to the leisure time that enables them to develop every aspect of their personality and their social integration. Clearly, everyone is entitled to exercise this right to personal development. The right to tourism is a concrete expression of this general right, and social tourism is underpinned by the desire to ensure that it is universally accessible in practice'. This view is also apparent in the approach to social tourism in Brazil (Almeida, 2011). Both definitions refer to the right or entitlement to travel participation. George (1999, p. 35) defines entitlement as 'based on the application of a rule according to its terms, without regard to individual qualities that the rule ignores'. The entitlement exists without restrictions on those who qualify for it, the rule is universal: purely by being part of the disadvantaged, a person can be entitled to public support (in this case social tourism).

Others however argue tourism participation via social tourism is a 'desert' rather than a right. George (1999, p. 34) defines desert as an implication of moral responsibility, which presupposes freedom. This view of social intervention is more in line with a neoliberal ideology: being part of society comes with a number of moral responsibilities – only those who fulfil these responsibilities 'deserve' support. Whereas a right/entitlement is universal, a desert is not: it depends on the characteristics and behaviour of the person in question. A person who has been made redundant when a company closes down may be seen to 'deserve' benefits from the government for a limited period whilst looking for other employment: this is because the person has fulfilled his or her responsibility to society by showing willingness and ability to work and by paying taxes whilst in employment. This does not mean that every person who is out of work is necessarily seen as equally 'deserving' of these benefits: the long-term unemployed for example may be seen by some

as having lost their right to full benefits, by not fulfilling their duty to society whilst unemployed. Desert is thus linked to individual qualities, which may mean someone has 'deserved' a certain reward, whereas another person has not. 'The guiding principle of public action is not solidarity but compassion; its goal is not to reinforce social bonds, and still less to reduce inequalities, but at best to relieve the most glaring destitution and to demonstrate society's moral sympathy for its deprived yet deserving members' (Wacquant, 2009, p. 42). In terms of social tourism (if it is supported at all by governments under the growing influence of neoliberalism), this means that whereas some individual cases may be deemed 'deserving' of the intervention, this cannot be seen as an entitlement based on a general rule. Chunn and Gavigan (2004, p. 231) argue that a shift towards more neoliberal policies has resulted in a 'huge expansion in the category of undeserving poor. Indeed, virtually no one is considered "deserving"; even those who do receive social assistance are viewed as temporary recipients who must demonstrate their willingness to work for welfare and who ultimately will be employed as a result of skills and experience gained through workfare and other government-subsidised programmes. Thus, sole-parent mothers who historically were more likely to be deemed "deserving" than were childless men and women are no longer so privileged'. This attitude has become more prominent in social tourism provision in many countries, as will be discussed in the 'Interactions' section of this chapter.

Motivations

There are *social* and *economic* motivations for the provision of social tourism. Social tourism may be proposed as a factor in the reduction of social exclusion, and/or may be seen as a mechanism to sustain jobs in the low season and provide an income stream for host communities.

The term 'social exclusion' was originally coined in France in 1974 to refer to various categories of people who were unprotected by social insurance at the time but labelled as 'social problems', for example: disabled people, substance abusers, delinquents, single parents etc. However, in the 1980s, this stigmatising and narrowly social view was superseded as the term became central to French debates about the nature of the 'new poverty' associated with technological change and economic restructuring (Rodgers *et al.*, 1995, p. 1) The literature shows that, despite the growing use and apparent acceptance of the term social exclusion, there are still many (contested) definitions of what it means exactly and confusion about the relationship between social exclusion and poverty (Hodgson and Turner, 2003, p. 266). Walker and Walker define social exclusion as 'a dynamic process of being shut out, fully or partially, from any of the social, economic, political and cultural systems which determine the social integration of a person in society' (Walker and Walker in Hodgson and Turner, 2003, p. 266). The UK Index of Multiple Deprivation, developed by the University of Oxford, measures social exclusion in terms of six 'dimensions': income, employment, health deprivation and disability, education and training, housing, and geographical access to services (Miller, 2003, p. 5).

In social tourism, participation in travel is seen as a mechanism that can help reduce social exclusion. According to Hughes (1991, p. 196), 'holidays cannot be dismissed lightly as a "frivolous pursuit" but should be seen "more as an investment in the well-being and social fabric" of society. The claim that non-participation in holidays is a social welfare issue with health and social care implications is particularly employed in the context of children and families' (Haukeland, 1990; cited in Corlyon and La Placa, 2006). The value of leisure, as part of the individual and collective needs of a society, complementing work, reinforcing group or family relationships, providing therapy or even a preventative medicine to the pressure of everyday living is increasingly recognised by both governments and labour organisations (Shaw and Williams, 2002). Jolin (2004) moreover asserts that social tourism, by its ambition to democratise tourism, contributes to the fight against inequality and exclusion and supports social cohesion.

Social tourism initiatives can also be motivated by economic objectives. The economic contribution of social tourism has been recognised by the European Economic and Social Committee (EESC), which states that social tourism is: 'an effective way of including new groups of people in tourism-related activities, thus contributing to the growth of an economic sector which ... has a direct impact on the creation of wealth and jobs in the interests of society as a whole ... the industry itself must realise that such access, besides being a social responsibility, is a business opportunity and competitive advantage' (EESC, 2006, pp. 15–16). An example of this emphasis on the potential economic motivations for social tourism provision is the Calypso programme of the European Commission for Enterprise and Industry. This programme aims to develop social tourism programmes and exchanges between different European countries. Four key target groups have been identified: senior citizens, families in difficult personal or financial circumstances, persons with disabilities and young people. The social aims of personal development, well-being, European citizenship and learning are highlighted, but the economic aims of the programme are more specifically defined (see Focus Box 1). The programme aims to generate economic activity and growth across Europe, reduce seasonality, create and sustain more and

---

Focus Box 1: The IMSERSO programme in Spain

A much cited example of the economic benefits of social tourism is the IMSERSO programme in Spain, which offers domestic holidays for senior citizens in coastal areas during the shoulder season. The holidays are financed through contributions by beneficiaries (70 per cent) and the public sector (30 per cent). The public sector investment however yields cost savings and earnings: the scheme allows for longer seasons and increased employment in the coastal regions; and the tourist expenditure may lead to higher tax income. Around 300 hotels participate in the scheme, which has benefited around 1 million participants in the 2008–2009 season and has been estimated to generate or maintain 79,300 jobs. The Spanish government has allocated €105 million for the 2009–2010 season, and it claims that every Euro invested yields 4 Euros in tax, spend and reduction in benefit payments (www.imserso.es). To stimulate similar initiatives throughout Europe, the European Commission for Enterprise and Industry launched the Calypso programme in 2008, which aims to produce social tourism exchanges between different European countries (Minnaert *et al.*, 2010).

better jobs in the tourism sector, and assist in the development of small emerging destinations on a regional level (ec.europa.eu).

Interactions

The way social tourism products are provided can differ greatly, however most delivery mechanisms are comprised of three elements: demand, mediator and supply (see Fig. 2.1). The demand side refers to the specific target group the initiative is aimed at – the type of disadvantage or exclusion it aims to address. Some social tourism initiatives are specifically focused on senior citizens, teenage mothers or substance abusers; others operate across different target groups. The supply side refers to the tourism attraction or accommodation facility where the social tourism experience takes place. The facilitator is the organisation that connects demand and supply, and that aims to remove the (financial, physical and/or psychological) barriers the target audience may experience.

Social tourism initiatives can be facilitated by the public or the voluntary sector. In Anglo-Saxon countries, charities usually play a key role, whereas in mainland Europe and several countries in Latin America, the public sector is a key stakeholder. In those countries, social tourism is provided at either very limited cost to the state, or in ways which simultaneously stimulate the local

economy and increase the income of the state via taxation and a reduction of unemployment benefits. Where the public sector plays a role, the concept of social tourism has been implemented in different ways to suit national contexts: several countries operate holiday voucher schemes (for example France and Hungary, see Focus Box 2), other countries have established public–private partnerships (for example Spain, Portugal and Flanders, Belgium, see Focus Box 3) (McCabe *et al.*, 2011).

In Anglo-Saxon countries, social tourism is not facilitated by the state, but via charitable organisations. In the UK for example, the Family Holiday Association promotes the quality of family life for parents and children who experience disadvantage as a result of poverty through holidays and other recreational activities (www.familyholidayassociation.org.uk). In 2014, the charity provided fully funded, domestic holidays for over 2500 families. The public sector's interest in social tourism has been limited, although the concept was referred to in the 'Tomorrow's Tourism' policy of 1999: 'The government is determined to help people – the elderly, people with disabilities, single parent families, families with young children, carers, and people with low incomes – who find difficulty in taking holidays or leisure breaks' (DCMS, 1999, p. 27). In the follow-up policy, 'Tomorrow's Tourism Today' (2004) and

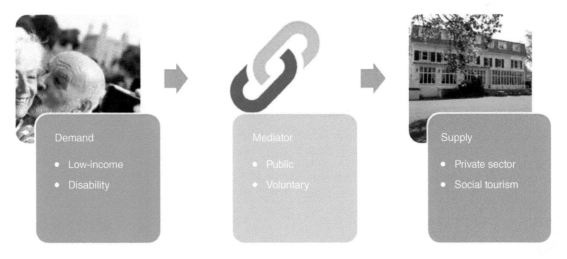

Fig. 2.1. The three elements in social tourism provision

subsequent policies however, the concept was no longer referred to.

Impacts and Insights

A growing body of research evidence indicates that social tourism can generate a range of benefits for beneficiaries. Minnaert et al. (2009), Minnaert (2008) and McCabe (2009) have conducted research into the social impacts of participation in social tourism by low-income beneficiaries, and have found evidence of benefits ranging from increases in self-esteem, improvement in family relations and widening of travel horizons to more pro-active attitudes to life, unplanned learning and behaviour change, and participation in education and employment.

Social tourism has been shown to lead to increases in social capital (Minnaert, 2008; Minnaert et al., 2009; McCabe, 2009; Minnaert et al., 2010). As social isolation is a common problem for disadvantaged families, holidays can be particularly valuable where they lead to an expansion of social networks or a strengthening of social ties. Minnaert et al. (2009) found that group holidays were particularly useful for this purpose as they encourage intense contact with other holidaymakers, often from similar geographical and social backgrounds. After the holidays, many of the adults responded to keep in touch via telephone or to pay each other visits. Minnaert et al. (2010) include examples of similar impacts of group holidays on disadvantaged children in Dublin.

Multiple studies have shown that social tourism can contribute to an increase in family capital (Minnaert, 2008; Minnaert et al., 2009; McCabe, 2009; Minnaert et al., 2010). In each of these studies,

L. Minnaert

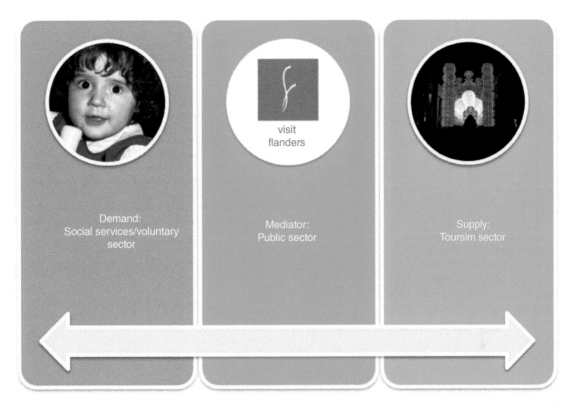

Fig. 2.2. Visit Flanders, a public sector body, liaises between state social services/voluntary sector organisations and the tourism industry to enhance social tourism provision.

social tourism beneficiaries reported that the holiday allowed the family members to spend quality time together away from the problems and the routine of the home environment; in McCabe's (2009) study this was evaluated as the second biggest benefit of the holiday, reported by 76% of the surveyed social tourism beneficiaries. On holiday, families may engage in new activities, or do things together they would not do at home. In many cases, this resulted in improvements in family relations: between the parents and the children, the adults as a couple or between siblings. In some cases, the holiday was also used to allow the children to adjust to new family members or a new family structure (McCabe, 2009).

The effect of the holiday on the well-being of the children is both an important motivation and an often-reported outcome of the holiday (Minnaert, 2008; Minnaert *et al.*, 2010). It was reported that the ability to go on a holiday allowed many children to gain confidence, make new friends and feel more integrated into school life after the experience.

Many parents commented how on the first day of school for example, the children would often be asked to draw a picture or say a few words about their holidays – in many cases however the children of low-income or disadvantaged families have not been away, even on a day trip, and may feel a particular sense of exclusion. The holiday experience in these cases can be a source of pride and happy memories after the experience. In McCabe's (2009) study, the 'opportunity for fun and happy memories for the children' was evaluated as the most important benefit of the holiday, reported by 80% of the social tourism beneficiaries. Parents also often emphasized that the inability to afford a holiday resulted in feelings of shame and embarrassment for them, illustrating that 'poverty can seem like personal failure in a society that views success in terms of conspicuous consumption' (Walker and Collins, 2007, p. 208).

Minnaert (2012) highlighted that social tourism also offers opportunities for learning and behaviour change via tourism. Although it is generally accepted that some forms of tourism can lead to learning (for example educational and special-interest holidays), the learning opportunities of leisure holidays are not always acknowledged, as there are often no formal learning activities involved. For non-educational forms of tourism, learning is often not seen as a motivation for the holiday. On the contrary, the holiday is usually mainly seen as a time for rest and relaxation, and learning can be seen as the opposite of this. However, social tourism has been shown to offer opportunities for learning a new skill, or a new way of looking at certain areas of life. The study highlights that holidays can offer valuable moments for reflection, and social tourism participants may use these to formulate aspirations or assess existing attitudes. In some cases, the changes in behaviour resulting from the holiday were small but meaningful: beneficiaries may for example be willing to use public transport after their vacation, whereas they were reluctant to do so before, thus potentially reducing their level of isolation. Minnaert (2012) also reported that social tourism participants were often more likely to take up further support offerings (such as courses, counselling sessions, or budget guidance) after the social tourism experience. The fact that these support opportunities were available before the holiday, but the participants did not take them up until afterwards, highlights the role of the holiday as a possible catalyst in attitude and behaviour change.

Questions

1. Do you feel participation in tourism should be an entitlement or a desert?
2. Do you think social tourism has a role in contemporary society?
3. If so, who should be the main facilitator, the public or the voluntary sector?

Further Reading and Website Links

Hughes, H. (1991) Holidays and the economically disadvantaged. *Tourism Management* 12, 193–196.
McCabe, S., Minnaert, L. and Diekmann, A. (2011) *Social Tourism in Europe: Theory and Practice*. Channel View Publications, Bristol.
Minnaert, L., Maitland, R. and Miller, G. (2011) What is social tourism? *Current Issues in Tourism* 5, 403–415. www.oits-isto.org

References

Almeida, M. (2011) Case study: the development of social tourism in Brazil. *Current Issues in Tourism* 14(5), 483–489.
Assipova, Z. and Minnaert, L. (2014) Tourists of the world, unite! The interpretation and facilitation of tourism towards the end of the Soviet Union (1962–1990). *Journal of Policy Research in Tourism, Leisure and Events* 6(3), 215–230.
Bélanger, C. and Jolin, L. (2011) The International Organisation of Social Tourism (ISTO) working towards a right to holidays and tourism for all. *Current Issues in Tourism* 14(5), 487–492.
CESR (1999) *Le tourisme social et associatif dans la région de Nord-Pas-de-Calais*. CESR, Nord-Pas-de-Calais, France.
Chauvin, J. (2002) *Le tourisme social et associatif en France*. l'Harmattan, Paris.
Chunn, D. and Gavigan, S. (2004) Welfare law, welfare fraud and the moral regulation of the 'never deserving' poor. *Social & Legal Studies* 13, 219–243.
Corlyon, J. and La Placa, V. (2006) *Holidays for Families in Need: Policies and Practice in the UK – Final Report to the Family Holiday Association*. Policy Research Bureau, London.
Deakin, N., Davis, A. and Thomas, N. (1995) *Public Welfare Services and Social Exclusion. The development of consumer-oriented initiatives in the European Union*. European Foundation for the Improvement of Living and Working Conditions, Dublin, Ireland.
Department of Culture, Media and Sports (DCMS) (1999) *Tomorrow's Tourism*. DCMS, London, UK.
European Economic and Social Committee (EESC) (2006) *Opinion of the Economic and Social Committee on Social Tourism in Europe*. EESC, Brussels.
Eurostat (2016) *Tourism Statistics – Participation in Tourism*. Available online: http://epp.eurostat.ec.europa.eu/statistics_explained/index.php/Tourism_statistics_-_participation_in_tourism.
George, R. (1999) *In Defence of Natural Law*. Clarendon Press, Oxford, UK.
Haukeland, J. (1990) Non-Travelers: The flip side of motivation. *Annals of Tourism Research* 17, 172–184.
Hodgson, F. and Turner, J. (2003) Participation not consumption: the need for new participatory practices to address transport and social exclusion. *Transport Policy* 10, 265–272.
Hughes, H. (1991) Holidays and the economically disadvantaged. *Tourism Management* 12, 193–196.
Hunzicker, W. (1951) *Social Tourism: Its Nature and Problems*. AIEST (International Tourists Alliance Scientific Commission), Geneva, Switzerland.
International Labour Organisation (1936) *Holidays with Pay Convention*. ILO, Geneva, Switzerland.
ISTO (2003) *Statutes*. ISTO, Brussels, Belgium.

Jolin, L. (2003) *Le tourisme social, un concept riche de ses évolutions, Le tourisme social dans le monde*, Téoros, Edition spéciale, 40ème anniversaire, 141.

Jolin, L. (2004) *L'ambition du Tourisme Social: un Tourisme pour Tous, Durable et Solidaire*. Available at: http://www.oits-isto.org (accessed 9 November 2017).

Lanquar, R. and Raynouard, Y. (1986) *Le Tourisme Social*. Presses Universitaires de France, Paris, France.

McCabe, S. (2009) Who needs a holiday? Evaluating social tourism. *Annals of Tourism Research* 36(4), 667–688.

McCabe, S., Minnaert, L. and Diekmann, A. (2011) *Social Tourism in Europe: Theory and Practice*. Channel View Publications, Bristol, UK.

Miller, J. (2003) Travel chances and social exclusion. Resource paper. Moving through nets: the physical and social dimensions of travel. 10th International Conference on Travel Behaviour Research. Lucerne, 10–14th August 2003.

Minnaert, L. for Tourism Flanders (2008) *Holidays Are For Everyone. Research Into the Effects and the Importance of Holidays for People Living in Poverty*. Tourism Flanders, Brussels.

Minnaert, L. (2012) 'Social tourism as opportunity for unplanned learning and behavior change', *Journal of Travel Research* September (51), 607–616.

Minnaert, L., Maitland, R. and Miller, G. (2009) Tourism and social policy. *Annals of Tourism Research* 36(2), 316–334.

Minnaert, L., Quinn, B., Griffin, K. and Stacey, J. (2010) Social tourism for low-income groups. In: Cole, S. and Morgan, N. (eds) *Tourism and Inequality*. CAB International, Wallingford, UK.

Minnaert, L., Maitland, R. and Miller, G. (2011) What is social tourism? *Current Issues in Tourism* 5, 403–415.

Rodgers, G., Gore, C. and Figueiredo, J. (ed.) (1995) *Social Exclusion: Rhetoric, Reality, Responses*. International Institute for Labour Studies, Geneva, Switzerland.

Sharpley, R. (1999) *Tourism, Tourists and Society*. Elm Publications, Huntingdon, UK.

Shaw, G. and Williams, A.M. (2002) *Critical Issues in Tourism: a Geographical Perspective*, second edition. Wiley-Blackwell, Oxford, UK.

Veal, A. (2010) *Leisure, Sport and Tourism: Politics, Policy and Planning*. CAB International, Wallingford, UK.

Wacquant, L. (2009) *Punishing the Poor: The Neoliberal Government of Social Insecurity*. Duke University Press, Durham, NC, USA.

Walker, R. and Collins, C. (2007) Families of the poor. In: Scott, J., Treas, J. and Richards, M. (eds) *The Blackwell Companion to the Sociology of Families*. Blackwell Publishing, Malden, MA, USA.

http://www.ec.europa.eu (accessed 22 December 2016).

http://www.familyholidayassociation.org.ukw (accessed 22 December 2016).

www.holidayparticipation.be (accessed 22 December 2016).

www.imserso.es (accessed 22 December 2016).

www.vakantieparticipatie.be (accessed 22 December 2016).

3 Family Tourism

Carol Southall

Learning Objectives

- To consider the growth and development of family tourism in a UK context
- To realise the importance of the family tourism market to the tourism industry
- To consider macro-environmental factors impacting on engagement with family tourism

Introduction

Holidays play an important role in family life, allowing family members to spend quality time together and consequently strengthening family relationships. Holidays can of course have the opposite effect: when estranged family members come together in a relatively confined space for a specified period of time, having previously only engaged in daily routine and independent activity, it can cause conflict. However, for most families, an opportunity to reconnect on holiday offers a welcome respite from daily routine and monotony.

> Families are made of an array of individuals of different age, gender and social position, each of whom have different holiday experiences and aspirations. Such differences are evident in the conflicts that regularly shadow family holidays. Being together for two weeks might reinforce a sense of familyness, but it might also generate suspicion and discomfort (Rosenblatt and Russell, 1975). Beneath the image of a united, stable, loving family there are multiple conflicts and tensions: Holidays that do not match up to expectations; conflicting interests; parents that are tired of being with their children all the time; wives that feel frustrated with their husband's inclination to do nothing; all these tensions also form part of the family holiday. (Obrador, 2012, p. 415).

In recent years 'the family' has become much more diverse in terms of its composition or 'make-up', and it is growing acceptance of this diversity which confirms the ongoing significance of the family tourism market to the tourism industry. Until relatively recently family tourism was an under-researched area, which is somewhat surprising given the importance of the family holiday in enabling quality time together unencumbered, at least in theory, by the stresses of daily life. As the 21st century progresses so the composition of families will become ever more diverse, as has been the case in more recent decades. Increasingly society is adapting to 'new' family norms, and industry must seek to accommodate diverse and often intergenerational family groups.

Interestingly according to Carr (2011, p. 10) and supported by Schänzel et al. (2005):

> ...one of the limitations of the studies of children's and families' holiday experiences that have been undertaken to date is that the majority have tended to provide adult-oriented examinations, generally viewing children as passive objects and, as a result, rarely collecting any information directly from them.

This chapter aims to define and outline the nature of family tourism, exploring key concepts such as definitions and constitution of the family, current trends in family tourism, historical development and changing holiday patterns, as well as macro-environmental factors impacting on family tourism, such as legislation (from a UK Government perspective), social tourism, health consciousness, technology and the global economy. The future of family tourism is also considered, focusing on '...capturing the diverse needs of children and adults of different ages, from diverse ethnic backgrounds and with diverse family structures' (Schänzel and Yeoman, 2015, p. 145).

According to Schänzel et al. (2012) family tourism is one of the most important sectors of the worldwide tourism industry, accounting for around 30% of the worldwide leisure travel market. Undoubtedly 'Families represent a large and growing market for the tourism industry' (Schänzel and Yeoman, 2015, p. 141). Numerous studies (Durkin, 2007; McCabe et al., 2007; Hilbrecht et al., 2008; McCabe, 2009; McCabe et al., 2010; All Party Parliamentary Group on Social Tourism, 2011; Minnaert, 2012) have recognised the potential social and educational benefits of tourism for families, as well as the importance of tourism as a tool to combat social exclusion (Minnaert *et al.*, 2006). According to *The Guardian* (2005) 'Holidays can improve physical and mental health and help families develop positive relationships' and it is family relationships, as well as the importance of tourism to the enhancement of those relationships, that will be explored more extensively within this chapter.

> …a family's identity (how they view themselves as a group and their comfort with that viewpoint) will play into how they use non-work or non-school time. Some families are all about day trips, whereas others load their travel and tourism experience into a longer and more intense window of time. (Mancini *et al.*, 2012, p. 312)

What is clear is that family tourism '…is predicted to grow at a faster rate than all other forms of leisure travel, partly because it represents a way to reunite the family and for family members to spend time with each other, away from the demands of work' (Schänzel *et al.*, 2012 *in* Schänzel and Yeoman, 2015, p. 141).

Key Concepts: 'Family', 'Family Type', 'Family Holidays' and 'Family Tourism'

Before exploring the nature of family tourism, it is important to clearly define what is meant by the key concepts of 'family', 'family type', 'family holidays' and of course 'family tourism'.

Powell *et al.* (2010, p. 1) describe 'family' as a 'societal cornerstone' and refer to '…abundant literature dating back at least to the sociologist Émile Durkheim (1897/1977) [which] contends that family is a primary institution into which people feel socially integrated and that this connectedness is consequential for the well-being of family members and the well-being of society'. Thus what is clear is that social integration, connectedness and well-being are essentials underpinning the family structure as indeed they are essentials supporting participation in the tourism and travel experience.

There are numerous definitions of family, many of which focus on the inclusion of children in the 'family' unit and some that recognise the 'diversity of family forms' (Powell *et al.*, 2010, p. 5). The diverse nature of families will be discussed later in this chapter, but it is important to note that there is an abundance of social science literature in particular that explores the definition of the family in some depth.

According to the Office for National Statistics (ONS) (2011, p. 18):

> a family is defined as a group of people who are either: a married, same-sex civil partnership, or cohabiting couple, with or without child(ren), a lone parent with child(ren), a married, same-sex civil partnership, or cohabiting couple with grandchild(ren) but with no children present from the intervening generation, or a single grandparent with grandchild(ren) but no children present from the intervening generation.

Furthermore the ONS (2011, p. 18) defines '*family type*' as:

> …the classification of families into different types distinguished by the presence, absence and type of couple relationship, whether a married couple family, a same-sex civil partnership family, a cohabiting couple family, or a lone parent family.

As Carr (2011, pp. 9–10) puts it:

> Irrespective of whether the family is defined in a nuclear, immediate or extended sense, a constant feature of them all has traditionally been the presence of at least one child and an adult responsible for the care of this child (i.e. an adult who is responsible for undertaking the role of care and provision traditionally associated with the concept of the parent). Consequently…the family is simply defined as consisting of at least *one adult and one child*…

According to Schänzel *et al.* (2005) family holidays involve a family group (of at least one adult and one child) undertaking leisure travel away from home for more than one day. Schänzel *et al.* (2012, p. 3) further defined 'family holidays' as '…time spent together as a family group (which may include extended family) doing activities different from normal routines that are fun but that may involve compromise and conflict at times.' 'Family holidays serve the purpose of (re)connecting people through tourism that can be seen as a social practice that involves networking, social capital formation and social obligations' (Schänzel, 2013).

Fundamentally, family tourism involves the participation of the family unit, in all its forms, in diverse forms of tourism activity over an extended period of time (Southall, 2012).

Family structure: types of families

The idealised view of the nuclear family that underpins the package holiday contrasts with both the lived experiences of families and the diversification in the nature of the family. (Obrador, 2012, p. 415)

In the course of the last five decades there have been numerous and significant demographic changes worthy of note in the context of family tourism. In part these demographic changes have also helped shape the family unit into the diverse structure it is today. The 'family' is an institution that has been changing and evolving for centuries. Bronfenbrenner (Bronfenbrenner and Morris (2006), cited in Parke (2013)) developed an ecological theory according to which children and families are embedded in a 'chronosystem', meaning that they are affected by changes that occur over time.

As Parke (2013, p. 1) says, 'Society has developed a cultural image of a perfect or ideal family…The cultural embodiment of this "ideal" family is the nuclear family form consisting of two heterosexual parents who conceive and rear their biological children, and is the template against which other family forms are judged'. What is clear, however, is that '…this particular family form (the heterosexual nuclear family) is fast becoming less prevalent and coexists with a wide variety of other family forms' (Parke, 2013, p. 5). As new family forms become more common and challenge this definition of an 'ideal' family, the added effects of changes in demographics and technology have also served to redefine the 'ideal' family. These include an increase in divorce and remarriage, changing employment patterns, same-sex parenting and increasing recognition of culturally diverse family variations globally (Parke, 2013).

According to Carr (2011, p. 9), 'It is important to recognise that the immediate family and the notion of spending leisure time in this unit is a modern western construct that is not necessarily shared throughout the Middle East, Asia or even southern Europe'; rather it is the extended family that plays a more significant role in these regions. 'This means that definitions and understandings of family holiday experiences must be culturally grounded and spatially differentiated' (Carr, 2011, p. 9).

For many years the definition of 'family' has focused on heteronormative conceptions that include marriage, children, gendered roles and heterosexual relationships (Powell et al., 2010; Hughes and Southall, 2012). In recent years there has been increasing evidence of emergent advocacy of a more all-encompassing definition of the word family that challenges this narrow hegemonic vision (Powell

et al., 2010). Mancini et al. (2012, p. 310) note that 'From a human development and family science perspective, families cannot be viewed in homogenized ways but rather their substantial variations and diversities must be accounted for. This includes most particularly the disparities many families face geographically, economically, and socially.' As Carr (2011, p. 9) points out, however, the tourism industry is slow to react to this de-homogenization, with holiday companies continuing to cater primarily for 'the idealised nuclear family, even to the extent of charging room supplements to those who do not conform to the nuclear family standard'.

Whatever the make-up of the modern family, it is increasingly interdependent and relies on the cooperation of others to care for and raise children (Parke, 2013).

Statistics relating to families

Life expectancy

According to Bennett et al. (2015) life expectancy in the UK in 2012 was 79.5 years for men and 83.3 years for women. Having already increased between 1981 and 2012 by 8.2 years for men and 6 years for women, it is estimated that by 2030 national life expectancy will reach 85.7 years for men and 87.6 years for women. It is predicted that by 2050 25% of the UK population will be aged over 65 (Parliament, 2010). This is confirmation of an ageing population and this longevity means that grandparents will continue to enjoy more time with their grandchildren taking partial or full responsibility for childcare whilst parents are working, and participating in family holidays with their children and grandchildren as an extended family unit. This is supported by Schänzel and Yeoman (2015) in their reference to the increasing 'verticalisation' of the family and the growing importance of grandparents in both childcare and the lives of their grandchildren.

Overseas and inbound visitation

In 2015, UK residents made 65.7 million visits abroad, an increase of 9.4% on 2014. Visits abroad to friends or family increased by 11% between 2014 and 2015 (Office for National Statistics, 2015a). Additionally, the number of overseas residents visiting friends and relatives in the UK grew by 7.1% from a record high in 2014 of 9.8 million

C. Southall

visits to 10.5 million visits in 2015. Spending by overseas residents visiting friends and family also saw a small rise in 2015, growing from £4.6 million to almost £4.8 million (ONS, 2014a, 2015b). The most popular reason for overseas visitors travelling to other areas of England, outside London, was visiting friends and relatives, with 38% of inbound visitors travelling for this purpose in 2015. Globally, mass migration over the course of the past fifty years has led to a significant increase in diasporic communities, with immigrants frequently opting to return home to visit friends and family and vice versa.

These statistics evidence the growing importance of the family tourism market, both domestically and internationally, as well as the significant economic value of the market to the UK.

Key markets

Key UK inbound markets for visiting friends and family include the Irish Republic, Poland, Spain, Germany, Australia and the USA (see Table 3.1). Visitors from the Irish Republic were much more likely to be in the UK to visit friends and family than for a holiday or business reasons, while over a third of visitors from Poland and Spain were visiting friends and family. Australian visitors were the least likely to be visiting on business but the most likely to be visiting friends and family (ONS, 2015b). Again this supports the assertion (Schänzel and Yeoman, 2015) that family tourism, both out- and inbound is a significant growth market.

Trends in family tourism spending

Trends in family tourism spending are an important consideration in the context of family tourism, and data on UK household expenditure and consumption enables further understanding of this key market, '…as out of home expenditure is a key indicator of family tourism, whether it is day trips or overnight stays' (Yeoman, 2012).

Statistics indicate that household spending on recreation and culture has increased significantly over the past decade, with almost a third of recreation and culture spending on holidays. According to the 2014 Family Spending Report published by the Office for National Statistics (ONS, 2015c), the average weekly household expenditure in the UK in 2014 was £531.30, a decrease from £539.80 per week at its peak in 2006 but an increase of £14 from 2013.

In 2014 transport had overtaken housing as the highest expenditure category, averaging £74.80 per week, a growth of £4.40 per week on 2013 but a decrease from £88.00 per week in 2001/2. Recreation and culture was third in terms of household expenditure in 2014, averaging £68.80 per week, with package holidays accounting for 33% of this amount at £23.10. Also significant was expenditure on restaurants and hotels, fifth on the list at £42.50. The combined categories of transport, recreation and culture and restaurants and hotels amounted to 35% of household expenditure in the UK in 2014 (at the time of writing, statistics were unavailable for 2015) (ONS, 2014b; 2015c).

In summary, people are living longer, travelling more to visit friends and relatives and spending a significant proportion of the household budget on leisure activities.

Demographic changes important in the context of family tourism

Family tourism is shaped by demographic changes and changes in social structures (Schänzel and Yeoman, 2015). These include:

Table 3.1. Reasons for visiting the UK. (Data from ONS, 2015b)

	Visiting friends and family (VFR) Visits (thousands)	Holiday Visits (thousands)	Business Visits (thousands)
Republic of Ireland	1,028	555	693
Poland	636	233	776
Spain	749	855	456
Germany	729	1,550	826
Australia	458	434	73
USA	838	1,363	764

- a rise in working parents, in particular working mothers;
- fathers playing a more active role in childrearing, in part due to an increase in working mothers;
- couples marrying older and having their first child later, or cohabiting without marriage;
- new routes to parenthood for same-sex and infertile couples, including adoption;
- an increase in the number of single parent families;
- higher divorce rates;
- an ageing population resulting in growing numbers of elderly people, many of whom are grandparents who actively help care for their grandchildren, and participate in multigenerational family trips; and
- growing numbers of stepfamilies.

Motivations: Benefits of Family Tourism

Social capital is described by Minnaert et al. (2009, p. 329) as 'the valuable relations between the individual and the world surrounding [them]'. Social capital thus refers to the relationships between people and the subsequent result of those relationships. According to Shakya (2014, p. 7) '...the concept of social capital acknowledges the importance of social relations in development...However social capital can also be detrimental from the perspective of individuals who are excluded from its benefits.'

In the context of the World Bank's 'Social Capital Initiative' (SCI), developed in the 1990s, the social capital of a society has been defined as 'the institutions, the relationships, the attitudes and values that govern interactions among people and contribute to economic and social development (Grootaert and van Bastelaer, 2001, p. 4). Social capital creates value in the form of trust, reciprocity and cooperation for those who are connected through various networks.

Parke (2013) discusses the importance of social systems and networks for families and refers to parents as 'managers of social opportunities' for their children. According to Parke (2013) an important product of this social connectedness and family network is the acquisition of social capital. Tourism is important 'for the reproduction of social networks and relations of domesticity' (Obrador, 2012, p. 417).

Parke (2013) also discusses the importance of two forms of social capital: bonding capital, whereby people socialise with others of similar cultural and social backgrounds, e.g. same age, religion, personal characteristic or social interest; and bridging capital which involves engagement with dissimilar others. Parke (2013) argues that both forms of social capital are important to understand contemporary families. '...by exposure to dissimilar families, parents and children can gain new perspectives on how families can be organised and operate and gain new respect and acceptance of diverse family forms'. Furthermore, spending quality time together as a family can lead to an improvement in family relationships and a reduction in tension and stress, resulting in more positive and beneficial relationships between family members.

Zabriskie and McCormick (2001) suggest that purposeful leisure time spent with the family can help foster a good family life and support children's development. There are undoubtedly numerous benefits of participation in tourism, including individual benefits such as opportunities for bonding, learning, intercultural communication, strengthening of relationships, health, personal and social development and social connectedness (Shaw et al., 2008; McCabe et al., 2010; Carr, 2011; Schänzel, 2013). In a study on participation in social tourism and links with subjective well-being and quality of life, McCabe et al. (2010, p. 770) concluded that there was '...tentative evidence to suggest that... [holidays have] a positive effect on the emotional states of...respondents'. McCabe et al.'s (2010) research established that perceived emotional benefits of holidays included:

- opportunity to spend quality time together as a family;
- opportunity to spend time away from difficult/ stressful circumstances;
- to be better able to cope with situations and look forward to the future;
- the opportunity for fun and happy memories; and
- the opportunity to experience new places and different activities.

Minnaert et al. (2009, p. 324) also established increases in family capital following their study on 'the effects of social tourism on family capital', with improvements in family relations resulting in positive behaviour changes identified by respondents. Interestingly the behavioural changes identified were perceived as being 'directly linked to the holiday experience by the respondents: after they had spent time together on holiday and had engaged in new activities, this new behaviour pattern was repeated at home. This can be seen as a form of experiential learning'. The benefits of experiential learning are also explored by Waite *et al.* (2015) in their study on what children learn when camping, concluding that the camping experience enhances and enables children's learning by encouraging strong family bonds, exploration, play, freedom and independence, as well as offering new cultural experiences.

According to Schänzel (2013) '...parents are more deliberate about social identity formation whereas children seek fun and sociality'. Furthermore, '...the holiday experience may offer an ideal opportunity for children to experience unstructured play and the freedom to be, rather than the need to become' (Carr, 2011, p. 19).

In the UK, the charity sector is the main provider of social tourism, whereas in mainland Europe most provision is state supported (McCabe *et al.*, 2010). In their 2015 report, the Family Holiday Association (FHA) (Focus Box 1) identify that there are '...a wide range of lasting social, emotional and psychological benefits that taking a break as a family can bring'. Many families who are supported by the FHA are struggling with issues ranging from severe and sudden illness to bereavement and abuse. The report identifies significant changes in family members following a family holiday, including increased affection towards other family members, improved behaviour at school and at home and greater optimism for the future.

Changing patterns of holiday-taking

The family holiday was very much a part of working-class culture as far back as the 1800s, following the development of the railways, taking day-trippers away from the industrial cities of England and on to the coast (Southall, 2012). It was the entrepreneur Billy Butlin who was 'perhaps most influential in his impact on the British family holiday market' (Southall, 2012, p. 52), opening his first holiday camp in the north-east of England in the mid-1930s.

'The type of holidays offered by early entrepreneurs such as Butlin, and later Fred Pontin, enabled families to seek a brief respite from historically dark and depressing times. For the families not previously in a position to afford such luxuries as holidays, the camps offered a welcome break.' (Southall, 2012, p. 53)

Greater opportunities for family holidays outside the UK came with the advent of the package holidays of the 1960s, 70s and beyond, with destinations such as Spain quickly becoming popular with the masses.

The UK recession from 2008 impacted significantly on travel patterns, with a rise in domestic tourism and a decline in outbound international tourism. Interestingly households with children maintained trip levels, whereas 7% fewer trips were made by households without children in 2009 (Visit England, 2010). This period also saw the rise of the 'staycation' or UK domestic holiday. Although there has been a rise in outbound international tourism since 2009, the 'drivers' of domestic tourism appear to have changed, with less focus on cost and the domestic holiday or 'staycation' as the 'cheaper

---

Focus Box 1: The Family Holiday Association (FHA)

The Family Holiday Association (FHA) is the UK's only national charity dedicated to helping families get a break. Established in 1975 by Pat and Joan Laurance, the Association is a London-based registered charity which in 2015 has so far helped over 3500 families enjoy a short break or day trip, half of whom had never been on holiday together before. It receives no government funding and relies entirely on donations.

All families are referred by professionals in the community such as teachers, social workers, health visitors and other charities. Families can have a break at a UK holiday park; take part in a group trip; or use free tickets provided by a range of partners including National Express, Visit Kent, National Trust and First Great Western.

It regularly participates in research on the impact of social tourism, showing that spending quality time together as a family results in stronger, healthier and happier families and communities.

It was the secretariat for the All Party Parliamentary Group on social tourism, resulting in the report 'Giving Britain a Break'. Through its Holidays Matter network it raises awareness of the importance of breaks and works with a range of industry partners, charities and statutory organisations so that more people can benefit.

For more information visit http://www.FamilyHolidayAssociation.org.uk
Courtesy of Family Holiday Association

---

option', and more focus on convenience and a return to domestic destinations that hold some allure stemming from a previous visit. According to Visit England (2015):

Cost remains an important reason consumers holiday in England rather than abroad, but it is rarely the sole, or even the dominant driver. The growth in domestic holidays in recent years is driving repeat visits, as are the established trends of convenience, ease and liking England.

Whilst UK consumers are likely to remain cautious about their holiday plans, Visit England (2015) anticipate that people are likely to balance short breaks in England with longer holidays abroad, although 'In the longer term, it is possible that the staycation will rally [as] the length and depth of the [recession] ensured consumers were more likely to holiday in England, and their positive experiences of those trips will spur repeat visits and a legacy effect'. A survey of more than a thousand UK consumers by The Boston Consulting Group (2015) found that half expected to spend more holidays in the UK than in recent years; this is the case for 60% of families with children younger than 18. At the same time, consumers are increasingly opting for more short breaks rather than less frequent long trips.

Research published by Thomson Holidays in 2011 identified the importance and value of family time on holiday, whilst at the same time establishing that 20% of parents are unable to take enough time off work to have a holiday. 'Giving Britain a Break', the 2011 report published by Thomson, also found that on average over a quarter of working parents spend less than an hour a day together with their children, despite wanting more time. Time, according to Mancini *et al.* (2012, pp. 311–312) '...is a resource, and actually possessing little of it constrains what can be chosen for travel and tourism'.

A 2015 Tripadvisor poll indicates that British households increased their holiday budgets by 8% in 2015. Interestingly the TripBarometer study by the independent research firm Ipsos found that 38% of British households were likely to increase their holiday budget as compared with 32% of overseas travellers. The poll indicated that whilst for UK travellers, Australia and New Zealand are still dream destinations, 'staycations' are also still popular, with 49% of all holidays by British households taking place within the UK (Take the Family, 2015).

The strength of the pound was a contributory factor in the number of families booking overseas holidays in 2015. With sterling reaching an eight-year high against the euro, this made a considerable difference to the family holiday budget with families getting more for their money in 2015 (*Travel Weekly*, 2015). In June 2016 however, the 'Brexit' vote for UK withdrawal from the European Union had a significant effect on the strength of the pound, which eventually fell to a 3-year low against the euro in October 2016. This meant that foreign holidays became more expensive for British holidaymakers. A weaker pound however, means that the UK is now a cheaper destination for overseas tourists, with some estimates of a 20% increase in enquiries from Chinese visitors and a rise in overseas visitors travelling to UK destinations outside London (BBC, 2017).

In their focus on travel trends in 2015, ABTA confirm that holidaymakers are seeking value in their holiday purchases, and are seeking to combine holidays with wellness, family time, relaxation and new experiences. This remains the case in 2017, however, against a backdrop of uncertainty created by world events and political upheaval, it is likely that there will be a rise in domestic tourism in the UK, although people will continue to travel internationally, with almost a quarter of the UK population planning to spend more on holidays in 2017 (ABTA, 2017). The number of domestic holidays increased to 71% in 2016, up from 64% in 2015 with families remaining key to the domestic market (ABTA, 2017).

Impacts and Insights

Macro-environmental impacts on family tourism

A range of macro-environmental factors have impacted upon the family tourism market over the course of recent years, including, but not limited to: 'Brexit'; the economic climate; UK Air Passenger Duty; technological developments; increasing awareness of health and safety due to recent terrorist attacks, natural disasters and outbreaks of disease; government legislation (specifically that governing holidays in school time); and social exclusion. Some of these factors have already been noted however it is important to recognise the effect that the wider environment has on the family tourism market.

As previously noted and perhaps as a reflection of the current uncertainty in the economy, ABTA (2017) anticipates that families remain key to the domestic UK market, particularly families with young children. For those travelling overseas, the abolition of Air Passenger Duty (APD) for children under 12 from 1 May 2015 also provided some financial respite for families and supported family holidays and the visiting friends and relatives market (ABTA, 2015).

Increasing exposure to, and use of, social media from a young age will involve children more effectively in the holiday decision-making process. As a result of this exposure, children are more aware of destinations, and they are also likely to be more technologically aware than their parents, leading to greater acceptance on the part of their parents, of their contribution to the holiday decision process. Furthermore, according to ABTA (2011, p. 13), 'Social media platforms, such as Facebook, [have] revolutionized global relationships – and reconnected long-lost friends and family', which could lead to an increase in VFR tourism. The ability to reconnect and *remain* connected with friends and family through social media means that VFR tourism is more likely in order to maintain the social and physical connection.

A number of high-profile incidents globally have led to growing awareness of worldwide safety and security. For example, a number of holiday destinations were affected by terrorist attacks in 2016, including Paris, Munich, Brussels and Istanbul. The Zika virus in parts of the Americas, Asia and the Caribbean caused widespread global concern and natural disasters such as earthquakes and hurricanes caused devastation to destinations including Italy, New Zealand and the Caribbean (ABTA, 2017).

Whilst all macro-environmental factors are significant to a lesser or greater extent, one key factor is explored here in greater depth: the 'Gove effect' – school holidays and impact of government legislation.

The 'Gove effect' – school holidays and impact of government legislation

According to Mancini *et al.* (2012) both economic ability and time are concrete factors that help us to understand the family holiday experience. The academic year has had a significant impact on family tourism in the sense that increasingly it determines when families are able to travel and for how long.

Traditionally holidays taken in school holidays are more expensive than those taken during term-time.

Affordability is a key factor for many families in their choice of holiday and evidence suggests that holidays during term-time are significantly cheaper than those taken in school holidays. In an article on holiday costs, *The Guardian* (2014) carried out a cost comparison of holidays bookable before and during school holidays and found that in some cases the price of holidays almost doubled during school holidays, with most averaging an increase of around 30%. Clearly this is a result of supply and demand, however many families have sought to overcome this issue by taking children out of school during term-time.

Since September 2013, family holidays have been affected by what is commonly referred to as the 'Gove effect'. The former Secretary of State for Education, Michael Gove, introduced fines and possible prosecution (in the case of non-payment of fines) for parents taking children out of school during term-time. Prior to this, head teachers were able to grant up to 10 days for family holidays in term-time, but they may now only grant leave in 'exceptional circumstances' (*Daily Telegraph*, 2015). 'Statistics show a 17 percent year-over-year decline in overall school absences since the new rules were introduced' (Boston Consulting Group, 2015). The Tourism Society (2015) suggests that the 'Gove effect' has resulted in an £87 million loss of business to Devon and Cornwall's visitor economies alone, due to a decrease in the numbers of families taking holidays in the region during term-time. From the industry perspective, this means that peak holiday period price increases are needed to compensate for decreased holiday-taking during the shoulder- and off-peak periods.

> According to a survey of 54 travel companies by Travelzoo and the Chartered Institute of Marketing – Travel Industry Group, 85% of travel operators have seen an impact on their business since the law changed, with a quarter saying that they might have to raise prices during the summer holidays to counteract the drop-off of families travelling during term time. (Boston Consulting Group, 2015)

Future of family tourism

There is no doubt that the future of family tourism is changing. Key trends such as changes in school holidays, diverse family structures, intergenerational participation in family holidays, improvements in economic circumstances, safety and security concerns and changes in demographics will impact upon the family tourism market.

Indeed a number of trends in family tourism are identified (Schänzel and Yeoman, 2015, pp. 142–145) as being those that are likely to shape the future. These include:

- **changing family structures** – new focus on the prominence of intergenerational relationships and multigenerational travel;
- **immigration** – migration leading to continued growth in VFR market;
- **social capital and creating memories** – (re)connecting social relations on holiday and tourism participation providing opportunities for bonding, communication and strengthening relationships;
- **growing awareness and concern regarding safety and security** – parents seek reassurance through access to online forums in order to allay concerns;
- **experiential family holidays** – increasingly families are engaging in adventure tourism, involving participation in more authentic experiences;
- **children as sophisticated consumers** – the travel industry is recognising the growing distinction between children's ages and their specific consumer needs;
- **blended families** – the definition of family has changed and this has implications for family holidays;
- **new family markets** – with the emergence of growth economies from source markets such as the BRIC countries (Brazil, Russia, India and China) there will be an increasing need for recognition of cultural difference and the needs of these potential new family markets; and
- **gender** – changes in gender roles in contemporary society have led to equality at home, in the workforce and on holiday and activities are becoming less gender-specific.

The deregulation of school holidays will lead to the softening of the demand curve for peak-season holidays, as school heads determine changes in school holidays. This is likely to lead to an extension of the shoulder period and a shorter peak period, making holidays more affordable for families. The travel industry will need to adapt quickly to these changes by ensuring that they have sufficient consumer insight, developing 'forecasting tools' and investing in 'dynamic pricing software' to react quickly to changes. 'Dynamic pricing, enhanced

---

Focus Box 2: Key considerations for the travel industry as it reacts to changing demand.

Dynamic Pricing: As the travel demand curve flattens and consumers figure out how they want to use new holiday times and formats, it will be more difficult for travel companies to determine optimal price points through the year. Vacation periods will likely become more fragmented, resulting in a higher number of varying price points. Without historical patterns to look back on, the early years of the transition will be especially challenging. The ability to price dynamically – setting prices in real time based on shifting demand, competitors' actions, and other factors – will be key to maximizing revenues as well as occupancy and use rates. Companies that do not have dynamic pricing systems will need to invest in them, and those that do have them may need to enhance their systems' reactive capabilities.

Forecasting Tools: Until new holiday patterns emerge, insights from the past are going to be less valuable and forecasting will gain in importance. Forward-looking operators will build adaptive forecast models, collecting granular holiday-schedule data for the first few years and using this information to assess shifting demand.

Capacity Planning: Travel companies will face evolving needs for the variable portion of their service capacity, such as hotel and resort staff or the number of shifts for rail employees. Extra capacity will be needed for shoulder periods, and capacity may need to be lowered for traditional peak periods. Operators will likely also face difficulty in shifting capacity to meet changing demand, adding to operational complexity. For example, companies that are not open year-round and rely on recruiting students as temporary staff during peak holiday periods may find it more difficult to find workers if holidays no longer coincide.

Consumer Insight: Developing precise and detailed knowledge of guests' profiles, such as family makeup and places of residence, will become increasingly important to predicting demand. Making the effort now to capture such information as customers' postcode and the share of guests with school-age children for cross-reference with local school schedules will pay off down the road with the ability to more accurately anticipate demand patterns through the year.

Courtesy of Boston Consulting Group (2015)

C. Southall

forecasting capabilities, capacity management, and consumer insight will be key to winning in this shifting environment' (Boston Consulting Group, 2015; see Focus Box 2).

Future Research

There are many important areas for future research on family tourism. Firstly future research should focus on oriental or eastern ('other') discourse, particularly in view of the fact that the emerging economies of BRIC countries are likely to play a significant role in future tourism activity worldwide. It is insufficient to consider only the western-centric perspective, as the emerging markets will present additional, often cultural, challenges in the context of family tourism.

Future research is also needed on how families use tourism to perform their social obligations, i.e. on family life on the move. 'The social construction of privacy is another area that requires further exploration. While presented as a retreat from the harsh realities of public life, family vacations often involve an exposure of the family to an anonymous but sanitized public. There is no privacy for the family in their search of the ideal domestic life as they will be relaxing by the pool under the close inspection of other families' gazes.' (Obrador, 2012, p. 417).

Additionally the diverse nature of families will continue to evolve and it is imperative to consider the needs of contemporary families in the context of tourism, recognising the important role that children play in determining tourism engagement and participation.

According to Mancini *et al.* (2012, p. 310) tourism organisations '…should be intentional about promoting relational tourism, that is structuring family opportunities that provide them time for interaction and transaction within the family and between their family and other families who are involved in the same travel and tourism experiences.' It would be appropriate to explore how tourism organisations could and do promote 'relational tourism', and ways in which family opportunities are structured to provide maximum benefit.

Questions and Tasks

1. What is meant by 'new' family norms and how has the concept of family changed over recent decades?
2. Access Office for National Statistics (ONS) data on 'Travel Trends' and analyse 'overseas Residents visits and spending in the UK by purpose and region of visit' over a recent 5 year period, identifying changes in inbound VFR markets and considering reasons for these changes.
3. Consider the development of social media and its impact on family tourism.

Further Reading

Consultancy.uk (2015) BCG: The Impact of New UK School Holiday Legislation. Available at: http://www.consultancy.uk/news/1553/the-impact-of-new-uk-school-holiday-legislation (accessed 17 July 2015).

Minnaert, L., Maitland, R. and Miller, G. (2009) Tourism and social policy: the value of social tourism. *Annals of Tourism Research* 36(2), 316–334.

Obrador, P. (2012) The place of the family in tourism research; domesticity and thick sociality by the pool. *Annals of Tourism Research* 39(1), 401–420.

Parke, R.D. (2013) *Future Families: Diverse Forms, Rich Possibilities.* Wiley, Chichester, UK.

Schänzel, H.A., Yeoman, I. and Backer, E. (eds) (2012) *Family Tourism: Multidisciplinary Perspectives.* Channel View Publications, Bristol, UK.

Schänzel, H.A. and Yeoman, I. (2015) Trends in family tourism. *Journal of Tourism Futures* 1(2), 141–147.

References

ABTA (2011) Travel Trends Report 2011. Available at: http://www.onecaribbean.org/content/files/ABTA2011TravelTrendsReport.pdf (accessed 30 July 2015).

ABTA (2015) Travel Trends 2015. Available at: https://c0e31a7ad92e875f8eaa-5facf23e658215b1771a91c2df41e9fe.ssl.cf3.rackcdn.com/publications/Travel_Trends_2015_Report.pdf (accessed 30 July 2015).

ABTA (2017) Travel Trends 2017. Available at: https://abta.com/assets/uploads/general/ABTA_Travel_Trends_Report_2017.pdf (accessed 5 January 2017).

All Party Parliamentary Group on Social Tourism (2011) Giving Britain a Break: Inquiry into the Social and Economic Benefits of Social Tourism. The Stationery Office Limited, UK. Available at: http://d3n8a8p-ro7vhmx.cloudfront.net/appgonsocialtourism/pages/29/attachments/original/111031GivingBritainaBreak.pdf?1320318284 (accessed 17 July 2015).

BBC (2017) Brexit Britain: What Has Actually Happened so Far? 4th January 2017. Available at: http://www.bbc.co.uk/news/business-36956418 (accessed 5 January 2017).

Bennett, J.E., Li, G., Foreman, K., Best, N., Kontis, V., *et al.* (2015) The future of life expectancy and life expectancy inequalities in England and Wales:

Bayesian spatiotemporal forecasting. *The Lancet* 386, 163–170. Available at: http://www.thelancet.com/pdfs/journals/lancet/PIIS0140-6736%2815%2960296-3.pdf (accessed 29 July 2015).

Boston Consulting Group (2015) Uncertainty in UK Travel and Tourism: School's Out—But When? Available at: https://www.bcgperspectives.com/content/articles/transportation_travel_tourism_pricing_marketing_schools_out_but_when/ (accessed 28 July 2015).

Carr, N. (2011) *Children's and Families' Holiday Experiences*. Routledge, London, UK.

Daily Telegraph (2015) Michael Gove 'costing West Country Tourism £87 million'. Available at: http://www.telegraph.co.uk/travel/travelnews/11632658/Michael-Gove-costing-West-Country-tourism-87million-a-year.html (accessed 17 July 2015).

Durkin, C. (2007) Social Tourism. *The Therapeutic Care Journal*. Available at: http://www.childrenwebmag.com/articles/social-work/social-tourism (accessed 17 July 2015).

Grootaert, C. and van Bastelaer, T. (2001) *Understanding and Measuring Social Capital: a synthesis of findings and recommendations from the Social Capital Initiative* (Social Capital Initiative Working Paper No 24), World Bank, Washington DC, USA.

Hilbrecht, M., Shaw, S.M., Delamere, F.M. and Havitzb, M.E. (2008) Experiences, perspectives, and meanings of family vacations for children. *Leisure/Loisir Special Issue: Popular Leisure* 32(2), 541–571.

Hughes, H. and Southall, C. (2012) Gay and lesbian families and tourism. In: Schänzel, H., Yeoman, I. and Backer, E. (eds) *Family Tourism: Multidisciplinary Perspectives*. Channel View Publications, Bristol, UK.

Mancini, J.A., George, D.V. and Jorgensen, B.L. (2012) Relational tourism: observations on families and travel. In: Uysal, M., Perdue, R. and Sirgy, M.J. (eds) *Handbook of Tourism and Quality of Life Research: Enhancing the Lives of Tourists and Residents of Host Communities*. Springer, Dordrecht, Netherlands.

McCabe, S. (2009) Who needs a holiday: evaluating social tourism. *Annals of Tourism Research* 36(4), 667–688.

McCabe, S., Foster, C. and Urbino, M. (2007) Briefing Paper for Policymakers. Evaluating Stated Needs for Support for Holidays. Christel DeHaan Tourism and Travel Institute/Nottingham University Business School. Available at: http://www.breaksforall.org.uk/pdfs/Briefing_paper_sept_08.pdf (accessed 17 July 2015).

McCabe, S., Joldersma, T. and Li, C. (2010) Understanding the benefits of social tourism: linking participation to subjective well-being and quality of life. *International Journal of Tourism Research* 12, 761–773.

Minnaert, L. (2012) Social tourism as opportunity for unplanned learning and behavior change. *Journal of Travel Research* 51, 607–616.

Minnaert, L., Maitland, R. and Miller, G. (2006) Social tourism and its ethical foundations. *Tourism Culture & Communication* 7(1), 7–17.

Minnaert, L., Maitland, R. and Miller, G. (2009) Tourism and social policy: the value of social tourism. *Annals of Tourism Research* 36(2), 316–334.

Obrador, P. (2012) The place of the family in tourism research; domesticity and thick sociality by the pool. *Annals of Tourism Research* 39(1), 401–420.

Office for National Statistics (ONS) (2011) *2011 Census Glossary of Terms*. ONS, London, UK.

Office for National Statistics (ONS) (2014a) Travel Trends 2014. Available at: http://www.ons.gov.uk/ons/rel/ott/travel-trends/2014/rpt-travel-trends--2014.html (accessed 27 July 2015).

Office for National Statistics (ONS) (2014b) Family Spending 2014 Edition: A Report on the Living Costs and Food Survey 2013. Available at: http://www.ons.gov.uk/ons/rel/family-spending/family-spending/2014-edition/index.html (accessed 29 July 2015).

Office for National Statistics (ONS) (2014c) Chapter 4: Trends in Household Expenditure over Time. Available at: http://www.ons.gov.uk/ons/dcp171766_385969.pdf (accessed 29 July 2015).

Office for National Statistics (ONS) (2015a) Travel Trends 2015. Available at: https://www.ons.gov.uk/people-populationandcommunity/leisureandtourism/articles/traveltrends/2015 (accessed 5 January 2017).

Office for National Statistics (ONS) (2015b) Overseas Residents Visits and Spending in the UK by Purpose and Region of Visit. Available at: https://www.ons.gov.uk/peoplepopulationandcommunity/leisureandtourism/datasets/overseasresidentsvisitstotheuk (accessed 5 January 2017).

Office for National Statistics (ONS) (2015c) Family Spending 2015 Edition: A Report on the Living Costs and Food Survey 2014. Available at: https://www.ons.gov.uk/peoplepopulationandcommunity/personalandhouseholdfinances/incomeandwealth/compendium/familyspending/2015 (accessed 5 January 2017).

Parke, R.D. (2013) *Future Families: Diverse Forms, Rich Possibilities*. Wiley, Chichester, UK.

Parliament (2010) The Ageing Population: Key Issues for the 2010 Parliament. Available at: http://www.parliament.uk/business/publications/research/key-issues-for-the-new-parliament/value-for-money-in-public-services/the-ageing-population/ (accessed 29 July 2015).

Powell, B., Blozendahl, C., Geist, C. and Steelman, L.C. (2010) *Counted Out: Same Sex Relations and Americans' Definitions of Family*. Russell Sage Foundation, New York, USA.

Schänzel, H.A. (2013) The importance of 'social' in family tourism. *Asia-Pacific Journal of Innovation in Hospitality and Tourism* 2(1), 1–15.

Schänzel, H.A. and Yeoman, I. (2015) Trends in family tourism. *Journal of Tourism Futures* 1(2), 141–147.

C. Southall

Schänzel, H.A., Smith, K.A. and Weaver, A. (2005) Family holidays: a research review and application to New Zealand. *Annals of Leisure Research* 8(2–3), 105–123.

Schänzel, H.A., Yeoman, I. and Backer, E. (eds) (2012) *Family Tourism: Multidisciplinary Perspectives.* Channel View Publications, Bristol.

Shakya, M. (2014) Social Capital, Tourism and Socio-economic Transformation of Rural Society: Evidence from Nepal. Working Paper. Volume 208. Institute of Development Research and Development Policy, Ruhr-Universitat Bochum: IEE. Available at: http://www.development-research.org/images/pdf/working_papers/wp-208.pdf (accessed 17 July 2015).

Shaw, S.M., Havitz, M.E. and Delamere, F.M. (2008) I decided to invest in my kid's memories: Family vacations, memories and the social construction of the family. *Tourism, Culture and Communication* 8(10), 13–26.

Southall, C. (2012) UK family tourism: past, present and future challenges. In: Schänzel, H., Yeoman, I. and Backer, E. (eds) *Family Tourism: Multidisciplinary Perspectives.* Channel View Publications, Bristol.

Take the Family (2015) British Families Spending More on Holidays. Available at: http://www.takethefamily.com/news/british-families-spending-more-holidays (accessed 17 July 2015).

The Guardian (2005) Holidays can improve physical and mental health and help families develop positive relationships. Government urged to back 'social tourism' Available at: http://www.theguardian.com/society/2005/feb/08/socialexclusion.politics (accessed 17 July 2015).

The Guardian (2014) Holiday Costs: Term-Time versus School Holidays. Available at: http://www.theguardian.com/travel/2014/feb/04/taking-kids-out-of-school-before-end-of-term (accessed 17 July 2015).

Travel Weekly (2015) Pound's Strength Offers UK Holidaymakers Extra Value. Available at: http://www.travelweekly.co.uk/Articles/2015/07/15/55934/pounds+strength+offers+uk+holidaymakers+extra+value.html (accessed 17 July 2015).

Tourism Society (2015) Solutions to the Gove Effect. Available at: http://www.tourismsociety.org/event-details/495/solutions-to-the-gove-effect.htm (accessed 17 July 2015).

Visit England (2010) The UK Tourist Statistics 2009. Available at: https://www.visitengland.com/sites/default/files/uk_tourist_2009_0.pdf (accessed 30 July 2015).

Visit England (2015) Beyond Staycation April 2015 (prepared by Trajectory). Available at: https://www.visitengland.com/sites/default/files/february_2015_final_builds_off_for_website.pdf (accessed 30 July 2015).

Waite, S., Parkinson, G., Blackwell, I., Martignetti, D., Blandon, C. and Moyeed, R. (2015) *What Do Children Learn When Camping? Perceptions of Parents, Children and Teachers.* Plymouth University & The Camping and Caravanning Club, Plymouth, UK.

Yeoman, I. (2012) 2050: Tomorrow's Tourism. Available at: http://www.tomorrowstourist.com/familyholiday.php (accessed 29 July 2015).

Zabriskie, R. and McCormick, B. (2001) The influence of family leisure patterns on perceptions of family functioning. *Family Relations: Interdisciplinary Journal of Applied Family Studies* 50(3), 6–74.

4 Cathedral Tourism

Ade Oriade and Harry Cameron

Learning Objectives

- To understand the scope and nature of cathedral tourism
- To differentiate between wider religious tourism and cathedral tourism
- To identify major influencing factors of cathedral tourism development
- To understand the interface between cathedral tourism and other forms of tourism
- To comprehend the impact of cathedral tourism development on its locale

Introduction

People have always travelled for reasons pertaining to visiting religious places or taking part in religious activities. Visiting cathedrals is one of such activities and/or visits and it's often referred to as religious tourism. Visiting cathedrals for tourism and leisure purposes is gaining ground, with tourism planners, cathedral administrators, local government officials, consultants and academics rising to the occasion in terms of planning, visitor experience management and research. Like any other type of tourism, cathedral tourism is visitor-led, attracting a diverse group of people in terms of demographic characteristics, reason for visit and attitude. Similarly, as in most types of tourism development, it brings along impacts which often necessitate government intervention, local residents' social interaction and dependence on environmental resources.

This chapter explores the concept of cathedral tourism. It describes various types of cathedrals and discusses factors that have influenced the growth of cathedral tourism. It further explores the motivation for cathedral tourism and delineates the impacts it has on the economy, the environment and on the local community. The chapter also examines the various interactions between local polity and cathedral tourism. Finally, the chapter presents a number of insights which can form the basis of further analysis for the understanding of cathedral tourism as a concept and distinct niche tourism market.

Key Concepts

Visits to cathedrals are often embedded in the definition of religious tourism. The Churches Visitor and Tourism Association (2017) employs a supply side approach in defining religious tourism, stating it is 'promoting best practice in welcoming visitors to places of worship …[and] developing the tourism potential and visitor experience of a unique part of our historical and contemporary sacred heritage'. This type of visit may be linked to other types of tourism activities and concepts such as urban tourism, film tourism and a host of other forms of cultural and heritage tourism. A key concept in travel is motivation. Travel motivation is a key factor and driver of visitor behaviour. Motivation for cathedral tourism is discussed in detail later in the chapter. Due to the evolving nature of tourism consumption, the world has seen a shift in patterns necessitated by the advanced level of travel experience, the increased number of 'to-see' places and growing interest for specialist subjects.

Visits to cathedrals for tourism and leisure purposes are becoming more popular even among non-religious visitors, so, it would be questionable to restrict the delineation of cathedral visits to religious tourism. In this chapter cathedral tourism is defined as the visit to a cathedral and designated cathedral quarters for spiritual or leisure purposes, in order to acquire a unique visit experience as part of historical sacred and monument heritage.

A cathedral is the mother church in a diocese or principal church in a city. It is usually the seat of a residential bishop who has his official seat in Christian churches that have an episcopal form of governance (Encyclopaedia Britannica, 2015). The origin of the word cathedral can be traced to three languages: *cathedrale* from French, *kathredra* from Greek, and *cathedra* from Latin meaning throne or seat. Cathedrals generally are huge buildings and are sometimes used as the determinant of the designation of city status. Various Christian denominations such as Catholic, Anglican, Evangelical and Methodist have cathedrals. According to Robinson *et al.* (2013), cathedrals can be classified as: flagship cathedrals and minsters; cathedrals within cathedral quarters; cathedrals within other designated areas; and other popular church tourism destinations.

Flagship cathedrals and minsters

This category represents sites that attract large numbers of domestic and international visitors. Sites in this category usually are positioned in major destinations. Examples of cathedrals in this class include St Paul's Cathedral, London; Canterbury Cathedral, which also happens to be a UNESCO World Heritage Site; Cologne Cathedral, also a UNESCO World Heritage Site; and York Minister to mention just a few.

Cathedrals within cathedral quarters

Cathedral quarters are becoming a popular tool for place-making. Cathedral quarters are usually historic areas of cities which are seen as the centre of city culture. Derby Cathedral is in this category; rebuilt in 1725, and surrounded by an assortment of businesses, retail shops, restaurants, pubs and visitor attractions such as museums and theatres, it is truly the hub of the city's culture. Other cathedrals in this category include Lincoln and Norwich cathedrals.

Cathedrals within other designated areas

This category comprises cathedrals that have become part of other 'quarters' in some destinations such as Bury St Edmunds Cathedral, Durham Cathedral (World Heritage site) and St Chad's Cathedral, Birmingham (Birmingham Jewellery Quarter) among others. Cathedrals in this category are situated in and form part of historic towns or renowned quarters rather than the quarter being formed around them. St Chad's Cathedral is situated on the outskirts of Birmingham's world-famous Jewellery Quarter, which is over 250 years old and still houses the world's busiest Assay Office. The Jewellery Quarter attracts domestic and international visitors to its buildings of historical significance, e.g. the Museum of the Jewellery Quarter and over 400 shops of jewellery designers and manufacturers (Robinson *et al.*, 2013).

Other popular church tourism destinations

Voase (2007) drew a distinction between cathedrals that are iconic in terms of scale, quality and antiquity, and parish churches which in latter days were upgraded to cathedral status. This category is comprised of such upgraded cathedrals and popular churches. Robinson *et al.* (2013) noted that a number of particularly popular religious sites in the UK are churches, rather than cathedrals, and are usually smaller buildings, but still attract significant numbers of visitors. Examples include Westminster Abbey (had cathedral status for ten years), Tewkesbury Abbey and Bath Abbey. Bath Abbey, for instance, attracts over 420,000 visitors each year and is well known for its Romantic Tower Tours, which include exclusive use, champagne and the opportunity to chime the Abbey bells; the tour can be booked for £100.

Major Factors Influencing Cathedral Tourism Development

Primarily, a cathedral serves as a place of worship. With further analysis a number of other roles anchored to social-economic influence can be deduced. While it is evident that people primarily visit cathedrals for worship and prayer purposes, the argument that cathedrals bring other socio-economic benefits to visitors and the community in which they are located suggests that people visit them or 'manage' them for more than just religious reasons. It is evident that people also visit cathedrals for tourism and leisure purposes as well as taking part in formal worship or visiting for personal prayer and contemplation.

The following subsections describe the major factors that have contributed to the development of cathedral tourism.

Land mass and beacon

Cathedrals, wherever they are located, are usually one of the most prominent – if not the most prominent – landmarks in such locations. The space they occupy can neither be ignored nor overemphasised.

For example Cologne Cathedral dominates the Rhine city skyline at 157.38 metres in height and occupying 8000 square metres. Cathedral quarters normally form a unique area in the heart of most cities, defining a special meeting place or a gateway to the city. A key factor is the importance of cathedral townscape qualities, which adds to the historical importance and attractiveness of the location. The precincts of cathedrals usually occupy a significant portion of land within a quarter, provide important areas of green space within a town centre, and in most cases are in conservation areas. A typology for cathedrals: large of international importance, medium-sized historic, urban, medium-sized and modern, is useful when considering the space they can occupy in the landscape.

Many cathedrals are now adopting a commercial and professional approach to land use, utilising the large amounts of land surrounding them, improving and increasing income through hosting visitors and events. The main aim for some cities is to stimulate long-term regeneration, to create vibrant mixed-use quarters that will improve the quality of the buildings, but also provide new settings for offices, shops, hotels and other leisure uses. Cathedral precinct typology should be aimed at a suitable land-use mix that retains a peaceful but animated setting, and also fosters a suitable environment for a city centre residential community, where the community and visitors want the surrounding urban area to be architecturally sympathetic to the cathedral as well as replete with multiple shopping, drinking and eating opportunities (Voase, 2007). The setting at Exeter is a good example where the cathedral is the heart of a creative and interesting quarter.

Architecture

For many cities and regions of the world the most dominant and iconic architectural feature is the cathedral. Tulban (2011) noted that the relationship between tourism and architecture is symbiotic. On one hand, architectural monuments such as cathedrals, owing to their history, beauty and celebrity, became touristic objectives; and on the other hand, architecture is in the heart of tourism services. St Basil's Russian Orthodox Cathedral, which is the icon of Russia, is a good example of the first aspect. The style, colours, patterns and shapes of the tulip domes are the culmination of a style that is unique to Russian architecture and is one of Moscow's most popular tourist attractions.

St Peter's Basilica in St Peter's Square, the Vatican, shown in Fig. 4.1, is probably the most photographed religious site in the world because of its monumental architectural statement. The Basilica lists among its architects the famous Italian sculptor, painter, architect, poet, and engineer, Michelangelo.

Cathedrals display a wide variety of architectural styles from the Byzantine style of the Hagia Sophia, Notre Dame's Gothic, and the Romanesque example of Pisa Cathedral, to the Renaissance of St Paul's and Brunelleschi's Santa Maria del Fiore in Florence. Gaudi's gothic and curvilinear Art Nouveau styled Sagrada Família is Barcelona's number one tourist attraction; so also is the sixties modernism of Liverpool's Roman Catholic Cathedral (Robinson et al., 2013). In popular song the city of Liverpool has 'a cathedral to spare', with the modern Catholic cathedral and the largest Anglican cathedral in Europe dominating the skyline of the city. In the Middle Ages and up to the Reformation in the 1500s, the Church enjoyed enormous power and wealth, and cathedrals are eloquent symbols of their dominant place in society. The towering magnificence of many cathedrals has dominated skylines for thousands of years: for example the medieval cathedral at Ely in England is visible for miles and often referred to as 'The Ship of the Fens'. The dominant Romano-Byzantine style of the Basilica de Sacre-Coeur, consecrated in 1919, dominates the landscape of Paris from the summit of Montmartre. Another remarkable cathedral worth mentioning in terms of design is the Mosque-Cathedral of Cordoba in Spain. With a rich and complex history the 'cathedral' combines Gothic, Renaissance and Baroque styles in the design of the main Christian part.

Art and artefacts

A number of cathedrals round the world are important works of art in their own right and most of these are homes to masterpieces, harbouring paintings, sculptures, ornaments and other forms of art decorations. Some of these artworks might have had different intended roles to what is perceived and consumed nowadays. For instance, it is believed in some quarters that connection to works of art can enable human beings to achieve the highest possible standards in their faith journey. In most cases, therefore, artists are engaged to produce work which would instil acceptable doctrines in believers, demonstrating to them the expectations of the Church. To this end, visual art was a potent

Fig. 4.1. St Peter's Basilica. (Courtesy: Jolly Janner [Public domain], via Wikimedia Commons)

means of conveying essential faith teachings and messages to the faithful.

In contemporary tourism, the various works of art, particularly medieval ones, are now the subject of experiential consumption which may stimulate some affective and cognitive feelings and attitudes in visitors. Some cathedrals, e.g. Gloucester Cathedral and Liverpool Cathedral, hold contemporary art collections and frequent exhibitions to emphasise the connection between art and religious faith, and possibly to encourage more visits.

Historical importance

The history of cathedrals is always fascinating, as they have many stories surrounding their construction, purpose, administration and representation. Their historical and heritage significance is exemplified in the number that have been designated UNESCO World Heritage Sites. For example, the Cathedral of Bern was designated a UNESCO World Heritage Site in 1983, the Mosque-Cathedral of Cordoba in 1984 and Cologne Cathedral in 1996.

Often prominent people and noblemen are buried in cathedral vaults or chapels, most of whom form an important part of the history of religion, politics, science and economics. No doubt scholars in these spheres of endeavour will make the journey to the resting place of their 'heroes' to pay homage or just to satisfy their curiosity. St. Peter's Basilica is a good example of where notable religious figures of history, such as St Peter, one of the twelve Apostles of Jesus Christ and the first Pope and Bishop of Rome, were buried. Another good example is Sir Isaac Newton, the notable British scientist, buried in Westminster Abbey. Newton's marble monument stands in the nave against the choir screen close to his grave. The cathedral of Santiago de Compostela has been part of a major historical pilgrimage route since the Middle Ages because it is the reputed burial-place of St James the Greater, another Apostle of Jesus Christ. It is an impressive structure measuring 318 feet long and 72 feet high; it is a mixture of Romanesque, Baroque, and Gothic styles and was built between 1075 and 1211.

No doubt the histories behind most of the cathedrals make them an attraction for a curious tourist or scholar. Their dominance at the time of their construction is often phenomenal. For example, Speyer Cathedral represented the ultimate symbol of medieval imperial power. No wonder, either, that they took so long to construct; their size and grandiose design are often magnificent. The building of Cordoba Cathedral spans nearly two centuries of changing architectural styles, while construction on the Basilica de la Sagrada Família started in 1882, but is still going on, and is speculated to finish sometime within the first four decades of the 21st century. Figure 4.2 shows the Basilica with cranes in the background. In another instance, the construction of the Cathedral of Bern took generations and series of builders to complete; its construction started in 1421 and was completed in 1893. In some cases construction works are disrupted. In Britain, the stories of war, arson, looting and political upheavals accentuate the general history behind Anglican cathedrals. These stories are often the focal point for interpretation in guided tours. A good example of a cathedral with an enormous number of stories behind it is Lincoln Cathedral, reputed to have been through a series of building disasters and mishaps in its near 1000 years of existence (BBC, 2014).

Economic impact

There is no doubt that cathedrals generate substantial economic benefits to the local areas in which they are situated. A number of studies (e.g. Shackley, 2006; Globe Economic Development Consultants, 2008; Robinson *et al.*, 2013) have looked at the economic significance of cathedrals within their geographical settings. The manners in which these impacts are generated include direct means resulting from cathedrals' employment and procurement activities; in addition, economic benefits are generated through the spending of visitors to cathedrals. According to Shackley (2006) many of the 42 Anglican cathedrals in England are major visitor attractions welcoming around 10 million visitors

per year. Shackley (2006) found they generate about £150 million per annum within their urban economies and employ 1885 people on a full-time basis. It must be noted that donations do form part of cathedrals' income but it has been found that a very small proportion of the revenue received by cathedrals is donations. This buttresses the argument that the cost of conservation and maintenance of cathedrals is likely to be through the generation of substantial revenue from visitors, either through entrance fees or sale of merchandise.

Cathedrals and visits to cathedrals also stimulate indirect and induced impacts through further spending generated by the direct spending of original visitors to cathedrals and further employment within the local economy. Robinson *et al.* (2013) in their Lichfield Cathedral study observed that the Cathedral pays £832,000 in wages and salaries out of which £482,000 is absorbed by the local economy. A central component of the procurement spending of the Cathedral pertains to expenditures for maintenance, repairs and restoration together with expenditure to purchase goods meant to be resold at the Cathedral Shop or Café. It must be noted that some degree of leakage effects are accounted for as not all employees are local residents, coupled with the fact that not all procurement spending involves only goods and services originating from the local economy. In other words, the full intricate nature of economic impact of tourism is at play; hence managers need to respond to all aspects and develop plans that will enable optimisation of positive economic impacts.

The use of the cathedral as a venue

Diversification is a buzzword that has been made popular over recent years as a result of the global economic recession experienced by many countries between late 2008 and 2012. Some countries, like the UK, are yet to experience full recovery. Diversification is a strategy adopted by an organisation when entering into a new market or industry. It is a means of reducing risk by exploring other viable areas of their core or related business. Suffice to add that diversification permeates all areas of business endeavour, however, diversification in tourism has been markedly noted, particularly during the recession period.

Cathedrals, being used for their original purpose or otherwise, are increasingly diversifying into

A. Oriade and H. Cameron

Fig. 4.2. Basilica de la Sagrada Família, still under construction. (Courtesy: Paolo da Reggio [Public domain], via Wikimedia Commons)

other service areas. The use of cathedrals as venues for events is one of the popular diversification options commonly seen nowadays. Apart from the fact that through this means the cathedral earns more income, it makes cathedrals more accessible and open to people who would not have visited one. To this end, diversification into event organisation and venue hire businesses makes cathedrals more popular and enhances visitor numbers and repeat business.

The link with other forms of tourism and economic activities

The link cathedral tourism has with other forms of tourism and economic activities has contributed immensely to its development. Typical examples of such relationships include links with film making, cultural tourism and film tourism. However, the notion of film tourism and its viability has been questioned by authors such as Heitmann (2010), arguing that films as part of the media are an extension of our individual worldview and as such do not create a new one. Heitmann (2010) further argues that film could be taken as a trigger for the type of tourism that it stands for: for example 'Braveheart' and 'Lord of the Rings' putting the natural scenery of the Scottish highlands and New Zealand on the map, thereby encouraging nature tourism.

The above augment cannot be far from true for some of the world's well known cathedrals, and of course for the justification of cathedral tourism. Globe Economic Development Consultants (2008) noted that Lincoln Cathedral, being a location for two films, 'The Da Vinci Code' in August 2005 and 'Young Victoria' in September 2007, benefited significantly from media interest and increased visitor numbers. During the making and prior to the release of 'The Da Vinci Code' the Cathedral opened for almost four weeks for the making of the film, welcoming large numbers of visitors to the city. On release of the film, the city enjoyed phenomenal worldwide media attention. Over 100 journalists and broadcasters from countries such as Singapore, South America and Japan came to Lincoln and the Cathedral visitor figures increased by 20% over 2006's visitor numbers (Globe Economic Development Consultants, 2008).

Other economic activities such as destination marketing and branding can be inferred. The presence of a cathedral and participation in cathedral tourism may also have wider impacts on the attractiveness of a city and for example, may lead to an increase in investment in the local economy.

Religious importance

Even though it is obvious that visits to cathedrals are primarily for worship and/or prayer, it is worth discussing here how religious importance attached to cathedrals has contributed to the development of cathedral tourism. Pilgrimage has always been a vital part of religious faiths. Trips to cathedrals are no exemption from this for Christians. The desire of people of faith to grow in their relationship with God is commonly viewed as a journey, and going on pilgrimage is a way of allowing the physical journey to enhance the spiritual journey of the mind. To this end, people embark on journeys to holy places. The need to travel brings a host of necessities with it, such as: transportation, need for accommodation and food, and spiritual blessing at the destination. In terms of transportation, people in the past travelled on foot or using horses. Today, it is far different: all the available means of transportation are also accessible to religious travellers. For amenities at the destination, people on pilgrimage have to make use of catering and accommodation facilities. A typical example is the St George's Cathedral Pilgrim Guest House in Jerusalem, which has been offering accommodation to pilgrims since 1923. The guest house today caters for both business and leisure visitors, nonetheless, the primary intended objective was to cater for religious people on pilgrimage. Whilst at the destination and on pilgrimage, pilgrims require spiritual leaders who will offer intercessorial blessings/prayers on their behalf or as a congregation. The role of spiritual leaders also entails leading sessions for thanksgiving and prayers for safe arrival and setting out. They also lead on spiritual obligatory performances.

Motivations

The key question underlying the concept of motivation is: why do people travel or visit places (in the case of this chapter, cathedrals)? Iso-Ahola (1982) described motivations as internal factors that arouse, direct and integrate visitors' behaviour. Suffice to note that individual visitors may have several factors driving them to visit a place. These factors would differ from context to context and individual to individual. Efforts have been made to understand travel motivation as this aids marketing effort, product development and demand forecast. Huang and Hsu (2009) noted that travel motivation theoretical themes such as Travel Career Ladder and Travel Career Patterns frameworks, and Plog's allocentric/psychocentric typologies (Plog, 1974, 1987, 2001) emerged from Maslow's (1970) hierarchy of needs theory. Please see further reading for details of travel motivation theoretical frameworks.

Understanding tourists' motivations remains elusive to tourism scholars despite the research in the topic area (Huang and Hsu, 2009). This is true of motivation for cathedral visitors. As Olsen (2013) notes there are a few, simplistic typologies of cathedral visitors which fail to capture the entire spectrum. Hughes *et al.* (2013) however, pointed out that factors that motivate visitation (apart from religious reasons) are: 'spur of the moment decision' (which usually accounts for majority of visits); family connections with site (e.g. visiting ancestors' gravestones); important and prominent people who were connected with the site; and personal interest in architecture and/or art works such as stained glass, sculpture and paintings.

As already established, the principal activity of cathedral is prayer and worship, so it is not surprising to know that studies found that a religious reason is one of the motives behind why people visit cathedrals. In the past and even today people tend to visit a cathedral because it is the seat of the bishop and they want to hear sermons from the head of the church in that diocese. Shackley (2002) advocates a two-category cathedral visitor motivation framework:

1. Visitors whose main motivation to visit cathedrals is religious.
2. Visitors whose motive to visit is founded on historic and architectural interests.

While these two categories have been empirically established, the latter is more prominent. Hughes *et al.* (2013) contend that the majority of cathedral visitors tend to be motivated by historic and architectural interests or by recreational or educational reasons, rather than religious reasons, and do not want to be labelled as pilgrims.

Another important motivating factor for cathedral visitation is the connection with history. According to Voase (2007), visitors to cathedrals seek a sense of connectedness with the founders and the builders of cathedrals; visitors want to experience the feelings and convictions that led their ancestors to invest their time and wealth in such a way. Voase's (2007) study suggests that cathedral visits are characterised by a desire to seek connection through contemplation. Sightseeing, another motivating factor for cathedral tourism, is capable of bringing about connection and contemplation as individuals wander about at their own pace soaking in the beauty of the site, separated in their thoughts and appreciation of the objects from the rest of the crowd.

Writing about motivation will not be complete without mentioning where the visitors come from and their composition. In the UK, visitors to cathedrals tend to be mainly domestic visitors. Studies found that people visit either as part of a small group comprised of friends and family or with a tour group, with only a few visiting cathedrals alone. It was also found that cathedral visits are secondary to visiting the city in which the cathedral is located (Voase, 2007; Robinson *et al.*, 2013). However, cathedral visits are well established; visitors expect a range of facilities such as information, parking, tours, and coffee and book shops (Shackley, 2006). No doubt visitors will expect the cathedral to be in harmony with the surrounding environment architecture, with complementing retail and hospitality opportunities. A good example of a cathedral with modern catering facilities is Norwich Cathedral, with its two-storey refectory that won two categories (Gold and the Commercial and Public Access awards) in the National Wood Awards in 2004.

Interactions with Destination Polity

Whilst some efforts have been expended on exploring the social and economic impacts of cathedrals and their role within cities, there is little research specifically focusing on economic impacts of cathedrals within the destinations where they are located. A report commissioned to examine the future role of Anglican cathedrals recognised that tourism is of great significance to England's cathedrals, firstly as part of their mission of teaching, evangelism and witness, and secondly as a source of income through donations, admission fees, retailing and catering. Cathedrals also play a major part in the nation's tourism industry through the number of visitors they attract (particularly those from overseas), the contribution they make to the stock of Britain's and other countries' heritage, and the wider economic benefits they generate through the impact on sales and employment generated in the wider local economy due to the activities of visitors.

The interactions cathedrals have with politics are well documented. The Church in most nations, e.g. Britain, Italy and Israel to mention but a few, had so much power and influence. For instance in the UK the magnitude of the Church's power was so considerable that it controlled one third of the country's wealth before Henry VIII confiscated much of its lands and stopped most of the privileges it was enjoying (BBC, 2014). The relationship has not been entirely negative, though. With the realisation of cathedrals' potential as heritage resources and their prospect of enhancing the tourism industry, the role of government policies has been protective of cathedrals, thereby encouraging cathedral tourism development. For instance, since 1937 the London Corporation has followed a policy known as the 'St Paul's Heights' to protect and enhance important views of the cathedral. This policy is in line with the Mayor's strategic view protection in the London Plan, outlined in detail in the London View Management Framework.

Impacts and Insights

In recent times our knowledge of the impacts of cathedrals has been broadened. Equally, some insights have been gained about their importance in the contemporary consumption environment, and the complexity of keeping them viable has led to innovative and creative methods of managing them and obtaining resourcing.

Tourism Resource

It is generally agreed that tourism relies on the attractiveness of a destination's resources. According to Godfrey and Clarke (2000) tourism resources can be divided into two major classes – principal and supporting resources. Principal resources are those that have the strongest pulling power and usually represent the key motivating factor in the tourist travel decision process. On the other hand, supporting resources are the type of resources that supplement destinations' main resources often adding to their appeal. These are usually not a primary motivator for travel. Undoubtedly, this classification can be problematic. For instance, on one hand, an individual may be attracted and travel to Lichfield purposely to see the Cathedral, in which case the cathedral is a principal resource. On the other, another individual may visit Lichfield Cathedral as a supplementary call to their visit to

the National Memorial Arboretum; thus, conversely, the Cathedral becomes a secondary resource in this case.

At a more extensive level, tourism resources can be further divided into five categories: natural, cultural, events, activities and services. Examples of natural tourism resources will include beaches, waterfalls, snow, flora and fauna. In the event category, examples like festivals and sporting events can be cited. Examples of activity may include winter sports and volunteering, while the service category will include medical services (medical tourism) and a host of others. Cathedrals as a tourism resource can be grouped under the cultural category.

Although the central function of a cathedral is the preservation of religious tradition and the provision of a space for worship, prayers and meditation, industry managers and religious leaders are increasingly justifying cathedrals as a principal tourism resource, citing that major cathedrals are the main reason why people visit the cities and towns in which they are located. It is not surprising these days to see studies being commissioned and conducted investigating this subject. Without doubt managers are making efforts to attract more visitors. Olsen (2013) notes that cathedrals are progressively being considered by government officials and tourism stakeholders as tourism attractions as a result of their important role in the heritage tourism industry, and subsequently in England's overall tourism strategy.

Visitors nowadays also see cathedrals as tourism resources, whether principal or secondary. According to Hughes *et al.* (2013) research in British cathedrals indicates that many visitors regard religious sites such as cathedrals as leisure or recreational attractions. In their study of Canterbury Cathedral in the UK, they found that visitors to the site felt it was essential to provide directional signage, displays and exhibits, value for money, attendants and equal access. Visitors tend to crave information on the cathedral's history, architecture and artwork, as well as stories regarding people connected with the site.

Visitor management dilemmas

The growing popularity of tourism at religious sites such as cathedrals presents challenges to managers in terms of visitor management. As noted earlier, visitors are demanding value for money. They want an experience that equals that obtainable from contemporary visitor attractions. Some of the difficulties relating to management of visitors and

A. Oriade and H. Cameron

their experience at cathedrals are accentuated by the fact that cathedrals are not primarily meant for visitation by tourists. Even though cathedrals in their design are meant to accommodate a large body of people and possibly traffic, they are not designed to accommodate people moving in different directions all at one time. Oriade *et al.* (2010) pointed out that one of the major operational issues is the tricky nature of prediction of demand, particularly where visitors' arrival is variable. Experienced managers are able to determine when human traffic will build up and put in place measures to prevent bottlenecks; this will be of particular importance at flagship cathedrals attracting appreciably large number of visitors.

One question relating to visitor management in cathedrals is the question of whether cathedrals should charge an entrance fee or not. The majority of cathedrals do not charge entrance fees, however, they expect visitors to make donations. It is easy to note role incompatibilities which arise as a result of this dual status of cathedrals as places of worship and visitor attractions, and this undoubtedly poses some dilemmas for managers. Voase's (2007) study

suggests that visitors see cathedrals as some sort of 'public territory', built by the preceding generations, and entry to such should not attract any obligatory charges.

Centre of social interaction and relaxation

People are increasingly recognising cathedrals' integral place at the heart of cities. Local residents and church administrators are progressively seeing cathedrals as hubs for community and social engagement. From a social perspective, cathedrals make a significant contribution by creating opportunities for education, relaxation and bonding. Most cathedrals are well loved by their local communities, i.e. congregation members, employees (comprising paid staff and volunteers) and local residents, who often describe their local cathedral with affection and a sense of ownership. Surprisingly, very few cathedrals take optimal advantage of this fact. Apart from emphasising the education aspect by encouraging school visits, and promoting their cafes and catering offers, the opportunity for bonding and social interaction is less emphasised. Figure 4.3 is a

Fig. 4.3. The Tegucigalpa Cathedral. (Courtesy: Stefan Zeugner [Public domain], via Wikimedia Commons)

picture of the front area of Tegucigalpa Cathedral in Honduras, full with people relaxing and interacting.

The Manchester Cathedral Development Project perhaps aims to explore this area judging by the inclusion of 'New Social Space' in the list of what the project aims to achieve. The focus on community benefits (and the conscious emphasis laid on this by highlighting that the renewing of the Cathedral and its immediate environment will promote social inclusion, enhance training and employment, boost tourism in the region, and stimulate arts, music, worship and heritage) possibly sums up the role of the cathedral as a total package in the 21st century.

Sustainability

The subject of the main focus of cathedral tourism – cathedrals – is a major area for disquiet when it comes to sustainability. By their nature cathedrals are very delicate resources, hence can be very expensive to maintain and prone to damage when exposed to usage (e.g. excessive visitation, other than that for which they were originally meant).

Governments in some cities and countries put in place regulations to protect cathedrals and resources within them. London's 'strategic view protection' policy is one such good example. While height protection and views should be an important consideration, controversy still arises when new developments are to be considered in the immediate vicinity of a cathedral. Architecture and development, arguments over traditional classical styles and modernist plans, and which ones work in the built environment, is always a design contest. However a greater challenge, common with many historic structures, is the issue of wear and tear. Cathedrals in northern Europe have suffered extensive weathering by atmospheric pollutants. The exterior stonework and statues are being eroded by the pollutants present in acid rain. Consequently many medieval cathedrals have had to have extensive renovation programmes, involving in many cases very expensive funding campaigns. As part of Canterbury Cathedral's renovation, six of the stained glass windows that have been removed for repairs to surrounding stonework have been on fund-raising exhibition at New York's Metropolitan Museum.

Summary

It is evident that cathedral tourism is a growth area and there is no doubt that people, in the future, will continue to visit cathedrals for historic, architectural, recreational, educational, and of course, religious reasons. Although it is often discussed under the umbrella of religious or faith-based tourism, it is argued here that this is an area worth recognising as a bona fide niche market. As the socio-economic impacts of this sector continue to become more apparent, church administrators and tourism managers will also continue to harness the opportunities presented by the market. However, managers, administrators, marketers and planners need to bear in mind that the development of the sector is not without its dilemmas, chief among such quandaries being issues of sustainability and visitor management. Balancing the needs of the worshipper and the tourist is another area worth careful consideration.

Questions and Activity

1. What would you consider the impacts of a Flagship Cathedral to be? Discuss the various impacts identified in this chapter.
2. Take a trip to any cathedral of your choice and conduct observational research identifying what can be classified as tourism resources. Categorise them using examples of typologies used in the chapter.
3. What are the main challenges facing cathedral tourism development?

Further Reading

Fletcher, J., Fyall, A., Gilbert, D. and Wanhill, S. (2013) *Tourism: Principles and Practices*, 5th edn. Pearson Education, Harlow, UK.
Raj, R. and Griffin, K.A. (eds) (2015) *Religious Tourism and Pilgrimage Management: An International Perspective*, 2nd edn. CAB International, Wallingford, UK.
Robinson, P., Luck, M. and Smith, S.L.J. (2013) *Tourism*. CAB International, Wallingford, UK.

References

BBC (2014) The Cathedrals of Britain. http://www.bbc.co.uk/history/british/architecture_cathedral_01.shtml (accessed 23 November 2016).
ECOTEC (2004) *The Economic and Social Impacts of Cathedrals in England*. ECOTEC Research and Consulting Ltd, London, UK.
Encyclopaedia Britannica (2015) Cathedral. http://www.britannica.com/EBchecked/topic/99526/cathedral (accessed 23 November 2016).

A. Oriade and H. Cameron

Globe Economic Development Consultants (2008) *The Economic and Social Impact of Lincoln Cathedral*. Globe Regeneration Ltd, Lincoln, UK.

Godfrey, K. and Clarke, J. (2000) *The Tourism Development Handbook: A Practical Approach to Planning and Marketing*. Thomson, London, UK.

Heitmann, S. (2010) Film tourism planning and development – questioning the role of stakeholders and sustainability. *Tourism and Hospitality Planning & Development* 7(1), 31–46.

Huang, S. and Hsu, C.H.C. (2009) Travel motivation: linking theory to practice. *International Journal of Culture, Tourism and Hospitality Research* 3(4), 287–295.

Hughes, K., Bond, N. and Ballantyne, R. (2013) Designing and managing interpretive experiences at religious sites: visitors' perceptions of Canterbury Cathedral. *Tourism Management* 36, 210–220.

Iso-Ahola, E. (1982) Towards a social psychology theory of tourism motivation: a rejoinder. *Annals of Tourism Research* 9(2), 256–262.

Jones, R.C. (no date) In Summer at Midday. http://www.robertcjones.co.uk/Birmingham Cathedral Churchyard, UK.html (accessed 4 January 2015).

Olsen, D.H. (2013) A scalar comparison of motivations and expectations of experience within the religious tourism market. *International Journal of Religious Tourism and Pilgrimage* 1(1), 40–61.

Oriade, A., Robinson, P. and Gelder, S. (2010) Delivering live events. In: Robinson, P., Wale, D. and Dickson, G. (eds) *Events Management*. CAB International, Wallingford, UK.

Robinson, P., Oriade, A., Southall, C. and Dimos, C. (2013) *An evaluation of the economic impact of Lichfield Cathedral upon the local economy of the City of Lichfield - Project Report*. University of Wolverhampton. Available at: http://eprints.staffs.ac.uk/1859/ (accessed 23 November 2016).

Shackley, M. (2002) Space, sanctity and service: the English cathedral as heterotopia. *International Journal of Tourism Research* 4(5), 345–352.

Shackley, M. (2006) Costs and benefits: the impact of cathedral tourism in England. *Journal of Heritage Tourism* 1(2), 133–141.

The Churches Visitor & Tourism Association. About Us. Available at: http://cvta.org.uk/about-us/ (accessed 15 November 2017).

Tulban, N. (2011) Architecture and tourism. *Journal of EcoAgriTourism* 7(2), 67–71.

Voase, R. (2007) Visiting a cathedral: the consumer psychology of a 'Rich Experience'. *International Journal of Heritage Studies* 13(1), 41–55.

5 Islamic Tourism

Nazia Ali

Learning Objectives

- To understand the tourist behaviours, experiences and motivations of the global Muslim diaspora
- To learn about Islamic tourism as a special interest global tourism market in Muslim and non-Muslim countries
- To discover the relationship between Islam, Islamic Civilisation identity, Shariah Law and spirituality in creating and consuming Islamic tourism
- To critically inspect the factors that could potentially impact upon the development of Islamic tourism

Key Concepts

This chapter engages with the following key concepts.

- Islamic Tourism: a form of tourism that is principally created, consumed and practised by people and populations following the theology of Islam, referred to as Muslims.
- Islamic Tourists: Muslims encountering, experiencing and participating in Islamic Tourism are referred to as Islamic Tourists.
- Shariah-Compliant: The Islamic Law – *Shariah* – prescribed in religious texts (i.e. the Quran and Hadith), which sets out the 'way of life' for Muslims to adhere by.
- Organisation of Islamic Cooperation (OIC): The OIC currently comprises 57 member states from the Muslim world, which seek to bring together, advance and promote the global Islamic community.

Major Factors

Understanding Islam and tourism

The relationship between religion and tourism, and also hospitality and events, is well established and has been considered in many secular and non-secular contexts, with a particular focus on heritage, pilgrimage, rituals, spirituality and traditions (Vukonić, 1996;

Timothy and Olsen, 2006; Raj and Morpeth, 2007; Scott and Jafari, 2010a; Stausberg, 2011). Religious tourism is defined as 'a form of tourism where people of a particular faith travel to visit places of religious significance in their faith' (El-Hanandeh, 2013, p. 53). The theoretical, conceptual and empirical underpinnings of religion and tourism found in the aforementioned texts, to mention but a few, further inform the associations of tourism with Islam. Thus, Islam and tourism can be closely aligned with the importance of pilgrimage-related journeys, namely the obligatory *Hajj* to Mecca (Saudi Arabia) (Henderson, 2011; El-Hanandeh, 2013; Jafari and Scott, 2014). The connection between tourism and Islam is exemplified by Jafari and Scott (2014, p. 6) 'tourism and Islam "naturally" fit together, as the latter "expects" pilgrimage by its adherents to Makkah'. However, tourism mobilities inspired by Islam are not limited to the obligatory *Hajj*, as there is also *Umarh*, a non-obligatory, but recommended, 'lesser' pilgrimage to Mecca; *Ziarat*, involving visiting local and regional holy places and sites, such as shrines and mosques; and *Rihla*, which entails travelling for the search of knowledge (Haq and Wong, 2010).

Defining Islamic tourism

The definitions of Islamic tourism are wide and varied, and embody various references to Muslims as participators, Islamic countries as tourist locations, activities with cultural, economic and religious dimensions, products consumed, and service encounter management (Duman, 2011). Carboni *et al.* (2014, p. 2) defined Islamic tourism as 'tourism in accordance with Islam, involving people of the Muslim faith who are interested in keeping with their personal religious habits whilst travelling'. Shakiry (2006) noted that Islamic tourism cannot be confined to such categories as religious tourism because 'it includes all kinds of family tourism that respects religious principles as well as tourism aimed at the discovery of old civilizations and their heritage, visiting cities and countries to come to know them to rest, or for recreation and treatment'. Islamic tourism could also be considered as synonymous with forms of tourism referred to as Halal tourism (Battour *et al.*, 2010), Islamic hospitality (Stephenson, 2014) and Muslim tourism (Wang *et al.*, 2010), as central to the interpretations of these niche markets are also Islamic beliefs, principles and values or Shariah compliance in terms of creation, consumption and practice. Moreover, the Organisation of Islamic Cooperation (OIC) identified major components of Islamic tourism as Shariah-compliant hotels and sport facilities, Halal food and drinks, and family-dedicated leisure areas (OIC, 2014).

Tourism mobilities of the Islamic tourist

According to the *Global Tourism Impact of Muslim Tourism Report 2015* by Salam Standard the international Muslim tourist market is worth US$138 billion in 2015 (cited in TTG Asia, 2016) and by the end of the decade is estimated to rise to US$200 billion. In 2010 there were about 1.6 billion Muslims across the world, which was 23% of the world's population and is likely to increase by 35% to 2.2 billion by 2030 (Pew Research Center, 2011). Therefore, based on the given statistics, there are likely to be vast numbers of Islamic tourists encountering, experiencing and participating in Islamic tourism. Islamic tourists, also referred to as Muslim tourists, journey to Muslim countries as these destinations complement and preserve their Islamic identity and deliver the tourism product, service or experience in accordance with Shariah Law for their families. Many of these places are member states of the OIC, for example the Kingdom of Saudi Arabia, Republic of Indonesia, the United Arab Emirates (UAE), Malaysia (See Focus Box 1) and Republic of Turkey (Crescent-Rating, 2014a). However, tourism mobilities

---

Focus Box 1: Malaysia: top ranking destination for Islamic tourism (2014)

The OIC member state Malaysia was ranked the top halal-friendly destination for Muslim tourists in 2014 in the CrescentRating's Halal Friendly Travel (CRaHFT) Ranking. The criteria for selection includes suitability as a family holiday destination, the level of services and facilities it provides for Muslim travellers, and the marketing initiatives of the destination. Malaysia has held the top rank position for three consecutive years since 2011, beating other OIC nations (Turkey in 2011, Egypt in 2012 and 2013, and United Arab Emirates in 2014) to the number one position. (CrescentRating, 2014a).

Malaysia is an Islamic nation and Islam is the state religion, and exists alongside other world religions such as Buddhism, Christianity and Hinduism.

The Islamic Tourism Centre of Malaysia introduces itself, on its web-page, as a 'Muslim-friendly destination'. This claim is justified by the nation having the 'necessary ingredients of an ideal Islamic tourism destination' (e.g. halal food, prayer facilities and Islamic attractions) and has a 'rich Islamic history and heritage', which appeals to Muslims. The marketing campaign is directed at Muslim and non-

Muslim tourists to the country seeking to explore and learn about Islam through such representations as 'Islamic architectural heritage, halal gastronomic delights, vibrant Islamic festivals and world-class Islamic events'. (Islamic Tourism Centre of Malaysia, 2015).

Islamic tourists can explore and experience many aspects of Islamic tourism in Malaysia such as mosque trails, Islamic museums, Islamic tours, and Islamic events. There is also a directory which the Islamic tourist can refer to for a Muslim-friendly experience, comprising travel agencies, hotels, airlines, certified halal organisations (e.g. food premises, consumer products and slaughterhouses) and places to purchase various Islamic heritage and cultural souvenirs from (Islamic Tourism Centre of Malaysia, 2015). The Islamic tourism products, services and experiences are more than extensions of Islam in Malaysia, but rather embodied into the daily 'way-of-life' in the nation. There is clearly a symbolic relationship between Islam and tourism in Malaysia, which appeals to and caters to the needs of the Muslim and non-Muslim tourist.

---

of the Islamic tourist are not limited to OIC destinations as Muslims also travel to non-OIC nations such as Singapore, South Africa, the United Kingdom, Australia and India (CrescentRating 2014a).

This way of life is a reflection of their daily life guided by beliefs (*Iman*) and practices (*Amal*), as non-tourists, and there is a desire to continue to be Shariah-compliant and practise their religion as tourists. As Battour *et al.* (2011, p. 528) noted 'Islamic religious attributes are bound to be very important considerations when a Muslim decides to travel abroad.' Islamic tourists are motivated to travel to tourist destinations, such as OIC nations, that do not separate the way-of-life from the personal, private and public domains. For example Muslims visiting the Sultanahmet Mosque, popularly referred to as the Blue Mosque (Istanbul, Turkey) are informed of the five daily prayer times and can perform prayer as shown in Fig. 5.1, and during prayer times the Blue Mosque is closed to visitors. These intra-Islamic tourism mobilities echo what was referred to in earlier tourism and travel literature as the 'tourist bubble' (Smith, 1977) or 'home-grown bubble' (Graburn, 1977) whereby holidaymakers search for or enter environments abroad that are reflective of their ways-of-life at home.

Motivations

Islamic 'ways-of-life'

The motive for travel by Muslim people and populations in tourism literature focuses extensively on the obligatory pilgrimage – the fifth pillar of Islam – the *Hajj* to Mecca (Saudi Arabia). However, travel is not limited to the religious as Islam encourages Muslims to travel, as endorsed in the Quran, to see and appreciate the creations of Allah (*Subhanahu Wa Ta'ala/swt*) (Zamani-Farahani and Henderson, 2009). This travel should be in accordance with Shariah teachings, which forbids Muslims to visit places where immoral or sinful acts take place that infringe on the Islamic way-of-life and its associated beliefs and practices (Battour *et al.*, 2010) or 'Islamic religiosity' (Zamani-Farahani and Musa, 2012). These motives for participation in Islamic tourism cannot be separated into the religious and the secular because according to Hassan 'Muslims do not distinguish between the religious and the secular but consider Islam to be a complete way of life' (1999, cited in Scott and Jafari, 2010a, p. 4).

Islamic identity

Muslims are motivated to participate in Islamic tourism to learn about and express their identities in places beyond their immediate settlement. Islamic identity, despite national, cultural, racial, political and denominational differences, has core characteristics that unite the global Muslim community. *Ummah* are the five mandatory pillars of faith: (i) belief in one God – Allah (*swt*), (ii) performing the daily prayer five times a day, (iii) helping the poor through alms and charitable donations, (iv) fasting during the month of Ramadan, and (v) *Hajj* to Mecca. The Holy Book, the Quran, is recited and respected by Muslims all across the globe and scriptures from the Quran are narrated during birth, marriage and death ceremonies, and also within the Quran is a source for Shariah Law. To be in a destination with other Muslims who share common characteristics of religious identity is a motivating factor to engage in Islamic tourism. Bogari *et al.* (2004) discovered that motivations for domestic tourism among Saudi tourists were driven by 'cultural value' and 'religious' push and pull factors. Also the Quran encourages Muslims to travel for learning, gaining knowledge and enjoyment (Carboni *et al.*, 2014). Figure 5.2 shows Muslim women viewing an exhibition on Islam inside the Blue Mosque in Istanbul (Turkey). This display inside the Blue Mosque performed an educational function as Islamic tourists learnt about, for example, the genealogy of the 25 prophets mentioned in the Quran, viewed English translations of Quranic verses, and images of Muslims performing prayer in the Blue Mosque.

Safety and Security

Tourist mobilities of Muslim diasporas can be led by geographies of identity as it is not uncommon for tourists to journey to places where people share the same identity characteristics, such as religion, to feel safe and secure in destinations where their presence as Muslims is not implicated with the politics of space. The identity of Muslims has been subject to scrutiny following the 11 September terrorist attacks on the World Trade Center by Al-Qa'ida. This incident of 9/11 resulted in a widespread distrust of Muslims in non-Islamic countries, reinforcing a 'dread or hatred for Islam – and therefore fear or dislike of all or most Muslims' (Ansari, 2002, p. 4). Another feature of Ansari's

Fig. 5.1. Prayer times at the Blue Mosque, Istanbul (Turkey).

(Ansari, 2002) observation has been a consequent growth in evidence of Islamophobia. In particular Muslim travellers journeying to non-Muslim nations in the post-9/11 global–local political climate have encountered Islamophobic attitudes, behaviours, practices and surveillances (Stephenson and Ali, 2010). Muslim tourists entering non-Muslim countries have been welcomed with hostile and inhospitable environments should they 'fit' the profile of the 'archetypal terrorist' (Bazian, 2014). The 'archetypal terrorist' is an amalgamation of tangible (i.e. physical markers such as language, dress, men with beards, and women with *hijabs*) and intangible connotations that are reflective of the stereotypical creations or imaginaries of a terrorist. For instance, airports are 'problematic sites' as

Fig. 5.2. Muslim women tourists at the Blue Mosque in Istanbul (Turkey).

authorities have repeatedly singled out Muslim travellers in 'stop and question' security measures, resulting in humiliation, distress and fear (Blackwood *et al.*, 2013). Nevertheless desire to travel to non-

Muslim nations is evident. Little research to date can be found that explains the rise of Islamic tourists to non-OIC countries, however a possible explanation could be the cosmopolitan nature of

N. Ali

cities such as Brisbane, Melbourne and Sydney, which collectively appreciate and promote Islamic culture (Stephenson, 2014). Also, Islamic tourism considered in the context of visiting friends and relatives (VFR) tourism can occur in non-Muslim nations when religious obligations to travel unite the Muslim diaspora, such as the obligatory funeral prayers (*Salāt ul-Janaza*) and associated ceremonies (Sattar *et al.*, 2013).

Interactions

Importance of civilisation identity

Muslims are obliged to travel the world in order to discover Islam and its associated civilisations as a means to enhance or seek knowledge and appreciate the boundless beauty of the world created by Allah (swt). As the entry on travel by Staples (2009, p. 672) in the *Encyclopaedia of Islam* reiterates:

> Muslims have travelled the world for centuries to visit holy sites and search for knowledge […] The Prophet Muhammed (d. 632) also urged his followers to travel in search of knowledge, 'even as far as China' and many Muslims wandered from Morocco to China and beyond in their search for deeper insight and spiritual wisdom.

Islamic civilisations are represented and present in a variety of contexts such as art, architecture, culture, history, language, literature/text, science, scriptures, rituals and traditions. Islam and civilisations are located across the globe – in the Arab world, Persian Empire, Turkey, Africa, the Far East, Asia and Central Europe. This further promotes the conceptualisations of the *Ummah*, which connects the global Muslim diaspora with the past, people, places and the present in the Muslim and non-Muslim worlds. Countries, especially in the Muslim world, have the 'soft power' of Islamic civilisational identity to encourage interactions with Islamic tourism products, services and practices. A series of global events as part of the *1001 Inventions: Discover a Golden Age – Inspire a Better Future* are held to showcase Muslim achievements across the world in science, technology and culture from the 7th century onwards (see http://1001inventions.com/). However, locating a distinct civilisational identity and balancing this with the cultural identities of a nation can be politically implicated. As Hoffstaedter (2009, p. 527) observes in his research investigating *Mak Yong*, a dance drama performance as a contested art space in Malaysia: 'art forms such as *Mak Yong* have been pulled into a political tussle over ownership and power to demarcate what is or should be Islamic, Malay or Malaysian'.

Spiritual enrichments and connections

Places for spiritual enhancement and sanctuary, beyond the obligatory pilgrimage – the *Hajj* (Mecca, Saudi Arabia), can be experienced at non-obligatory sites and spaces referred to as *Ziarat* (visits to shrines/graves) in Islamic teachings. Ali's (2008) study of return visits of the UK Pakistani diaspora to Pakistan noted first-generation Pakistanis visited the graves of Sufi *pirs* (saints/holy men) and when visiting a shrine, Pakistanis engage in ritualistic activities such as offering prayer, laying flowers on tombs, placing embroidered shawls on shrines, listening to *qawali* (mystical songs) or leaving a charitable donation. Although visiting shrines of *pirs* is not a religious duty or obligation, Pakistani respondents in Ali's (2008) study recognised the importance of paying homage to *pirs* for spiritual aid and guidance. There are numerous shrines constructed across Pakistan for Sufi mystical devotion, which are integrated into the religious backdrop of Pakistani life. Pakistani respondents returning to Pakistan offered prayer at the following tombs of Sufi *pirs*: Baba Pir Shah Ghazi Dumerie Sarkar near the Mirpur district in Azad Kashmir, and Mian Mir and Data Ganj Baksh in Lahore. Shrines of prominent Sufi saints, scholars and poets can be found in OIC nations, for example Rumi's shrine in Konya (Turkey) and non-OIC countries, for example Moinuddin Chishti's tomb in Ajmer (India). Thus, Muslims visit shrines of Sufi *pirs*, poets and mystics central to symbolic representations of Sufi philosophical teachings of Islam and Muslim heritage across the globe, and therefore having close associations with Islamic tourism. However, spiritually enriched interactions associated with Sufism can also be categorised as 'Sufi Tourism', which according to Abeddour (2011), in his analysis of the impact of Sufism on tourism in Morocco, is 'spiritually motivated travel to explore religious locations such as tombs of saints, great scholars and righteous people'.

Non-Muslim tourists and Islamic tourism

Although focused specifically on Muslims and their participation in Islamic tourism, non-Muslims also participate in Islamic tourism, therefore interpretations of Islamic tourism/tourists can be extended to non-Muslims travelling in the Muslim world (Zamani-Farahani and Henderson, 2009). Hosts in Muslim countries deliver the Islamic tourism product, service and experience, and are religiously obligated to look after their guest whether followers of Islam or not – the same principles apply. The *Hadith* states 'He, who believes in Allah (*swt*) and the Last Day, let him show hospitality to his guest...' Non-Muslim tourists' interaction with OIC places (e.g. Malaysia, United Arab Emirates and Turkey) and their people and populations is a complex and tense one, especially when local religious beliefs, customs and values are compromised and behaviour of non-Muslims and/or Western tourists is considered to be incompatible with the Islamic backdrop of the nation, as many authors have noted (Din, 1989; Henderson, 2003; Timothy and Iverson, 2006). Nevertheless Muslim tourist destinations have attempted to balance the triangular relationship between Islamic (Muslim) tourists, Islamic (non-Muslim) tourists and locals. A sign at several entrance points to the Sultanahmet Mosque, iconically referred to as the Blue Mosque, reminds visitors to show respect by wearing the correct attire – men should fully cover their legs and women should wear a headscarf and ankle length skirt – items can be borrowed free of charge from the mosque. To respect prayer the Blue Mosque is closed to visitors during prayer times, and inside the mosque noticeboards inviting tourists 'To Understand Islam' by contacting the Islamic Information Centre are displayed. Moreover, Turkish hospitality, in the Islamic orient, to non-Muslims is reflected on by an American freelance writer, Amy Lysen (2013) in her travel blog:

> Turkey was nothing that I expected or I could have ever imagined; but as soon as I met the people of Istanbul I immediately felt at home [...] I was lucky to meet people who cared about me and never expected anything back. Their warmth and compassion welcomed me, a total stranger. I was just one of thousands of tourists passing through, but they made me feel like it was their personal duty to take care of me [...] The Turkish have perfected the art of hospitality in so many ways.

Impacts and Insights

Marketing Islamic tourism

Islamic tourism as a special interest or niche market targeting mainly the global Muslim diaspora has to be marketed, communicated and branded to attract tourists. Although Muslims are aware of their religiously oriented journeys through various Islamic teachings and texts, the rankings produced by CrescentRating (2014a) indicate OIC countries have entered a 'place war' for this lucrative segment and there is a need to market Islamic tourism. The World Travel Market (2007) alerted the Muslim world, ten years ago, to the potential for Halal tourism within and beyond the Middle East. Moreover, where Western tourist destinations fall short of Shariah compliance, Muslims, especially the non-liberals, turn to OIC countries. Therefore 'Islamic attributes' set the foundations for destinations to design marketing programmes to attract/target Muslim tourists (Battour *et al.*, 2011, p. 528). For Islamic marketing and branding to be targeted at Muslims it needs to differ from the traditional Western theories and practices of marketing and branding as it 'seeks to address the needs of Muslim markets' (Temporal, 2011, p. xiii) and recognises the symbolic relationship of marketing and branding with the Muslim faith (Yusof and Jusoh, 2014). CrescentRating (2014b) sets out *Successful Destination Marketing Strategies for Muslim Travellers,* which include:

- understanding the preferences, motivations, decision making and travel planning processes;
- identifying visitor markets that are reflective of the destination and aligned with community values;
- implementing Strategic Marketing Plans, and engaging Muslim travellers in key promotional and advertising campaigns; and
- developing cooperative marketing programmes with tourism organisations and businesses.

However, non-Muslim tourists travelling to OIC destinations seeking religious/faith-based or cultural experiences should not be overlooked, as Islamic tourism co-exists with other tourist market segments (e.g. event tourism, food tourism, dark tourism). Therefore, marketing and branding strategies should be inclusive of their needs and wants, but at the same time not comprising the Shariah compliance expectations of Muslim tourists.

Terrorism and Islamic tourism destinations

Muslim countries have been subjected to attacks claimed by Islamic militant (e.g. Islamic State) or terrorist (e.g. Al-Qa'ida) groups, consequently casualties (death or injury) are mainly Muslim – although no distinction has been made to date of Islamic tourists and hosts. A few years ago Malaysian authorities uncovered a planned terrorist attack in the capital city Kuala Lumpur by individuals with suspected links with Islamic State (Isis) (Parameswaran, 2015). It can be argued that terrorist threats in a top-ranking Islamic tourism country can have wider implications on Malaysia's destination image and ability to attract Muslim and non-Muslim tourists. Islamic civilisation identity has also been under threat and implicated in militant and terrorist attacks in Muslim nations (i.e. Syria, Iraq and Tunisia) as Islamic State has destroyed artefacts in museums and libraries – on the premise that exhibiting and gazing on them is un-Islamic. Sufi shrines have been demolished in Syria and Libya by Isis, which are of religious, cultural and spiritual significance to Muslims. Although no statistical evidence can be found of the economic impact of terrorist attacks and presence of Isis on Islamic tourism in the Muslim world, it can however be argued that continued destruction of visitor attractions of religious and spiritual importance casts a shadow on future developments. However, terrorism is not the only movement diminishing symbols and sites associated with Islam and Muslim Heritage as commodification and commercialisation is also playing a role. As Ziauddin Sardar (cited in Sparrow, 2014) discusses the destruction of historical and ancient sites in Mecca:

> The house of Khadijah, the first wife of the Prophet Muhammad, has been turned into a block of toilets […] The Makkah Hilton is built over the house of Abu Bakr, the closest companion of the prophet and the first caliph […] the Saudis have turned the spiritual heart of Islam [into] an ultramodern, monolithic enclave, where difference is not tolerated, history has no meaning, and consumerism is paramount.

The future of Islamic tourism

It appears that travel movements of Islamic tourists to Muslim countries are under surveillance by national and international authorities, as there are suspicions that travellers from the West are joining the Isis movement. This echoes the travel environments Muslims found themselves travelling in post-9/11, however this time the terrorist threat is to the Muslim world. The British media reports claim that British Muslim men and women are travelling to Syria and Iraq to join Isis so as to engage in jihad (Mendick *et al.*, 2014). A few years ago three British schoolgirls, one aged 16 and two aged 15, journeyed to Sanliurfa in south-east Turkey, close to the Syrian border, and are believed to have crossed over to Syria (Agence France-Presse, 2015). Consequently these complex travels of Muslims in the Islamic world may impact upon future developments of global Islamic tourism movements. Also, rather than travelling to OIC countries, Islamic tourists may, owing to the possibility of Islamic militant or terrorist attacks, turn to non-OIC nations (e.g. Singapore, South Africa and the United Kingdom) for the Islamic tourism experience. Although non-OIC countries are not politically Islamic States, Republics or Kingdoms, they nevertheless have a large Muslim diaspora with histories of migration tied to OIC nations. In the United Kingdom, the National Census 2011 found 2.7 million residents in England and Wales identified themselves as Muslim – the second largest religious group (Office for National Statistics, 2015). There is potential for Islamic tourism to grow across non-OIC nations (as well as OIC nations) by engaging stakeholders (e.g. Muslim tourists, transport sector, visitor attraction managers, hospitality industry, tourism intermediaries, private/public organisations, and OIC members) to work collaboratively to cater for the Muslim traveller.

Questions

1. For countries in the non-Muslim world seeking to develop Islamic tourism as a niche market, what would you advise them to do and not to do?

2. Can non-Islamic tourists visiting Islamic destinations, shrines and sites be considered as Islamic tourists? Justify your response.

3. What does the future hold for Islamic tourism and its OIC countries implicated by global political climates such as terrorism? Discuss.

Further Reading

Al-Hamarneh, A. and Steiner, C. (2004) Rethinking the strategies of tourism development of the arab world after September 11, 2001. *Comparative Studies of South Asia, Africa and the Middle East* 24(1), 173–182.

Eid, R. and El-Gohary, H. (2015) The role of Islamic religiosity on the relationship between perceived value and tourist satisfaction. *Tourism Management* 46, 477–488.

Neveu, N. (2010) Islamic tourism as an ideological construction: a Jordan case study. *Journal of Tourism and Cultural Change* 8(4), 327–337.

Websites

International Conference on Halal Tourism 2017: http://icoht2017.issconference.net/.

Islamic Tourism Centre of Malaysia: http://itc.gov.my/.

Muslim Heritage: http://www.muslimheritage.com/.

References

Abeddour, Y. (2011) *Sufi Tourism in Morocco: The Impact of Sufism on Tourism*. Available at: https://mrmorocco18.wordpress.com/2011/02/01/sufi-tourism-in-morocco-the-impact-of-sufism-on-tourism/ (accessed 28 April 2015).

Agence France-Presse (2015) Man suspected of helping UK schoolgirls join Isis is Syrian, says Turkey. *The Guardian,* 13 March 2015. Available at: http://www.theguardian.com/world/2015/mar/13/man-uk-schoolgirls-join-isis-syrian-turkey-intelligence-agency (accessed 29 April 2015).

Ali, N. (2008) The Significance of Ethnic Identity upon Tourism Participation within the Pakistani Community. PhD Thesis, University of Bedfordshire, Luton, UK.

Ansari, H. (2002) *Muslims in Britain*. Minority Rights Group International, London, UK.

Battour, M.M., Ismail, M.N. and Battor, M. (2010) Toward a halal tourism market. *Tourism Analysis* 15, 461–470.

Battour, M., Ismail, M.N. and Battor, M. (2011) The impact of destination attributes on Muslim tourist's choice. *International Journal of Tourism Research* 13, 527–540.

Bazian, H. (2014) The 'Randomness' of Islamophobia at US airports. *Turkey Agenda,* 3 September 2014. Available at: http://www.hatembazian.com/content/the-randomness-of-islamophobia-at-us-airports/ (accessed 26 April 2015).

Blackwood, L., Hopkins, N. and Reicher, S. (2013) I know who I am, but who do they think I am? Muslim perspectives on encounters with airport authorities. *Ethnic and Racial Studies* 36(6), 1090–1108.

Bogari, N.B., Crowther, G. and Marr, N. (2004) Motivation for domestic tourism: a case study of the Kingdom of Saudi Arabia. *Tourism Analysis* 8, 137–141.

Carboni, M., Perelli, C. and Sistu, G.C. (2014) Is Islamic tourism a viable option for Tunisian tourism? Insight from Djerba. *Tourism Management* 11, 1–19.

CrescentRating (2014a) *Top Halal Friendly Destinations –* 2014. Available at: http://www.crescentrating.com/crahft-ranking-2014/item/3602-crescentratings-top-halal-friendly-holiday-destinations-2014.html (accessed 16 Feburary 2015).

CrescentRating (2014b) *Destination Marketing*. Available at: http://www.crescentrating.com/destination-marketing.html (accessed 28 April 2015).

Din, K. (1989) Islam and tourism: patterns, issues and option. *Annals of Tourism Research* 16, 542–563.

Duman, T. (2011) Value of Islamic Tourism Offering: Perspectives from the Turkish Experience (online), paper presented at the World Islamic Tourism Forum (WITF), Kuala Lumpur, Malaysia, 12–13 July. Available at: http://www.iais.org.my/e/attach/ppts/12-13JUL2011-WITF/ppts/Dr%20Teoman%20Duman.pdf (accessed 15 Feburary 2015).

El-Hanandeh, A. (2013) Quantifying the carbon footprint of religious tourism: the case of Hajj. *Journal of Cleaner Production* 52, 53–60.

Graburn, N.H.H. (1977) Tourism: the sacred journey. In: Smith, V.L. (ed.) *Hosts and Guests: The Anthropology of Tourism*. University of Pennsylvania Press, Philadelphia, USA, pp. 17–31.

Haq, F. and Wong, H.Y. (2010) Is spiritual tourism a new strategy for marketing Islam? *Journal of Islamic Marketing* 1(2), 136–148.

Henderson, J.C. (2003) Managing tourism and Islam in Peninsular Malaysia. *Tourism Management* 24, 447–456.

Henderson, J.C. (2009) Managing tourism and Islam in peninsular Malaysia. *Tourism Management* 24, 447–456.

Henderson, J.C. (2011) Religious tourism and its management: the Hajj in Saudi Arabia. *International Journal of Tourism Research* 13, 541–552.

Hoffstaedter, G. (2009) Contested spaces: globalization, the arts and the state in Malaysia. *Ethnicities* 9(4), 527–545. DOI: https://doi.org/10.1177/1468796809345606

Islamic Tourism Centre of Malaysia (2015) *Discover Malaysia: Your Muslim-friendly Destination*. Available at: http://itc.gov.my/tourists/welcome-to-malaysia-the-land-of-truly-asia/ (accessed 17 February 2015).

Jafari, J. and Scott, N. (2014) Muslim world and its tourisms. *Annals of Tourism Research* 44, 1–19.

Lysen, A. (2013) Turkish hospitality: a non-muslim's discovery. *OnIslam*. Available at: http://magiccityistanbul.blogspot.co.uk/2013/12/turkish-hospitality-non-muslims.html (accessed 15 November 2017).

Mendick, R., Verkaik, R. and Ross, T. (2014) Muslim MP: 2,000 Britons fighting for Islamic State. *The Telegraph*, 23 November 2014. Available at: http://www.telegraph.co.uk/news/worldnews/islamic-state/11248114/Muslim-MP-2000-Britons-fighting-for-Islamic-State.html (accessed 29 April 2015).

OIC (2014) OIC member states consider ways of boosting Islamic tourism. *Newsletter*, 2nd June, Jakarta: Indonesia. Available at: http://www.oic-oci.org/topic/?t_id=9111&t_ref=3650&lan=en (accessed 15 February 2015).

Office for National Statistics (2015) What does the Census tell us about religion in 2011? Available at: http://www.ons.gov.uk/ons/rel/census/2011-census/detailed-characteristics-for-local-authorities-in-england-and-wales/sty-religion.html (accessed 29 April 2015).

Parameswaran, P. (2015) Malaysia says new terror group trying to create Islamic State. *The Diplomat,* 8 April 2015. Available at: http://thediplomat.com/2015/04/

malaysia-says-new-terror-group-trying-to-create-islamic-state/ (accessed 28 April 2015).

Pew Research Center (2011) *The Future of the Global Muslim Population*. Available at: http://www.pewforum.org/2011/01/27/the-future-of-the-global-muslim-population/ (accessed 17 February 2015).

Raj, R. and Morpeth, N. (eds) (2007) *Religious Tourism and Pilgrimage Management*. CAB International, Wallingford, UK.

Sattar, Z., Hannam, K. and Ali, N. (2013) Religious obligations to travel: first generation Pakistani migrants from Newcastle upon Tyne. *Journal of Tourism and Cultural Change* 11(1–2), 61–72.

Scott, N. and Jafari, J. (eds) (2010a) *Tourism in the Muslim World*. Emerald, Bingley, UK.

Scott, N. and Jafari, J. (2010b) Introduction: tourism and Islam. In: Scott, N. and Jafari, J. (eds) *Tourism in the Muslim World*. Emerald, Bingley, UK pp. 1–13.

Shakiry, A.S. (2006) 'Islamic Tourism' for whom? *Islamic Tourism*, Issue 23, May-June. Available at: http://www.islamictourism.com/PDFs/Issue%2023/English/6%20ITP.pdf (accessed 15 February 2015).

Smith, V.L. (1977) Introduction. In: Smith, V.L. (ed.) *Hosts and Guests: The Anthropology of Tourism*. University of Pennsylvania Press, Philadelphia, USA, pp. 1–14.

Sparrow, J. (2014) If great architecture belongs to humanity, do we have a responsibility to save it in wartimes? *The Guardian*, 7 October 2014. Available at: http://www.theguardian.com/commentisfree/2014/oct/07/-sp-if-great-architecture-belongs-to-humanity-do-we-have-a-responsibility-to-save-it-in-war-times (accessed on 28 April 2015).

Staples, E. (2009) Travel. In: Campo, J.E. (ed.) *Encyclopaedia of Islam*. Infobase Publishing, New York, USA, p. 672.

Stausberg, M. (2011) *Religion and Tourism: Crossroads, Destinations and Encounters*. Routledge, London, UK.

Stephenson, M.L. and Ali, N. (2010) Tourism, travel and Islamophobia: Post 9/11 journeys of Muslims in non-Muslim states. In: Scott, N. and Jafari, J. (eds) *Tourism in the Muslim World*. Emerald, Bingley, UK, pp. 235–251.

Stephenson, M.L. (2014) Deciphering 'Islamic hospitality': developments, challenges and opportunities. *Tourism Management* 40, 155–164.

Temporal, P. (2011) *Islamic Branding and Marketing: Creating a Global Islamic Business*. John Wiley, Singapore.

Timothy, D.J. and Iverson, T. (2006) Tourism and Islam: consideration of culture and duty. In: Timothy, D.J. and Olsen, D.H. (eds) *Tourism, Religion and Spiritual Journeys*. Routledge, London, UK pp. 186–205.

Timothy, D.J. and Olsen, D.H. (eds) (2006) *Tourism, Religion and Spiritual Journeys*. Routledge, London.

TTG Asia (2016) Global Muslim travel market worth US$138 billion and growing. 16 December 2016. Available at: http://ttgasia.com/article.php?article_id=28539 (accessed 3 January 2017).

Vukonić, B. (1996) *Tourism and Religion*. Pergamon, Oxford, UK.

Wang, Z., Ding, P., Scott, N. and Fan, Y. (2010) Muslim tourism in China. In: Scott, N. and Jafari, J. (eds) *Tourism in the Muslim World*. Emerald, Bingley, UK, pp. 107–119.

World Travel Market (2007) *WTM Global Trends Report 2007*. Euromonitor International, London, UK.

Yusof, M.Y.L. and Jusoh, W.W.J. (2014) Islamic branding: the understanding and perception. *Procedia – Social and Behavioural Sciences* 130, 179–185.

Zamani-Farahani, H. and Henderson, J.C. (2009) Islamic tourism and managing tourism development in Islamic societies: the cases of Iran and Saudi Arabia. *International Journal of Tourism Research* 12, 79–89.

Zamani-Farahani, H. and Musa, G. (2012) The relationship between Islamic religiosity and residents' perceptions of socio-cultural impact of tourism in Iran: Case studies of Sarein and Masouleh. *Tourism Management* 33, 802–814.

6 Literary Tourism

Graham Busby

Learning Objectives

- To understand what is encompassed by the term literary tourism
- To learn how literature and tourism are linked
- To discover how literary tourism develops

Introduction

This chapter adopts a number of sub-headings in order to examine the phenomenon of literary tourism: key concepts, major factors, motivations, interactions, impacts and insights. It cannot be denied that literature creates 'places' to be visited. These may be places of the imagination, based on genuine locales, or explicitly accurate destinations. Mention Thoreau and for some Concord, Massachusetts, along with nearby Walden Pond spring to mind. For others the association might be Sherlock Holmes and Baker Street, or Shakespeare and Stratford upon Avon. A comprehensive list of places associated with writers and their work would indeed be very long.

It is not surprising then that Ousby (1990) discusses literary tourism as a form of special interest tourism and believes that many churches, which house famous writers' graves, are tourist destinations. The late Malcolm Bradbury could be said to have made a pastiche of this in his novel *To The Hermitage*, in the early part of which the principal character is searching for the grave of René Descartes in Stockholm, whilst on route to Saint Petersburg to take part in The Diderot Project.

Key Concepts

Literary tourism – what is it? To state that it is tourism based in some way upon literary output misses some key facets. For example, each and every reader of a text may see something others do not. Literary tourism is, axiomatically, about creativity and imagination; there is an 'emotional engagement' (Robinson and Andersen, 2002, p. 17) and creation

of special meanings for the individual (Squire, 1994a). Whilst there may not always be an obvious direct link between reading and tourism, research into the relationship should not be ignored (Robinson, 2002).

According to Herbert (2001) and Squire (1996) the phenomenon of literary tourism is about visiting places celebrated for their connections with literary figures. Other facets will become apparent, in due course. Certainly, it has long been recognised that places associated with works of literature can be commodified by the tourist industry to attract increased numbers of visitors (Robinson and Andersen, 2002). This can be achieved through various forms, including 'package trails of fictionally derived experiences' (Robinson and Andersen, 2002, p. 15), as evidenced by the Thomas Hardy Trail, developed by West Dorset Tourism, which encompasses various sites associated with the author's life and works, upon which many of Hardy's books were based, blurring the boundaries between what is real and what is metaphorical (Herbert, 1995). Such trails, which are socially constructed, are in a sense typical of the packaging ideology which Busby and O'Neill (2006) determine to be consistent with modern tourism. The Harry Potter map, developed by Visit Britain, is an example of a destination marketing organisation providing the potential for tours of film locations which originate from novels (Busby and George, 2004). Having researched packaged trails, MacLeod *et al.* (2009) take this further and propose a typology of biographical, literary landscape, and generic literary trails.

With literary tourism, the concept of authenticity is particularly salient (Fawcett and Cormack, 2001). On most occasions this will be authenticity of the setting. When a set has been recreated or moved, for example, Thomas Hardy's study in Dorchester Museum (Watson, 2006), this is a form of *staged authenticity* (MacCannell, 1989) whereby tourists are looking for authentic experiences, but are given contrived ones; MacCannell believes all tourists are looking for the original – or the authentic. Authenticity within tourism has become a much debated phenomenon with MacCannell's (1989) view of authenticity as solely object-related being challenged by many authors as too simplistic to define the tourist experience. Bruner (1994; cited in Wang, 1999) challenges this view and develops a notion of *constructive*, or *symbolic authenticity*. This is the concept that objects may appear authentic because of society making them so, believing that authenticity can be subject to tourists' individual perceptions. Cohen (1988) believes that if the objects visited are considered by the tourist to be authentic, then they are authentic, whether they are the originals or not. Both interpretations above stem from the perspective of toured objects. However, Wang (1999) suggests both objective and constructive authenticity are to do with toured objects, and not those of tourist experiences, and suggests *existential authenticity* as an alternative.

Existential authenticity is the belief that the objects being viewed, or activities undertaken by the tourist, do not have to be authentic at all. The authenticity comes from the experiences of visitors when undertaking liminal tourist activities. Wang (1999) further categorises this into *intrapersonal* and *interpersonal authenticity*, the former being bodily feelings evoked by existential authentic experiences, and the latter being authentic bonding between people as a result of visiting a toured object.

Relating this to literary tourism, Lincoln Cathedral is a prime example of what is termed a 'runaway production location' (Beeton, 2005); this is where movies and TV series are filmed in a location mocked-up to be another. *The Da Vinci Code* bestseller novel featured Westminster Abbey although the film used Lincoln Cathedral.

Tooke and Baker (1996) believe that visitor numbers increase to the place that is being represented, that is Westminster Abbey and not the location itself, i.e. Lincoln Cathedral, (see also 'Cathedral Tourism' chapter, this volume). This is elaborated upon further by Tooke and Baker (1996) with the case of *Cadfael*, which involves the tales of a medieval monk detective, set in Shrewsbury. *Cadfael* was originally a series of novels, written by Ellis Peters (the pen name of Edith Pargeter), and attracted visitors to Shrewsbury long before the television series was made; however, Tooke and Baker (1996) reported a substantial increase in numbers to the town following airing of the television series. This would not be considered surprising had the filming of the series

not taken place in Hungary (Busby and Hambly, 2000), again raising questions of authenticity. This is closely related to constructive authenticity (Wang, 1999), whereby an object or destination is socially constructed, in this case by movie producers, as authentically somewhere else.

Arguably, authenticity is most to the fore in the writer's home. Whilst Hardy's study has been moved to a local museum, Charles Darwin's can still be viewed *in situ* at Down House, Kent, for example. Sir Walter Scott "invented the genre of the writer's house in Britain" (Watson, 2006, p. 93), although pilgrimages to sites associated with authors predate him, however, as visits to Shakespeare sites in Stratford upon Avon began in the 18th century (Watson, 2006). Washington Irving was a notable 19th century visitor; in terms of authenticity, he referred to liking Shakespeare's chair. 'It is the custom of every one that visits the house to sit (in the chair): whether this be done with the hope of imbibing any of the inspiration of the bard I am at a loss to say'; he was assured that 'such was the fervent zeal of devotees, that the chair had to be new bottomed at least once in three years'; more pertinently, Irving (1998, p. 226) said he was '…ever willing to be deceived, where the deceit is pleasant and costs nothing' – an early example of interpersonal existentialist authenticity, probably.

Major Factors

Technology, film and creative cultural tourism development are three factors of supreme importance in the advance of literary tourism. Technology, initially, in the form of the World Wide Web has enabled common-interest groups to promote their enthusiasms; for example, The Arthur Ransome Society encourages interest in the children's genre of storytelling, particularly salient because many of the settings can be identified, despite being written in the 1930s. The Society organises member's weekends for the devotee. Writing a few decades later, Malcolm Saville used easily identifiable settings and the eponymous Society organises events to experience them. Development of 'apps' for smartphones have enabled Destination Marketing Organisations to inform visitors of specific locations and backgrounds; one example to illustrate this is to be found in Reykjavik, Iceland (https://www.mobogenie.com/download-literary-reykjav-k-1272150.html).

As the 20th century progressed, settings used by film and television producers began to appeal to a wide range of viewers. Whilst many film scripts are not written by the original author of a novel, the release stimulates interest; however, one particular exception to this is the novel *Wakolda*, written by Lucía Puenzo who also wrote the script and directed the movie (www.imdb.com/title/tt1847746/), set around Bariloche, Argentina. As research by Busby and O'Neill (2006) shows, the type of visitor to a setting after release of a film may be qualitatively different to a few years earlier following publication of a novel. Film can also lead to what Busby and Laviolette (2006, p. 148) term film-induced literary tourism: 'the viewer has read the author's works after viewing what may have been changed by the screenplay...measurement of this type...is dependent on substantial on-site empirical research, such as that conducted on the Greek island of Cephalonia in the wake of production of the film *Captain Corelli's Mandolin*', adapted from the novel by Louis de Bernières (O'Neill *et al.*, 2005).

Creative cultural tourism (Richards and Wilson, 2006) is tourism which utilises destination-based cultural capital in a creative form. The resources may be tangible or intangible and can be commodified. These are either latent (almost always tangible elements) or potential cultural capital (Busby and Meethan, 2008). In the 1990s, the literary connection between author Daphne du Maurier and the Fowey area of Cornwall was still potential cultural capital. In 1997 Restormel Borough Council launched the first Daphne du Maurier Festival of Arts and Literature and, in so doing, created *Daphne du Maurier Country*, with concomitant road signs stating this (Busby and Hambly, 2000).

Whilst the term *creative cultural tourism* may not have been to the fore in developers' minds, the creation of *countries* associated with an author is clearly useful for marketing purposes and a large number exist in the United Kingdom. To cite from fiction, in his novel *To The Hermitage*, Malcolm Bradbury (2000, p. 154) suggests 'you can start your Yorkshire tour in Brontë Country, where the signs are in Japanese, go on to Bradford which is Priestley Country...then head for James Herriott Country (no people, just animals). On to Castle Howard (Brideshead Country) and to the coast at Whitby (Dracula Country). Then if you head northward you'll soon find yourself among the aspiring maid-servants of Catherine Cookson Country. Go south to the Humber...this can be instantly recognized as Philip Larkin Country'. This range of genres from fiction illustrates the diverse appeal of literary

tourism and is far from exhaustive: crime fiction has created *Agatha Christie Country* in south Devon (Busby *et al.*, 2003) and poetry *Yeats Country* in County Sligo, Ireland (Wallace, 2009), see Fig. 6.1. As another example, travel writing provides 'a vehicle through which places ...have been reinterpreted and communicated to wider audiences illustrated by the work of Bill Bryson' (Busby and Klug, 2001, p. 321), leading to another form of literary tourism.

Motivations

Clearly, literature is a strong motivator for visits to places associated with literary figures (Busby and Shetliffe, 2013), yet what may generate this motivation is a search for personal cultural capital; this is a concept that is acquired by the individual and not necessarily via formal education; uncertificated education may be of equal importance (Busby and Meethan, 2008). Personal cultural capital is, axiomatically, linked to education and this helps to explain results obtained in a survey concerning The Diary of Anne Frank (see Focus Box 1).

As with many forms of tourism, there can be multiple motivations. The example of the Anne Frank House encapsulates both literary tourism and dark or thanatourism; some visitors may be motivated by one form to a greater extent than the other. A similar example is seen with the concept of religious tourism; in a study of two remote Exmoor churches, in England, Brice *et al.* (2003) discovered that more than 16% of visitors (*n* = 414) to Oare were motivated by the Victorian novel *Lorna Doone*, written by R.D. Blackmore and published in 1869. Of course, it is translation to large and small screen, as well as incorporation in the BBC's Big Read, that has kept this work in the mind of the public for so many years after first appearing (http://www.bbc.co.uk/arts/bigread/top200_2.shtml). Daphne du Maurier has already been mentioned and some visitors to Lanteglos church, in Cornwall, are motivated by the knowledge that she was married there (Busby, 2004). There are, then, multiple motivations at work as far as visitors are concerned.

Interactions

Interactions are partly stimulated by the plethora of specialist guidebooks for literary visitors. Intriguingly, Eagle and Carnell (1977, p. v) assert

Fig. 6.1. Signpost in Yeats Country, County Sligo.

Focus Box 1: Anne Frank's Diary and tourism

Anne Frank kept her diary from 12 June 1942 to 1 August 1944. 'Initially, she wrote it strictly for herself... one day in 1944... a member of the Dutch government in exile, announced in a radio broadcast from London that after the war he hoped to collect eyewitness accounts of the suffering of the Dutch people... which could be made available to the public. As an example, he specifically mentioned letters and diaries' (Frank and Pressler, 2001, p. v). This inspired Anne Frank and she was convinced that her diary should be published in due course. Having started it aged thirteen, she died in Belsen concentration camp aged fifteen.

The Anne Frank House, in Amsterdam, opened in 1960 and provides a space to commemorate the life of Anne and her family. Readers of The Diary are presented with somewhere to undertake a pilgrimage to because Anne Frank 'is simultaneously "the Holocaust's most famous victim", "the most famous child of the twentieth century", and "her face with the sad shy smile is one of the icons"' of the last century (Cole, 1999, p. 23).

In a survey concerning The Diary ($n = 331$), nearly 60% of respondents were graduates and just under 50% had read the book. However, what was of particular interest was the influence of the book as motivator; while respondents who had read the book identified that they were encouraged to visit the site, this perception differed remarkably from the responses of those who had not read it – instead, they perceived that reading The Diary would deter them from the site (significant at the 99.9% level) – this seems quite stark as an implication (Busby and Devereux, 2015).

In 2015, there were 1,268,100 visitors to The Anne Frank House, an increase of 40,600 on the previous year. Numbers have steadily climbed since the property opened and there is no diminution of interest (Anne Frank House, 2016).

that their guide was originally intended to indicate 'those places where something relevant to literature… could be seen, but so many buildings have been demolished… that it has been necessary to add the word 'gone' after the description… and leave the rest to the reader's imagination' – truly suitable for those in search of existential authenticity.

To cite another guidebook, Frank Morley's (1980, p. 167) *Literary Britain* organises much of its content along the key roads: A1, A2, A3, A4, A5 and A6; with Jane Austen, Walter Scott, Richardson, Fielding, Dickens, Thackeray and Eliot being associated with a small area around the A3 in western Surrey; Morley 'wonders what radioactivity worked in this strip'. Interactions stimulated by literature and maps or illustrations can be susceptible to overt promotion by the relevant destination marketing organisation; for example, the page facing the author details of 'international bestseller' *The Guernsey Literary and Potato Peel Pie Society* emphasises accommodation and travel deals on the Visit Guernsey website (Shaffer and Barrows, 2009).

Undoubtedly, novelists deliberately cultivate subjectivity, which distinguishes literature from factual writing (Pocock, 1981), and can lead to misleading impressions of a destination being portrayed (Robinson, 2002). Fictional works create fictional characters and events, which exist in fictional worlds. Rojek (1993) terms such literary landscapes 'escape areas', indicative of the new post-modern realities which blur the boundaries between the real and the imaginary (Urry, 1990; Beeton, 2001). This inspires tourists to explore worlds as depicted in literature, correlating imagined locations with some markers of reality (Robinson, 2002). The best-selling Harry Potter novels have created what Sharp (2000) terms 'imaginative geographies'.

The expansion of the literary tourism market is likely to be *ad hoc*, opportunistic and idiosyncratic, with tourism development likely to reflect wider sociocultural trends regarding access, transport and improved information flows (Robinson and Andersen, 2002). Though Riley (1994) states there is a decreasing reliance on written information to gather knowledge, Robinson and Andersen (2002) are confident that we will continue to inhabit a culture of books and literature, despite the rise in hyper- and virtual realities.

Mention has already been made of the link between technology and literary tourism, therefore, it is interesting to note how some once popular authors have 'reappeared', to be enjoyed by a contemporary audience. John Higgins has created the website http://www.victorcanning.com in order to provide background details on the eponymous author and to link to print-on-demand website www.lulu.com. Many of Canning's novels feature readily identifiable places and in creation of the website, John Higgins visited Florence (*The Chasm*), Angers (*The Boy on Platform One*) and Majorca (*The Manasco Road*), besides many English trips to confirm this. A key point is that Canning's work sold in the hundreds of thousands of volumes between the 1930s and 1980s and the website now receives 'hits' daily from all over the world (Higgins, personal communication, 2014).

Critically, literary places are not historical accidents, they represent a merger of the real and imagined; they are 'social constructions, created, amplified, and promoted to attract visitors' (Herbert, 2001, p. 313). In our 'been there, done that', 'tick-box' culture, such creations can generate kudos and cultural capital (Bourdieu, 1986) at various levels, and in re-narrating holiday experiences, literary connections are rarely omitted. Johnson's (1986) 'circuit of culture' explores ways in which meanings are encoded by producers and promoters of (literary) visitor attractions, and decoded by visitors. The circuit is often adapted for the study of literary places (Squire, 1994b; Herbert, 1996) and conceptualises the interrelationships between tourism, culture and society (Squire, 1994b).

To take an example already referred to, an *agency*, Restormel Borough Council, has created (*production*) the annual Daphne du Maurier Festival of Arts and Literature – which provides a range of events, over 170 at the 2007 festival, this leads on to *texts*, in the circuit. Given the phenomenological perspective and individuals' levels of personal cultural capital, these *texts* lead to manifold *readings* which, in turn, have an *impact* (including repeat visitation) and lead to slightly changed *production* in following years. Attendance at this annual festival illustrates participation in two of the forms of special interest tourism in this book – the occurrence of both literary and festival tourism. As has been mentioned, there are also crossover points between literary, film and cathedral tourism. Children feature large in Lake District holidays that take in tours of Arthur Ransome's *Swallows and Amazons* locations, demonstrating the crossover between family and literary tourism. In fact, if we consider the importance of the media in tourism, some forms of special interest tourism particularly interlock; for example, celebrity chef Rick Stein has had a significant influence on gastronomic tourism through his published books and filmed appearances (Busby *et al.*, 2013). Interactions, then, undoubtedly have impacts.

Impacts and Insights

The impact of literature has been implicitly addressed already. However, it is useful to focus on one location in order to consider how it can outweigh significant historical incidents. Forgotten by many, yet famous in his day, Arthur Mee (1947, p. 254) states 'What do they know of England who do not Whitby know?' The small Yorkshire town is famous for several events: the Synod of Whitby, in 664, is a key date in ecclesiastical history for the Roman date for Easter was chosen and, thence, England became attached to the Roman Catholic Church. In his substantial novel *Credo*, Melvyn Bragg uses this event as a key component; 'Bega had known that there would be a synod and a debate at Whitby, but only as she travelled there did she begin to realise the size and importance of the event' (Bragg, 1996, p. 509). Several hundred years later, locally born James Cook (Captain Cook that is) sailed from here – the discoverer of many lands is commemorated by a bronze statue and in other ways (see http://www.captcook-ne.co.uk/ccne/cookne/whitby.htm and http://www.cookmuseumwhitby.co.uk). Indeed, the appellation *Captain Cook Country* has been shown by Prentice (2004) to have quite a high level of recognition.

However, the Synod of Whitby and the Captain Cook connection pale into insignificance when compared with a fictional creation and link to the town. In his introduction to the Wordsworth Classics edition of *Dracula*, Rogers (2000, p. vi) claims that the character '...has probably been the most widely popularised anti-hero in the whole of Western culture. More than two hundred and fifty films and innumerable stories and comics owe their inspiration to his figure...'. This novel has been translated into 44 languages besides English (Rogers, 2000), a testament to its influence. Whilst Transylvania (in Romania) springs readily to mind in the story, Dracula lands, in the form of a dog, from the schooner *Demeter* as it crashes onto the shore at Whitby during a storm, the immense dog 'Making straight for the steep cliff, where the churchyard hangs over the laneway to the East Pier so steeply that some of the flat tombstones... actually project over where the sustaining cliff has

fallen away...' (Stoker, 2000, p. 67). Many aspects of Whitby feature in the novel written by Bram Stoker whilst staying in The Royal Hotel (http://whitby.co.uk/dracula, 2010). Stoker has had a significant impact on tourism to a small town in East Yorkshire and Duncan Light (2007) has illustrated how many Romanian sites have come to be associated with Dracula in relatively recent times as a result of tourist demand while, perhaps surprisingly, Stoker never visited Romania. This is also a good example of where the fictional creation becomes significantly more important than the author: The Bram Stoker Experience (museum) opened in Dublin in 2003 and closed in 2008, due to lack of demand (Laing and Frost, 2012).

Turning to insights in literary tourism, the children's fiction of Arthur Ransome has already been mentioned. To the initiated, it's worth noting that illustrations form a key element in the reading experience; furthermore, 'when trying to find exact locations for Ransome's stories, explorers should refer to both the text and illustrations' (Wardale, 2006, p. 103). Whilst much exists for the literary tourist to discover, in the right setting, there may still be transposition: Wardale (2001), for example, indicates that The Roaring Donkey inn, featured in one of Ransome's Norfolk Broads novels, is actually many miles away. Of course, books such as Wardale's show that the public is actually interested in location-seeking. Illustrations enhance text. So does presence of a map or more than one. Harry Thompson's (2005) Man Booker Prize long-listed novel *This Thing of Darkness* provides the reader with four maps, enabling clear plotting of where activities occur in South America. Thompson's story is based on real events whereas Charles Cumming's (2012) *The Spanish Game* is pure fiction although it contains a detailed map of central Madrid and has the imprimatur of being one of a few featured in *Reading on Location – Great Books Set In Top Travel Destinations* (Moncada and Quin, 2011): everything the literary tourist needs in order to visit the spot.

Conclusion

Literary tourism may be undertaken by the well educated visitor searching for a deeply meaningful experience. On the other hand, children in search of places associated with the novels of Arthur Ransome may not be well educated (yet) although

Case Study 1: Destination image – Toronto in literature

Toronto is a global city on virtually any basis, whether in Sassen's (1991) terms or by dint of its cosmopolitan nature with one hundred and fifty languages being spoken by residents (City of Toronto, 2009). It needs to be emphasised that Toronto is, to all intents and purposes, a comparatively young city; this becomes all the more significant when one stops to consider what exactly influences representations of any given settlement; nearly all European cities have many centuries of heritage and this produces multiple representations based on both tangible and intangible heritage. Toronto has little in the way of built heritage which is more than one hundred and twenty years old; similarly, the intangible heritage is 'young' and, principally, based on the traditions of in-migrants. In other words, whilst the city is not a 'blank canvas', it is argued that literature can significantly influence representations, particularly given the absence of substantial built and intangible heritage.

The literature confirming the influence of destination image upon tourist behaviour is extensive (Pike, 2004; Yüksel and Akgül, 2007; Chen and Tsai, 2007; Busby and Haines, 2013). In tourism research, the key question is, of course, how is destination image created? Developing the concept from the work of Gunn and Gartner, Ateljevic (2000) suggests that the images upon which destination choices are based can be classified as: the organic, the induced and the complex.

The organic image is created by informal, non-commercial sources of information which may include word-of-mouth testimony; importantly, it is information which is not controlled by destination promoters.

Fig. 6.2. Project Bookmark Canada: panel showing excerpt from Ondaatje's *In The Skin Of A Lion* at the eastern end of the Prince Edward Viaduct.

Continued

G. Busby

Case Study 1: Continued.

The induced image is the result of marketing professionals; however, as Tasci and Gartner (2007, p. 414) point out, 'mutual exclusivity' between the two forms of image is almost non-existent as a result of 'skillful media relations' by marketing professionals. In recent years the image of Toronto has, arguably, been influenced by its depiction in works of fiction.

A number of novels have been examined for their portrayal of locations within the Greater Toronto area. As Alistair MacLeod (1999, p. 3) states, in *No Great Mischief*, 'Regardless of the route of entrance, the realization of the city of Toronto is always something of a surprise'; in his novel, as in Michael Ondaatje's *In The Skin Of A Lion*, it is the underbelly of the city which is illustrated. Nonetheless, it paints a picture of the city and it creates what Rojek (1997, p. 55) terms a 'pot pourri', a truly organic image of Toronto, constructed from 'representational files'.

Table 6.1. Toronto in literature – a selection

Date of publication	Title	Author
1981	*The Rebel Angels*	Robertson Davies
1987	*In The Skin Of A Lion*	Michael Ondaatje
1993	*The Robber Bride*	Margaret Atwood
1999	*No Great Mischief*	Alistair MacLeod

Ondaatje's novel is set during construction of the Bloor Street Bridge, also known as the Prince Edward Viaduct; and this feature plays a large part. 'The book is a fictionalized account of the lives of immigrant labourers who constructed many of Toronto's landmarks in the early 20th century. Project Bookmark Canada selected a passage from the novel for their inaugural plaque, which was unveiled at the east end of the Viaduct' in April 2009 (Willis, 2009). The passage starts 'Then there was no fear on the bridge. The worst, the incredible had happened. A nun had fallen off the Prince Edward Viaduct before it was even finished' (Ondaatje, 1988, p. 33). The key character Nicholas Temelcoff is famous on the bridge, 'He is given all the difficult jobs… he descends into the air with no fear. (p.36)… Below him is the Don River, the Grand Trunk, the CN and CP railway tracks, and Rosedale Valley Road' (p.44). See Fig. 6.2

The Toronto Observer commented 'Project Bookmark Canada is an extraordinary way to commemorate not just our authors but our public places… What Mr. Ondaatje said in his book is that before a city can be seen it has to be imagined' (Willis, 2009).

This is the creation of organic destination image in action and Malcolm Bradbury (1996) pays homage to these authors in his *Atlas of Literature* which identifies Toronto locations. This particular atlas illustrates the international nature of literature and its influence on visitors.

---

the experience is just as meaningful. What has helped to popularise many aspects of literary tourism has been driven by changes in technology, not only in the form of television and cinema, although these media have brought many literary works to much wider audiences. The advent of the World Wide Web provides a platform for the truly special-interest tourist with 'apps' to download providing an immediate resource and social media sites to permit the portrayal of affinity by readers.

A wide range of genres has been seen to stimulate literary tourism, some leading to a greater volume of visitors than others, and the scope for creating or expanding literary places is evident, as is the potential for contested meaning at such sites. Whilst the impacts, in terms of visitor numbers, are usually manageable, the financial benefits can help to address issues of tourism seasonality, as seen with The Daphne du Maurier Festival in Cornwall, held in an off-peak month.

Questions

1. Does one genre motivate literary tourism more than any other?
2. Is visiting Stratford-upon-Avon about more than literary tourism?
3. Does it matter if pulp fiction creates literary tourism?

Further Reading and Website Links

Müller, D.K. (2006) Unplanned development of literary tourism in two municipalities in rural Sweden. *Scandinavian Journal of Hospitality and Tourism* 6(3) 214–228.

Ridanpää, J. (2011) Pajala as a literary place: in the readings and footsteps of Mikael Niemi. *Journal of Tourism and Cultural Change* 9(2) 103–117.

Smith, K.A. (2003) Literary enthusiasts as visitors and volunteers. *International Journal of Tourism Research* 5(2) 83–95.

www.lithouses.org

This website features properties associated with literary figures in some way; these include birthplaces, such as Dr Johnson's in Lichfield, to long-term homes, such as Robert Graves, in Mallorca. The website illustrates the importance of a range of literary genres.

www.georgeborrow.org

The website belongs to the George Borrow Society, a common interest group which holds regular meetings, not only in the UK, and publishes a bulleting twice a year. Interest continues unabated in this Victorian character and the website is useful as it illustrates a niche within the special interest tourism form of literary tourism, those interested in a long-dead travel writer.

www.arthur-ransome.org.uk

Best known as the writer of the twelve Swallows and Amazons stories, Arthur Ransome's influence continues as illustrated by the Lake District National Park Authority's webpage on him. The locations are still sought after today.

www.witchend.com

This is the website of the Malcolm Saville Society; he was a well known author of children's fiction but, crucially, the locations in both urban and rural areas can easily be found. As with Arthur Ransome's stories, those of Malcolm Saville remain in the imagination of many from introduction in childhood.

References

Anne Frank House (2016) Visitor numbers. Available at: http://www.annefrank.org/en/News/Press/Visitor-numbers (accessed on 22 December 2016).

Ateljevic, I. (2000) Tourist motivation, values and perceptions. In: Woodside, A.G., Crouch, G., Oppermann, M. and Sakai, M. (eds) *Consumer Psychology of Tourism, Hospitality and Leisure*. CAB International, Wallingford, UK, pp. 193–210.

Beeton, S. (2001) Smiling for the camera: the influence of film audiences on a budget tourism destination. *Tourism, Culture and Communication* 3(1), 15–26.

Beeton, S. (2005) *Film-induced tourism*. Channel View, Clevedon, UK.

Bourdieu, P. (1986) *Distinction – a social critique of the judgement of taste*. Routledge, London.

Bradbury, M. (1996) *The Atlas of Literature*. De Agostini Editions, London, UK.

Bradbury, M. (2000) *To the Hermitage*. Picador, London, UK.

Bragg, M. (1996) *Credo*. Sceptre, London, UK.

Brice, J., Busby, G. and Brunt, P. (2003) English rural church tourism: a visitor typology. *Acta Turistica* 15(2), 144–162.

Bruner, E.M. (1994) Abraham Lincoln as authentic reproduction: a critique of postmodernism. *American Anthropologist* 96(2), 397–415.

Busby, G. (2004) The contested Cornish church heritage. In: Payton, P. (ed.) *Cornish Studies*. University of Exeter Press, Exeter, UK. 12, pp. 166–183.

Busby, G. and Devereux, H. (2015) Dark tourism in context: The Diary of Anne Frank. *European Journal of Tourism, Hospitality and Recreation* 6(1), 27–38.

Busby, G. and George, J. (2004) The Tailor of Gloucester: Potter meets Potter – literary tourism in a cathedral city. *Conference Proceedings – Tourism and Literature, Harrogate*, 22–26 July.

Busby, G. and Haines, C. (2013) Doc Martin and film tourism: the creation of destination image. *Tourism* 61(2), 105–120.

Busby, G. and Hambly, Z. (2000) Literary tourism and the Daphne du Maurier festival. In: Payton, P. (ed.) *Cornish Studies*. University of Exeter Press, Exeter, UK. 8, pp. 197–212.

Busby, G. and Klug, J. (2001) Movie-induced tourism: the challenge of measurement and other issues. *Journal of Vacation Marketing* 7(4), 316–332.

Busby, G. and Laviolette, P. (2006) Narratives in the net: fiction and Cornish tourism. In: Payton, P. (ed.) *Cornish Studies*. University of Exeter Press, Exeter, UK. 14, pp. 142–163.

Busby, G. and Meethan, K. (2008) Cultural capital in Cornwall: heritage and the visitor. In: Payton, P. (ed.) *Cornish Studies*. University of Exeter Press, Exeter, UK. 16, pp. 146–166.

Busby, G. and O'Neill, K. (2006) Cephallonia and Captain Corelli's Mandolin: the influence of literature and film on British visitors. *Acta Turistica* 18(1), 30–51.

Busby, G. and Shetliffe, E. (2013) Literary tourism in context: Byron and Newstead Abbey. *European Journal of Tourism, Hospitality and Recreation* 4(3), 5–45.

Busby, G., Brunt, P. and Lund, J. (2003) In Agatha Christie country: resident perception of special interest tourism. *Tourism* 51(3), 287–300.

Busby, G., Huang, R. and Jarman, R. (2013) The Stein effect: an alternative film-induced tourism perspective. *International Journal of Tourism Research* 15(6), 570–582.

Chen, C.F. and Tsai, D. (2007) How destination image and evaluative factors affect behavioral intentions? *Tourism Management* 28(4), 1115–1122.

City of Toronto (2009) City of Toronto Immigration and Settlement Portal. Available at: http://www.toronto.ca/immigration/diversity_imm.htm (accessed 26 January 2009).

Cohen, E. (1988) Authenticity and commoditization in tourism. *Annals of Tourism Research* 15(3), 371–386.

Cole, T. (1999) *Selling the Holocaust: From Auschwitz to Schindler – How History is Bought, Packaged and Sold*. Routledge, New York.

Cumming, C. (2006) *The Spanish Game*. HarperCollins, London, UK.

Eagle, D. and Carnell, H. (1977) *The Oxford Literary Guide to the British Isles*. Oxford University Press, Oxford, UK.

Fawcett, C. and Cormack, P. (2001) Guarding authenticity at literary tourism sites. *Annals of Tourism Research* 28(3), 686–704.

Frank, O.H. and Pressler, M. (2001) *The Diary of a Young Girl – Anne Frank – the Definitive Edition*. Penguin, London, UK.

Herbert, D.T. (1995) Heritage as literary place. In: Herbert, D. (ed.) *Heritage, Tourism and Society*. Mansell, London, UK. pp. 32–48.

Herbert, D.T. (1996) Artistic and literary places in France as tourist attractions. *Tourism Management* 17(2), 77–85.

Herbert, D. (2001) Literary places, tourism and the heritage experience. *Annals of Tourism Research* 28(2), 312–333.

Irving, W. (1998) *The Sketch-Book of Geoffrey Crayon, Gent*. Oxford University Press, Oxford, UK.

Johnson, R. (1986) The story so far and further transformation. In: Punter, D. (ed) *Introduction to Contemporary Studies*. Longman, Harlow, UK. pp. 277–313.

Laing, J. and Frost, W. (2012) *Books and Travel: Inspiration, Quests and Transformation*. Channel View, Bristol, UK.

Light, D. (2007) Dracula tourism in Romania – cultural identity and the state. *Annals of Tourism Research* 34(3), 746–765.

MacCannell, D. (1989) *The Tourist: A New Theory of the Leisure Class*. Schocken, New York, USA.

Macleod, A. (1999) *No Great Mischief*. McLelland & Stewart, Toronto, Canada.

MacLeod, N., Hayes, D. and Slater, A. (2009) Reading the landscape: the development of a typology of literary trails that incorporate an experiential design perspective. *Journal of Hospitality Marketing and Management* 18(2–3), 154–172.

Mee, A. (1947) *The King's England – Yorkshire: North Riding*. Hodder & Stoughton, London, UK.

Moncada, L. and Quin, S. (2011) *Reading on Location – Great Books Set In Top Travel Destinations*. New Holland, London, UK.

Morley, F. (1980) *Literary Britain*. Hutchinson, London, UK.

Ondaatje, M. (1988) *In the Skin of a Lion*. Picador, London, UK.

O'Neill, K., Butts, S. and Busby, G. (2005) The Corellification of Cephallonian tourism. *Anatolia* 16(2), 207–226.

Ousby, I. (1990) *The Englishman's England*. University Press, Cambridge, UK.

Pike, S. (2004) *Destination Marketing Organizations*. Elsevier, Oxford, UK.

Pocock, D.C.D. (1981) *Humanistic Geography and Literature*. Croom Helm, London, UK.

Prentice, R. (2004) Tourist familiarity and imagery. *Annals of Tourism Research* 31(4), 923–945.

Richards, G. and Wilson, J. (2006) Developing creativity in tourist experiences: a solution to the serial reproduction of culture? *Tourism Management* 27, 1209–1223.

Riley, R.W. (1994) Movie-induced tourism. In: Seaton, A.V. (ed.) *Tourism: State of the Art*. John Wiley, Chichester, UK. pp. 453–458.

Robinson, M. (2002) Between and beyond the pages: literature–tourism relationships. In: Robinson, M. and Andersen, H.C. (eds) *Literature and Tourism, Essays in the Reading and Writing on Tourism*. Thomson, London, UK. pp. 39–79.

Robinson, M. and Andersen, H.C. (2002) Reading between the lines: literature and the creation of touristic spaces. In: Robinson, M. and Andersen, H.C. (eds) *Literature and Tourism: Essays in the Reading and Writing of Tourism*. Thomson, London, UK. pp. 1–38.

Rogers, D. (2000) Introduction. *Dracula*. Wordsworth Editions, London, UK.

Rojek, C. (1993) *Ways of Escape: Modern Transformations in Leisure and Travel*. Macmillan, Basingstoke, UK.

Rojek, C. (1997) Indexing, dragging and the social construction of tourist sights. In: Rojek, C. and Urry, J. (eds) *Touring Cultures – Transformations of Travel and Theory*. Routledge, London, UK. pp. 52–74.

Sassen, S. (1991) *The Global City*. Princeton University Press, Princeton, USA.

Shaffer, M.A. and Barrows, A. (2009) *The Guernsey Literary and Potato Peel Pie Society*. Bloomsbury, London, UK.

Sharp, J. (2000) Towards a critical analysis of fictive geographies. *Area* 32(3), 327–334.

Squire, S.J. (1994a) The cultural values of literary tourism. In: Timothy, D. (ed.) *The Heritage Tourist Experience: Critical Essays*. Ashgate Publishing Limited, Aldershot, UK, pp. 401–418.

Squire, S.J. (1994b) The cultural values of literary tourism. *Annals of Tourism Research* 21, 103–120.

Squire, S. (1996) Literary tourism and sustainable tourism: promoting 'Anne of Green Gables' in Prince Edward Island. *Journal of Sustainable Tourism* 4(3), 119–134.

Stoker, B. (2000) *Dracula*. Wordsworth Editions, London, UK.

Tasci, A.D.A. and Gartner, W.C. (2007) Destination image and its functional relationships. *Journal of Travel Research* 45(4), 413–425.

Tasci, A.D.A., Gartner, W.C. and Tamer Cavusgil, S. (2007) Conceptualization and operationalization of destination image. *Journal of Hospitality and Tourism Research* 31(2), 194–223.

Thompson, H. (2005) *This Thing of Darkness*. Headline, London, UK.

Tooke, N. and Baker, M. (1996) Seeing is believing: the effect of film on visitor numbers to screened locations. *Tourism Management* 17(2), 87–94.

Urry, J. (1990) *The Tourist Gaze*. Sage, London, UK.

Wallace, C. (2009) Yeat's country and 'Yeat's Country': conceptualizing literary spaces. *Journal of Tourism and Cultural Change* 7(1), 48–60.

Wang, N. (1999) Rethinking authenticity in tourism experience. *Annals of Tourism Research* 26(2), 349–370.

Wardale, R. (2001) *Arthur Ransome's East Anglia*. Poppyland Publishing, Cromer, UK.

Wardale, R. (2006) *In Search of Swallows and Amazons – Arthur Ransome's Lakeland*. Sigma Leisure, Wilmslow, UK.

Watson, N. (2006) *The Literary Tourist*. Palgrave Macmillan, Basingstoke, UK.

Willis, L. (2009) Bloor Street Viaduct bridges history, culture, life and death. *The Toronto Observer*, Available at: http://torontoobserver.ca/2009/04/24/bloor-street-viaduct-bridges-history-culture-life-and-death/ (viewed on 14 January).

Yüksel, A. and Akgül, O. (2007) Postcards as affective image makers: an idle agent in destination marketing. *Tourism Management* 28(3), 714–725.

7 Music Tourism

Allan Watson

Learning Objectives

- To understand music tourism as a rapidly expanding and diverse tourist niche, which has spread to many locations across the globe
- To understand motivations for musical tourism ranging from pilgrimage and 'nostalgia consumption' to contemporary live music performance and festivals
- To discover how music is being used as part of the tourism strategies employed by local governments in the belief that it can provide economic benefits
- To recognise that alongside the positive impacts of music tourism, there can come a number of associated negative impacts on local society and culture

Key Concepts

This chapter is concerned with music tourism as a form of special interest cultural tourism. It will focus in particular on the links between music, heritage, nostalgia, pilgrimage and place, as well as on the role of contemporary music in fostering festival and live music tourism. The chapter considers the use of both music heritage and contemporary music scenes in place branding and marketing, and the relationships between music tourism, sustainable economic development and gentrification.

Major Factors

In a relatively recent transformation, music – in different genres and guises – has become a new rationale for travel and a market for tourists in a rapidly expanding industry (Gibson and Connell, 2007).

Music tourism can be considered as a type of special interest cultural tourism, in the sense that it can be seen as an extension of a tourist's special interest in certain forms of musical expression (Moscardo et al., 2009). It incorporates a range of different activities including music festivals and other live performance events (for example concerts and operas), and travel to destinations linked with historical or contemporary music scenes where tourists may visit music museums, participate in music heritage trails (see Roberts, 2014), or visit iconic sites such as recording studios or the once-homes of famous artists. It is a rapidly expanding and diverse tourist niche, which has been especially successful in those countries with both mature tourism and music industries (Leaver and Schmidt, 2009). Yet music tourism has also spread to many locations across the globe, from live music performances in major world cities to the indigenous music of rural landscapes, from the musical heritage of post-industrial cities (see for example Brocken, 2015, on Liverpool) to the hedonistic dance music of club culture and beach parties (see Gibson and Connell, 2003a).

As a form of special interest tourism, music tourism involves a distinct and particular set of motivations for travel, and involves a particular set of activities. At a personal level, people develop an intimate relationship with music, and it forms an important part of individual identity. Music therefore has an emotive power, evoking personal memories, and allowing people to recall particular periods of their lives. As Connell and Gibson (2003) note, music tourism taps into this, providing people with opportunities to relive their emotional attachments to music. The role of music in creating a 'story of self' is one of the main motives for travel (Bolderman and Reijnders, 2016). This may include visiting particular places and sites associated with favourite performers; places where they lived, produced music, performed, and even died. Given the strong attachment between particular styles of music and particular places, music tourism may also involve visiting particular places associated with particular musical scenes and 'sounds'. But, as Gibson and Connell (2007) suggest, music tourism is extremely varied, and although nostalgia is a part of many travels, it is not exclusively so. Music also plays a key role in new tourist experiences – in the creation of new memories and new emotional attachments to sites, places and people. Music tourism therefore includes activities such as visiting sites of live performance, including music festivals and locations associated with new forms of music and subcultural experiences, and travelling to experience places based upon cultural meanings associated with music.

The economic opportunities presented by this relatively new form of special interest tourism are increasingly being recognised. For those places with musical heritage or contemporary live music scenes, it is argued that music tourism presents an opportunity to enhance or rejuvenate a place's brand, bolster tourism market share, and shape the development of infrastructure that supports tourism more generally (Gibson and Davidson, 2004). Thus, increasingly, music is being used as part of the tourism strategies employed by local and national governments and tourist promotion boards (see, for example, Prior, 2015, on Iceland). Indeed, estimates of the economic impact of music tourism in certain locations are impressive; in 2007 the Memphis Convention and Visitors Bureau estimated that the city's music tourism industry had attracted around one million visitors and a spend of US$3billion. Yet despite this, music tourism has received scant attention from tourism scholars (Gibson and Connell, 2007). The purpose of this chapter is to examine the motivations, activities and impacts of music tourism as a form of special interest tourism, and in doing so, consolidate the small body of literature that has developed in this area.

Motivations

As Connell and Gibson (2003) note, inherent in some forms of music tourism is the notion of pilgrimage, whereby tourists visit particular places and sites associated with particular performers who hold a particularly important meaning for them. Highlighting the quasi-religious faith often held in the power of music icons, they point to the emergence of a set of 'sacred' locations – sites which particular artists occupied or passed through, or often died at. As such, these are sites which have been transformed from seemingly meaningless, ordinary locations into sites of significant cultural meaning. There are many prominent examples, perhaps the most notable of which relate to the death of these icons: Elvis Presley's grave at Graceland in Memphis; John Lennon's Imagine memorial at Strawberry Fields in

Central Park, New York (close to the Dakota building in which John Lennon lived and was murdered, Focus Box 1); Jim Morrison's grave at Père Lachaise Cemetery in Paris (Fig. 7.1); and Jimi Hendrix's resting place at Greenwood Memorial Park in Seattle (Connell and Gibson, 2003).

These 'sacred' sites are not limited to sites of death, memorial and remembrance, however. There are a wide range of other sites, including sites of life, music production and performance that attract pilgrims. There is a significance attached to the places where these artists lived, for example. Here one can point again to Graceland, as well as the childhood homes of the Beatles in Liverpool. The recording studios in which artists produced their music have also become sites of pilgrimage – in particular Abbey Road Studios in London, in which the Beatles produced much of their music; Sun Studios in Memphis, in which Elvis Presley had his early recording experiences; and more contemporary sites of music production such as Windmill Lane in Dublin, the studio at which U2 produced many of their most well known records (see Gibson, 2005). As Herbert (1996, p. 77) suggests, visiting allows 'contact with places closely associated with admired individuals, allows sight of, and perhaps the chance to touch, artefacts or memorabilia; the setting enhances the experiential quality of these contacts'. Indeed, the common act of scrawling graffiti at these sites – something that is now an accepted part of attending sites such as Abbey Road Studios or Jim Morrison's grave in Paris – allows the expression of feelings in a way that is also a lasting reminder of presence at these places (Alderman, 2002). Through such acts, fandom does not simply respond to music spaces and places, it *creates* them (Brocken, 2015). Furthermore, as Bolderman and Reijnders (2016) suggest, the embodied experience of 'being there', often with other fans, can act as an anchor point in a continued emotional connection to the related place, forming an extension to personal life narratives and identities.

Fans, however, of course have different levels of 'involvement' with an artist, ranging from the dilettante to the highly devoted (Thorne and Bruner, 2006), and so will have differing levels of motivation for visiting particular sites. At the extreme end of the scale, the pilgrimages of highly devoted fans carry high levels of meaning and emotion – they are what Leaver and Schmidt (2009) term 'high involvement consumers'. However for the majority of music tourists, their visits to locations associated

Fig. 7.1. Grave of Jim Morrison, Père-Lachaise Cemetery, Paris (Source: Wikimedia Commons).

with bands might be more appropriately considered as a form of 'nostalgia consumption' (Dann, 1994) rather than a pilgrimage *per se*. Such nostalgia tourism involves visiting sites as a way of revisiting particular memories and emotions associated with music from a particular period of life – a search for authenticity and a 'contextual understanding' of the lives of particular artists and the development of particular music scenes. As Fremaux and Fremaux (2013) suggest, as there are particularly strong links between music heritage and nostalgia, nostalgia can be very positive and attractive for tourist agencies in building music tourism attractions. This is especially the case where a location can claim a strong link with a particular artist or music scene. Since the 1980s for example, the city of Liverpool

Focus Box 1: Strawberry Fields as a place of secular pilgrimage

Strawberry Fields is a memorial to songwriter and Beatles' member John Lennon located in Central Park in New York. Kruse (2003) highlights how this memorial has become one of a number of places associated with Lennon and the Beatles that has undergone sacralisation as part of the sanctification of John Lennon by many fans. As a site of 'cultural religion' (Alderman, 2002), Kruse notes how Strawberry Fields has become a place of secular pilgrimage, something which is especially marked each year on 8th December, which is the anniversary of Lennon's death.

Kruse notes how Strawberry Fields has become a focus for a variety of discourses related to John Lennon's life and music, and that through these discourses; especially those related to peace; the significance of Strawberry Fields reaches beyond direct references to Lennon or the Beatles. The experience of pilgrims visiting Strawberry Fields, Kruse suggests, is not generalisable, but instead involves a multitude of interpretations, with visitors having 'a depth of sentiment that reaches beyond the scope of rock music to a confluence of historical reflection, idealism, and timeless hope for peace' (Kruse, 2003, p.157). Thus, 'Strawberry Fields becomes a memorial to more than a popular songwriter; it becomes a shrine to the youthful idealism of the 1960s' (Kruse, 2003, p.159).

has been building a highly lucrative music tourism industry around its association with arguably the world's most famous group, the Beatles. This particular focus for tourism has not only been successful in its own right (see Case Study 1), but is also an important component of a wider strategy for growing cultural tourism, something given renewed impetus following the award of European Capital of Culture in 2008.

Another type of music tourism relates not to heritage, nostalgia, and place *per se*, but to contemporary music scenes and live music performances in the form of gigs and festivals. The potential economic benefits of live music tourism are increasingly being recognised. A study produced by UK Music in 2013, for example, identified that 6.5 million music tourists attend a festival or gig, and that this generated £2.2 billion in spending; £1.3 billion of this came from direct spend by music tourists, such as buying tickets and paying for accommodation; with £914m coming from indirect music tourism spend along the supply chain generated by the tourists. This type of music tourism, they suggest, offers 'astounding regional tourism benefits' and the 'potential to fuel tourism throughout the country' (www.ukmusic.org/research/report-archive/wish-you-were-here-2013, accessed 1 October 2014), pointing to record demand for a number of major UK festivals including Glastonbury. They do also note, however, that music tourism is disproportionately focused on London, which attracts 28% of all music tourists to the UK.

Quinn (2006) argues that increasingly there is a very strong association between festivals and tourism,

and that 'abundant evidence is now available to show that countless festivals are marketed as tourist attractions and draw definable tourist flows' (2006, p. 289). Felsenstein and Fleischer (2003) note that the most obvious reasons for the popularity of local festivals being used as a tourism promotion tool relate to, first, the way in which festivals increase the demand for local tourism; and second, that successful festivals can help 'recreate the image of a place or contribute toward the exposure of a location trying to get on the tourism map' (Felsenstein and Fleischer, 2003, p. 385).

As an important form of cultural festival, live music festivals are increasingly being used as instruments for promoting tourism and boosting regional economies. Gibson and Davidson (2004) for example, point to the importance of the annual Country and Western Music Festival in Tamworth, New South Wales, in the city's emergence as Australia's 'country music capital'. The leading event of its type in Australia, the festival attracts 60,000 visitors every year and includes a 10-day programme, 2400 events, 116 venues and 1000 artists (Gibson and Davidson, 2004). Tamworth's status as 'country music capital', they suggest, has been deliberately created as an outcome of strategic place marketing by tourism authorities, with the festival becoming central to the town's identity and tourism marketing strategies and being brought 'into the broad orbit of local economic development strategies' (Gibson and Davidson, 2004, p. 393).

Successful examples such as Tamworth have given further credence to the idea that music

Case Study 1: Beatles tourism in Liverpool and Hamburg

Given the status of the Beatles as arguably the world's most famous band, it is not surprising that tourism related to the band provides one of the most prominent examples of music tourism. Beatles tourism stretches across a variety of locations and sites associated with the band: most prominently, the city of Liverpool in which the band members were born and spent their early career together; Abbey Road Studios in London, at which the band were to record many of their albums; the Strawberry Fields memorial in Central Park, New York, close to the Dakota building in which John Lennon lived and was murdered; and the port of Hamburg in Northern Germany, where the Beatles regularly performed during their early career. For both the cities of Liverpool and Hamburg, their association with the Beatles has become part of an explicit music tourism strategy.

In the case of Liverpool, Kruse argues that 'the marketing of the Beatles ... has become a well-coordinated

and highly lucrative industry" (2005, p. 89). As Cohen (1997) suggests, the death of John Lennon in 1980 triggered an urgent desire on the part of many Beatles fans to travel to Liverpool, and despite early scepticism from local public sector organisations about the merits of promoting the Beatles as a tourist attraction (Cohen, 2007), the subsequent decades have seen the successful commercialisation of the link between the Beatles and their home city. Kruse (2005) highlights how the landscape of Beatles places is composed of a patchwork of commercial and vernacular places that may be authentic, replicated, or historically unrelated, but which are woven together as a unified landscape by narratives from the local tourism industry, or what Brocken (2015) terms an agreed 'mono-history'. This narrative, Kruse argues, is a largely romantic and nostalgic one relating to the early years of the Beatles' career which was focused in Merseyside.

Fig. 7.2. Beatles imagery, HMV store, Liverpool (Source: Author).

Continued

An example of the high level of commercialisation that Beatles tourism has brought to the urban landscape is Cavern City Tours Ltd (see Brocken, 2015), a company which owns the Cavern Club (now a replica of the original, which had previously been demolished), the Cavern Pub, The Beatles Story museum, and the Magical Mystery tour. Surrounding these sites are a plethora of shops selling Beatles souvenirs and memorabilia, as well as bars, clubs, pubs and exhibitions where Beatles music is played (Cohen, 1997), while Beatles imagery is common place across the city (Fig. 7.2). More recently, in 2008, the upmarket Hard Day's Night hotel opened, offering a range of Beatles-themed luxury rooms as well as Paul McCartney and John Lennon suites.

A series of other, non-centralised vernacular sites form part of the Beatles landscape alongside these highly commercialised sites, most notably the family homes of Paul McCartney in Forthlin Road (acquired by the National Trust in 1995) and John Lennon in Menlove Avenue (donated to the National Trust in 2002 by Yoko Ono). Other vernacular places feature in the Beatles landscape that are ordinary and unremarkable other than that they have been given meaning through Beatles songs. Most notable in this respect are Penny Lane and the Strawberry Field children's home. Such sites form part of commercial Beatles tours, but are also sought out by tourists independently.

The other major location with which the Beatles had a strong connection during the early stages of their career was Hamburg in Germany, with the live music scene of the port having a significant influence on the band's image and sound. However, as Fremaux and Fremaux (2013) suggest, Hamburg's role in the Beatles' legacy has been overshadowed by the strong cultural ownership of the band that has been claimed by the tourism industry in Liverpool since the 1980s. Indeed, the city was relatively slow to recognise the potential for tourism related to its connection to the Beatles, and Fremaux and Fremaux note that it would not be until May 2009 that Hamburg would begin to reclaim this heritage through the opening of the Beatlemania Museum in the St. Pauli district of the city. Slightly earlier, in September 2008, the dedication of the Beatles-Platz had marked the first formal commemoration of Beatles-related sites in the district. These developments, they argue, signalled a new initiative to rebrand Hamburg as a place for family-friendly tourism.

festivals can be used as a springboard for wider developments in music tourism, prompting other cities to follow suit. Baerenholdt and Haldrup (2006) for example point to the example of Roskilde, Denmark, which since 1971 has hosted the famous Roskilde Festival, one of the largest music festivals in Europe and the largest in Northern Europe. Based on the strong association with rock music that the festival has given to Roskilde, a development project called 'Rock City' was initiated, which involved construction of a museum and experience centre for rock music. However, the project is more ambitious than this alone, and looks to integrate these facilities with a broader complex (known as 'Music City') that includes hotel and conference facilities, retail, a research and education institution, and housing areas and facilities for private businesses (Baerenholdt and Haldrup, 2006).

Alongside festivals, as Gibson and Connell (2003b) note, another crucial element of tourist consumption is popular music produced specifically for youth markets. They point in particular to that music informed by the attitudes and styles of backpacker cultures, which involve 'conjunctures of fashion, language ... recreational activities (scuba diving, rock climbing, clubbing, drug-taking) and music tastes' (Gibson and Connell, 2003b, p. 167). They note how Byron Bay, Australia, has become part of an international network of dance music sites closely associated with routes of backpacker culture, which include Goa in India (see Saldanha, 2002a, b), and Koh Samui and Koh Phangan in Thailand. These have become places where backpackers go to experience electronic psychedelic music and drug culture at beach dance parties. More generally, the youth dance music tourism market is one which has become increasingly commercialised over the last three decades, as package tour operators have taken advantage of the fact that young people are often keen to travel to pursue their interest in dance music, and are a target audience with high disposable incomes and much leisure time. This was especially the case in Europe, in which a number of key dance music tourism destinations would emerge. The island of Ibiza in particular would emerge as the central location for dance music tourism (Focus Box 2), especially for the UK youth tourism market (Sellars, 1998).

Focus Box 2: Ibiza, dance music and UK youth tourism

Sellars (1998) describes how, through the early 1990s, there was a move towards young people from the UK taking holidays to pursue their interest in dance music, which involved following their favourite DJs to wherever in Europe, or the world, they might be playing. This form of musical tourism was to quickly become commercialised on a large scale. It would first occur through established nightclubs in particular destinations attracting particular DJs and hosting popular club nights from the 'superclubs' of the UK. Music tourism would then quickly become subject to packaging by tour operators, who were both very astute in marketing these holidays, and also highly aware of what youth tourists wanted in terms of music, clubs, bars, drink and fashion:

> The brochures depict the type of images and text that young people of today can relate to

and indeed desire, the majority of pages being dominated by young people having lots of 'fun in the sun' and then fun on the dancefloor (Sellars, 1998, p. 614)

This is nowhere more marked than in Ibiza, which remains the number one European destination for dance music tourism. Sellars describes how big-name night clubs from the UK run nights in the main clubs in Ibiza, such as Cream, Ministry of Sound, and Manumission. These, she argues, act as a 'pull-factor' so that dance music tourists have invariably followed these nights to Ibiza. Location, in this instance, seems to be a more minor attraction, given that 'brochures do not depict the scenic and cultural values of the resort, but show packed night clubs with beautiful people in skimpy outfits' (Sellars, 1998, p. 613).

Interactions

As more and more cities have opened up their cultural activities to tourists and embraced tourism as part of economic development and urban regeneration strategies, it has become increasingly important for places to create a distinct 'place identity' (Robins, 1991) in order to retain or increase market share. Given that music reflects aspects of the place in which it is created (Cohen, 1997) – and therefore each city has its own unique sound, musical heritage and/or contemporary live music scenes – music has been identified as important by many locations in respect of creating a unique place identity. As Gibson and Connell (2003b) suggest, 'music is both a key cultural industry and a text through which places are known and represented, providing a new source of images and sounds for tourism promotion' (2003b, p. 166).

Atkinson (1997) for example describes how, in the 1980s, as New Orleans positioned itself to develop a tourism industry in order to drive urban regeneration, it found itself in competition with other cities to attract visitors for entertainment and leisure activities. She describes how research was commissioned to discover what distinctive quality of the city would be most competitive, and it was found that discretionary tourists list 'excitement' most often as the goal of their travels. It was considered that New Orleans' music scene, with its

characteristics of spontaneity, celebration and participation, fed into this, and so it was decided to exploit the city's music image for the purposes of tourism (Atkinson, 1997; see also Meadows, 2014, Focus Box 3). Music would subsequently become central to the packaging of New Orleans as 'the birthplace of jazz' (Connell and Gibson, 2003). It is a strategy that would seem to have been successful: drawing on data from the US Travel Data Service, Cohen (1997) reports that in 1990, the total primary and secondary spending of the visitor industry was US$3.2 billion, of which US$593.6 million was calculated to be spending attracted by music, with music tourism creating 38,000 jobs. Atkinson (1997) reports that in 1990 the New Orleans Jazz and Heritage festival alone had an economic impact of roughly US$71.6 million.

Other cities have also, through their tourism strategies, employed music in producing a unique 'brand' to appeal to tourists, perhaps none more so than Nashville, Tennessee. Connell and Gibson (2003) describe how, the self-appointed 'home' of country and western music has, through preserving and commercialising its musical heritage, 'cemented its reputation in the music world as the centre of country music production' and simultaneously 'marketed this reputation in the tourist world through constructions of spectacle' (2003, p. 240). The city has attracted millions of tourists who come to visit the various museums, souvenir shops, performers' homes and country music-based theme park, and to take part in line-dancing (Connell and Gibson, 2003). But the most successful example of an explicitly music-based tourism strategy can be found in the case of Memphis, the world's most iconic and commercially significant location for musical tourism (Gibson and Connell, 2007, Focus Box 4). As noted earlier, the Memphis Convention

---

Focus Box 3: Music tourism in New Orleans

In her analysis of the role of music in the place packaging of tourism in New Orleans, Atkinson (1997) describes how, due to its history of racial and cultural mixing – Africans, Italians, Spanish and French – New Orleans has a very particular historical identification with music. The city's role in the evolution of jazz, she points out, gave the city an international association with jazz music that still persists today. It is not only the uniqueness of the music itself that marks New Orleans' musical association, however, but also its performance. Cultural mixing has resulted in a heritage of musical performance on the street, in the forms of street bands, 'second-line' parades (in which people dance behind a brass band as it moves down the street), and jazz funerals. The expectations of visitors are then shaped as much by the contemporary performance of musical heritage as they are by the music. These expectations are met in that, as Atkinson describes, the streets of the old French Quarter are still often the place of music and celebration:

> Entertainment spills outside buildings on to the sidewalks and courtyards of the Quarter, extending the tourist space to include the streets and *banquettes*, liberating the tourist, who can now 'own' the entire space... 'Private' cultural celebrations, such as neighbourhood jazz funerals and parades, have no boundaries between locals and tourists. (Atkinson, 1997, p. 94, emphasis in original)

Tourists, then, become a part of the revelry, and therefore active participants in shaping their own tourist experience. Music, Atkinson argues, acts as a sign that a space is open to occupation by tourists, marking spaces where revelry is permitted. Music is also used to lure tourists to new spaces that have been created by the riverside explicitly for them, with bands and street musicians serenading visitors.

Focus Box 4: Music tourism in Memphis

Much of the success of Memphis' music tourism strategy can be attributed to Graceland, the once home and now burial place of Elvis Presley. Graceland opened in 1982 and is estimated to attract some 600,000 visitors annually (Leaver and Schmidt, 2009), making it the most important single destination for music tourists in the world. But while Graceland attracts huge visitor numbers and forms an important part of the city's tourism campaigns, there is more to Memphis in terms of music tourism than Graceland alone. Gibson and Connell (2007) describe Memphis as a city:

> ...literally re-made through music: it defines tourist and non-tourist spaces, reverberates though key cultural districts and is central to how certain destinations (such as Graceland) secure their emotive and commercial significance (Gibson and Connell, 2007, p. 171)

Whilst being strongly linked to Elvis Presley, Memphis is famous more generally as a centre of rhythm and blues. As Gibson and Connell describe, the city's African-American population and their music scenes were focused on the Beale Street precinct of the city, and it is this precinct (following demolition, and then reconstruction) that would subsequently become a music-based tourist landscape, seeing the construction of shopping malls, museums and hotels, as part of the wider commodification of tourism. Music plays a central role in the attraction of tourists to the precinct:

> Nowadays, music fills the streetscape, marking Beale Street as a tourist space in contrast to surrounding neighbourhoods... Music acts as an aural lure for restaurants, cafes and nightclubs all capitalizing on the city's reputation (Gibson and Connell, 2007, p. 182)

In an example of how a successful music tourism industry can stimulate wider urban renewal, Gibson and Connell describe how Beale Street has become an 'anchor' for the renewal of Memphis' entire downtown, which seeks to create a wider cultural and entertainment precinct.

A. Watson

and Visitors Bureau (2007) estimated that the city's music tourism industry had attracted around one million visitors and a spend of US$3billion.

As Connell and Gibson (2003) suggest, outside the West, however, only a few locations across Asia, Latin America and the Caribbean have stimulated significant music tourism. They point, for example, to the music tourism that has developed in South America around traditional forms of music, especially in Cuba around the revival of rumba music and the Buena Vista Social Club (see for example Perna, 2014), and in Argentina around tango. In both cases music has provided an important image for these countries that make them legible as cultural destinations to tourists, and thus has stimulated tourism more broadly.

Music tourism of course overlaps with some of the other forms of special interest tourism considered in this volume. Perhaps most significant are interactions between music tourism and festival tourism. Studies into the motivations of music festival attendees by Pegg and Patterson (2010), Gelder and Robinson (2009) and Bowen and Daniels (2005) for example, have highlighted that a 'festival atmosphere' that offers opportunities for socialising and new non-musical experiences is of high importance over and above the music, and as such events managers cannot rely solely on the theme of the event itself. Research by Green (2002) and Nurse (2002) focusing on the Caribbean has highlighted the overlap of musical tourism, festival tourism and carnival tourism, and their importance in destination marketing and international recognition. Given that music tourism can be seen as a strategy in which creative resources are deployed to generate distinctive place-identities (Richards, 2011), it also overlaps with other forms of creative special interest tourism such as film and theatre/opera tourism.

Impacts and Insights

Increasingly music is being used as part of the tourism strategies employed by local governments and tourist promotions boards, in the belief that it can provide economic benefits (through both direct and indirect tourist spend), social benefits, and act as a catalyst for urban regeneration. Such a position has been supported by a number of academic studies, such as that by Leaver and Schmidt (2009) who argue that music tourism 'offers towns and cities the opportunity to further develop elements of their

tourist based economies' (2009, p. 228). Yet, there remain a number of issues with regards to music tourism that require continued critical consideration from academics and policy makers.

First is the issue of understanding the likely economic benefits and impacts that come from music tourism strategies. This is not straightforward. Because the motivations and activities of music tourists are quite varied, as Gibson and Connell (2007) note, music tourism is difficult to define, and therefore it is difficult to conduct straightforward economic or social impact analysis. Further, they note that in the literature that has considered music tourism studies, cultural issues have tended to dominate analysis while studies on the economic dimensions of music analysis are rare. While figures for large music tourism locations such as New Orleans and Memphis, provided earlier in this chapter, are impressive, economic analysis of a wider range of music tourism locations and sites is required in order to fully understand how successful music tourism strategies might be in a variety of locations. The failure of the National Centre for Popular Music, which opened at a cost of £15m in March 1999 in Sheffield, UK, only to close a little over a year later due to low visitor numbers, is a case in point. As Long (2014, p. 54) suggests in his analysis of recent strategies around music tourism in the same city, there is 'a need to reflect on the local specificity of place history, economy and cultures in devising local music (and tourism) plans and strategies'.

Further, and with specific regard to tourism driven by music festivals, many festivals only exist because of generous public funding. As Moscardo et al. (2009) note, the role of festivals as image-maker is often highlighted by government funding agencies, and as such, Moscardo et al. argue that these agencies often provide public financial assistance to festivals based on 'beliefs about the ability of music events to raise the profile of a region and change its image in a way that will make it more attractive to tourists' (2009, p. 8). However, a number of academics have argued that available evidence supports only temporary image enhancement from festivals (see for example Prentice and Andersen, 2003; Quinn, 2005). Further, for O'Sullivan and Jackson (2002), while festival tourism can benefit local tourism-related business, income generation alone is not enough, and in order to contribute sustainable localities a 'spread of benefits for residents and businesses should be sought' (O'Sullivan and Jackson, 2002, p. 327). Such a perspective is supported by Felsenstein and Fleischer (2003) who argue that:

> A large local, expenditure driven, multiplier generated by a festival is not, in itself, a sufficient indicator of local gain. It says little about the costs involved in producing an event, the distribution of local gains to local people, or how much better off the local area would be in the absence of the festival (2003, p. 385).

Examining the contribution of a festival to local tourism, then, requires a more nuanced assessment that looks at impacts in a variety of spheres, especially, Felsenstein and Fleischer argue, where expectations of local economic income and employment obfuscate negative economic, social and environmental impacts.

Second then, and related to the above, there is a need to better understand the social impacts of music tourism on the locations in which it is focused. This is especially the case when music tourism strategies are developed as part of wider strategies for urban renewal. As Gibson and Connell (2007) note, while music tourism may result in changes to an area that bring back vitality, it can also result in the displacement of poorer residents from the inner city due to residential property market dynamics – a process that has come to be described as 'tourism gentrification'. They point to both New Orleans and Harlem as examples of locations in which the urban renewal stimulated by cultural tourism has had negative impacts on black residents through rising rent costs.

In a more detailed appraisal of gentrification in New Orleans' Vieux Carre (French Quarter) in which the city's music tourism is predominantly focused, Gotham (2005) suggests that tourism gentrification is not only residential, however, but also commercial. The transformation of the Vieux Carre into an entertainment destination, he argues, 'enhances the significance of consumption-orientated activities in residential space and encourages gentrification' (Gotham, 2005, p. 1114). As such, the development of music tourism as a key component of a wider tourism strategy in New Orleans has been complicit in pricing out working-class residents and as such eroding the very bohemian and musical character of the quarter that attracts tourists so strongly in the first instance. Thus, in considering music tourism specifically, and cultural tourism more generally, it is important to recognise that alongside the positive impacts to local economy, real estate and retail sector, can come negative impacts on local society and culture. Greater research and appraisal of the impact of existing music tourism strategies are needed in this regard to ensure that such strategies are not to the long-term detriment of local society and the cultural creativity that enabled music tourism to flourish in particular locations in the first instance.

Questions

1. What is the range of motivations for travel amongst music tourists?
2. In what ways is it thought music can be used to enhance place image and stimulate local economic development?
3. For what reasons might we question whether music tourism represents a mechanism for providing sustainable local economic development?

Further Reading

Readers are referred to *On the Road Again: Music and Tourism* by Chris Gibson and John Connell (Channel View Press, 2003). This book represents the first, and to date only, truly comprehensive analysis of the full global extent of music tourism. The book contains elements of historical and contemporary research and covers a range of diverse international case studies. With specific reference to Liverpool, readers are referred to Michael Brocken's *The Twenty-First Century Legacy of the Beatles: Liverpool and Popular Music Heritage Tourism* (Ashgate, 2015), which traces the historical development of Beatles tourism in the city. Readers interested in musical tourism in and around the Caribbean should refer to *Sun, Sea, and Sound: Music and Tourism in the Circum-Caribbean* edited by Timothy Rommen and Daniel Neely (Oxford University Press, 2014), which contains a range of chapters covering the Caribbean, Cuba, Brazil and the USA.

References

Alderman, D. (2002) Writing on the Graceland wall: on the importance of authorship in pilgrimage landscapes. *Tourism Recreation Research* 27(2), 27–33.

Atkinson, C.Z. (1997) Whose New Orleans? Music's place in the packaging of New Orleans for tourism. In: Abram, S., Waldren, J. and Macleod, D.V.L. (eds) *Tourists and Tourism: Identifying with People and Places.* Berg, Oxford, UK, pp. 91–106.

Baerenholdt, J.O. and Haldrup, M. (2006) Mobile networks and place making in cultural tourism. *European Urban and Regional Studies* 13(3), 209–224.

Bolderman, L. and Reijnders, S. (2016) Have you found what you're looking for? Analysing tourist experiences of Wagner's Bayreuth, ABBA's Stockholm and U2's Dublin. *Tourist Studies* 17, 164–181, (doi:10.1177/1468797616665757).

Bowen, H. and Daniels, M. (2005) Does the music matter? Motivations for attending a music festival. *Event Management* 9(3), 155–164.

Brocken, M. (2015) *The Twenty-First Century Legacy of the Beatles: Liverpool and Popular Music Heritage Tourism.* Ashgate, Farnham, UK.

Cohen, S. (1997) More than the Beatles: popular music, tourism and urban regeneration. In: Abram, S., Waldren, J. and Macleod, D.V.L. (eds) *Tourists and Tourism: Identifying with People and Places.* Berg, Oxford, UK, pp. 71–90.

Cohen, S. (2007) *Decline, Renewal, and the City in Popular Music: Beyond the Beatles.* Ashgate, Farnham, UK.

Connell, J. and Gibson, C. (2003) *Sound Tracks: Popular Music, Identity and Place.* Routledge, London, UK.

Dann, G. (1994) Tourism: the nostalgia industry of the future. In: Theobold, W. (ed.) *Global Tourism: The Next Decade.* Butterworth Heinemann, Oxford, UK, pp. 55–67.

Felsenstein, D. and Fleischer, A. (2003) Local festivals and tourism promotion: the role of public assistance and visitor expenditure. *Journal of Travel Research* 41, 385–392.

Fremaux, S. and Fremaux, M. (2013) Remembering the Beatles' legacy in Hamburg's problematic tourism strategy. *Journal of Heritage Tourism* 8(4), 303–319.

Gelder, G. and Robinson, P. (2009) A critical comparative study of visitor motivations for attending music festivals: a case study of Glastonbury and V Festival. *Event Management* 13(3), 181–196.

Gibson, C. (2005) Recording studios: relational spaces of creativity in the city. *Built Environment* 31(3), 192–207.

Gibson, C. and Connell, J. (2003a) *On the Road Again: Music and Tourism.* Channel View Press, Clevedon, UK.

Gibson, C. and Connell, J. (2003b) 'Bongo fury': tourism, music and cultural economy at Byron Bay, Australia. *Tijdschrift voor Economische en Sociale Geografie* 94(2), 164–187.

Gibson, C. and Connell, J. (2007) Music, tourism and the transformation of Memphis. *Tourism Geographies* 9(2), 160–190.

Gibson, C. and Davidson, D. (2004) Tamworth, Australia's 'country music capital': place marketing, rurality, and resident reactions. *Journal of Rural Studies* 20, 387–404.

Gotham, K. (2005) Tourism gentrification: the case of New Orleans Vieux Carré (French Quarter). *Urban Studies* 39(10), 1735–1756.

Green, G.L. (2002) Marketing the nation: carnival and tourism in Trinidad and Tobago. *Critique of Anthropology* 22(3), 283–304.

Herbert, D. (1996) Artistic and literary places in France as tourist attractions. *Tourism Management* 17(2), 77–85.

Kruse, R.J. (2003) Imagining Strawberry Fields as a place of pilgrimage. *Area* 35(2), 154–162.

Kruse, R.J. (2005) The Beatles as place makers: narrated landscapes in Liverpool, England. *Journal of Cultural Geography* 22(2), 87–114.

Leaver, D. and Schmidt, R.A. (2009) Before they were famous: music-based tourism and a musician's hometown roots. *Journal of Place Management and Development* 2(3), 220–229.

Long, P. (2014) Popular music, psychogeography, place identity and tourism: the case of Sheffield. *Tourism Studies* 14(1), 48–65.

Meadows, R. (2014) "Jockomo fee na nay!": Afro-Caribbean and Afro-Creole sensorialities and the festivalization of New Orleans's music tourism. In: Rommen, T. and Neely, D.T. (eds) *Sun, Sea and Sound: Music and Tourism in the Circum-Caribbean.* Oxford University Press, Oxford, UK, pp. 238–264.

Memphis Convention and Visitors Bureau (2007) *Memphis Convention and Visitors Bureau Economic Impact Study.* Memphis Convention and Visitors Bureau, Memphis, TN, USA.

Moscardo, G., McCarthy, B., Murphy, L. and Pearce, P. (2009) The importance of networks in special interest tourism: case studies of music tourism in Australia. *International Journal of Tourism Policy* 2(1/2), 5–23.

Nurse, K. (2002) Bringing culture into tourism: festival tourism and Reggae Sunsplash in Jamaica. *Social and Economic Studies* 51(1), 124–1473.

O'Sullivan, D. and Jackson, M.J. (2002) Festival tourism: a contributor to sustainable local economic development? *Journal of Sustainable Tourism* 10(4), 325–342.

Pegg, S. and Patterson, I. (2010) Rethinking music festivals as a staged event: gaining insights from understanding visitor motivations and the experiences they seek. *Journal of Convention & Event Tourism* 11(2), 85–99.

Perna, V.A. (2014) Selling Cuba by the sound: music and tourism in Cuba in the 1990s. In: Rommen, T. and Neely, D.T. (eds) *Sun, Sea and Sound: Music and Tourism in the Circum-Caribbean.* Oxford University Press, Oxford, UK, pp. 44–70.

Prentice, R. and Andersen, V. (2003) Festival as creative destination. *Annals of Tourism Research* 30(1), 7–30.

Prior, N. (2015) 'It's a social thing, not a nature thing': popular music practices in Reykjavík, Iceland. *Cultural Sociology* 9(1), 81–98.

Quinn, B. (2005) Arts festivals and the city. *Urban Studies* 42(5–6), 927–943.

Quinn, B. (2006) Problematising 'festival tourism': arts festivals and sustainable development in Ireland. *Journal of Sustainable Tourism* 14(3), 288–306.

Richards, G. (2011) Creativity and tourism: the state of the art. *Annals of Tourism Research* 38(4), 1225–1253.

Roberts, L. (2014) Marketing musicscapes, or the political economy of contagious magic. *Tourist Studies* 14(1), 10–29.

Robins, K. (1991) Tradition and translation: national culture in its global context. In: Corner, J. and Harvey, S. (eds) *Enterprise and Heritage.* Routledge, London, UK.

Saldanha, A. (2002a) Music tourism and factions of bodies in Goa. *Tourist Studies* 2(1), 43–62.

Saldanha, A. (2002b) Trance and visibility at dawn: racial dynamics in Goa's rave scene. *Social & Cultural Geography* 6(5), 707–721.

Sellars, A. (1998) The influence of dance music on the UK youth tourism market. *Tourism Management* 19(6), 611–615.

Thorne, S. and Bruner, G.C. (2006) An exploratory investigation of the characteristics of consumer fanaticism. *Qualitative Market Research* 9(1), 51–72.

8 Film Tourism

W. Glen Croy

Learning Objectives

- To distinguish special interest film tourism
- To differentiate tourists at film sites
- To compare film tourist motivations and experiences
- To illustrate film tourism impacts

Introduction

Film tourism is a special interest phenomenon. The attraction of film (including movies, television and similar media) related sites has been widely reported in the general media, and garnered research interest (by example, a number of journal special issues, including: *Tourism Culture and Communication, 6*(3), 2006; *Tourist Studies, 6*(1), 2006; *Tourism Review International, 13*(2), 2009; *Worldwide Hospitality and Tourism Themes, 3*(2), 2011; *Tourism Review International, 15*(3), 2011; *Tourism and Hospitality Planning and Development, 7*(1), 2010; *Tourism Review International, 16*(2), 2012; *Tourism Analysis, 20*(3), 2015). Some of this attention, particularly from the general media, has even indicated that film tourism may be a mass and significant form of tourism.

Nonetheless, the research is highlighting the exceptional nature of film tourism, and the localised impacts. Only a small minority of films appear to generate tourist demand (Croy and Heitmann, 2011). An exceptional example of film tourism is that of *Close Encounters of the Third Kind* (1977), in that the site of the closing scenes had a 74% increase in visitor numbers the year after its release (Riley *et al.*, 1998). The localised impact of film tourism is in that the influential reach of film appears to take place within a tourist destination, as compared to in the generating region (Croy, 2011). As Macionis and Sparks (2009, p. 99) found, the majority of film site visits occur when already at the destination, and 'there are only a very small percentage of tourists … who travel to a location for the prime reason of visiting a film site'. Whilst the research is

indicating that film tourism is a niche experience, how can we understand the tourists that partake in these experiences?

To gain a better understanding of special interest film tourists and tourism, this chapter presents key concepts and analyses existing studies. The analysis investigates major factors including the variety of film tourist types, and how they are characterised to identify special interest film tourists and the scale of special interest film tourists so as to determine the size of such interest. The chapter then specifically examines special interest film tourist motivations and their experiences. An overview of special interest film tourism impacts and insights are presented. Finally, conclusions are drawn presenting the place of special interest film tourism in tourism.

Key Concepts

The first key concept to be understood is film tourism. Beeton (2005, p. 11) defines film tourism as 'visitation to sites where movies and TV programmes have been filmed [and set], as well as to tours to production studios, including film-related theme parks'. Logically, there can be and is a lot of overlap with many other natural and built icons that tourists visit. For example, the Eiffel Tower in Paris has featured in many films (e.g. *The Man on the Eiffel Tower* (1949), *Funny Face* (1957), *The Great Race* (1965), *A View to a Kill* (1985), *Moulin Rouge* (2001), *Rush Hour 3* (2007), *Ratatouille* (2007), *Hugo* (2011), *Sherlock Holmes: A Game of Shadows* (2011), *I Have to Buy New Shoes* (2012)), though is also an attraction in its own right. All the same, any visit to the Eiffel Tower is film tourism by definition 'visitation to sites where movies and TV programmes have been filmed', even if the tourists visiting have not seen or been motivated by these films. In this chapter the focus is on tourists that have film as a central role in visitation.

Other special interest film tourism key concepts include destination image formation, motivations, and decision-making. Films are argued to play an early and influential role in destination image formation about places, people and societies. Films are often the first extended exposure to new locations around the world (i.e. more than the 1 minute news clip), and audiences are able to distinguish between fiction and reality within films to glean much about the place. The destination image is a foundation for motivations, even if not associated specifically with the film, and then decision-making. Overall, film sites can attract a number of tourists, though this may not be specifically due to the film. Nonetheless, film may have played a subtle role influencing the tourists' destination image, motivations and decision-making, at a level not even apparent to tourists.

Major Factors

The major factors are who is a film tourist and what are the variety of film tourist types.

Film tourists

First, it is important to note that there is a small group of *film business tourists*, whose employment is film, and they travel for this. Film business tourists exist throughout the film production process, from pre-production, production and post-production. Such film business tourists include location scouts, producers, directors, actors, film crew, special effects, public relations, marketing and catering. In addition, there are also film business tourists for launches, premiers, festivals and fairs. Additionally, film commentators and reviewers, cinema operators, film commissioners, film funding and purchasing agencies, and the like may also need to travel for their employment. *Film business associated tourists*, those in film-related employment such as celebrity, attendance at premiers, festivals and fairs, and paparazzi, could also be included in the fringe of this category. As per the general understanding of business travel, these film business tourists are travelling due to their employment commitments.

The remainder of the chapter will focus on the discretionary film tourist, those that have at least a perceived choice in the selection of their experiences.

Film tourist types

Not all film tourists are the same: there are different types. As Rittichainuwat and Rattanaphinanchai

(2015) discuss, there have been three main studies presenting film tourist types (Macionis, 2004; Connell and Meyer, 2009; Croy and Heitmann, 2011).

Macionis (2004) proposed a motivation-based model of film tourists, including three types. Starting with those with the highest interest in film were 'specific film tourists', 'who actively seek out places they have seen in film' (p. 87). Those with an expected moderate interest in film were classified as 'general film tourists', characterised by 'those who are not specifically drawn to a film location but who participate in film tourism activities while at a destination' (p. 87). Those with the least interest in film are the 'serendipitous film tourist', being 'those who just happen to be in a destination portrayed in a film' (p. 87). Connell and Meyer (2009, p. 199), extending Macionis' (2004) typology, found an even more film-interested group of tourists, the 'elite film tourist', who was 'visiting purely to view the filming location with no other motive'.

Croy and Heitmann (2011), using the cultural tourist typology of McKercher and du Cros (2003), continued with the importance of film in the destination decision (as an indicator of motive), and added a shallow to deep experience dimension to the film tourist typology. They presented five types of film tourists starting with 'purposeful film tourists' who have deep film experiences, and for whom film had high importance in the destination decision. 'Sightseeing film tourists' also had film as of high importance in the destination decision, but have shallow filmic experiences. 'Casual film tourists' also had shallow experiences and film only had a moderate importance in the destination decision. 'Incidental film tourists' also had a shallow experience and film was of low importance in the destination decision. For Croy and Heitmann's (2011) 'serendipitous film tourists', film was of low to moderate importance in the decision, though through the encounter, a deep experience was had.

The typologies show a diversity of film motivations, importance and experiences being had by tourists, and, for many, in a shared space. A film location may have tourists who travelled around the world to be right there, and beside them a tourist who has low (or no) awareness of the film and is only incidentally at that place. One tourist may be having a deep filmic experience and another a very shallow film experience. Whilst they are all part of the film tourist typology, not all of them are considered special interest film tourists.

Film Tourist Motivations

Evidently, film has varying levels of influence as a motivator. This is demonstrated in the importance of film in destination decisions. Those with film as high importance on the decision are the special interest film tourists, and their motivations and experiences are investigated in greater detail in this section.

Film importance in destination decisions

Special interest film tourists are characterised by having film as high importance in selecting the destination: Macionis' (2004) specific film tourists, Connell and Meyer's (2009) elite film tourist, and Croy and Heitmann's (2011) sightseeing and purposeful film tourists. Additionally, for those with a special film interest, a deep filmic experience would also be expected. How many tourists at these film sites are special interest film tourists? In short, not many.

Much of the earlier research on film tourism compared pre- and post-film release demand as an indicator of tourist motivation (for example, Riley and Van Doren, 1992; Tooke and Baker, 1996). The change in visitation levels in their reported cases did indeed provide strong circumstantial evidence of an impact of film, and they were film tourists, though could not distinguish as to the specific film tourist types. Whilst recognising films played a motivating role, the interpretations were that the tourists were attracted by the locations of 'idyllic or extraordinary landscape qualities', as compared to the films *per* se, though with the caveat that further research was needed 'to verify these assertions' (Riley and Van Doren, 1992, p. 274). Similarly, Tooke and Baker (1996, p. 94) concluded that subsidies should be considered for 'locations which display attractive national landscapes or urban vistas', again implying it is the location featured in film, as compared to the film that generated visitation. Continuing this theme, when questioning visitors influenced by *The Lord of the Rings* as to what specifically encouraged them to travel to New Zealand, 86% noted 'the scenery' (Croy, 2004). Similarly, Hudson *et al.* (2011, p. 185) found that 'landscape and scenery were the two most important items inspiring the participants to visit' when assessing the influence of film on viewers' desire to travel to the location. With a supposed emphasis on the location in driving the decision, as compared to the film (film raised awareness of the idyllic landscapes, which motivated and drove tourist decisions),

these tourists would be Croy and Heitmann's (2011) casual, incidental and serendipitous film tourists, not special interest film tourists.

Following this, further studies have investigated the motivations and decision-making of tourists at film sights. Particularly of interest is the proportion of special interest film tourists for whom film was of primary importance in the destination decision.

Busby and Klug (2001) surveyed Notting Hill visitors shortly after the release of the film of the same name. They found that whilst 55% of respondents had seen the film, only 5.3% had *Notting Hill* as the reason for visiting the area. Oviedo-García *et al.* (2016), in their study of visitors to Seville found '16.2% of respondents noted film as an influence on their decision to visit Seville', though further clarified, not necessarily as a main reason. di Cesare *et al.* (2009), in their study of the Campania and Piedmont regions of Italy, found that 83% of respondents' travel desire had been moderately or highly induced by film. Nonetheless, only 4% of respondents had film as a high influence on destination choice. Two-thirds of di Cesare *et al.*'s (2009) respondents were obtained at filmed sites, and the other third from key tourist sites. Macionis and Sparks (2009), in their test of Macionis' (2004) motivational model, undertook a mailing list survey of those with an expressed interest in travel and film. Of the respondents, 4% had visited a film site with film being a primary reason.

Rittichainuwat and Rattanaphinanchai (2015) in their study of Thai tour group participants to Korea, explicitly including film site visits, found that 10.5% self-identified as specific film tourists. However, 12% of respondents noted their purpose of the trip was film tourism (as compared to vacation, business, visiting friends and relatives and the like). It is of interest that only 3% identified themselves as specific film tourists and noted their purpose for the travel as film.

Connell and Meyer (2009) investigated the mostly daytrip visitors to the Isle of Mull, finding that 69% of respondents would not have visited except for *Balamory* (2002–2005). They found that 70% had the television programme being a primary reason, and divided these into the specific film tourist (36%), and the elite film tourist (*Balamory* was the only reason, 34%). Nonetheless, they also noted that most visiting Mull were on a day visit as part of a larger holiday (81%), so the influence of film in the overall destination decision may have been less. Croy and Buchmann (2009) found that for tourists on a *The Lord of the Rings* (2001–2003) film tour, whilst most were international visitors, film was not the reason they visited New Zealand. Additionally, even though it was a film-specific tour, a third of the participants had not engaged with the books or films, and did not identify themselves as film tourists.

Carl *et al.* (2007) also investigated tourist motivations to participate in three *The Lord of the Rings* film tours. About three-quarters of the respondents had watched the films. They found, for the day trips, that a film tour 'was an interesting addition to their itinerary' (p. 56), complementing their primary motivation to experience New Zealand. However, for the multiday tour, they were primarily motivated to experience Middle Earth, the film locations and sets. Even lower proportions were found when investigating the role of *The Lord of the Rings* on New Zealand tourism demand, with only 0.3% of respondents noting the films as a main (though not primary) reason for visiting the country (Croy, 2004). At least 74% had watched at least one of the films and 88% knew they were filmed in New Zealand, however 80% stated the films were not a reason for travelling to New Zealand.

These studies indicate that whilst tourists visit film locations, and are aware of films linked to the locations, in the most part they are not motivated by film, nor is film important in the destination decision. The cases of *Balamory* and the Isle of Mull and the multiday tourists on *The Lord of the Rings* tour are exceptional, even compared to other film-specific tours. In both of these exceptional cases, the visit to the destination would not have occurred except for the film relationship.

These findings indicate a hierarchy of film tourist site types. For a film site, which will be shared by the typology of film tourists, special interest film tourists appear to be about 5% of visitors (Table 8.1). A proportion of these film site tourists are those that participate in film tours, as part of a larger non-film trip. Even for these film tour participants, only a small proportion of about 10% would be special interest film tourists. Of note, even in the film tour participants, a large minority had not even watched the films, indicating that they would be incidental or serendipitous film tourists. These sites also attract those undertaking specific tours and travel just to see these film spaces, all of which are special interest film tourists. As such, of the roughly 5% of special interest film tourists, a

Table 8.1. Special interest film tourists in film experience contexts

Context	Incidental film tourists	Special interest film tourists
Nation	80%	0.3%
Film site	45%[#]	5%
Film tour	25–33%[#]	10%
Film trip		100%
	No/Low ⟵⟶ High	
	Importance of film in destination decision	

[#]Percentage that had not watched the film: there may be more than had seen the film, though it still had low importance in the destination decision.

greater concentration will be found in the film tour participants at the site, which would be a smaller proportion of overall visitors.

Of course, Table 8.1 is a generalisation of current empirical findings. Nevertheless, it does provide a contrast to the often reported direct impact of film on tourism. Whilst the direct impact of film on tourist travel decisions has been found to be small, given the proportions that had been exposed to the films, film would likely play other roles in destination image formation and decision-making (Croy, 2010, 2011). Consistent with the propositions of earlier studies, it appears that the 'place' featured in films, including 'location, scenery, destination attributes', (Macionis, 2004, p. 90), is the main motivator for most film tourists (as compared to the performance or personality). As further research is undertaken, it will be valuable to compare the contexts and types of film tourists they attract.

Special interest film tourism

Special interest film tourism is indeed a niche area. In this section further investigation of the characteristics of the special interest film tourist motivations, and their filmic experience, will be undertaken.

Special interest film tourists

Whilst small in number, there are special interest film tourists. The majority of film tourists are motivated by place, which may lead to considering special interest film tourists being motivated more by 'performance (storylines or plot, themes, genres), and personality (cast, celebrity, characters)'

Focus Box 1: Film tourism in New Zealand

New Zealand has often been noted as a primary example of film tourism, particularly the association with *The Lord of the Rings* and *The Hobbit* (2012–2014). Nonetheless, the demonstrable influence of the films on visitation are slight: there are not many people travelling to New Zealand just because of the films (Croy, 2004). There are however people who are now more aware and favourable towards New Zealand as a tourism destination due to the films, and this is becoming increasingly recognised and celebrated (Croy, 2010; NZIER, 2014). It is also noted that film specific tours and attractions are increasingly popular, also reflecting growth in some areas' tourism activity (e.g. Matamata, which includes the Hobbiton village and has witnessed growth in visitation, NZIER, 2014).

Using the period surrounding *The Hobbit* films, international tourist numbers increased from 2.45m in 2008 to 3.13m in 2015 (Statistics New Zealand, 2016a). All the same, national tourism patterns, such as guest nights, remain relatively stable over the same period (5.5 nights in 2008 to 4.7 nights in 2015 according to Statistics New Zealand, 2016b). This indicates, that whilst international tourist numbers are increasing, tourists are not staying longer. Consequently, if they are partaking in film activities, these are as a substitute for other activities. This also indicates that as areas become more popular due to film, such as Matamata, then this is at the expense of other areas. Overall, it indicates that there may be activity substitution and spatial displacement occurring due to film tourism.

Even so, films have been shot in New Zealand for over 100 years, though not always the setting (Fig. 8.1). The number of films and exposures this creates provides great opportunity to develop a familiar and complex image of New Zealand in the potential tourists' minds. The films also provide the opportunity to develop a range of tourist experiences in the country, as standalone film attractions, though also integrating with the regions and other attractions. However, as the number of films and experiences grows, so

Fig. 8.1. Deer Park Heights, Queenstown, New Zealand. The immediate pictured area has been the setting for *The Rescue* (1988), North Korea, *The Lord of the Rings* and *The Hobbit*, Middle Earth, and *X-Men Origins: Wolverine* (2009), Canada. (Source: Glen Croy)

Continued

does the opportunity to overwrite the communities' stories and experiences of their home.

Tourism New Zealand has done a textbook job at connecting *The Lord of the Rings* and *The Hobbit* films to New Zealand through image management and media investment. New Zealand is now known internationally as the Home of Middle Earth. Now, for the communities, can New Zealand be known for other things? Here too, Tourism New Zealand uses its website to drive those investigating the Home of Middle Earth to become aware and enthralled by other aspects of the country. Also, through the tourists' experiences on the film tours, other insights to the country, places and cultures become apparent. Despite this, how could the local tourism organisations and communities' best communicate their story with tourists, especially as tourists have the preconceived notions of place and people developed through the influential exposure to film?

(Macionis, 2004, p. 90). Connell (2012, p. 1016) highlights, expectedly, that tourism sites associated with a specific film 'may be appealing to a particular demographic, then the results of such studies may not be transferable to other film locations'. Connell's early study, with Meyer (2009), on *Balamory*, highlights that the 91% were groups with children, and two-thirds of the children aged between 2 and 6 years, reflecting the audience demographic. Nonetheless, this was the demographics of the whole sample.

Croy and Buchmann's (2009) study of film tour participants, in comparison to traditional high country recreationists, found they were largely international, slightly more likely to be female, and aged from mid-20s to mid-40s. Again, this was the film-tour profile as a whole. Carl *et al.* (2007) also found that almost all participants were international, marginally more likely to be female, and the majority were between 16 and 35. Echoing this, Rittichainuwat and Rattanaphinanchai (2015) also found a greater portion of females (over two-thirds), with the majority aged 20–39 years. They also found their sample was largely single and highly educated, with almost 90% having a university degree (all were international). Interestingly Busby and Klug (2001) in their sample of Notting Hill visitors found slightly more males, although most were below 44 years, international and with a university education.

These studies give the profile of visitors to film sites, and participants in film tours, though only a starting indication of the special interest film tourist. There are studies that have focused specifically on the special interest film tourist. Three key examples are Roesch's (2009) study of a *Star Wars* (1977–2016) tour, Buchmann *et al.*'s (2010) study of *The Lord of the Rings* tours, and Yen and Croy's (2016) study of Taiwanese Korean-drama tourists. Roesch (2009) studied 17 participants on a weeklong *Star Wars* tour in Tunisia. The participants were all international, aged 21–50, mostly solo and male, and had a variety of education levels. Three females participated, two just to accompany their partners (the fans) and spend time with them and see the country; even some on the tour were not special interest film tourists. This was the third edition of a fan-organised tour as there were no commercial *Star Wars* tours available at any of the film sites, in America or Tunisia. Buchmann *et al.* (2010) investigated 33 special interest film tourists' experiences over three 15-day *The Lord of the Rings* trips. All were international visitors, highly educated, and most were either 21–30 or 51–60 years. Yen and Croy (2016) surveyed 390 participants of *Hallyu* (Korean-drama/TV/music) fan websites that had also visited the film sites in Korea. Sixty per cent of the respondents were female, two-thirds between 21 and 30 years, and the vast majority were either at university or had completed a degree.

Beyond the demographics, which broadly reflect the films' audiences (Connell, 2012), further insights are available. Roesch (2009) found that the film was a cult or classic (he also looked at shorter *The Lord of the Rings* and *The Sound of Music* (1965) tours). Participants owned and had watched the *Star Wars* films, including the 'special features', many times, and many owned further books about the films. They also engaged in websites about the films. It appears they identified themselves as major fans, one even travelling to both premières of *Star Wars: The Phantom Menace* (1999) in London and Los Angeles in the same week. As indicated, they undertook extensive pre-travel research on the films and locations, and often the relationship to favoured characters influenced the decision. Three of the 17 participants were repeating the tour. All bookings were made at least a couple of months in advance, and most a year in advance.

For the Buchmann *et al.* (2010) *The Lord of the Rings* special interest tourists, again they had viewed the films and seen the 'special features'. The participants also drew from the book and all had engaged to some extent with it. Many sought a fellowship of likeminded people through the tour. The participants looked forward to seeing film sites; their motivations were across a continuum from those driven by the film to those driven by the country. Most were in the middle. Interestingly again, those wanting to see the country (through a *film tour*) may be reflecting the coupled-participants of the *Star Wars* tour. Buchmann *et al.* (2010) also identified that all participants perceived that New Zealand was an authentic representation of Middle Earth, and had some emotional attachment to it as Middle Earth. Furthermore, most did not identify themselves as fans, yet travelled a very long way to participate in a film tour. On this final point, whilst appreciating the partner-of-fans segment, I assume the fandom may be understated. Participants may perceive 'extreme' fans as a relative point, even encounter these extreme examples on the tour and or at the locations, and compare themselves to these instead of their affinity with the films or the broader population.

Yen and Croy's (2016) sample was purposefully selected from those that were not only active viewers, but also active followers of the characters, actors, and interactive with other fans through these fan websites. Using scales, the participants' celebrity involvement and worship scores were found. Celebrity involvement (a motivation, arousal or interest in activities associated with a celebrity (after Havitz and Dimanche, 1997)) was low, and celebrity worship was moderate. Involvement was a measure of the role of the celebrity in the respondents' everyday life, and influence on identity. As per the Buchmann *et al.* (2010) findings of self-identified fans, maybe fandom does not play such a significant role. Whilst the levels of celebrity involvement and worship were low and moderate, Yen and Croy (2016) did find that there was a relationship between them and destination image, indicating a positive and significant influence of the films on respondents' perceptions of the destination.

Regarding special interest film tourists, the current indicative empirical research shows that they reflect the audience demographic, and have further specifying characteristics. The films are of a 'cult' nature, which appears consistent with the film tourism studies in the literature. Whilst this may appear a redundant point, with cult films representing films with dedicated fan following, most films with just box-office success are not apparent as film tourism cases. All the same, is this through the choice of the researchers, or that the phenomena are only present in cult-film circumstances? The special interest film tourists have viewed the films multiple times, and sought out and viewed the 'special features'. Many have also obtained resources beyond the films, including through fan and social media websites. The engagement with the films and other resources positively changed their perceptions of the locations. Interestingly, whilst many self-identified themselves as fans, this was not universal. As compared to Table 8.1, it was not the expected 100% of participants on film trips that were special interest film tourists. Overall, the special interest film tourists share similar characteristics to other visitors, and additionally have had extended and more intense engagements with the films, to an extent that influences their perception of the place visited.

Special interest film tourism experiences

Tourist experiences at film sites, like film tourists, vary. Connell and Meyer (2009) found that the desired experiences were related to *Balamory*, and the more the trip was driven by the television programme, the more problematic it was, as there were not many *Balamory* activities for children to do. For adults, the scenery and actual township were the most satisfying parts of the experience, while for children it was the coloured houses reflected in the television programme. Roesch (2009), in the reflections of short *The Lord of the Rings* and *The Sound of Music* tour participants, noted the experience was driven by image collection, and as part of a larger journey to the area. The images collected were an immediately shared and celebrated aspect of the tour, including, for some, recreating shots. Nonetheless, for *The Sound of Music* tours, the film was the main reason for visiting that part of Austria. *The Lord of the Rings* tours appeared to have deeper experiences, maybe due to their smaller size, than the larger (and shorter) *The Sound of*

Music tours. Both tours were mainly participated in by fans, though there were also non-fans and people who had not seen the films. It is of note that the actors and celebrities were not a focus or desired aspect of the experiences, though nevertheless featured during tour dead-times, filled with 'behind the scenes' and technical insights.

In *The Lord of the Rings* tours noted by Croy and Buchmann (2009), the guided experience is film-centred, though very much also engaging in the scenery and landscape of the high country. The scenery and high country was a primary reason for some participants joining the tour, and the focus of post-visit discussion on the way back. The participants were social during the tour, though not necessarily about the films. Carl *et al.* (2007) noted the experiences were seeing the filmed sites, the landscape and scenery, and actually being in Middle Earth. Where the film could not be located by obvious visual cues, then tourists appeared less satisfied. Contrastingly there were others that preferred a wholly natural site. Nonetheless, most were satisfied due to three experiential elements: the local and guide hospitality and knowledge; the beauty of the landscape; and immersion in the film experience and sets.

For film tourists, there appear to be some relatively shallow expectations, leading to a deeper scenery or location experience, as compared to deep film experiences. Is this the same for the special interest film tourists? Yen and Croy (2016) did not investigate the film experiences of the respondents, as such the focus will be on the Roesch (2009) and Buchmann *et al.* (2010) study findings.

Roesch's (2009) *Star Wars* participants' experience was in the identification and recollection of film sites, and then collection of the resembling images of the film, aided by provided maps and photos. The film sites were experienced as sacred places, places of immersive reflection to take in the atmosphere of the filmic experience. The atmosphere added important elements to mentally imprinting the experience, particularly the natural scenery and heat of the desert, with the omission of set-structures, requiring the mind to reconstruct the seen-environment as the film. For some, the mental imagery progressed to simulating the characters in the film presented location, even if just mentally. Others recreated shots, in some cases using miniatures and props, and re-enacted scenes, or their own interpretations of them. As well as the photos, films and memories, many also collected sand as

mementoes of their tour, the film and the represented planet. Many also took deteriorating set features as souvenirs. For many of the participants, solitude or at least only small numbers of others, was important. Added insights on locations, such as technology use, and spatial and temporal discrepancies, were positive knowledge elements of the participants' experiences, providing further 'place insiderness' (Roesch, 2009, p. 160).

As place insiders, there was intense sharing of film information and experiences, and using this to further inform and enhance the film trip experience, no doubt largely facilitated by the extended time together. The shared investment and emotionally active following of the films further tightened the socialised bond between participants; being part of an exclusive community. Additionally, the guide was part of the community, an included member. The tour, understandably, also had much downtime, even at the filmed sites, where the participants disengaged from the film and location to socialise.

Roesch (2009) noted the negative elements of the tour were the lack of solitude, especially to interpret and experience the sights/sites, and the competition for image collection sites. The rare encounters with other tourists were unwanted and interrupted the sights and filmic experience. The other tourists were derided as they were perceived not to have the fan knowledge and hence respect for the locations, as demonstrated by being a participant on this trip (as compared to a general sightseeing tour of the local desert). At other multiparty sites, without the contest for the film specific sites, the feelings of privilege and derision were not apparent. Local-trip participant interactions, when based upon selling goods, were not appreciated. However, in other local interactions when further insights to the films were provided, even if as a process of sale, then this was positively perceived.

For *The Lord of the Rings* tour participants, the scenery was a constant film and country experience (Buchmann *et al.*, 2010), see Fig. 8.2. Carl *et al.* (2007) also found that the multiday film tourists were especially satisfied by the New Zealand landscape. Buchmann's *et al.* (2010) participants were impressed by the scenery, and could imagine it was being Middle Earth; participants even eagerly pursued the interplay between the imaginary and real. As proposed by Buchmann *et al.* (2010) the connection between the real and imaginary has been emphasised and reinforced through tourism and airline advertising, so this closure of the image circle in experience is not too surprising (also see Croy, 2010). The close connection with the films, noted as spiritual, appeared to be the lens of experience, seeking the adventure and fellowship themes of the film in their tour experience. As such, the experience, for some, appears to match that of a pilgrimage, being in the specific locations to simulate the depicted experiences.

The role of the other participants was important in co-creating and sharing the 'spiritual' experience in the physical place. The bringing together the mentally engaged with the physical location created an embodiment experience for participants (Buchmann *et al.*, 2010), emphasising the importance of the mythical themes to the participants as more than just film experiences. Similarly to the *Star Wars* participants, having the experience of place, including the weather and the encompassing scenery, further

enhanced the embodiment experience. Buchmann *et al.* (2010) additionally identified that the extensive time together created a community, constructing and reinforcing an immersive experience through sharing knowledge, experiences and interpretations. Again, on these trips, the guides and drivers were members of the community, significantly due to the sincerity and passion they demonstrated.

The special interest film tourist experience is based upon extensive pre-engagement, consequently meaning a more informed and informative on-site experience. The experience is driven by physically locating the film and embodying the imagined with the real. The locating also draws in the discovered spectacular actual location, including sensual experience of place, and it is the embodiment for a spiritual realisation, whilst appreciating the location-realness. The process enhances the film insiderness, and is

Fig. 8.2. Franz Josef Glacier, West Coast, New Zealand, access point for Mt Gunn, a White Mountains' Beacon in *The Lord of the Rings: The Return of the King* (2003). (Source: Glen Croy)

further reinforced and emphasised by the immersion with actively participating others. As compared to other film tourists, there is a deeper experience, founded on an already deeper knowledge, attachment and engagement with the films. Due to the deeper engagement and sharing this with similar others, the experience is also more immersive. The immersion in the film-community provides further opportunity for insights beyond the even uncommonly known, reinforcing a distinction between the insiders and outsiders. The special interest film tourist really reflects the 'new-tribe' noted by Connell (2012, p. 1018), bound by a common filmic-affinity, searching for locations and in the process making previously 'unremarkable places become remarkable'. Whilst the tribe is small, their experience is one of spiritual embodiment.

Interactions

As indicated in the example of the Eiffel Tower, film sites are often pre-existing tourist sights and sites, as such there are many overlaps and interactions with other special interest tourism areas. For example, Gloucester Cathedral was also used to film aspects of three *Harry Potter* films (2001, 2002, 2009); film theme parks are a popular family tourism destinations (e.g. Disneyland, Universal Studios); royal palaces and families have featured strongly in film and are tourist attractions (e.g. *The Last Emperor* (China, 1987), *Mrs Brown* (Scotland, 1997), *Anna and the King* (Thailand, 1999), *The Princess Diaries* (USA, 2001), *King Arthur* (UK, 2004), *The King's Speech* (England, 2010), *Grace of Monaco* (Monaco, 2014)); dark tourism sites are also known through film (e.g. *The Longest Day* (1962), *Schindler's List* (1993), *Pearl Harbor* (2001), *World Trade Center* (2006), *The Boy in the Striped Pyjamas* (2008)); many literary tourism sites become further famous through film (e.g. *Anne of Green Gables* (1908, 1985), *The Da Vinci Code* (2003, 2006)), and some relocated (e.g. *The Lord of the Rings* (1954)); and films such as *City of God* (Rio de Janeiro, 2002) and *Slumdog Millionaire* (Mumbai, 2008) have reportedly generated pro-poor tourism activities.

Impacts

Special interest film tourism evidently has impacts on tourists. Film tourism, in the broader sense, also has impacts on the destination, host community, environment and film industry. Croy *et al.* (in press) provide an overview of the film tourism stakeholders and impacts. They conclude that increased visitation due to film results in impacts and the destination management organisation needs to take leadership in managing these. All the same, they highlight that the film tourism impacts are 'similar to general tourism impacts, though magnified by the film's profile in the community and potential tourist audience'.

Conclusion

The growing interest in film tourism is dispelling the social-truth of film tourism as a mass tourism phenomenon. Film tourism is instead localised in impact and exceptional, it is in fact a special interest experience. Whilst recognising film business and film business associated tourists, the focus was on discretionary film tourists. Film tourists exist across a typology, from those incidentally at a film site, to those for whom film is the primary purpose for the destination choice. There are not many special interest film tourists, and instead film is more a vehicle to become aware of the scenery and landscape. The empirical research indicates that even at a film site, the percentage of special interest film tourists to be as low as 5%. Even on film tours only about 10% of participants may be special interest film tourists.

Special interest film tourists, unsurprisingly, reflect the demographic characteristics of the audience. The films are classic or cult and the tourists have watched them many times. Additionally, the special interest film tourists engage beyond the films, through books, websites, 'behind the scenes' videos and the like. With the extensive pre-engagement, the special interest film tourist experience is deep. The mix of real locations and filmic images generated a sensual embodying experience. Sharing the experience with well informed and passionate others creates a sense of tribe.

Overall, special interest film tourism is small in scale, though very intense. It is an experience that includes very high pre-site film engagement, often over an extended time. The on-site experience is deep and immersive, combining the film with location and likeminded fellows. Finally, the vast majority of film tourists, whilst still visiting the sites, are not as engaged, and film is much less important to their on-site experience and destination choice.

Questions

1. For the last place you visited on holiday, had you seen this in film (movies and or television) before? How influential was film as a motivation and decision-making factor? Do you know of anyone that has visited this place specifically due to its film portrayals?

2. Identify a destination that you have seen portrayed in at least five movies. List the destination's main tourist attractions and recall if these were also portrayed in the movies. Do you think these attractions would be as popular with tourists even if they were not portrayed in movies?

3. For your favourite movie, list all of the additional information you have engaged with (e.g. 'behind the scenes', director, producer or actor commentary, blogs, fan-groups, books...). Have you also been motivated to visit the destination where it was filmed or set just because of the film? Compare with your classmates what further information they have engaged with, and if they have been motivated to visit the movie site.

Further Reading

Beeton, S. (2016) *Film-Induced Tourism*, 2nd edn. Channel View Publications, Clevedon, UK.

Croy, G. and Heitmann, S. (2011) Tourism and film. In: Robinson, P., Heitmann, S. and Dieke, P.U.C. (eds) *Research Themes for Tourism*. CAB International, Wallingford, UK, pp. 188–204.

Hudson, S. (2011) Working together to leverage film tourism: collaboration between the film and tourism industries. *Worldwide Hospitality and Tourism Themes* 3(2), 165–172.

References

Beeton, S. (2005) *Film-Induced Tourism*. Channel View Publications, Clevedon, UK.

Buchmann, A., Moore, K. and Fisher, D. (2010) Experiencing film tourism: authenticity and fellowship. *Annals of Tourism Research* 37(1), 229–248.

Busby, G. and Klug, J. (2001) Movie-induced tourism: the challenge of measurement and other issues. *Journal of Vacation Marketing* 7(4), 316–332.

Carl, D., Kindon, S. and Smith, K. (2007) Tourists' experiences of film locations: New Zealand as 'Middle-Earth'. *Tourism Geographies* 9(1), 49–63.

Connell, J. (2012) Film tourism: evolution, progress and prospects. *Tourism Management* 33(5), 1007–1229.

Connell, J. and Meyer, D. (2009) *Balamory* revisited: an evaluation of the screen tourism destination-tourist nexus. *Tourism Management* 30(2), 194–207.

Croy, W.G. (2004) *The Lord of the Rings, New Zealand, and Tourism: Image Building with Film*. Department of Management, Faculty of Business and Economics. Monash University, Melbourne, Australia.

Croy, W.G. (2010) Planning for film tourism: active destination image management. *Tourism and Hospitality Planning and Development* 7(1), 21–30.

Croy, W.G. (2011) Film tourism: sustained economic contributions to destinations. *Worldwide Hospitality and Tourism Themes* 3(2), 159–164.

Croy, W.G. and Buchmann, A. (2009) Film-induced tourism in the high country: recreation and tourism contest. *Tourism Review International* 13(2), 147–155.

Croy, G. and Heitmann, S. (2011) Tourism and film. In: Robinson, P., Heitmann, S. and Dieke, P.U.C. (eds) *Research Themes for Tourism*. CAB International, Wallingford, UK, pp. 188–204.

Croy, W.G., Kersten, M., Mélinon, A. and Bowen, D. (in press) Film tourism stakeholders and impacts. In: Lundberg, C. and Ziakas, V. (eds) *Handbook of Popular Culture and Tourism*. Routledge, Oxford, UK.

di Cesare, F., D'Angelo, L. and Rech, G. (2009) Films and tourism: understanding the nature and intensity of their cause-effect relationship. *Tourism Review International* 13(2), 103–112.

Havitz, M.E. and Dimanche, F. (1997) Leisure involvement revisited: conceptual conundrums and measurement advances. *Journal of Leisure Research* 29(3), 245–278.

Hudson, S., Wang, Y. and Gil, S.M. (2011) The influence of a film on destination image and the desire to travel: a cross-cultural comparison. *International Journal of Tourism Research* 13(2), 177–190.

Macionis, N. (2004) Understanding the film-induced tourist. In: Frost, W., Croy, G. and Beeton, S. (eds) *International Tourism and Media Conference Proceedings*. 24–26 November 2004. Tourism Research Unit, Monash University, Melbourne, Australia, pp. 86–97.

Macionis, N. and Sparks, B. (2009) Film tourism: an incidental experience. *Tourism Review International* 13(2), 93–102.

McKercher, B. and du Cros, H. (2003) Testing a cultural tourist typology. *International Journal of Tourism Research* 5(1), 45–58.

NZIER (2014) *2013 Western Market Visitor Growth: What Explains the Increase in Advanced-Economy Visitors?* NZIER, Wellington, New Zealand. Available at: http://nzier.org.nz/static/media/filer_public/8b/f7/8bf74d73-e8a6-436d-bda6-206b4132c0e2/understanding_western_market_growth.pdf (accessed August 2017)

Oviedo-García, M.A., Castellanos-Verdugo, M., Trujillo-García, M.A. and Mallya, T. (2016) Film-induced tourist motivations. The case of Seville (Spain). *Current Issues in Tourism* 19, 713–733.

Riley, R.W. and Van Doren, C.S. (1992) Movies as tourism promotion: a 'pull' factor in a 'push' location. *Tourism Management* 13(3), 267–274.

Riley, R.W., Baker, D. and Van Doren, C.S. (1998) Movie induced tourism. *Annals of Tourism Research* 25(4), 919–935.

Rittichainuwat, B. and Rattanaphinanchai, S. (2015) Applying a mixed method of quantitative and qualitative design in explaining the travel motivation of film tourists in visiting a film-shooting destination. *Tourism Management* 46, 136–147.

Roesch, S. (2009) *The Experiences of Film Location Tourists*. Channel View Publications, Clevedon, UK.

Statistics New Zealand (2016a) *Infoshare: International travel and migration – Visitor arrival totals (Annual-Dec)*. Available at: http://www.stats.govt.nz/infoshare/default.aspx (accessed 15 November 2017).

Statistics New Zealand (2016b) *Infoshare: International travel and migration – Visitor arrivals by country of residence, purpose and length of stay (Annual-Dec)*. Available at: http://www.stats.govt.nz/infoshare/default.aspx (accessed 15 November 2017).

Tooke, N. and Baker, M. (1996) Seeing is believing: the effect of film on visitor numbers to screened locations. *Tourism Management* 17(2), 87–94.

Yen, C.H. and Croy, W.G. (2016) Film tourism: celebrity involvement, celebrity worship and destination image. *Current Issues in Tourism* 19(10), 1027–1044.

9 Carnival Tourism

Violet Cuffy

Learning Objectives

- To gain understanding of the history and evolution of modern day street carnivals
- To create an awareness of the key dimension of Caribbean-based carnivals working in unison to create effective street festivals
- To gain an appreciation for the importance of the socio-cultural and economic impacts of carnival tourism to the wide range of stakeholders involved in this unique festival
- To obtain insight of the importance of the traditional and heritage elements of carnival to carnivalists and other key stakeholders

Introduction

Festivals that celebrate, commemorate and perform aspects of local, regional and international cultures are now a universal phenomenon (Long *et al.*, 2004). Carnival is one such well established festival sub-niche and is widely utilised as a tourism development strategy by many destinations worldwide. As such it is now a global sensation with different countries having their own unique versions and interpretations of the festival (Broadmeadow, 2014). The London Development Agency (2003) describes Carnival as an international arts festival which offers the visitor a truly global culinary map alongside arts and crafts, music, clothing and a range of other items.

From a historic standpoint the roots of carnival can be traced back to the Roman pre-Lenten Catholic celebrations (Taylor, 1986). Significantly, Fraser (1978) suggests it originated from the January New Year Roman festival of the Kalends, which then spread throughout the entire Roman Empire (Cowley, 1991). It later developed into a Catholic celebration preceding the beginning of the Lenten fast from the early 12th century (Mauldin, 2004).

Currently, there are numerous versions of carnival in cities across the world, as there are many ways of analysing carnivals in cities hosting this marvellous spectacle (Connor and Farrar, 2004). However, very little emphasis has been placed on its distinct dimensions from the perspective of a Special interest tourism (SIT) product. Hence, this chapter offers further insight into carnival tourism as a unique niche product. The focus here is on this 'special interest tourism' street festival, adopted and transformed by Caribbean nationals as a distinctive identifier of their West Indian heritage and culture.

Key Concepts

Conceptual and historic background

Historically the concept of special interest tourism (SIT) emerged as a major segment of tourism in the 1980s (Read, 1980). SIT is described as the provision of customised leisure and recreational activities based on specific demand and interests of a particular segment of individuals and groups (Douglas *et al.*, 2001). Special interest tourism involves travel for distinct purposes motivated by unique interests and particular tourist activities in another destination. According to Swarbrook and Horner (1999) this may involve engaging in existing interests, or developing a new interest in a novel or familiar location. Within this particular type of tourism the destination is of secondary focus while the interest or activity takes centre stage. In that regard the special interest activity is the motivator for travel.

In a seminal piece Read (1980) defines SIT as the hub around which the total travel experience is planned and developed. Stebbins (1992) later adds it is a means of finding personal fulfilment; while according to the World Tourism Organisation (1985) those involved tend to exercise the same profession or have a common hobby. Further, special interest tourists demonstrate the desire for authenticity and real experiences that offer them active identification with host communities in a non-exploitative manner (Douglas *et al.*, 2001).

Also of relevance here, are two additional motivators of SIT tourists, emotion and escape, previously cited by Weiler and Hall (1992).

Whatever the overall motivation for engaging in SIT, Brotherton and Himmetoğlu (1997) cite four core typologies of the typical tourist within this market as follows:

- *The Dabbler*: travellers looking for a change of interests or activity
- *The Enthusiast*: tourists who have started to progress from the sampling phase
- *The Expert*: tourists who have a high level of knowledge and skills of the choice of activity
- *The Fanatic*: tourists who demonstrate extreme devotion possibly even eccentric or impractical beyond what is generally regarded as normal limits to the activities or interests.

They further offer a tourism interest continuum 'GIT – MIT – SIT' to help explain the distinguishing characteristics between special interest, general and mixed tourists. For the purpose of this chapter the defining features of the typical SIT tourist are delineated in Table 9.1.

Both the public and private sector conceive challenges with such small scale, personalised tourism products. Among the main arguments are: (i) inability of local communities to manage the tourism industry and to be self-sustaining; (ii) economies of scale of individual operators generally are inadequate to implement sustainable practices; (iii) SIT is a high-risk strategy that has emerged from the shift from traditional mass tourism to more sophisticated and better-informed tourists.

Arguably, SIT is a complex phenomenon, often small scale in nature, labour-intensive and challenged by issues of management of impacts, indigenous ownership and control, preservation and development of cultural heritage among many other concerns faced by larger organisations within the tourism industry (Douglas *et al.*, 2001). Regardless, a common argument raised, as explained by Trauer (2006) is SIT has the benefit of being opposite to general interest, mixed interest and mass tourism; focuses on new forms of tourism; and addresses the needs of tourists and hosts in areas of cultural, heritage, festivals and events tourism among others. Trauer proposes the SIT Interactive System, shown in Fig. 9.1 as a framework for conceptualising the complex interdisciplinary system which encompasses the various dimensions of the SIT environment.

The above illustrated system demonstrates the integral role of a range of elements within the overall environment including technology, politics, ecology, socio-economy, culture, supply and demand, personal factors and importantly the media on SIT as a distinct product area.

The next sections will examine how these underpinning concepts help explain the intricacies of the street festival carnival, the special interest tourism product of concern in this chapter.

Table 9.1. Characteristics of the special interest tourists. Source: adapted from Brotherton and Himmetoğlu (1997).

Distinctive characteristics of the special interest tourists
Constitute a minority of the travelling population
Are usually from middle to upper class socio-economic groups
Are generally less price sensitive than general/mixed interest tourists
Tend to be experienced and sophisticated travellers
Have high expectations in relation to the activities/interests but not necessarily in terms of accommodation facilities
Are adventurous, allocentric, types of people who do not like to follow the majority
Have no specific social obligations for their holidays, and do not feel the need to choose the 'socially acceptable' quality
Are likely to see the special interest holiday as an extension of their home-based leisure choice and activities
View alternate destinations as contexts for the pursuit of their special interest.

The carnival tourism interactive system

Festivals and special events feature highly among the growing types of tourism attractions (Gursoy *et al.*, 2014). Long *et al.* (2004) suggest that international tourism stimulated by globalisation has led to the shift of festivals from parochial localised events to global attractions. Undoubtedly, as shown in Fig. 9.2 carnivals represent an expression of diasporic cultures and identities visible beyond their local communities and thus attract the media, tourism marketing agencies, governments and their relevant tourism departments in advancing this unique SIT.

Based on the seminal works of the theorist Mikhail Bakhtin (1984a, b), carnivalesque presents a framework for advancing the historic phenomenon

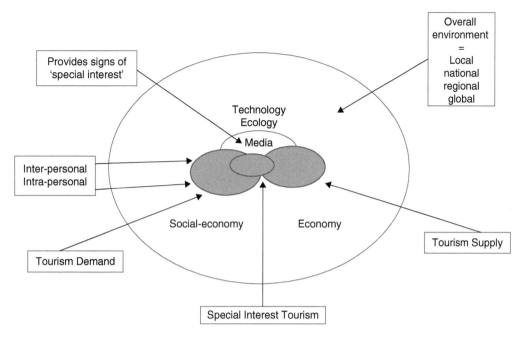

Fig. 9.1. SIT Interactive System. (Source: Trauer, 2006)

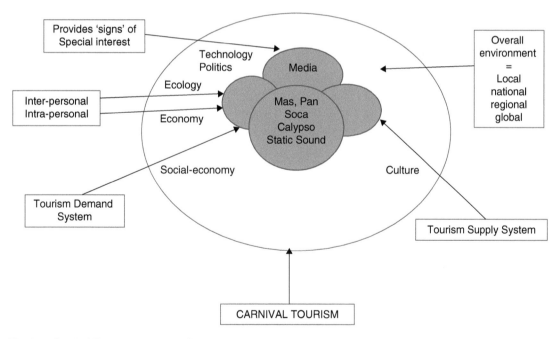

Fig. 9.2. Carnival Tourism Interactive System. (Adapted from Trauer, 2006)

around which this festival is understood. As in the SIT framework it offers insight into the political, legal and ideological authority where the church and state regulations are temporarily averted through

the extremes of social liberation enjoyed during carnival season. Unquestionably, carnival with its various dimensions (Mas, Pan, Soca, Calypso and Static sounds), systems and rituals rooted in the local cultures and heritage presents a dynamic SIT product worthy of further exploration.

Carnivals are commonly used as a tool for city regeneration and creation of cultural capitals, a phenomenon now often explored by carnival destinations. This is particularly evident 'in large cities that are gateways to immigration where street festivals and carnivals bring together members of carnivalesque and cultural minorities, some of whom may be recent arrivals, while others may have settled for several generations' (Ferdinand and Shaw, 2012, p. 9).

As such Rao (2001) suggests that festivals provide a specified time and place within which families can demonstrate their commitment to the collective. This is particularly true within carnival communities where an integral dimension of the festivity is that participants form and join Mas Bands, Steel Bands and Calypso Tents building a strong pseudo-family culture within these structures.

In a study of six festivals in the Caribbean, inclusive of Trinidad's Carnival, Nurse (2001) highlights that these special interest festivals typically at the national and regional level:

- Generate new tourism demand from the short-break travel market, as well as diasporic and intra-regional tourist groupings often omitted in tourist marketing plans.
- Account for a significant share of total visitor expenditure.
- Attract tourists who tend to be quite knowledgeable about the art form, culture and heritage; thus, they tend to spend more on local goods and services and are usually repeat visitors and good word of mouth promotion for local events.
- Tend to attract international media and thus enhance the local image and attractiveness as a tourist destination.
- Facilitate development and export of the art form by creating new clients, markets and media exposure. In addition, such events stimulate infrastructure development, heritage conservation and investment into the arts.
- Contribute to the wider economy through tax receipts, generate employment and sectorial linkages and spillovers in areas such as hospitality, media, advertising, car rental, transport, the music industry and merchandise.
- Create a synergistic relationship between tourism and community development as cultural confidence, image and national identity is enhanced alongside growth and success of such events.

Further, the importance of carnival in the international tourism market is evidenced from the formation of organisations such as the Federation of European Carnival Cities (FECC) founded in 1980 to promote carnival internationally. Much later on, the year 2000 marked the introduction of the Foundation of European Carnival Cities which was registered in May 2004 in Luxembourg. FECC boasts of over 500 members and organisations representing 100 cities in 52 countries within its network. Currently, FECC holds two major events each year which bring carnivalists from around the world together to showcase their craft and carnival products.

Major Factors

The history of Caribbean-based carnivals which are the focus of this chapter credit much of their advancement on the island of Trinidad (Nurse, 1999; Connor and Farrar, 2004) and Brazil (Nurse, 2004) which developed a multifaceted festival that emerged out of slavery as a form of rebellion against the oppressive European colonialism of Trinidad (Hill, 1972). It is therefore widely claimed (Jackson, 1988; Nurse, 2004; Ferdinand and Williams, 2013 among many others) that there is a direct line of descent between Notting Hill (for example, and other international carnivals) and the earliest form of carnival originating in the Caribbean (LDA, 2003), most notably Trinidad. According to the London Development Agency 2003 report, and demonstrating an exemplary carnivalesque culture:

> During the era of slavery black people were forbidden to play musical instruments and wear costumes, apart from during the period of carnival, in those times an imported European version. With the repeal of slavery, slaves took to the streets in song and dance including in their own culture and using their artistic skills to mimic their masters, pouring scorn on the system that enslaved them for so long. In so doing slaves would dress like their masters and powder their faces or make masks representing distorted images of the former owner, as if to signify the evil inherent in those acts of possession or as a token of ridicule. (LDA, 2003, p. 10)

It is not surprising then, that the Trinidad and Tobago carnival has a long history with a far-reaching global presence and multiple offshoots worldwide (Nurse, 1999). What makes Trinidad's carnival unique is that it embraces indigenous diversity and cultures, and celebrates local traditions. Moreover traditionally, masquerade costumes, songs and music have embodied the socio-political and economic environment of the community. It is this strong carnival heritage and cultural tradition that has been exported to the Western world wherever Caribbean nationals have migrated and formed new diaspora settlements.

Typically, modern day carnivals still linked to the Roman Catholic traditions take place pre-lent, but some Caribbean-based carnivals, adapting to the local environment, may be held at other times of the year (see Table 9.2) as in the case of Notting Hill (Focus Box 1), Leeds, Caribbana in Canada, and Labour Day in New York among a few others. Interestingly, the archetypal Caribbean-based carnival is not a singular art form but an integrated framework for live performances that are rooted in several other art forms involving the human body, space and time (Wong, 2014). Such carnivals are generally developed around five disciplines: Mas (Masquerade), Calypso, Pan (steel bands), static sound systems and Soca (a blend of sound and calypso) forming its own intricate Interactive System, as illustrated in Fig. 9.2.

Besides, carnival celebrations reflect the diverse cultures of communities both local and international, through tourist interaction with carnivalists and the host country. Additionally, Carnival signals a temporary suspension of regulatory forces, while offering participants (locals and tourists alike) an opportunity to transgress societal conventions (Bakhtin, 1984a, b), facilitating true visitor–host integration rarely observed elsewhere. This is best explained by what Wong (2014) describes as the interplay of the four Ms of Carnival – Masquerade, Movement, Music and Mayhem in the public realm. A phenomenon, colloquially known among carnivalists as the 'baccanal of the canaval'!

Hence, Wong suggests, what commenced as the freedom of expression of a people, soon turned into the basis of the global carnival industry recognisable

Table 9.2. Caribbean-based Carnivals. (Approximate dates are given for the concluding festivities. Carnival season may last for over a month prior to the concluding festivities, and the exact dates vary from year to year)

Location	Festival	Timing
Anguilla	Anguilla Summer Festival	early August
Antigua & Barbuda		
Antigua	Antigua Carnival	early August
Barbuda	Caribana	early June
Aruba	Carnival Pre-Lent	
The Bahamas	Junkanoo	late December/early January
Barbados	Crop Over	early August
Belize	Carnival	September
Bonaire	Carnival	Pre-Lent
British Virgin Islands		
Tortola	BVI Emancipation	early August
Virgin Gorda	Virgin Gorda Easter Festival Celebrations	late March/early April
Cayman Islands	Batabano	late April/early May
Cuba		
Cuba	Carnival of Santiago de Cuba	July
Cuba	Havana Carnival	July/August
Curacao	Carnival	Pre-Lent
Dominica	Carnival	Pre-Lent
Dominica Republic	Dominican Independence Day	February
Grenada		
Carriacou	Carnival	Pre-Lent
Grenada	Spicemas	early August
Guadeloupe	Carnival	Pre-Lent
Guyana	Mashramani (Mash) Carnival	Pre-Lent, Guyanese Republic Day
Hati	Kanaval, Carnival	Pre-Lent
Jamaica	Bacchanal	Late March/early April
Martinique	Carnival	Pre-Lent
Montserrat	Montserrat Festival	early January, New Year's Day
Puerto Rico	Carnaval de Ponce, Carnival	Pre-Lent

today. He argues, the skills of costume making, steel band drumming and calypso became established as essential to the carnival tradition. Today it occupies a unique and established place in the national cultural and tourism calendar worldwide.

However, in recent years, there has been a noticeable filtration of the emerging and contemporary culture of 'bikini, beads, and feathers' style masquerade costume which many lament does not reflect the cultural authenticity of the art form (see Cuffy, 2014). Nevertheless, Wong (2014) argues that this transformation is essentially the voice of the younger generation. Debatably, this new trend reflects how society has evolved and the extent to which Carnival has been commodified for global consumption, or to coin a term used by Lancaster (2004), the impact of *when spectators become performers*. It is from this background that this chapter explores the key elements of this niche market as a contemporary special interest tourism product.

Motivations

Generally, the festival and special events industry touches virtually every life worldwide several times over and accounts for trillions of US dollars annually (Kline and Oliver, 2015). It is uncontested that as a SIT product, the carnival industry has developed way beyond small local traditional celebrations to the realm of international events taking centre stage on the calendar of national tourism events, and now forms part of many destination marketing strategic plans.

However, the growth of a thriving international Caribbean-based carnival industry relies not only on the presence of Caribbean nationals in the foreign metropole but importantly on their persistent desire as dislocated nationals to want to cultivate and perpetuate their cultural heritage (Scher, 2004). As such it is widely held that the Caribbean diaspora (particularly from Rio de Janeiro's and Trinidad's carnivals) are pillars of the New World carnivals wherever they are located (Crichlow and Armstrong, 2012). Presented below are accounts of some of the most well know 'exported' Caribbean-based carnival destinations within this niche market, as cited in the London Development Agency 2003 report and Porto (2010).

Toronto Carnival, Caribbana

Toronto's international carnival draws an estimated one million people from Canada, the United States, the Caribbean and other overseas countries and acts as a showcase for Toronto's brand as the world's most culturally diverse city (LDA, 2003).

Labour Day, New York

Grown from a community event to the largest event of its kind in the United States, with an estimated attendance of three and a half million people, and an annual revenue of US$300 million. The parade has been part of an action to promote tourism and increase the economic impact of cultural events and tourism for the Caribbean and to exploit the celebration of Caribbean cultural heritage for the community based around Brooklyn (LDA, 2003).

Mardi Gras, New Orleans

Held 47 days preceding Easter the festival began as a simple masquerade ball, but over the years has evolved into a complex set of public masquerade balls, street processions and private parties. Most of the parades and balls are sponsored by entities called Krewes. At the time of the LDA report, Mardi Gras had an estimated economic impact of between US$840 million and US$1 billion (LDA, 2003).

Rio de Janeiro, Brazil

The Brazilian carnival is intrinsically linked to Brazil's image as a people and a country. Results of a study conducted in 2006 cites carnival as a positive and important travel motivator for Brazil that serves as a key reason for repeat visit. From a cultural perspective carnival brings together the differences across the Brazilian territories, largely due to the fact that it is celebrated by all sections of the population (Porto, 2010).

Interactions

There are a number of sub-sectors which are closely linked to hosting a successful carnival festival. Some are more central to the main events, as with the music industry, while others like travel and accommodation serve more of a supporting role as discussed below.

Real Mas, Dominica

Travel

A large number of visitors travel to the island for carnival by air and a small number by sea from the neighbouring Caribbean islands or day cruises. Due to limited international air access travel to the island during the period can be strained. Locals tend to travel by car or bus. Therefore the travel sector accounts for a significant portion of the carnival economy.

Accommodation and hospitality

The Caribbean is well known for its warm and friendly hospitality, and the carnival season is one time when this is truly experienced. In addition to the traditional hotel and bed and breakfast accommodation there is a marked increase in home stays and house shares particularly among returning Dominicans.

Food and drink

Another key element of the carnival is the Caribbean cuisine. The traditional street stalls are a key part of the carnival spirit offering a wide range of local food and drink. It is also a time when local restaurants and food providers experience extremely high demand.

Music tourism

In Dominica, as elsewhere, the music industry is a core dimension of the entire celebrations with distinct events and music competitions forming a central part of the festive session. Musicians represent a distinct industry which exists beyond carnival yet is well integrated into pre-events and the street parade. Many artists are involved in creating new productions annually for the season. However, the on-going challenge is to develop music with an international appeal and cultural relevance outside the festive season. Nevertheless, the diaspora serve as a promising market for this sector.

Impacts and Insights

As discussed above, many major cities have employed carnival as a tourism strategy for its wide-ranging impacts and benefits (Nurse, 2004). This will now be discussed under the broad areas of the socio-cultural, political and economic dimensions of Caribbean-based carnivals, all key elements of the Carnival Tourism Interactive System (Fig 9.2).

Economic

Newer carnivals are increasingly being established for utilisation as pivotal elements of destination marketing strategies. In many cases this is observed where cultural and heritage tourism is used as a tool to boost the local economy and to aid the seasonal and geographical spread of tourism (Long and Perdue, 1990). In the United Kingdom as elsewhere, carnival has historically been used as a central aspect of regeneration projects in major cities such as London and Leeds, as well as smaller, less known destinations such as the Isle of Wight, Bridgwater Guy Fawkes Carnival and Luton. However, there has been a new appreciation of this potential leading to an array of young and less internationally renowned carnivals in other countries such as in France (Nice), the Seychelles and Nigeria to name a few.

Regardless, Taylor (1986, p. 38) much earlier on cautioned that 'taking carnival seriously is a full time job..... it means penetrating a vast network of cottage industries, ranging from costume construction and boot-making to steel-tempering and music arranging, which hold the carnival together in an astonishing display of skilled and ingenious craft.' Today this demands large economic investment and support on behalf of the artists and the destination alike. Unfortunately, most carnivalists and their relevant structures are underfunded and operate on minimal budgets. The ongoing challenge is achievement of economic sustainably. This demands development of strong stakeholder networks and partnerships, with equally strong governance and management systems which would facilitate viable business and entrepreneurial type operations.

Socio-cultural

On one hand, carnival contributes to social cohesion through community celebration. It contributes to a sense of pride of place, ethnic identity and sense of belonging among locals and visitors alike. There is usually a sense of goodwill, jubilation and extreme public elation during carnival celebrations overriding barriers between races, the police, class and other social boundaries. The role of the carnival culture on the national scale, for instance, participation of carnivalists in the Queen's Jubilee in 2002 and the London Olympics in 2012 in the UK, gives some insight into its positive social significance within countries where it is hosted.

On the other hand, community issues and extreme anger may arise due to the sheer volume of visitors descending on the local community over the two days of carnival. This puts great strain on the fabric and infrastructure of the local community. Stress is generally

Fig. 9.3. Carnivalists at Notting Hill.

experienced on public transport, security, food supply, toilet facilities, emergency services and the ever contested use of the streets normally reserved only for the parade or costume processions and affiliated carnival activity; often to the disdain of some segments of local residents who are non-participants. In addition, there is the issue of noise and negative effects of the vibrations of static sound systems during the street parties, not to mention the misuse of street corners and front gardens as impromptu toilets by the revellers.

However, smaller traditional, and for the most part less commercialised and commodified carnivals such as in the Commonwealth of Dominica tend to have more social buy-in across a wider cross-section of the host community. Besides, patrons can live in a false reality of social cohesion during the carnival celebrations as demonstrated in this tourist experience in Brazil,

> I also like the idea of dancing. I recently returned from Brazil, where I learned the Samba and where every year during Carnival the social in-cohesion of

that country's skewed wealth distribution – rivalling South Africa's as the worst on the planet – is momentarily obliterated in the world's biggest dance festival. (Labonte, 2004, p. 120)

In contrast to the distinct demarcation of social class observed by this tourist experience above, what follows is a synopsis of the most spontaneous Caribbean Carnival, celebrated in the nature isle, the Commonwealth of Dominica (Case Study 1).

Political

Conventionally, carnival is marked by duality, plus a highly contested social and political history (Cohen, 1980; Bakhtin, 1984a; Jackson, 1988; Humphrey, 2001; Riggio, 2004; Churchill, 2006; Sujoldžić, 2010; Bogad, 2012; Ferris, 2012; Matheson and Tinsley, 2014; Wong, 2014). As elsewhere, carnival in Dominica is often marked by the rejection of power, structure and authority. Also typical is the

V. Cuffy

Focus Box 1: Notting Hill Carnival

According to Ken Livingstone, Mayor 2003, The Notting Hill carnival is widely acknowledged as Europe's largest street festival and is a key signifier of London's status ranking among the largest and most spectacular of world festivals. This view is supported by Ferris (2012) who describes it as the largest street theatre in Europe. It also plays a key role in enhancing London's international tourism offer and image as a cosmopolitan and culturally diverse city (Livingstone, 2003). Moreover, it is the largest single public event staged on a regular basis in London (LDA, 2003). It is no surprise then, that the word carnival is now synonymous with Notting Hill; and that it has become a significant (albeit tourism-focused) symbol of London and Great Britain, and thus, an event on top of the list of the tourism calendar (Wong, 2014).

Notting Hill carnival unlike many other carnivals elsewhere is not held as a pre-lent festival but rather is celebrated the last weekend in August each year, largely due to the extreme cold in mid-February (Broadmeadow, 2014). The outdoor street procession, food stalls and the numerous static sound systems that are nestled within the carnival route that circulates through Notting Hill in West London are a testament to the energy and commitment of Claudia Jones, a political activist and writer who founded the carnival; and organiser of the first (indoor) carnival in response to the racist intimidation and violence from white youth against West Indians that escalated in the summer of 1958 (Ferris, 2012, pp.121).

Carnival is now a vibrant, ethnically diverse celebration, which enjoys a strong sense of ownership from a number of Londoners; it is recognised for its economic contribution and importance for London's image, the sense of identity it sustains for London's diverse communities and for social cohesion (LDA, 2003).

As cited in the LDA 2003 report carnival enjoyed an estimated figure of attendees in 2001 of 1.16 million and a £45 million spend from patrons over the three days. Notting Hill carnival also positively influences spending patterns of attendees throughout the rest of the year, with 52% more likely to buy more Caribbean food items and products that were launched at the carnival after attending (LDA, 2003).

For London, carnival is a major economic generator contributing £93 million and supporting 3000 full time equivalent jobs. It is one of the most spectacular of tourist attractions drawing visitors from within the UK and from overseas; making a significant contribution to London's place as a world leading tourism destination. It supports a variety of business activities – street traders, teaching of carnival, show casing skills at other festivals, costume designers, mas bands, and boosting sales for local restaurants, cafes, pubs and retail businesses in the location. Practitioners provide the vital creative content, and the goodwill of people providing skill, labour and resources to make it a reality. It is an important cultural event for London, enjoyed by Londoners and visitors across ethnicity, age and socio-economic background alike. Michael Ward, LDA Chief Executive (Ward, 2003).

---

element of role reversals, masking, role play, rituals, imagery, excessive consumption and acting as celebrations (Broadmeadow, 2014). Still lingering on in most transplanted Western carnivals are the negative impacts of remnants of racial discrimination, marginalised societies and the struggles associated with colonisation; all of which continuously resurface (Cohen, 1980; Dunn, 1992; Bogad, 2012) in the ongoing discourse around carnival. Nevertheless, this is less evident in island carnivals such as Dominica.

Furthermore, in modern-day Western cultures, the commodification of carnival allows the festival to be regulated and productively used to enable continual growth of capital. And thus,

> people can have the illusion of freedom, if they can get wasted regularly, they don't seek the desire to organise carnival to parody the state, and enact role reversal in the traditional sense. Capitalism seeks to combine Dionysian and his opposite Apollo, [the conflict of freedom and work] together, to keep everyone working towards continual growth…[with the] state as regulator. (Broadmeadow, 2014, p. 6)

This phenomenon arguably further perpetuates the contested dimensions of carnival management by the local authorities as against the carnivalists.

Arguably, according to Scott (1990) the safety valve theory may explain the actions of the elite and their sustained negative perception of carnival as a potential excuse for disorder, noise and violence necessitating excessive and continuous surveillance. These external pressures all give rise to equal ongoing and increasing levels of event regulations and professionalism that impinge on the essence of carnivalesque (Matheson and Tinsley, 2014), the art form and the spirit of carnival.

Case Study 1: Carnival in the Commonwealth of Dominica

Coined as 'The Real Mas', the Commonwealth of Dominica is among the few remaining Caribbean islands with the strong elements of traditional rituals still featuring prominently in its carnival celebrations. Further, it is among the few where locals and tourists alike can enjoy the spontaneity of the live street events and non-commodified or highly commercialised nature of the street parades. In contrast to highly staged parades elsewhere, it is not unusual for onlookers to themselves be moved into joining in on the parade either by the force of the spirit of carnival or being invited to do so by the revellers themselves.

Dominica's Carnival is currently held during the traditional pre-Lenten season, though in recent years there has been much debate about shifting the date to overcome competition from the vast number of Carnivals happening simultaneously around the globe but more particularly closer to home in the sister Caribbean island, Trinidad and Tobago.

Visitors to Dominica can anticipate a season of activities including calypso competitions, Queen, Teenage and Princess Pageants, community level shows, and pre-carnival street jump-ups in various communities, which culminate with the main two days of street parades. The typical calendar of activities of the various sub-groups of art forms is as follows:

Parade and Opening of Carnival

This marks the opening of the carnival season with a major parade of all participants in various events for that season: The Queen Contestants, Calypsonians, Princess Show Contestants, and representations of some of the main bands. Plus, spectators are treated to Sensay and Black Devils; Moko Jumbies (stilt walkers), cheerleaders, advertising floats from the business community; Lapo Kabwit bands, live brass bands and the modern day Sound Systems among other revellers.

The most symbolic event is the handing over of the keys to the City by the Mayor of the City Council to the Chairperson of the Carnival Organising Committee. This event also has legal implications as it marks the onset of a period where artists (particularly Calypsonians) are 'supposedly' protected from

Fig. 9.4. The Sensay.

Continued

V. Cuffy

Case Study 1: Continued.

legal regulations attributed to libel and slander resulting from the lyrics of their compositions.

Key Carnival Events

Carnival Princess Show:
Usually held on the first Sunday after opening.

The Stardom Calypso Tent: (Every Wednesday from January)
A series of Calypso shows, offering a mixture of serious political commentary, local social scandals and humour; it is a very popular weekly feature of the season among locals and visitors alike.

Showdown Mas Camp (Every Friday from January)
A more recent Calypso tent offering an alternate or additional weekday night out for calypso patrons.

Teenage Pageant
Usually held on the second Sunday of the season.

Lagoon Street Jam
A prominent item on the agenda on the Monday night preceding the last weekend of Carnival. It is a free event and enjoys much support from returning diaspora tourists who often book their travel to arrive in time for this gathering. Often this is where one meets individuals from the diaspora visiting home for the season. It is a night to enjoy the Calypso hits, the latest Soca releases, the local cuisine and lots of the local beer, Kubuli and alcohol.

Kiddies Carnival
Event for the young in age and at heart.

The National Queen Show
A central feature where a number of young ladies vie for the title of Miss Dominica. The winner enjoys a reign of one year and is expected to take part in regional pageants held during other Caribbean Carnivals.

National Calypso Finals
A major event where the finalists from various rounds of eliminations, quarter-, and semi-finals compete for the title of Calypso King or Queen.

Stardom 'King of the Tent'
The event where a winner for the season is chosen based on popularity.

Showdown Mas Camp 'Champ of the Camp'
A similar event where a winner for the season is chosen based on popularity.

Fig. 9.5. The Black Devils.

Continued

Case Study 1: Continued.

Mini Carnival - Bord La Mer
A free street event held on the city's Bayfront.

Rotary's Souse & Punch (held each year on the last Sunday before Carnival)
A pre-carnival Souse & Punch day party held at the popular Layou River Hotel.

The Street Parades

Carnival Street Parades
Carnival Monday and Tuesday or Jump Up. Two days of parades and when everyone takes to the streets

Carnival Monday Street Parade

J'Ouvert
4 am to 6 am – Lapo Kabwit (traditional drums and tin bands); **6 am to 8 am** – Hifi Bands; **10 am to 12 Noon** – Traditional Old Mas Costume bands (Sensay, Darkkies, Black Devils, Ban Mouve, etc.) and School Bands; **2 pm to 10 pm** – T-Shirt Bands with Hifi; Open to general public participation usually by about 5pm

Carnival Tuesday Street Parade:
10 am – A parade of winners of all competitions held over the season: Carnival King & Queen, Princess, and Miss Teen Dominica; plus other contestants from the range of events showcase their costumes; also, traditional Costume Bands; and other groups and gangs.

Throughout the two days of street processions judges at various key locations across the city judge the parades as well as listen very keenly for the most played and popular Calypso on the streets for awarding the title **Road March Song**.

These main parades are held in the city, Roseau, however many villages put on their own events and small costume processions over the season.

Vaval: Wednesday after Carnival
A traditional culminating event is held in some villages on the West coast – Dublanc and in the Kalinago (Carib) Territory – on Ash Wednesday, burying (or burning) of the 'spirit' of Carnival and signalling the onset of Lenten season.

Adapted from: http://www.avirtualdominica.com/

Conclusions

The question that this chapter raises is how to advance carnival, a special interest tourism product, engaging sustainable systems and approaches that satisfy the needs and developmental goals of all stakeholders involved – carnivalists, government and its relevant authorities and services, the host community and importantly the tourists?

In discussing the evils of the commodification of carnival in the capitalistic society, one may agonise that:

What carnival remains, in parts of the world have themselves become spectacles – specialist performances watched by spectators – with police lines and barriers placed between the parade and audience. Thus, the vortexed, whirling, uncontrollable state of creative chaos is shoe-horned into neat straight lines and rectangles. A visit to many contemporary carnivals sanctioned by the state (such as Carnival in Rio de Janeiro, or Notting Hill Carnival in London) where consumption and corporate sponsorship has taken over from the creativity and spontaneity [as in Dominica], is enough to illustrate how carnival under capitalism has lost it vitality. But carnival has been with us since time immemorial and it has always refused to die. Reappearing in different guises across the ages, it returns again and again. Freed from the clutches of entertainment, the anti-capitalist movement have thrown it back into the street, where it is liberated from commerce for everyone to enjoy once again. (Notes From Nowhere, 2003, p. 177)

In acknowledging the numerous socio-economic benefits of advancing a destination level carnival tourism agenda, what needs to be further considered is the case for ethical tourism development measures that ensure the carnivalists and the art form are fully supported. The continuing financial struggle of artists and their respective camps in the five disciplines (Mas, Pan, Static sound, Calypso and Soca) year after year to stage this massive street theatre still remains. This scenario tends to support the view of many carnivalists and writers like Michael La Rose (2014) that this is evidence of the ill-distributed, misdirected, or as many argue, leakage of the financial gains away from the festival creators, the carnivalists, to over-policing and other necessary but over-budgeted council management expenses. Notwithstanding this fact the chronic structural management and governance issues that permeate the carnival body itself pose deep-rooted 'wicked' problems for the artists and key stakeholders.

A lack of understanding or acknowledgement of the history and heritage of Caribbean-based carnivals contributes its own unique dilemmas when engaging carnival for tourism. A study of the development of the emblematic carnival observed today will help one appreciate that carnival is not designed to be constrained in a park or an illusory building-based space; rather it is framed for the streets, the social landscape that connects the carnivalists to the world (Ferris, 2012). Yet, the fight for right to the streets, and claims laid by the host community remains a contested issue, particularly in the case of Notting Hill (Cuffy, 2014; La Rose, 2014).

Regardless, as carnival advances as an art form and an international tourism business, governments worldwide continue to capitalise on its benefits as a core calendrical destination marketing strategy. Besides, change always comes hand in hand with development and progress. Nevertheless, it is incumbent that the overriding attitude of the game changers is not to throw caution to the winds. For without the Caribbean artists there can be no Caribbean-based carnival; without the authentic spirit of the Caribbean 'canaval' on the street, there can be no carnival!

Hence this chapter argues in favour of adopting a set of ethical sustainable carnival tourism principles which could be advanced in addressing the ongoing challenges of the 'canaval'. This would have to involve measures at the core pillars of sustainability previously discussed – economic, socio-cultural and the local political environment, as well as supporting the five core carnival disciplines. Much research has dealt with and engaged in elements of the discourse around the sustainability of carnival, but in this current era it is now opportune to further explore the *business of carnival tourism*.

Questions

1. How best can carnival be developed into a sustainable business which addresses the needs and dimensions of indigenous carnivals?

2. How can tourists be further educated to engage in carnival, its history and culture beyond the basic information of the baccanal?

3. Why is an understanding of the concept of carnivalesque so integral to carnival movers and shakers in the advancement of the commodification of the carnival tourism agenda?

Further Reading

Cuffy, V. (forthcoming) *Carnival. Culture and Tourism.* CAB International, Wallingford, UK.

Mauldin, B. (ed.) (2004) *Carnaval.* University of Washington Press, Seattle, Washington, USA.

Smith, M. (2003) *Issues in Cultural Tourism Studies.* Routledge, London, UK.

Riggio, M.C. (2004) *Carnival Culture in Action.* Routledge, New York, USA.

Acknowledgements

I wish to extend special acknowledgment to Wendy Walsh at www.avirtualdominica.com for her kind support in completing this chapter and her continued work in the promotion of Dominica's history, tourism and cultural heritage.

References

Bakhtin, M. (1984a) *Rabelais and His World* (H. Iswolsky, Trans.) Indiana University Press, Bloomington, Indiana, USA

Bakhtin, M. (1984b) *Problems of Dostoevsky's Poetics (Theory and History of Literature)*, 1st edn. (C. Emerson, Trans) Manchester University Press, Manchester, UK.

Bogad, L.M. (2012) Carnivals against capital: radical clowning and the global justice movement. In: Crichlow, M.A. (ed.) *Carnival Art, Culture and Politics: Performing Life.* Routledge, London, UK.

Broadmeadow, M. (2014) *Under the Influence, Extended Carnival in Capitalist Society.* MFA, Fine Art, Goldsmiths. Available at: http://www.academia.edu/7732383/Under_the_Influence_Extended_Carnival_in_Capitalist_Society (accessed 1 February 2017).

Brotherton, B. and Himmetoğlu, B. (1997) Beyond Destinations: Special Interest Tourism. *Anatolia: An International Journal of Tourism and Hospitality Research* 8 (3), 11–30.

Churchill, N. (2006) Dignifying carnival, the politics of heritage recognition in Puebla, Mexico. *International Journal of Cultural Property* 13(1), 1–24.

Cohen, A. (1980) Drama and politics in the development of a London carnival. *MAN, New Series* 15(1), 65–87.

Connor, G. and Farrar, M. (2004) Carnival in Leeds and London, UK: making new black British subjectivities. In: Riggio, M.C. (ed.) *Carnival: Culture in Action – the Trinidad Experience.* Routledge, London, UK.

Cowley, J. (1991) Carnival and other seasonal festivals in the West Indies, USA and Britain – selected bibliographical index, *Bibliographies in Ethnic Relations* No. 10, Centre for Research in Ethnic Relations, September 1991, University of Warwick, Coventry, UK.

Crichlow, M.A. and Armstrong, P. (2012) Carnival praxis, carnivalesque strategies and Atlantic interstices. In: Crichlow, M.A. (ed.) *Carnival Art, Culture and Politics: Performing Life*. Routledge, London, UK.

Cuffy, V. (2014) Notting Hill Carnival, is it Time for a Tourism Strategy?, *Carnival Grooves, Notting Hill Carnival Edition,* Soca News (Joseph Charles Publishing), London, UK pp. 14–15.

Douglas, N., Douglas, N. and Derrett, R. (2001) *Special interest tourism: context and cases*. John Wiley & Sons, Australia.

Dunn, C. (1992) Bahian carnival: a stage for *afro-hispanic review. African-Brazilian Culture* 11(1/3), 11–20.

Federation of European Carnival Cities (FECC) Available at: http://www.carnivalcities.com (accessed 5 July 2015).

Ferdinand, N. and Shaw, S.J. (2012) Events in our changing world. In: Ferdinand, N. and Paul, J.K. (eds) *Events Management: An International Approach*. Sage, London, UK, pp. 5–22.

Ferdinand, N. and Williams, N. (2013) Festival internationalization: towards a network interpretation. *Tourism Management* 34, 202–210.

Ferris, L. (2012) Incremental art, negotiating the route of London's Notting Hill carnival. In: Crichlow, M.A. (ed.) *Carnival Art, Culture and Politics: Performing Life*. Routledge, London, UK.

Fraser, J.G. (ed.) (1978) *The Illustrated Golden Bough* (abridged, M. Douglas, illustrated S. MacCormack) Macmillan, London, UK.

Gursoy, D., Kim, K. and Uysal, M. (2014) Perceived impacts of festivals and special events by organizers: an extension and validation. *Tourism Management* 25(2), 171–181.

Hill, E. (1972) *The Trinidad Carnival Mandate for a National Theatre*. University of Texas Press, Austin, TX.

Humphrey, C. (2001) *The Politics of Carnival: Festive Misrule in Medieval England*. Manchester University Press, Manchester, UK.

Jackson, P. (1988) Street life: the politics of Carnival. *Environment and Planning D: Society and Space* 6(2), 213–227.

Kline, C. and Oliver, J. (2015) Beyond economic benefits: exploring the effects of festivals and events and community capitals. In: Moufakkir, O. and Pernecky, T. (eds) *Ideological, Social and Cultural Aspects of Events*. CAB International, Wallingford, UK, pp. 171–181.

Labonte, R. (2004) Social inclusion/exclusion: dancing the dialectic. *Health Promotional International* 19(1), 115–121.

Lancaster, K. (2004) When spectators become performers: contemporary performance-entertainments meet the needs of an "unsettled" audience. *Journal of Popular Culture* 30(2), 75–88.

La Rose, M. (2014) We Stand on the Shoulders of Giants – Notting Hill Carnival, a Celebration of 50 Years. *Carnival Grooves, Notting Hill Carnival Edition,* Soca News (Joseph Charles Publishing), London, UK, pp. 5–8.

Livingstone, K. (2003) Mayor Foreword, The Economic Impact of Notting Hill Carnival, *CONNECTION*, August 2003, London Development Agency, London.

London Development Agency (LDA) (2003) The Economic Impact of Notting Hill Carnival, *CONNECTION*, August 2003, London Development Agency, London, UK.

Long, P.T. and Perdue, R.R. (1990) The economic impact of rural festivals and special events: assessing the spatial distribution of expenditures. *Journal of Travel Research* 28(4), 10–14.

Long, P., Robinson, M. and Picard, D. (2004) Festivals and tourism: Links and developments. In: Long, P. and Robinson, M. (eds) *Festivals and Tourism: Marketing, Management and Evaluation*. Centre for Tourism and Cultural Change, Oxford, pp. 1–14.

Matheson, C.M. and Tinsley, R. (2014) The carnivalesque and event evolution: a study of the Beltane fire festival. *Leisure Studies* 35(1), 1–27. DOI:10.1080/02614367.2014.962591.

Mauldin, B. (ed.) (2004) *¡Carnaval!* University of Washington Press, Seattle, Washington, USA.

Notes From Nowhere (eds) (2003) *We are Everywhere. The Irresistible Rise of Global Anticipation*. Verso, New York, USA.

Nurse, K. (1999) Globalisation and Trinidad carnival: diaspora, hybrid and identity in global culture. *Cultural Studies* 13(4), 661–690.

Nurse, K. (2001) *Festival tourism in the Caribbean: An Economic Impact Assessment*. Institute of International Relations, University of the West Indies, Prepared for: Inter-American Development Bank, Washington DC. USA.

Nurse, K. (2004) Trinidad carnival: festival tourism and cultural industry. *Event Management* 8(4), 223–230.

Porto, A.F. (2010) *Culture and Tourism: Perspectives of Foreigners on the Brazilian Carnival*. Open access, DOI: 10.2495/ST100361.

Rao, V. (2001) Celebrations as social investments: festival expenditures unit price variation and social status in rural India. *The Journal of Development Studies* 38(1), 71–97.

Read, S.E. (1980) *A prime focus in the expansion of tourism in the next decade: special interest travel*. In: Hawkins, D.E., Shafer E.L. and Rovelstad, J.M. (eds) Department of Human Kinetics and Leisure Studies, George Washington University, Washington, D.C., pp.193–202.

Riggio, M.C. (2004) Time out or time in? The urban dialectic of carnival. In: Riggio, M.C. (ed.) *Carnival: Culture in Action: The Trinidad Experience. (Worlds of Performance Series)*. Routledge, New York, USA, pp. 13–30.

Scher, P. (2004) *Carnival and the Formation of a Caribbean Transnation*. University Press of Florida, Florida, USA.

Scott, J.C. (1990) Domination and the arts of resistance. *Hidden Transcripts*. Yale University Press, New Haven, Connecticut, USA.

Stebbins, R.A. (1992) *Amateurs, Professionals, and Serious Leisure*. McGill-Queen's University Press, Montreal, Canada.

Sujoldžić, A. (2010) The politics of Carnival. *Book of Abstracts, European Association of Social Anthropologists 11th Biennial Conference 'Crisis and imagination' (Maynooth, Irska, 24th–27th August, 2010)*, European Association of Social Anthropologists, pp. 147–147.

Swarbrooke, J. and Horner, S. (1999) *Consumer Behaviour in Tourism*. Butterworth Heinemann, Oxford, UK.

Taylor, J. (1986) *Masquerade: the Visitor's Introduction to Trinidad and Tobago. (Macmillan Caribbean Guide)*. Macmillan, London, UK

Trauer, B. (2006) *Conceptualizing special interest tourism - frameworks for analysis*. Tourism Management 27 (2), 183–200.

Ward, M. (2003) Chief Executive Foreword, The Economic Impact of Notting Hill Carnival, *CONNECTION*, August 2003, London Development Agency, London, UK.

Weiler, B. and Hall, C.M. (1992) *Special Interest Tourism*. Belhaven Press, London.

Wong, A. (2014) Carnival's Contributions to Britain, Presentation, Carnival Village Trust Awards 2014, Recognising Achievement, Celebrating Excellence. Tabernacle, Powis Square, London 9th August, 2014. http://www.avirtualdominica.com/.

World Tourism Organisation (1985) *The State's Role in Protecting and Promoting Culture as a Factor of Tourism Development and the Proper Use and Exploitation of the National Cultural Heritage of Sites and Monument for Tourism*. World Tourism Organisation, Madrid.

10 Sports Tourism: Golf

Claire Humphreys

Learning Objectives

- To understand the concept of sports tourism as a sub-sector of special interest tourism
- To recognise the variety of sports tourism market segments through an examination of the realm of golf tourism
- To be aware of the impacts of the golf tourism industry for destinations
- To appreciate some of the trends affecting golf tourism

Key Concepts

Sports tourism has, in the past three decades, seen significant growth in attention from the academic community, with Weed (2009) identifying a number of markers that denote maturity as an academic field. Although research has moved on to consider aspects such as behaviours, impacts, policy and provision (Weed, 2006), much of the early work considered definitional issues (Glyptis, 1982; Redmond, 1991; Jackson and Glyptis, 1992), using either 'sport tourism' (Hall, 1992; Gibson, 1998b; Pigeassou, 2004), 'sports tourism' (Priestley, 1995; Kurtzman and Zauhar, 1997) and, in the work of Gammon and Robinson (2003), distinctions between 'sports tourism and tourism sport'. Critiques of these definitions have been presented (Faulkner *et al.*, 1998), with Weed (2005, p. 234) concluding that the concept should reflect '*more than the sum of* sport and tourism'.

Sports tourism is a three-dimensional concept consisting of travel to play sport, travel to watch sport and travel to sports attractions (Delpy, 1998; Gibson, 2006), thus encompassing all forms of sporting activity (Deery *et al.*, 2004). The travel element is significant in that it acknowledges the interaction between the activity and the location or place. Thus Weed and Bull (2004, p. 37) propose that sports tourism should be defined as 'a social, economic and cultural phenomenon that stems from the unique interaction of activity, people, and place'. Furthermore distinctions between competitive/non-competitive sport (Hinch and Higham, 2001) and the casual/avid-connoisseur participant exist (Standeven and De Knop, 1999; Ritchie *et al.*, 2002). The sports tourist is complex, with demand for sports-related vacations affected by social class, lifestage, ethnicity and gender – with males more likely than females to participate (Humphreys, 2014).

Sports tourism is important for many holiday destinations, accounting for up to one-quarter of tourism receipts (Tassiopoulos and Haydam, 2008). Sporting mega-events (such as the FIFA Football World Cup and the Olympic Games) attract large numbers of tourists, bringing both spectators and participants to the host destinations as well as influencing image and appeal for future visitation (Visit Scotland, 2012). In a joint statement the IOC and UNWTO asserted that 'tourism and sport are interrelated and complementary' (UNWTO and IOC, 2004), important in terms of their value for destination development and social engagement.

Major Factors: a Focus on Golf Tourism

The value and scale of the sports tourism industry is difficult to accurately predict due to the diversity of sports activities, events and attractions. However the focus on golf tourism in this chapter is justified because, with an estimated market worth in excess of US$25 billion (Mintel, 2010) generated from the 80 million golfers worldwide, it is perhaps the largest sector of the sports tourism industry. And while the sport has historically been perceived as elitist, the past 30 years has seen greater diversification in the characteristics of the golf player – and consequently the golf tourist (Humphreys, 2016a)

In recent years golf holiday sales have increased (KPMG Golf Business Community, 2013b), with dedicated tour operators serving expanding global markets. Its importance has encouraged regions to develop strategies to expand provision and initiate efforts to enhance golf tourism reputations (Humphreys, 2011). This has included the development of new courses, increased promotion and the hosting of professional golf events. Golf destinations comprise a bundle of attributes (such as course quality, golf facilities, accommodation quality, climate and hospitality) which appeal to participants (Barros *et al.*, 2010). Thus variations in supply offer appeal to the different segments of demand.

Motivations: Demand for Golf Tourism

Segmentation of tourist markets uses characteristics such as geographic, socio-demographic and lifespan (Gibson *et al.*, 1998; Dolnicar and Kemp, 2008; Middleton *et al.*, 2009) to break the vast consumer market into discrete groups on which to tailor marketing efforts. Additionally sport-related characteristics further refine segments. For example Weed and Bull (2004, p. 77) propose that sports tourists can be categorised based on levels of participation from incidental through sporadic, occasional, regular and committed, to the driven sports tourist for whom sports participation is 'professionally significant'. Distinction has also been made between active participants and passive spectators of sports events and competitions (Gibson, 1998a; Pitts, 1999; Green and Jones, 2005). Such characteristics can be applied directly to golf tourists, with Hennessey *et al.* (2008) proposing three golf tourist groupings – infrequent, moderate and dedicated – where infrequent golfers play five or fewer rounds per annum while dedicated golfers are deemed to be those who have played over 25 rounds per year and are considered devoted to the game. Moital and Dias (2012) also distinguish between 'hard-core' golf tourists and 'recreational' golf tourists on the basis of main purpose of travel, concluding that recreational tourists play less frequently and are less likely to book golf tee times in advance of the trip.

Several 'golfographic' variables (handicap, golf membership, years of play and number of golf trips taken) and the ability to play to handicap influence the number and variety of courses played while on vacation (Petrick, 2002; Hennessey *et al.*, 2008). Furthermore, in her investigation of golfer characteristics and destination selection, Humphreys (2013) identifies multiple factors influencing golf tourism participation. These include the centrality

of golf in the holidaymaker's life, the effort to which a golfer would go to in order to create opportunities to play while on vacation, frequency of participation, engagement with skill development and competitions, preparedness to compromise over course complexity and the influence of others in the travel group. Thus it is evident that golf tourists are not one homogeneous group.

Of the 80 million golfers playing globally, the biggest golf markets are located in the USA and Canada (Fig. 10.1). These two countries, along with the UK, have significant levels of domestic as well as international golf tourism. The Scandinavian, German and Austrian markets are also strong, particularly for international trips (KPMG Golf Business Community, 2013a).

Golf tourists are seen as high spenders, with golfers spending at 120% of the level of other tourists (Mintel, 2012; KPMG Golf Business Community, 2013a), not just to golf facility providers but also to upscale accommodation, restaurants, golf and non-golf retailers, and other amenity providers (KPMG, 2008). However, competition for leisure time and holiday expenditure comes from other sports. For example, in the USA the growth of cycling as a competitive sport for middle-aged men is impacting the core market for golf, with total golf participation declining from 25 million to 19 million players over the past decade (Euromonitor, 2014). Furthermore golf tourist demand is affected by other factors, such as price sensitivity (see Focus Box 1). Despite such pressures the USA remains the largest market, with around one-quarter of the world's golfers and half of the world's courses (*The Economist*, 2014).

Motivation for sports tourism participation is complex, in so far as the sports element may not be the dominant reason for participation in travel and some travellers do not directly acknowledge their true motivations (Bouchet *et al.*, 2004; Kurtzman and Zauhar, 2005). Motivations are shaped by numerous constraints and abilities to negotiate around such pressures (Jackson and Scott, 1999). Focusing on motivations for golf tourism, Kim and Ritchie (2010) conclude that five motivational push factors (business opportunity, benefits, learning and challenging, escape/relax, social interaction/kinship) and seven motivational pull factors (natural environment, golfing-related availability and accessibility, golf resort/course facilities and services, tourism attractions, tourism facilities and services, nightlife and entertainment, and price and ease of access) determine demand.

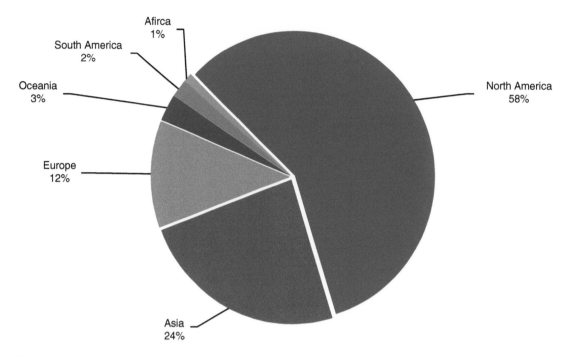

Fig. 10.1. Share of golfers by region

Focus Box 1: Factors influencing demand for golf tourism

Results of research from the KPMG Golf travel insights survey in 2013 identified key factors considered important for golf tourists. The survey examined the views of 110 golf tour operators from 38 countries, to identify key factors shaping golf destination choice:

- Price of package
- Quality of golf courses
- Accessibility
- Quality of accommodation
- Climate
- Number of golf courses
- Entertainment
- Golf tradition

Price has long been considered influential on tourism demand (Martin and Witt, 1988). It takes account of the cost of travelling to a destination, costs while at the destination and the effect of exchange rates (Crouch, 1994). The price of substitute destinations also shapes demand patterns.

For golf tourism specifically price sensitivity is influenced by the substitutability of destinations (Lo and Lam, 2004), with places that offer unique golf experiences being buffered against price pressures. The total cost of the trip is more significant than the individual elements of the trip, such as costs of accessing golf courses, transporting golf equipment as luggage, accommodation, travel and hospitality (Humphreys, 2013; Humphreys, 2016b) with perceived utility (based on expected satisfaction gained from consuming the range of products and services) influencing demand (Gratton and Taylor, 2000). Furthermore, market characteristics sway demand choices, with dedicated golfers more likely to select challenging and costlier courses than infrequent or moderate golfers (Priestley, 1995; Hennessey *et al.*, 2008).

C. Humphreys

While playing golf may be the dominant experience for some holidaymakers, in other cases the tourism experience may prevail (golf being one activity undertaken during the trip) (TIA, 2006). However, rarely does a single motive exist thus multiple motivations influence consumer behaviour for sports tourism (Gill *et al.*, 1996; Gammon and Robinson, 2003). Participation is thus shaped by a multitude of factors influencing the trip decision-making process (Humphreys and Weed, 2012), with a particular influence on whether and where to take a trip (Um and Crompton, 1990; Mansfield, 1992). Negotiating for golf to be incorporated in trips is a complex issue as 'the potential activities of all travel companions have to be met by a supply in a given destination (maximising utility for each travel companion)' (Bieger and Laesser, 2004, p. 368). Therefore attitudes towards golf, negotiation and compromise influence destination selection. Furthermore the expanding supply of golf tourism destinations and products allows a diversity of markets to be served.

Interactions

The standard format for golf courses is 18 holes (with 9-hole formats not uncommon). Several golf resorts comprise 27 or 36 holes of golf while popular golf destinations will see a number of courses clustered together. Examples of golf course clusters include Hilton Head and Myrtle Beach on the east coast of the USA and Hainan Island, China – home to the ten courses of Mission Hills resort and 14 other courses across the island. Most courses include holes of varied lengths but a small fraction of courses may focus only on short holes (known as 'par-3s'). These 'par-3' courses (sometimes called executive courses) take less time to play and are popular with those pressed for time or just starting to learn the game. However, historically such courses are less favourably received and thus less likely to appeal to the mainstream golf tourism market (Hudson and Hudson, 2010). There is a slight shift as executive courses use high-profile designers and major brand names to enhance their status. However, this still remains a very small segment of overall supply.

Golf tourism intermediaries are an important part of the supply chain, with golfers often using intermediaries because they are perceived to offer convenience of booking, good value and enhanced quality of experience (driven by their extensive product knowledge). Intermediaries contract with golf courses, allowing tee times to be booked on demand and packaged with accommodation and travel to create a holiday product, which the intermediary then markets to golfers. Consequently intermediaries play an important role in shaping the image, popularity and promotion of golf tourism destinations (Humphreys, 2014).

In 2016 the International Association of Golf Tour operators (IAGTO) had 655 specialist golf tour operators as members. These intermediaries, located in 61 counties, were estimated to sell 87% of global golf tourism packages (IAGTO, 2016) – with packaging usually comprising a 'pre-payment of green fees and pre-booking of tee-times, as well as transportation and accommodation' (Hudson and Hudson, 2014, p. 58). Intermediaries are likely to be used when golf tours are perceived as complex (perhaps international air travel is required, multiple courses are to be played or travel reservations are to be made in a foreign language). Alternatively intermediaries are employed by the group trip organiser to provide transparency of pricing and transfer of risk (Humphreys, 2014).

Impacts and Insights

The number of golf courses globally exceeds 34,000 (R&A, 2015), with Great Britain, New Zealand, Australia, Ireland, Canada, the USA and Sweden having the highest per capita density (Barton, 2009). The growth of the middle classes in India and China has encouraged the development of new courses in these regions, although in China this has largely been in contravention of government legislation. Despite a ban on new courses introduced in 2004 the number of courses tripled to in excess of 600 by 2011. However, notwithstanding booming participation levels, a government crackdown on illegally built courses has seen upwards of 10% of golf courses closed down, with the government arguing that courses place excessive strain on the country's land and water resources (Dasgupta, 2015). Despite India's long history of golf (the first courses opening at the end of the 19th century) this vast country has around 200 golf courses (half of which are located on military bases with limited public access). However, expansion in supply is occurring to cater to the growing demand from local golfers, with as many as 30 new courses forecast to be completed in the decade ending 2020 (KPMG, 2011).

The USA dominates global supply with 45% of the world's golf facilities (R&A, 2015), although one-quarter of these are private members clubs (with access limited to those paying membership fees) (National Recreation and Parks Association, 2012). There has been contraction in supply since 2008, with 500 courses closing over this period and forecasts suggesting upwards of another 150 closing over the next decade as the market seeks equilibrium (Gray, 2015). Europe has seen little change in supply over the past decade following twenty years of expansion (the number of courses doubling over this period). In 2015 in excess of 7000 courses were available, with a quarter located in England (KPMG Golf Advisory Practice, 2016). Although 16 courses closed in the UK in 2015 the same period saw eight new courses open in the Netherlands and four each in Slovakia and Latvia to offset any European decline.

The top five international destinations selected by golf tourists are Spain, Portugal, Scotland, Turkey and Ireland – with the large European market heavily influencing this. Thailand and Vietnam are also seeing some growth as golf tourism destinations as the Asian market continues to expand (KPMG Golf Business Community, 2013a).

The high value per tourist and growing participation levels have led many destinations to incorporate golf into local tourism strategies or policy (Australian Golf Industry Council, 2014). This is discussed further in Focus Box 2. The development of golf tourism requires more than course development; related infrastructure including accommodation, amenities and transportation may also require investment (Priestley, 2006).

The strategic development of golf tourism is not without controversy as the resources required to develop an extensive product can, as we mentioned earlier in the case of China, put pressure on scarce land and water resources. Markwick (2000), in her review of the debates related to golf tourism development on the Mediterranean island of Malta,

---

Focus Box 2: New Zealand International Golf Tourism Strategy

Tourism New Zealand developed a long term strategy for international golf tourism in 2013. This strategy acknowledged NZ$260 million of prior investment by the private sector in golf facilities and sought to expand its minimal share of a multi-billion dollar market. The strategy highlighted that New Zealand has a diverse range of courses (more than 400 in total), including many of high quality appearing on world ranking lists. It also acknowledged that it has a suitable year-round climate, products offering excellent value for money, courses which offer spectacular scenery and vistas, and a variety of complementary attractions suited to key golf markets (Tourism New Zealand, 2013).

The strategy sought to increase total spending by international golfers by 50%, recognising that, on average, international golfers visiting New Zealand spend more (NZ$3300) than non-golfers (NZ$2500) and stay longer (Tourism New Zealand, 2016). The strategy specifically targets the dominant markets of Australia, USA, China and Japan (see Table 10.1) and is supported with NZ$2 million of funding for international marketing (Caldwell, 2013).

In line with existing tourism marketing focused on '100% pure New Zealand', promotional efforts for golf tourism have focused on the natural landscape. To enhance the coherence of the golf tourism product in New Zealand the strategy has encouraged the development of 'golf trails' which combine golf with other

Table 10.1. Major markets for golf tourism to New Zealand.

Markets that provide the most golf tourists	Number of golf visitors	Percentage of total market
Australia	44,891	52
USA	8,848	9
China	4,494	5
Japan	2,332	3

Source: Tourism New Zealand, 2016

attractions as a scenic journey through the country. This has required coordination between Tourism New Zealand, regional tourism organisations (RTOs), and local golf operators. While there has been some success in developing and promoting such trails there is still work to do in terms of strategy recommendations, such as developing regional green fee passes to be used across multiple courses.

One barrier to expanding golf tourism in New Zealand is the lack of world-class tournaments hosted in the country. Such tournaments can confer quality on a destination as well as expanding media coverage viewed by key target markets. To counter this familiarisation tours have been developed (Golf Tourism New Zealand, 2014). Furthermore, information provided online has significantly increased, and a centralised online reservation system has been developed.

C. Humphreys

comments that conflicts can be appreciated in terms of the various economic and environmental benefits and disbenefits for local stakeholders. Economic benefits are frequently used as justification of the strategic development of golf tourism, with the direct revenues and golf tourism's contribution to employment and GDP espoused. Across the European, Middle East and African (EMA) region the golf industry generated €21 billion in direct revenue for the economy, of which almost 13% (€2.7 billion) was attributed to golf tourism directly, and €6.5 billion when indirect revenues in golf tourism are considered (KPMG, 2008). Golf tourism has also been used strategically to address seasonality of tourism demand (Garau-Vadell and Borja-Solé, 2008).

Although much of the debate on the impacts of golf tourism has focused on the negative environmental impacts of golf course development (Wheeler and Nauright, 2006), it is worth first appreciating that there are some positive outcomes of golf course development, including the reuse of degraded land and the wildlife habitats provided as a result of the natural landscapes maintained. Historically golf courses were shaped within existing landscapes; however recent trends have seen more manipulation of the natural environment as courses are developed and increased use of chemicals and water resources add further pressure. In recent years there has been greater attention on environmental sustainability of golf courses, reflected in the introduction in 1997 of the Sports Turf Research Institute (STRI) Golf Environment Awards and in 2008 the 'Green Golf' awards supported by *Golf Magazine*. The golf industry has also developed initiatives to promote sustainability (see Focus Box 3), including the development of certification programmes.

Golf courses are usually developed to serve the needs of the local market. However, it should be noted that golf tourism can directly encourage course development through increased demand (Completo and Gustavo, 2014). The American seaside resort of Myrtle Beach, for example, has almost 100 courses, far in excess of that needed to serve the resident population, developed to serve the demand from the millions of visitors the destination receives each year (Humphreys, 2016a). Furthermore, social impacts may be felt as tourists compete with the local population for use of golf (and non-golf) resources. This can place pressure on tee times, on-course experiences (perhaps seen

through slow play as tourists, who know little of the course, or wish to enjoy the beauty of the scenery, take additional time to play) and in the clubhouse after the game.

The supply of golf tourism facilities is changing as the golf industry caters to shifting consumer preferences, offering new amenities and styles of golf (Euromonitor, 2014). Executive courses were mentioned previously but technology is also playing a role, as golf simulators are further enhanced to create sensory experiences (Kurtzman and Zauhar, 2003). Simulators can provide a different type of golf experience without the requirement for large areas of green space. They are also not climate dependent and can operate year round in temperature-controlled environments. In Korea, for example, golfers 'facing steep green fees and onerous travel times to play on traditional, physical golf courses' instead visit golf-simulator cafes for practice and social engagement (Han *et al.*, 2013, p. 428). The outcome is that this may shape demand for golf–related travel. In conclusion changing demand trends can influence or be influenced by change in supply trends.

Trends and Issues

The trend bringing perhaps the greatest change to golf tourism is the growing number of participants in Asia. New players coming to the game add to the potential market for travel, particularly in countries where supply locally is limited, making it expensive to play. International travel for golf has seen strong market growth in China, India, to a lesser extent in Malaysia and the South American countries of Brazil and Argentina. In such cases it is the internationally renowned courses which shape destination selection, although visa regulations also heavily impact this (IAGTO, 2013). Destinations particularly benefiting from this growth are the USA and Scotland – reputedly the 'home of golf' (Butler, 2005; Visit Scotland, 2015).

In the mature markets of Europe and the USA there is a shortening of booking lead times as more golfers look for last-minute deals. This search for good value is coupled with an increasing demand for higher quality accommodation and courses which, combined, places intense pressures on the profitability of golf tourism suppliers. Prevalence of shorter trips (3–5 days) means that destinations with convenient proximity to local markets often gain, particularly when word-of-mouth

GEO is a not-for-profit organisation developed by business leaders to enhance sustainability within the golf industry. This sets standards and provides certification to encourage improved sustainability at existing courses, for new golf developments and in the operation of golf tournaments. This focuses on both environmental and social sustainability.

In partnership with the R&A (golf's governing body for Europe, Africa and the Asian-Pacific region) this organisation has encouraged more than 500 courses across the globe to participate in a practical online programme to plan and implement sustainable improvements to their business operations. Specifically the programme considers the protection of nature; efficient and responsible use of water; air, soil and water pollution controls; energy efficiency; ethics in supply chain decisions and positive and ethical engagement with local communities.

Golf courses in more than 50 countries have completed the GEO On-Course programme, with this certification having varying levels of prevalence.

As Fig. 10.2 shows, golf courses in Iceland have almost universal completion of this certification (93% of golf courses have participated) while in England, the country with the most courses in Europe, only 3.5% of golf courses have engaged with this certification programme. There is some, albeit limited, support from the world's top golf courses. *Golf Digest* publishes the world's top 100 golf courses and three of the top ten have completed the certification programme (Royal County Down, Ireland; Royal Dornoch, Scotland; and Royal Melbourne, Australia).

While Fig. 10.2 details the case in Europe, other places have similar experiences. For example in the USA around 0.3% of golf courses have completed this certification – a similar ratio to that of Germany. While the level of engagement with this sustainability initiative may be attributed to awareness of the programme, it may also be some reflection of attitudes towards and awareness of sustainability issues for golf courses in different regions of the world.

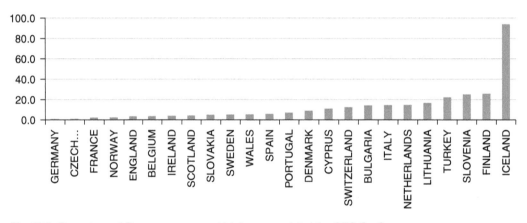

Fig. 10.2. Percentage of European courses which have completed the GEO On-Course programme.

discussion of experiences enhances reputations (Humphreys, 2011).

Trends in supply have seen new destinations opening up as countries with little tradition or reputation for golf (Vietnam and Morocco as examples) develop courses as part of a broader tourism strategy (HSBC, 2012). The successful implementation of such policies by other destinations encourages this – for example Mauritius has developed its

reputation as a golf destination, having embedded initiatives into the tourism strategy over a decade ago. Now around 60,000 golfers visit the island annually (Lemay, 2015) and its golf destination image was further enhanced when, in 2015, the island hosted a tournament which formed part of the European and Asian professional tour schedule. Professional golf events continue to be an important part of the golf tourism product, bringing large numbers of spectators to host destinations. Hosting the Ryder Cup at Celtic Manor brought 244,000 spectators and in excess of £82 million into the Welsh economy (BBC, 2011) while the Masters golf tournament, held annually in Augusta, Georgia, adds (according to historic estimates) US$109 million to the local economy (Golf 2020, 2010).

Conclusions

The demand for golf tourism is heavily influenced by the total number of people regularly playing the sport. While some regions see players leaving the game, this is countered by the growing appeal of the sport in developing nations. This may be further extended following the return, after an absence of 112 years, of golf to the Olympics in 2016. Spectating at golf events remains popular, with high-profile events televised to global audiences encouraging future visitation, as golfers consider the possibility of playing in the footsteps of professionals (Humphreys, 2013).

Golf tourists are generally high-spending and well educated, making them an attractive market for many destinations and thus government leaders appreciate the value of this market segment to the economy and destination development (Mintel, 2010). However as new golf destinations develop, so competition will increase, possibly to the detriment of those locations that fail to maintain quality in terms of courses and supporting tourist amenities, a key factor, alongside price, in the destination selection process. Supply will also need to adapt to the cultural expectations of the newly emerging markets travelling internationally to participate in golf tourism.

There is growing pressure to improve the sustainability of golf course operations, which may prove challenging for destinations that develop courses in climates which are less than conducive to the needs for large swathes of grassland. Furthermore many golf tourists seek warm, dry climates as ideal environments. Thus at times during the year some areas are seen as too hot, too wet or too cold to play, stimulating golf trips (often international) by players seeking better playing conditions. Thus markets from the UK, Scandinavia and Canada may choose to fly south in winter to find better golfing climates while those in South East Asia and the Middle East may fly to cooler regions in summer to avoid high temperatures and humidity.

Although executive courses may potentially encourage the local population to take up the sport or play more frequently, this does little to stimulate international golf tourism. Markets seek a variety of conveniently accessible courses, thus resorts with multiple courses or destinations which provide a high density of golf courses will remain attractive.

Despite competition from other sports the future of golf tourism is positive as market size expands and new destinations come on stream. However, markets seeking value for money and increased supply will mean golf courses – and the intermediaries that package these products – will be increasingly pressured on price. This will be coupled with the burden to maintain quality. Those places with a long tradition of golf, or an internationally renowned reputation, will perhaps be able to withstand intensive price pressures but the overall trip experience will remain important for the golf tourist.

Questions

1. What characteristics of the golf tourism market have encouraged Tourism New Zealand to develop a golf tourism strategy? How might market characteristics change over the coming decade?

2. China is developing its skilled golfers to compete for the sport's Olympic gold medal. However, it has banned the construction of new courses and is reducing the number of existing courses available. What might be the implication of large-scale course closure on the Chinese outbound golf tourism market?

3. To what extent do professional golf events affect the demand pattern for golf destinations?

Further Reading

Hudson, S. and Hudson, L. (2014) *Golf Tourism*, 2nd edn. Goodfellow Publishers, Woodeaton, Oxford, UK. [This book provides a clear overview of the sector, with commentary on demand, supply and impacts. It explains the planning and management of golf courses and examines the influence of golf events.]

Humphreys, C. (2014) Understanding how sporting characteristics and behaviours influence destination selection: a grounded theory study of golf tourism. *Journal of Sport & Tourism* 19, 29–54. [This paper examines the characteristics of the golf tourist and explores the relationship between golf trip behaviours and destination selection.]

Priestley, G.K. (2006) Planning implications of golf tourism. *Tourism & Hospitality Research* 6, 170–178. [This paper focuses on the development of golf courses and the policies linked to golf tourism strategies.]

Websites

International Association of Golf Tour Operators: www.iagto.com

Golf Environment Organisation: www.golfenvironment.org

Visit Scotland – golf tourism research: www.visitscotland.org/research_and_statistics/tourism_sectors/golf.aspx

Tourism New Zealand Golf: www.tourismnewzealand.com/markets-stats/sectors/special-interest/golf

Incredible India (National Tourist Board) Golf Tourism guidelines: www.incredibleindia.org/images/docs/trade-pdf/product/golf-tourism/golf-guideline.pdf

References

Australian Golf Industry Council (2014) *The Value of Golf Tourism to Australia*. AGIC, Melbourne, Australia.

Barros, C.P., Butler, R. and Correia, A.N. (2010) The length of stay of golf tourism: a survival analysis. *Tourism Management* 31, 13–21.

Barton, J. (2009) Planet Golf: Top 100 Courses Outside the U.S. [Online]. ESPN. Available at: http://sports.espn.go.com/travel/news/story?id=2360251 (accessed 13 November 2017).

BBC (2011) Ryder Cup Golf's '£82.4m Boost to Economy of Wales' [Online]. BBC Wales. Available at: http://www.bbc.co.uk/news/uk-wales-12834078 (accessed 26 May 2015).

Bieger, T. and Laesser, C. (2004) Information sources for travel decisions: toward a source process model. *Journal of Travel Research* 42, 357–371.

Bouchet, P., Lebrun, A.-M. and Auvergne, S. (2004) Sport tourism consumer experiences: a comprehensive model. *Journal of Sport Tourism* 9, 127–140.

Butler, R. (2005) The influence of sport on destination development: the example of golf at St Andrews, Scotland. In: Higham, J. (ed.) *Sport Tourism Destinations.* Elsevier Butterworth-Heinemann, Oxford, UK.

Caldwell, O. (2013) Strategy targets golfing tourists. *Otago Daily Times*, New Zealand, 14 August.

Completo, F. and Gustavo, N. (2014) Golf tourism destination management: looking for a sustainable demand: the case of Portugal. *Journal of Management and Sustainability* 4, 142–153.

Crouch, G.I. (1994) The study of international tourism demand: a review of findings. *Journal of Travel Research* 33, 12–23.

Dasgupta, S. (2015) China closes 66 golf courses as it steps up anti-graft fight. *The Times of India*, 31 March.

Deery, M., Jago, L. and Fredline, L. (2004) Sport tourism or event tourism: are they one and the same? *Journal of Sport & Tourism* 9, 235–245.

Delpy, L. (1998) An overview of sport tourism: building towards a dimensional framework. *Journal of Vacation Marketing* 4, 23–38.

Dolnicar, S. and Kemp, B. (eds) (2008) *Tourism Segmentation by Consumer-based Variables*. Routledge, New York, USA.

Euromonitor (2014) *World Travel Market Global Trends Report*. Euromonitor, London, UK.

Faulkner, B., Tideswell, C. and Weston, A. (1998) Leveraging tourism benefits from the Sydney 2000 Olympics: Keynote presentation, Sport Management: Opportunities and Change. Fourth Annual Conference of the Sport Management Association of Australia and New Zealand, 26–28 November 1998, Gold Coast, Australia.

Gammon, S. and Robinson, T. (2003) Sport and tourism: a conceptual framework. *Journal of Sport Tourism* 8, 21–26.

Garau-Vadell, J.B. and Borja-Solé, L.D. (2008) Golf in mass tourism destinations facing seasonality: a longitudinal study. *Tourism Review* 63, 16–24.

GEO (2015) *Directory* [Online]. Golf Environment Organisation. Available at: http://www.golfenvironment.org/directory (accessed 22 May 2015).

Gibson, H. (1998a) Active sport tourism: who participates? *Leisure Studies* 17, 155–170.

Gibson, H.J. (1998b) Sport tourism: a critical analysis of research. *Sport Management Review* 1, 45–76.

Gibson, H. (2006) *Sport Tourism: Concepts and Theories*. Routledge, Abingdon, UK.

Gibson, H.J., Attle, S.P. and Yiannakis, A. (1998) Segmenting the active sport tourist market: a life-span perspective. *Journal of Vacation Marketing* 4, 52–64.

Gill, D.L., Williams, L., Dowd, D.A., Beaudoin, C.M. and Martin, J.J. (1996) Competitive orientations and motives of adult sport and exercise participants. *Journal of Sport Behavior* 19, 307–318.

Glyptis, S. (1982) *Sport and Tourism in Western Europe*. British Travel Educational Trust, London, UK.

Golf 2020 (2010) *The Georgia Golf Economy*. Georgia Allied Golf Council, Georgia, USA.

Golf Tourism New Zealand (2014) *Golf Tourism New Zealand Progress Report*. GTNZ, Wellington, New Zealand.

Gratton, C. and Taylor, P. (2000) *Economics of Sport and Recreation*. Spon Press, London, UK.

Gray, R. (2015) *Golf Industry Looks to Hit More Green in '15* [Online]. Fox Business. Available at: http://www.foxbusiness.com/industries/2015/01/22/golf-industry-looks-to-hit-more-green-in-15/ (accessed 22 May 2015).

Green, B.C. and Jones, I. (2005) Serious leisure, social identity and sport tourism. *Sport in Society* 8, 164–181.

Hall, C.M. (1992) Adventure, sport and health. In: Hall, C.M. and Weiler, B. (eds) *Special Interest Tourism*. Belhaven Press, London, UK.

Han, H., Hwang, J. and Woods, D.P. (2013) Choosing virtual – rather than real – leisure activities: an examination of the decision–making process in screen-golf participants. *Asia Pacific Journal of Tourism Research* 19, 428–450.

Hennessey, S.M., Macdonald, R. and Maceachern, M. (2008) A framework for understanding golfing visitors to a destination. *Journal of Sport & Tourism* 13, 5–35.

Hinch, T.D. and Higham, J.E.S. (2001) Sport tourism: a framework for research. *International Journal of Tourism Research* 3, 45–58.

C. Humphreys

HSBC (2012) *Golf's 2020 Vision*. HSBC, London, UK.

Hudson, S. and Hudson, L. (2010) *Golf Tourism*. Goodfellow Publishers, Woodeaton, Oxford, UK.

Hudson, S. and Hudson, L. (2014) *Golf Tourism,* 2nd edn. Goodfellow Publishers, Woodeaton, Oxford, UK.

Humphreys, C. (2011) Who cares where I play? Linking reputation with the golfing capital and the implication for golf destinations. *Journal of Sport Tourism* 16, 105–128.

Humphreys, C. (2013) An Evaluation of the Relationships between Golfer Characteristics, Golfer Behaviours and Destination Selection. PhD Thesis, Canterbury Christchurch University, Canterbury, UK.

Humphreys, C. (2014) Understanding how sporting characteristics and behaviours influence destination selection: a grounded theory study of golf tourism. *Journal of Sport & Tourism* 19, 29–54.

Humphreys, C. (2016a) *The Business of Tourism*. Pearson Education, Harlow.

Humphreys, C. (2016b) Travelling with golf clubs: the influence of baggage on the trip decision-making process. *Journal of Sport and Tourism,* 21, 49–63.

Humphreys, C. and Weed, M. (2012) Golf tourism and the trip decision making process: the influence of life-stage, negotiation and compromise, and the existence of tiered decision making units. *Leisure Studies*, 33, 75–95.

IAGTO (2013) *Golf Tourism Report*. IAGTO, London.

IAGTO (2016) *IAGTO – The Organisation* [Online]. Available at: http://www.iagto.com/about (accessed 23 December 2016).

Jackson, G.A.M. and Glyptis, S.A. (1992) *Sport and tourism: a review of the literature. Report to the Sports Council*. Loughborough University, Loughborough.

Jackson, E.L. and Scott, D. (1999) Constraints to leisure. In: Jackson, E.L. and Burton, T.L. (eds) *Leisure Studies: Prospects for the Twenty-first Century*. Venture Publishing, State College, PA, USA.

Kim, J.H. and Ritchie, B.W. (2010) Motivation-based typology: an empirical study of golf tourists. *Journal of Hospitality & Tourism Research* 36, 251–280.

KPMG (2008) *The Value of Golf to Europe, Middle East and Africa: A Study on the Golf Economy*. KPMG Advisory, Hungary.

KPMG (2011) *Country Snapshot: India*. KPMG's Golf Advisory Practice, Budapest, Hungary.

KPMG Golf Advisory Practice (2016) *Golf Participation report for Europe*. Golf Benchmark, KPMG, Hungary. Available online at: http://static.golfbenchmark.com/media/3/0/0/4/3004.pdf (accessed 23 December 2016).

KPMG Golf Business Community (2013a) *Golf Travel Insights 2013*. KPMG, Hungary.

KPMG Golf Business Community (2013b) *Golf Travel Insights: Golf Benchmark* [Online]. KPMG Golf Business Community. Available at: http://www.iagto.com/ (accessed 3 August 2013).

KPMG Golf Business Community (2015) *Golf Participation in Europe 2015* [Online]. KPMG Golf Business Community. Available at: https://assets.kpmg.com/content/dam/kpmg/pdf/2016/07/golf-participation-europe-2015.pdf (accessed 13 November 2017).

Kurtzman, J. and Zauhar, J. (1997) A wave in time – the sports tourism phenomena. *Journal of Sport & Tourism* 4, 7–24.

Kurtzman, J. and Zauhar, J. (2003) Virtual sport tourism. In: Hudson, S. (ed.) *Sport and Adventure Tourism*. Haworth Hospitality Press, Binghampton, NY, USA.

Kurtzman, J. and Zauhar, J. (2005) Sports tourism consumer motivation. *Journal of Sport Tourism* 10, 21–31.

Lemay, C. (2015) *Mauritius Open: Sun, Sea and Sand Saves: How the Third Country to Adopt Golf Attracted the First tri-sanctioned Event* [Online]. Available at: http://www.golfmagic.com/news/golf-news/mauritius-open-sun-sea-and-sand-saves/21191.html (accessed 26 May 2015).

Lo, A. and Lam, T. (2004) Long-haul and short-haul outbound all-inclusive package tours. *Asia Pacific Journal of Tourism Research* 9, 161–176.

Mansfield, Y. (1992) From motivation to actual travel. *Annals of Tourism Research* 19, 399–419.

Markwick, M.C. (2000) Golf tourism development, stakeholders, differing discourses and alternative agendas: the case of Malta. *Tourism Management* 21, 515–524.

Martin, C.A. and Witt, S.F. (1988) Substitute prices in models of tourism demand. *Annals of Tourism Research* 15, 255–268.

Middleton, V., Fyall, A., Morgan, M. and Ranchhod, A. (2009) *Marketing in Travel and Tourism*. Butterworth Heinemann, Oxford, UK.

Mintel (2010) *Golf Tourism - International*. Mintel, London, UK.

Mintel (2012) *Sports Tourism Worldwide*. Mintel, London, UK.

Moital, M. and Dias, N.R. (2012) Golf tourists' satisfaction: hard-core versus recreational golf tourists. In: Shipway, R. and Fyall, A. (eds) *International Sport Events: Impacts, Experience and Identities*. Routledge, Abingdon, UK.

National Recreation and Parks Association (2012) *Course Numbers* [Online]. USA: NRPA. Available at: http://www.parksandrecreation.org/2012/March/Course-Numbers/ (accessed 29 May 2015).

Petrick, J.F. (2002) An examination of golf vacationers' novelty. *Annals of Tourism Research* 29, 384–400.

Pigeassou, C. (2004) Contribution to the definition of sport tourism. *Journal of Sport & Tourism* 9, 287–289.

Pitts, B.G. (1999) Sports tourism and niche markets: Identification and analysis of the growing lesbian and gay sports tourism industry. *Journal of Vacation Marketing* 5, 31–50.

Priestley, G.K. (1995) Sports tourism: the case of golf. In: Ashworth, G.J. and Dietvorst, A.G.J. (eds) *Tourism and Spatial Transformations: Implications for Policy and Planning*. CAB International, Wallingford, UK.

Priestley, G.K. (2006) Planning implications of golf tourism. *Tourism & Hospitality Research* 6, 170–178.

R&A (2015) *Golf around the World*. The R&A, St Andrews, Scotland, UK.

Redmond, G. (1991) Changing styles of sports tourism: industry/consumer interactions in Canada, the USA and Europe. In: Sinclair, M.T. and Stabler, M.J. (eds) *The Tourist Industry: An International Analysis.* CAB International, Wallingford, UK.

Ritchie, B., Mosedale, L. and King, J. (2002) Profiling sport tourists: the case of super 12 rugby union in the Australian Capital Territory, Australia. *Current Issues in Tourism* 5, 33–44.

Standeven, J. and De Knop, P. (1999) *Sport Tourism*. Human Kinetics, Illinois, USA.

Tassiopoulos, D. and Haydam, N. (2008) Golf tourists in South Africa: a demand-side study of a niche market in sports tourism. *Tourism Management* 29, 870–882.

The Economist (2014) Handicapped. 20 December.

TIA (2006) *TIA – Domestic Travel Fast Facts – Travel Trends from A to Z* [Online]. USA: Travel Industry Association. Available at: http://www.tia.org/pressmedia/domestic_a_to_z.html (accessed 11 November 2015).

Tourism New Zealand (2013) *New Zealand International Golf Tourism Strategy*. Tourism New Zealand, Wellington.

Tourism New Zealand (2016) Special Interest, Available online at: http://www.tourismnewzealand.com/markets-stats/sectors/special-interest/golf/ (accessed 23 December 2016).

Um, S. and Crompton, J.L. (1990) Attitude determinants in tourism destination choice. *Annals of Tourism Research* 17, 432–448.

UNWTO and IOC (2004) Joint message from the WTO secretary general and the IOC president for world tourism day 2004. *Sport and Tourism: Two Living Forces for Mutual Understanding, Culture and the Development of Society*. Available at: https://www.olympic.org/news/world-tourism-day-2004 (accessed 3 October 2017).

Visit Scotland (2012) *Sport Tourism – The Scale of Opportunity from Hosting a Mega Event*. Visit Scotland, Edinburgh.

Visit Scotland (2015) *Scotland: The Home of Golf* [Online]. Visit Scotland. Available at: http://www.visitscotland.com/see-do/activities/golf/home-of-golf/ (accessed 26 May 2015).

Weed, M. (2005) Sport tourism theory and method – concepts, issues and epistemologies. *European Sport Management Quarterly* 5, 229–242.

Weed, M. (2006) Sports tourism research 2000–2004: a systematic review of knowledge and a meta-evaluation of methods. *Journal of Sport and Tourism* 11, 5–30.

Weed, M. (2009) Progress in sports tourism research? a meta-review and exploration of futures. *Tourism Management* 30, 615–628.

Weed, M. and Bull, C. (2004) *Sports Tourism: Participants, Policy and Providers*. Elsevier Butterworth Heinemann, Oxford, UK.

Wheeler, K. and Nauright, J. (2006) A global perspective on the environmental impact of golf. *Sport in Society* 9, 427–443.

11 Adventure Tourism

RALF BUCKLEY

Learning Objectives

- To understand how the adventure tourism sector operates
- To learn what motivates adventure tourists and their guides
- To discover future trends and opportunities in adventure tourism

Key Concepts

In the commercial tourism industry, the term adventure is used principally to market products which centre on exciting client experiences, most commonly active and outdoors. Product design, scale, geography, infrastructure and prices differ enormously for different activities and market segments (Buckley, 2007). Adventure tourism includes many specialised subsectors (Table 11.1). It also includes products which are principally nature or wildlife-based, but which involve intense emotional experiences, remote locations, or a degree of risk (see Focus Box 1). There are strong overlaps between commercial adventure tourism, individual adventure travel, and non-commercial adventure recreation.

Some commercial adventure tour operators focus on a single activity, either at a single location or a set of different destinations. Others offer a portfolio of adventure activities, either at one icon site or worldwide. A number of tourist destinations promote themselves as adventure capitals, with multiple operators offering different activities at the same place (Buckley, 2006). The degree of integration in ownership and operation of transport, accommodation and activity components also varies greatly within the sector.

Adventure tourism has substantial cross-linkages with the clothing, entertainment, equipment manufacturing and property development sectors (Buckley, 2003, 2010a). The global scale of adventure tourism depends on exactly what is included or excluded, and on accounting approaches adopted, but annual turnover is estimated at around US$ one trillion (Buckley, 2009).

Major Factors

The adventure tourism sector is shaped by two major factors, reflecting demand and supply respectively. The first factor is increasing urbanisation in wealthier nations whose citizens have both time and resources to engage in commercial tourism. This includes newly wealthy market segments in newly industrialised nations such as the BRICS group (Brazil, Russia, India, China and South Africa) (Buckley, 1998; Buckley *et al.*, 2015). This urbanisation has created growing demand for outdoor experiences, which provide both individual excitement and social capital, supporting a commercial industry which provides the expertise, logistics, equipment and safety for such experiences.

The second major factor is geography, both physical and human. Natural environment, terrain and climate determine the best locations for different adventure activities at different levels of skill and difficulty (Buckley, 2006, 2010a). Human geography, including population, infrastructure and politics, determines how many potential clients can get to each site at what cost. Broadly, the adventure tourism industry includes high-volume short-duration products, commonly also low-skill and low-price, near to major population centres (Table 11.2); and low-volume, longer-duration products, typically high-skill and high-priced, in more remote locations (Fig. 11.1).

The industry can be seen as a pyramid, with a high-volume, low-skill, low-priced base supporting successively lower-volume, higher-skill and higher-priced components (Fig. 11.2). The apex consists of highly expensive, highly skilled one-off expeditions or extreme adventure sports endeavours, many of them sponsored, televised, and used to market products such as energy drinks which are not themselves part of the tourism sector. Similar approaches

Table 11.1. Adventure activities. (From Buckley (2006, 2010a))

Abseiling	Ice climbing	Sailing
Aircraft (aerobatic)	Jetboating	Sea kayaking
Ballooning	Kayaking	Shark watching
Blackwater rafting	Kiteboarding	Skiing
Bungee jumping	Langlauf skiing	Skydiving/ parachuting
Caving	Mountain biking	Snowboarding
Diving	Mountaineering	Snowshoeing
Expedition cruises	Off-road 4WD	Surfing
Gliding	Parapente/ paragliding	Whale watching
Hang gliding	Quad biking/ATV	Whitewater kayaking
Heliski/boarding	River expeditions	Whitewater rafting
Hiking	Rock climbing	Wildlife watching
Horse riding	Sailboarding	Zorbing

were used historically in tobacco advertising (Buckley, 2003). Whilst these linkages have long been apparent (Buckley, 2003), the details of financial flows, cross-ownership structures and competitive manoeuvring do not seem to have been investigated systematically.

Similarly, over recent decades, large-scale fixed-site adventure tourism corporations, such as ski resorts and yachting marinas, have changed their business models to rely much less on the activity itself, e.g. through lift ticket sales or berth rentals, and much more on capital gains through property development and real estate sales (Buckley, 2006).

Motivations

The motivations of adventure tourists have been studied quite intensively, and this field of research remains very active currently. Different individuals may have different motivations for different activities at different times, and any one individual may also have a combination of different motivations simultaneously. At least 14 major categories of motivations (Table 11.3) have been identified for people to take part in adventure tourism activities (Buckley, 2012). Commonly, these are divided into external or social motivations relating principally to interactions with other people either during a tour or after it ends; and internal or psychological motivations relating principally to emotional rewards. For the former, there are literatures relating to social capital

and so-called bragging rights; for the latter, there is an extensive literature addressing concepts such as flow, peak experience, thrill, embodiment, rush, fear and joy (Faullant et al., 2011; Buckley, 2012, 2015, 2016; Kerr and Houge Mackenzie, 2012; Schneider and Vogt, 2012; Tsaur et al., 2012; Carnicelli-Filho, 2013; Chen and Petrick, 2013; Tsaur et al., 2013; Hosany et al., 2014; Pomfret and Bramwell, 2014).

Interactions

Providing an adventure experience for an individual tour client typically involves a very large number of organisations and individuals, and successful interactions between each of these are critical to client safety and satisfaction (Buckley, 2010b; Deemer, 2014). Some of these components and interactions apply across all subsectors of the tourism industry: for example, the logistics of tourist transport, accommodation and catering; the legal aspects of permits and insurance; the details of product design, marketing and distribution; and quality control measures to provide service and satisfaction. Also in this category are the many interactions between primary retail tour operators and their suppliers and subcontractors, which reflect the business structure of the tourism industry.

Some aspects apply across outdoor tourism more broadly, such as dealings with landowners and land management agencies to provide access, licences and emergency services for adventure activities. Such arrangements sometimes involve conflicts between different user groups, e.g. between different activities, or between commercial tour operators and private recreational groups carrying out the same activity at the same site. There is an extensive literature on the origins, asymmetries and resolution of such conflicts. Many such studies are for competing recreational uses of public lands, but the types of interactions involved also apply for commercial adventure tourism (Buckley, 2010a; Newsome et al., 2011; Serenari et al., 2013; Newsome, 2014).

Once an adventure tour is under way, there is a separate set of interactions between the individuals involved. This includes interactions amongst the guides, interactions amongst the clients, and interactions between the guides and the clients. One component of such interactions, namely health and safety communications, was examined by Buckley (2010b) for the whitewater rafting and kayaking sector. A related component, namely the emotional experiences of guides, both in dealing with each

Focus Box 1: Shark watching

Different divers focus on different marine wildlife, from the tiny centimetre-long pink pygmy seahorse to whales and whale sharks. There is no official 'Big Five' of the underwater world, but at least on commercial dive tours, most instructors will point out whales and dolphins, turtles, and rays and sharks whenever they appear. Of course, there are many different species in each of these groups. Surface-based whale watching has a substantial commercial history in many parts of the world. More recently, commercial shark watching has grown greatly in popularity, with free-diving and cage-diving options on offer for different species and locations. Individual sharks are worth orders of magnitude more economically through dive tourism than through commercial fishing or shark finning. There is even a guide book to shark watching (Carwardine and Watterson, 2002). The shark watching tour industry has been summarised by Buckley (2010b). The different shark species watchable in different parts of the world are summarised in the table below, which is based on data from Carwardine and Watterson (2002).

Distribution of shark species watched by divers. (Data from Carwardine and Watterson (2002), pp. 89–139, and Buckley (2010a))

Shark species	Europe and UK	America and Caribbean	Middle East and North Africa	East and South Africa	Australia and NZ	Asia and Pacific Islands
Ragged-tooth		*	*	*	*	*
Thresher			*			*
Basking	*					
Mako	*	*			*	
Great white		*		*	*	
Scalloped hammerhead		*	*	*		*
Great hammerhead		*		*	*	*
Caribbean reef		*				
Ocean whitetip		*	*		*	
Silky		*	*			
Dusky		*				
Galapagos		*			*	
Grey reef		*	*		*	*
Silvertip		*	*		*	*
Blacktip reef		*	*	*	*	*
Bull		*		*		*
Bronze whaler		*		*	*	*
Lemon		*				
Tiger		*		*	*	*
Whitetip reef		*	*		*	*
Blue	*	*			*	
Whale		*		*	*	*
Nurse		*				
Zebra/Leopard				*	*	*
Horn		*				
Tawny		*				*

other and in dealing with clients, has been examined recently by Kerr and Houge Mackenzie (2012), Sohn and Lee (2012), Carnicelli-Filho (2013), and Tsaur and Lin (2014). In summary, guides are expected to display only upbeat, confident and positive emotions to clients, no matter what they may feel internally; and they are expected to manage or choreograph the emotions of their clients, so that the clients experience excitement but not panic. It is because of these various interpersonal interactions that adventure tour guides require so-called soft or people skills as well as hard activity skills.

Table 11.2. Activities at selected adventure destinations. (From Buckley (2006))

	Climbing	Ski	Rafting	Jetboat	Hiking	Biking	Horse ride	ORV tour	Helirides	Hang-gliding	Balloon	Skydive	Bungee	Diving	Sea kayak	Surf/sailboard
Queenstown, New Zealand		*	*	*	*	*	*		*	*	*	*	*			
Banff, Canada	*	*	*		*	*	*	*	*	*	*					
Bozeman, USA	*	*	*		*	*	*				*	*				
Interlaken, Switzerland	*	*	*		*	*	*			*	*	*	*		*	
Chamonix, France	*	*	*		*	*					*					
Kathmandu, Nepal	*		*		*	*	*									
Victoria Falls, Zambia			*	*			*		*	*			*			
Moab, USA	*	*	*		*	*	*	*	*		*	*				
Cairns, Australia		*						*			*	*	*	*		
Pacific Harbour, Fiji		*												*	*	*

Case study 1: Expansion of adventure tourism activities in the boardsports sector

Many commercial adventure tourism activities and products are based on boardsports. These include: skiing and snowboarding, surfing and stand-up paddleboarding, and sailboarding and kiteboarding. In the countries where they originated, skiing and surfing have long histories, but as worldwide commercial adventure tourism activities, their histories are quite brief. Snowboards, sailboards, kiteboards and stand-up paddleboards are even more recent in origin. The success, spread and ultimate scale of these new activities depend partly on cost and accessibility, but also on how easy they are to learn. The number of snowboarders rapidly overtook the number of skiers at many ski resorts worldwide, for example, but snowboarding has not replaced skiing, and the two coexist on the same slopes. The growth of snowboarding provided a major economic boost to ski resort corporations, since it greatly expanded client numbers, particularly in younger demographic groups. Snowboarding also provided new economic opportunities in equipment manufacture, with new companies such as Burton gaining global recognition. Snowboard design and technology also contributed to advances in ski equipment, notably the introduction of sidecut skis.

The evolution of surfboard design has been dependent on new materials and on increasing demand, which can support capital investment in more expensive production techniques. The earliest surfboards in Hawaii were long, finless and wooden, with a rectangular cross-section. These gave way to individually shaped foam and fibreglass boards, and thence to mass-produced carbon fibre boards. Plan shapes, cross-sections, and number of fins have diversified greatly. Sailboard construction, in contrast, started with blow-moulded plastic one-design, and branched out to include carbon/Kevlar construction for wave-jumping and speed-record boards, whilst retaining mass-produced plastic boards for the much larger flat-water sailboard market. Mast joints evolved from hinges to flexible couplings, masts from single-piece fixed-length construction to multi-piece adjustable-length, booms from fixed-length wooden to adjustable-length aluminium alloy, and sails from sailcloth to Mylar panels. In areas suitable for kiteboarding, sailboarding has fallen somewhat in popularity; but globally, it is a very high-volume activity, particularly popular on inland lakes in Europe.

Kiteboarding is more recent in origin, and has the advantage that the boards are much smaller and there is no mast, so kiteboarding equipment is easily transportable. It does require a degree of learned skill, and there is the potential for injury, so it is a 'serious leisure' (Stebbins, 1982) activity rather than a mass holiday option. It is a high-adrenaline activity, however, with indefinite opportunities for skill progression. As a result, it has grown very rapidly in popularity at both ocean and inland destinations, with or without surf. Numbers of commercial kiteboard tour operators have grown correspondingly, from almost none a

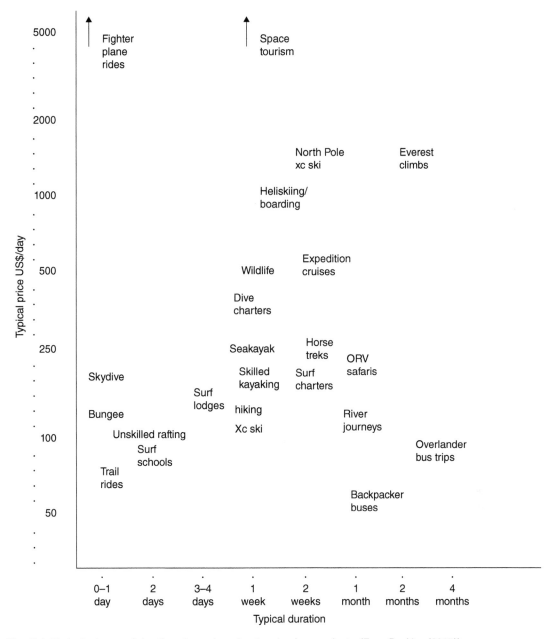

Fig. 11.1. Typical prices and durations for major adventure tourism products. (From Buckley (2006))

few years ago, to hundreds currently. Kiteboard tour destinations include well known high-wind sites such as Tarifa in Spain, oceanic islands such as Australia's Cocos and Lord Howe Islands, and newly developing destinations such as Hainan in China.

Stand-up paddle boards have entered the board-sports adventure tourism market at much the same time as kiteboards, but appeal to a far broader demographic. There are a few highly skilled individuals who ride these boards on large and potentially dangerous waves at famous surf breaks, and others

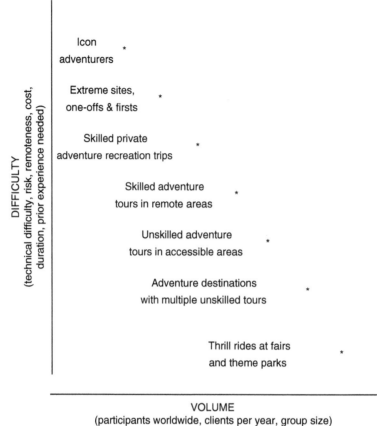

Fig. 11.2. The adventure activity pyramid: volume *vs* difficulty. (From Buckley (2006))

who paddle them down rivers more commonly frequented by whitewater kayakers. By far the majority of stand-up paddleboard sales, however, are to relatively unskilled individuals who want to paddle them on flat water, principally for fitness. In contrast to kiteboards, flat-water stand-up paddleboarding is available as an unskilled home or holiday activity to anyone with basic fitness and capability. Paddleboards are now manufactured in many different shapes and sizes, and most are inconveniently large, though not impossible, to transport as passenger baggage. Paddleboard rentals, however, are now available at many relevant tourist destinations. There are also inflatable paddleboards, constructed of the same materials as whitewater rafts and able to maintain a high degree of rigidity. These, however, are not yet available in high performance designs.

Overall, therefore, during the past couple of decades, the scale and diversity of boardsports in the adventure tourism subsector has grown greatly.

Historically, boardsports started solely with individual skiing and later surfing, and both of these were very different from modern variants. Early skiers used long wooden skis, tarred and waxed, with hiking boots, cable bindings and a single pole, illustrated by Fiennes (2011). Early surfers used very long plank-like wooden boards designed only to go straight down a wave and ride the whitewater into shore. The modern repertoire of manoeuvres was undreamt of. In a second phase, skiing grew in complexity from an individual backcountry activity, to mountain clubs with ski tows, thence to commercial ski lifts, ski resorts and now the very large mountain resort-residential developments which characterise the industry, and cater for snowboarders as well as skiers. Surfing and related activities have also grown rapidly, though following a different trajectory. Surfboards have evolved greatly in design and construction, and the number of surfers, surfing destinations, and commercial surf tourism

R. Buckley

Table 11.3. Motivations for adventure activities. (From Buckley (2012))

Internal, performance of activity

Thrill	Adrenalin, excitement
Fear	Overcoming fear
Control	Maintain physical and mental control of one's body
Skills	Using expertise to perform very difficult tasks
Achieve	Overcoming challenges to reach difficult goals
Fitness	Activity simply as a way to keep physically fit
[Risk]	[Danger as a direct motivation]

Internal/external, place in nature

Nature	Appreciation of beauty
Art	Perception of activity as artistic
Spirit	Activity as spiritual experience

External, social position

Friends	Enjoyment in sharing an activity with others
Image	Enhancing how one is perceived by others
Escape	A change from routine of home or work
[Compete]	[Competition against others]

Note: for those items shown in square brackets [ ], some studies did identify these factors as motivations, but others specifically excluded them – that is, participants explicitly denied that they were motivated by risk or competition respectively.

operators have all expanded greatly. This growth has been boosted still further through the addition of sailboards, kiteboards and stand-up paddleboards, all of which support large markets at inland and flat-water sites as well as coastal, island and surfing destinations. Links into the clothing, soft-drink, entertainment and advertising industries have strengthened, and boardsports activities have moved from an individual fringe or niche occupation, to a mainstream component of the adventure tourism sector.

Case study 2: Packaging heliski tours

Heliskiing and heliboarding are the top tier of the commercial ski tourism industry, providing clients with untracked powder snow at iconic ski destinations. Heliskiing is expensive, so clients must necessarily be relatively wealthy; and to make the expenditure worthwhile, they also need to be skilled skiers or snowboarders. Heliski tour operators worldwide are therefore essentially competing for the same relatively limited market. Part of this competition is

simply through snow quality and reliability: some areas are more famous than others. Part, however, is through service, safety and product packaging.

The principal differences between packages are firstly in length, i.e. the number of days skiing; and secondly in the inclusions and exclusions, what is paid as part of the package, and what is payable as extras. Broadly, there are three main categories: half-day to one-day introductory packages based at or near high-volume ski resorts; multi-day packages based at dedicated heliski lodges, for experienced clients; and various forms of exclusive, exotic or charter-based packages aimed at the most wealthy clients. Some operators offer products at all three levels.

At the introductory level, many packages are sold by number of runs, where a run is a single descent. This allows the operator to make each run short, in vertical metres, and hence cheap in helicopter time and fuel. These introductory packages typically include lunch, a shuttle pick-up, and use of avalanche transceivers, but not accommodation or ski rental. Most include three runs before lunch; and if enough clients are keen, they can purchase further runs in the afternoon. Marketing of these packages focuses principally on persuading resort skiers that heliskiing is within their expertise and budget.

The multi-day packages, which form the mainstay of the heliski industry, are commonly sold by total vertical metres rather than number of runs, and they are much more inclusive than the introductory packages. Whilst there are a few 4-day packages, the majority are 6 or 6.5 day packages based in dedicated lodges which in winter are accessible only by helicopter. They run shuttles on a 7-day rotation to bring clients in and take them out. The package price includes: a guaranteed minimum vertical metres of skiing or snowboarding; accommodation and meals; and in some cases, use of powder skis or snowboards.

Packages may differ in: the level of luxury in the ski lodge; the number of groups assigned to each helicopter; the number of guides with each group; minor inclusions and exclusions such as ski or snowboard tuning, guest laundry, etc.; loyalty programmes for multiple repeat clients; and perhaps most importantly, the number of vertical metres included in the package. For the world's two largest heliski operators, both based in the Canadian Rockies, one has historically offered a fixed quota of vertical metres skied, with extra charges if that quota is surpassed; whilst the other has offered unlimited vertical metres, but at a slightly higher price. In practice, however, there are many factors restricting the total vertical metres skiable in 6 days. Some, such as hours of daylight and snow and weather conditions, are outside the operator's control; others, such as the hours actually spent skiing, and the time for helicopter turnarounds, are subject to a certain degree of adjustment. Unlimited, in this context therefore, does not mean that the clients can ski as many vertical metres as they want, but simply that the pricing structure does not depend on the number of vertical metres actually skied.

At the luxury level, there are three main distinctions from the basic multi-day packages as above. The first is helicopter access. In luxury packages, the clients essentially charter a helicopter for their own exclusive use, rather than sharing it with two or sometimes three other groups. The guides and helicopter pilots are very efficient at cycling several groups simultaneously so there is minimal waiting time at pick-up points, but one way they do this is by stopping at intervals during each descent, to re-group. With a dedicated helicopter and a well matched group, if snow conditions are safe, then guides can pick long runs which the group can ski top to bottom without stopping, knowing that their helicopter will immediately collect them wherever they decide to halt.

The next level of luxury is a dedicated lodge as well as a dedicated helicopter, so that the group does not mix at all with mainstream clients, and can be provided with higher levels of service. In addition to larger and more luxurious rooms, this would typically include an a-la-carte menu rather than a buffet, and vintage wines included rather than purchased separately. These dedicated lodges may also include other activities such as indoor climbing walls in case there are days when the weather makes skiing impossible.

A third approach, for particularly wealthy clients, is to base the heliski operation on a luxury ocean-going yacht with its own helicopter. This allows the guides and clients to access slopes and runs which may never have been skied before. However, it also means that there is a reduced opportunity to follow the build-up of the snowpack during the season. At the lodge-based operations, guides can go out every morning before the clients, to dig snow pits and check avalanche risk. They also hold safety debriefings every evening, where they share information from the day's skiing and plan the following day. Over the course of the season, this gives them a detailed knowledge of potential avalanche risk in different sections of their skiing terrain. Specialised or exploratory operations which move into new terrain each day either from a boat, or by transporting a camp and mobile helicopter fuel tanks, will still dig snow pits every day, but do not have the same opportunity to build up a comprehensive picture of the season's snowfall and its subsequent metamorphosis into snowpack layers.

In addition to these differences in levels of luxury, different heliski operations offer different measures for avalanche safety. All of them equip their clients with avalanche transceivers. Most conduct training and practice search sessions using these transceivers, before boarding the helicopter for the first run. Some of the single-day operators, however, do not; and even for the multi-day operators, these practice sessions differ in thoroughness. Speed is critical in any avalanche rescue, so as a test, a guide will generally bury a transceiver in snow and require the clients to find it within a short and specified time period. In each heligroup, the guide will carry a radio, and also a small backpack containing a collapsible avalanche probe and a collapsible snow shovel. Some heliski operators check that their clients know how to use the radio, but others do not. Depending on the size of the helicopters used and hence the number of clients and guides in each, each group may have either one avalanche pack or two. If there are two, some operators have the second pack rotated between individual clients in each group, with the guide skiing at the front of the group, and that client skiing at the back. Other operators, in the same terrain and with the same helicopters, provide two guides per group, each with an avalanche pack. This increases safety, but also cost.

At least one operator provides specially designed and constructed avalanche packs to every client. These packs, which are firmly attached with a thigh and shoulder harness, contain avalanche wings as well as probe and shovel. These wings are like giant fabric balloons, operated by a small compressed air bottle, which expand very rapidly from the sides of the backpack when a ripcord is pulled. They are intended to increase the buoyancy of a skier caught in an avalanche, so that they are more likely to remain near the surface where injury risks are lower and rescue opportunities greater. The same company also fits tiny individually coded electronic responder devices in its avalanche transceivers, which enable a buried skier to be located and identified accurately from a helicopter hovering above. For skiers and snowboarders trapped in avalanches, the most immediate risk is suffocation, and there is a proprietary breathing device, the Avalung, which assists in extracting air from within the snowpack. Historically, it was up to individual skiers whether or not to purchase these devices; but currently, some heliski operators issue them to their clients as part of the package. Overall, there is a trend for new safety devices, once tested, to spread gradually throughout the sector, so that safety as a whole improves incrementally. During this process, however, differentials in safety practices between operators provide an important aspect of product differentiation.

Impacts and Insights

The social, economic and environmental impacts of adventure tourism can be considerable. Depending on exactly what is included, the annual global turnover of the outdoor tourism sector, much of it adventure-based, is estimated at around US$ one trillion (Buckley, 2009). There are many estimates of local economic scale, turnover and impact for different areas and activities. At some tourist destinations, the so-called adventure capitals, the entire local economy is supported through a portfolio of commercial adventure tourism activities. There are also many more destinations and local communities which rely heavily on a single adventure tourism activity such as skiing, surfing, whale watching or rock climbing. Seasonality, economic scale, employment and entrepreneurial activities, and economic multiplier effects may differ considerably between different destinations and communities.

Social impacts of adventure tourism also depend greatly on the destination and activity. New employment opportunities provide prosperity for some, and may indirectly fund social services for others, but can also introduce inequities and conflicts. The transfer of tacit knowledge between international visitors and local residents (Buckley and Ollenburg, 2013) can also generate new social opportunities and modify social structures. In many adventure tourism sectors with strong seasonality, skilled guides form a specialised social community with its own subculture, which maintains communications as it moves between sites and seasons. Commercial adventure tourism operators rely on this social coherence to provide skilled staff when they are needed (Buckley, 2006).

The environmental impacts of adventure tourism and adventure recreation, particularly in public protected areas, have also been studied extensively (Buckley, 2004, 2011, 2013; Burgin and Hardiman, 2012; Ong and Musa, 2012; Poudel and Nyaupane, 2013). Both the types and intensities of impacts differ greatly between activities and ecosystems, and also depend on season, visitor numbers, group size, infrastructure and equipment, land and visitor management practices, and individual visitor behaviour. There is an extensive literature in this field, commonly referred to as recreation ecology but also including commercial adventure tourism.

Our recent research in adventure tourism has indicated two particular insights which could catalyse significant future research. The first is essentially cultural. Adventure tourism operates within powerful cultural contexts, which differ substantially between countries. Some aspects are very broad, such as what activities, clothing and supervision are considered appropriate for men, women and children of various social, ethnic and religious backgrounds.

Other differences are driven by historical traditions and recent social changes. New wealth in the BRICS nations, as noted above, has increased domestic demand for adventure tourism in those countries, but the types and styles of activities preferred differ between cultures (Buckley *et al.*, 2015). The structures of adventure tourism products in businesses in China, for example, differ greatly from those in Western nations, even within the same subsectors (Buckley *et al.*, 2014a). Cultural differences in tourism interests have been shown for a number of tourism subsectors, and are routinely recognised by commercial tour operators (Buckley and Ollenburg, 2013), but to date have received relatively little attention in adventure tourism research.

The second insight relates to the emotional aspects of adventure tourist motivations. Emotional outcomes are not their only motivations, but especially for more highly skilled and specialised tours and tour clients, they may be the most significant. It is only recently, however, that these emotional experiences have been addressed directly through ethnographic, autoethnographic and other psychological research. Some of these experiences can be very intense, including fear of imminent death.

Adventure tourism thus provides opportunities for these very fundamental aspects of human experience to be studied in ethically and experimentally tractable circumstances (Buckley, 2014a). Such questions include not only the relationships between emotional and psychological experiences such as fear and joy (Faullant *et al.*, 2011), flow and thrill (Buckley, 2012), but potentially also more fundamental questions such as human perception of time (Arstila, 2012; Buckley, 2014b).

Questions

1. What distinguishes and defines adventure tourism, and why, and how? Is it the specific activities or setting, or is it factors such as risk or thrill?
2. Not everyone enjoys adventure, but some people are highly addicted. Where would you see yourself on that scale, and why?
3. How has adventure tourism evolved over recent decades, and how do you think it will change in the next few decades?

Further Reading

Beard, C., Swarbrooke, J., Leckie, S. and Pomfret, G. (2012) *Adventure Tourism: The New Frontier*. Routledge, London, UK.

Buckley, R.C. (2010a) *Adventure Tourism Management*. Elsevier, Oxford, UK.

Buckley, R.C. (2006) *Adventure Tourism*. CAB International, Wallingford, UK.

References

Arstila, V. (2012) Time slows down during accidents. *Frontiers in Psychology* 3, 196, DOI: 10.3389/fpsyg.2012.00196.

Buckley, R.C. (1998) Ecotourism megatrends. *Australian International Business Review*, December 1998, 52–54.

Buckley, R.C. (2003) Adventure tourism and the clothing, fashion and entertainment industries. *Journal of Ecotourism* 2, 126–134.

Buckley, R.C. (ed.) (2004) *Environmental Impacts of Ecotourism*. CAB International, Wallingford, UK, p. 389.

Buckley, R.C. (2006) *Adventure Tourism*. CAB International, Wallingford, UK.

Buckley, R.C. (2007) Adventure tourism products: price, duration, size, skill, remoteness. *Tourism Management* 28, 1428–1433.

Buckley, R.C. (2009) *Ecotourism: Principles and Practices*. CAB International, Wallingford, UK.

Buckley, R.C. (2010a) *Adventure Tourism Management*. Elsevier, Oxford, UK.

Buckley, R.C. (2010b) Communications in adventure tour products: health and safety in rafting and kayaking. *Annals of Tourism Research* 37, 315–332.

Buckley, R.C. (2011) Tourism and environment. *Annual Review of Environment and Resources* 36, 397–416.

Buckley, R.C. (2012) Rush as a key motivation in skilled adventure tourism: resolving the risk recreation paradox. *Tourism Management* 33(4), 961–970.

Buckley, R.C. (2013) Next steps in recreation ecology. *Frontiers in Ecology and the Environment* 11(8), 399.

Buckley, R.C. (2014a) Adventure tourism as a research tool in non-tourism disciplines. *Tourism Recreation Research* 39(1), 39–49.

Buckley, R.C. (2014b) Slow time perception can be learned. *Frontiers in Psychology* 5, 209, DOI: 10.3389/fpsyg.2014.00209.

Buckley, R.C. (2015) Adventure thrills are addictive. *Frontiers in Psychology* 6, 1915.

Buckley, R.C. (2016) Qualitative analysis of emotions: fear and thrill. *Frontiers in Psychology* 7, 1187.

Buckley, R.C. and Ollenburg, C. (2013) Tacit knowledge transfer: cross cultural adventure. *Annals of Tourism Research* 40, 419–422, DOI: 10.1016/j.annals.2012.08.010.

Buckley, R.C., McDonald, K., Duan, L., Sun, L. and Chen, L.X. (2014a) Chinese model for mass adventure tourism. *Tourism Management* 44, 5–13.

Buckley, R.C., Gretzel, U., Scott, D., Weaver, D. and Becken, S. (2015) Tourism megatrends. *Tourism Recreation Research* 40.

Burgin, S. and Hardiman, N. (2012) Extreme sports in natural areas: looming disaster or a catalyst for a paradigm shift in land use planning? *Journal of Environmental Planning and Management* 55(7), 921–940.

Carnicelli-Filho, S. (2013) The emotional life of adventure guides. *Annals of Tourism Research* 43, 192–209.

Carwardine, M. and Watterson, K. (2002) *The Shark-watcher's Handbook: A Guide to Sharks and Where to See Them*. Princeton University Press, Princeton, NJ, USA.

Chen, C.-C. and Petrick, J.F. (2013) Health and wellness benefits of travel experiences: a literature review. *Journal of Travel Research* 52(6), 709–719.

Deemer, E. (2014) In search of the snow leopard: a new take on conservation-based ecotourism for Natural Habitat Adventures. *Journal of Ecotourism* 1–7, DOI: 10.1080/14724049.2014.937439.

Faullant, R., Matzler, K. and Mooradian, T.A. (2011) Personality, basic emotions, and satisfaction: primary emotions in the mountaineering experience. *Tourism Management* 32, 1423–1430.

Fiennes, R. (2011) *Captain Scott*. Hodder & Stoughton, London, UK.

Hosany, S., Prayag, G., Deesilatham, S., Causevic, S. and Odeh, K. (2014) Measuring tourists' emotional experiences: further validation of the destination emotion scale. *Journal of Travel Research* 1–14, DOI: 10.1177/0047287514522878.

Kerr, J.H. and Houge Mackenzie, S. (2012) Multiple motives for participating in adventure sports. *Psychology of Sport and Exercise* 13, 649–657.

Newsome, D. (2014) Appropriate policy development and research needs in response to adventure racing in protected areas. *Biological Conservation* 171, 259–269.

R. Buckley

Newsome, D., Lacroix, C. and Pickering, C. (2011) Adventure racing events in Australia: context, assessment and implications for protected area management. *Australian Geographer* 42(4), 403–418, DOI: 10.1080/00049182.2012.619955.

Ong, T.F. and Musa, G. (2012) Examining the influences of experience, personality and attitude on SCUBA divers' underwater behaviour: a structural equation model. *Tourism Management* 33, 1521–1534.

Pomfret, G. and Bramwell, B. (2014) The characteristics and motivational decisions of outdoor adventure tourists: a review and analysis. *Current Issues in Tourism* 1–32, DOI: 10.1080/13683500.2014.925430.

Poudel, S. and Nyaupane, G.P. (2013) The role of interpretative tour guiding in sustainable destination management: a comparison between guided and nonguided tourists. *Journal of Travel Research* DOI: 10.1177/0047287513478496.

Schneider, P.P. and Vogt, C.A. (2012) Applying the 3M model of personality and motivation to adventure travelers. *Journal of Travel Research* 51(6), 704–716.

Serenari, C., Bosak, K. and Attarian, A. (2013) Cross-cultural efficacy of American low-impact programs: a comparison between Garhwal guide beliefs on environmental behavior and American outdoor travel norms. *Tourism Management* 34, 50–60.

Sohn, H.-K. and Lee, T.J. (2012) Relationship between HEXACO personality factors and emotional labour of service providers in the tourism industry. *Tourism Management* 33, 116–125.

Stebbins, R.A. (1982) Serious leisure: a conceptual statement. *The Pacific Sociological Review* 25(2), 251–272.

Tsaur, S.-H. and Lin, W.-R. (2014) Hassles of tour leaders. *Tourism Management* 45, 28–38.

Tsaur, S.-H., Yen, C-. and Hsiao, S-. (2012) Transcendent experience, flow and happiness for mountain climbers. *International Journal of Tourism Research* 15(4), 360–374.

Tsaur, S.-H., Lin, W.-R. and Liu, J.-S. (2013) Sources of challenge for adventure tourists: scale development and validation. *Tourism Management* 38, 85–93.

12 Shopping Tourism

Dallen J. Timothy

Learning Objectives

- To understand the importance of shopping as a tourist activity
- To understand the difference between shopping tourism and tourist shopping
- To learn about current and futuristic management and research trends in tourism and retail
- To recognise the variety of shopping types and activities related to tourism

Introduction

Retailing is one of the most ubiquitous elements of tourist destinations, and shopping is one of the most common activities undertaken by travellers. All destinations offer some form of retailing, and most regional plans include shopping opportunities for tourists, who tend to spend more money while travelling than they do at home. Tourists spend billions of dollars each year on shopping, beyond the cost of the trip itself. While most shopping research focuses on souvenirs, evidence suggests that tourists also spend considerable time and money in non-traditional tourism retail venues, such as department stores, outlet malls, supermarkets, farmers' markets and big-box/do-it-yourself stores. The economic importance of tourist shopping cannot be overstated, and the social and experiential significance of shopping for tourists is profound (Jansen-Verbeke, 1991; Coles, 2004; Timothy, 2005).

This chapter provides an overview of emerging trends in tourism and shopping research. These include demand characteristics, retail as a branding mechanism, unconventional retail spaces, the importance of souvenirs, the effects of globalisation, and shopping as cultural experience. Several of these issues were discussed elsewhere (Timothy, 2014), but this chapter contributes additional insight into these and other emerging trends that have heretofore not been well documented in the research literature, and concludes by summarising several gaps in knowledge that ought to be of interest to tourism scholars.

Key Concepts

With the 19th-century industrialisation of the Western world, people spent increasingly less time on survival and more time in leisure pursuits. This trend resulted in what Veblen (1934) termed the 'leisure class', for which fine wines, expensive foods and fine apparel became central to their lives. The leisure class has continued to grow with higher education levels and standards of living, although it now also includes the middle class. This materialisation process ushered in the age of mass consumption.

Two concrete manifestations of mass consumption are travel and shopping. These activities are complementary and relate in several ways. First, when people travel, they have a tendency to behave differently than they would at home (Mathieson and Wall, 1982; Carr, 2002), including in their patterns of consumption. For instance, conservative spending habits and inhibitions about high prices give way to hedonic, frivolous shopping that might normally be considered wasteful or excessive. At one extreme is the spontaneity exhibited by tourists who impulsively purchase a timeshare after attending a sales meeting (Woods, 2001). Simpler examples include paying too much for a drink, or purchasing unnecessary products.

Second, some consumers who normally enjoy shopping might have a more intense retail experience in a destination than they would at home, and those who ordinarily do not enjoy shopping at home might enjoy it while traveling (Timothy, 2005). Retail environments, merchandise selection and the freedoms associated with time and money during holidays can affect shopping tendencies for better or for worse.

Third, shopping tendencies or interests can determine destination choice. Shopping may provide the primary impetus for taking a trip. Certain places (e.g. New York, Paris and Dubai) have become destinations for groups or individuals whose main purpose is to shop (Henderson *et al.*, 2011; Kwek *et al.*, 2014). Package tours from Asia to the Mall of America or West Edmonton Mall have long been important products in North America (Timothy, 2005). Weekend spending jaunts in Europe became popular with low-cost airline flights between major European cities.

Fourth, retailing can also determine people's destination behaviour. As noted above, shopping can be a main travel motive, but shopping also provides an alternative or secondary activity for tourists once they are already in the destination for other reasons (Timothy, 2005). Finally, the previous points have elucidated various leisure shopping patterns, but utilitarian retailing is also an important part of tourism – before the trip, during the trip and after the trip. Pre-trip purchases (e.g. swimsuits, sunscreen, clothing) help travellers prepare for a journey (Coles, 2004). Likewise, many holiday-makers shop at supermarkets, pharmacies or department stores for practical items that become necessary during the trip.

Major Factors

The discussion so far has provided a different way of looking at the multifarious relationships between tourism and shopping, although it is clearly not an exhaustive list. In addition to understanding experiences, there are several trends and major factors that should be emphasised in any discussion about contemporary shopping.

Demand characteristics

Retail demand and its market characteristics are the most researched element of shopping and tourism, stemming from broader consumer behaviour traditions. Many studies have evaluated the relationships between intentions to shop, satisfaction, preferences, motivations and behaviours, and diverse intrinsic characteristics (e.g. age, gender, expenditures and reason for travelling) and extrinsic variables (e.g. quality of customer service, merchandise variety, retail environment, prices and destination attributes)(e.g. Dmitrovic and Vida, 2007; Tosun *et al.*, 2007; LeHew and Wesley, 2007; Kim *et al.*, 2011; Kinley *et al.*, 2012; Lehto *et al.*, 2013; Han *et al.*, 2014; Lin and Mao, 2015).

Predictably, Kim *et al.* (2011) found that based on extrinsic and intrinsic variables, satisfied Japanese shopper tourists, including those who were happy with the merchandise they bought and who spent the most money, had higher intentions to return to the destination than other tourists. Bojanic's (2011) study concluded that family lifecycle and age help determine the types of shops visited during holidays and the level of daily expenditures. Yüksel (2009) identified the physical shop environment, and Jones (1999) found attentive sales staff as enhancing the quality of the shopping experience.

These studies are important in establishing baseline knowledge about tourist shopping characteristics, behaviours and intensions. However, of greater concern are meta-factors that affect entire population cohorts or destinations more directly and holistically. One such issue is that nationality differences influence tourists' shopping behaviours and patterns (Wong and Law, 2003; Lehto *et al.*, 2013). One recent study (*Tourism Review*, 2014) shows that certain nationalities have different shopping destination preferences; the Chinese prefer Paris and Saudis favour London. This reflects national images of otherness, product offerings and socio-political connectedness between tourists' origins and destinations.

Similarly, much has been written about the reciprocal gift-giving cultures of East Asia and the social obligations associated with returning home with high-quality, name-brand and place-specific gifts for relatives, friends and co-workers (Park, 2000; Hobson and Christensen, 2001; Rosenbaum and Spears, 2005). In the more individualist societies of Europe and North America, socially prescribed gift giving is less important, and as a result, fewer North Americans and Europeans spend as much time and money on shopping as their Asian counterparts do (Timothy, 2005).

Cultural background and nationality may also influence the retail items selected during vacation shopping trips. In a Gambian case study, Thompson and Cutler (1997) discovered different merchandise preferences between tourist nationalities. They found that German tourists prefer bright colours, abstract designs and more frivolous items. British tourists, on the other hand, tend to buy more utilitarian objects such as chess sets and dishes. Scandinavians tended to favour more customary designs which they consider more authentic and local.

It is also important to note that different types of tourists shop for different items, depending on their travel purpose and the destinations or attractions they visit. Mass tourists, for instance, have a tendency to buy mass-produced items that represent iconic attractions (du Cros, 2013). Retailers cater to these consumers by providing superficial symbols that generally lack authenticity but are inexpensive and easy to transport (Paraskevaidis and Andriotis, 2015). Gastronomy enthusiasts are inclined to buy food products, recipe books and cooking accoutrements that will help them relive their experience or replicate something they enjoyed eating. Heritage tourists are known as avid shoppers for items that connect with the cultures of the destination (Timothy, 2011). Sacred souvenirs abound at pilgrimage destinations to help religious tourists remember the sacrosanct places they visited, rekindle the spirit they felt, or continue practising their faith at home (Shackley, 2006; Kaell, 2012).

Retail and shopping as a destination brand

Destinations use icons and images to 'brand' themselves as important places to visit. In doing this, a country or region can create a competitive advantage over other regions and emphasise its distinctiveness. Similarly, shopping has been used in many places as a focus of tourism marketing and has featured prominently in tourism policy making and promotional campaigns (Timothy, 2001; McIntyre, 2012; Lehto *et al.*, 2013; Rabbiosi, 2015). Besides its role as the major air hub of Southeast Asia, Singapore has positioned itself as a shopping hub, often in conjunction with its ease of access and proximity to nearby markets, such as China, Malaysia, Indonesia and Thailand (Henderson *et al.*, 2011).

From a tourism perspective, every place wants to be special, and this is no less true in the context of shopping. Superlatives for locations or buildings, such as the oldest, largest, easternmost, longest or smallest, are a well used means of buttressing a location's position in the world and a way of conveying its uniqueness. Recent years have seen a boom in constructing large-scale shopping malls with places scrambling to be the next 'largest shopping mall in the world' only to be outdone a few years later by a newer and larger retail centre somewhere else. This is nowhere more visible than in Asia and the Middle East (Howard, 2010; Meyer-Ohle, 2014). At the time of writing, the Dubai Mall was the largest shopping mall in the world in total area (1.124 million m²), while the New South China Mall was the largest in leasable space (659,612m²).

While some of the rentable space in many of these emerging megamalls remains empty for years, much of their appeal lies in their reputation as the 'largest', regardless of how this is measured. Part of their size-based appeal derives from other services beyond the shops themselves. Many megamalls now provide entire vacation experiences with self-contained hotels, restaurants, zoos, aquaria, indoor golf, indoor skiing, swimming pools and theatres (Butler, 1991; Goss, 1993).

Besides the well-malled landscapes of China and India, the United Arab Emirates hosts one of the largest critical masses of shopping centres. Shopping has long been an important part of the Dubai experience, even before the construction of its large malls, when it was known for gold bazaars. In 1996, however, Dubai initiated the Dubai Shopping Festival (DSF) to build a network among the city's retailers (malls, stores and traditional souks) and other service providers and to help attract consumers from abroad (Alhosani and Zaidan, 2014; Peter and Anandkumar, 2014). Since that time, the festival alone has drawn between three and four million international shopping enthusiasts each January/February. The 20th anniversary of the DSF was celebrated in January 2015 with citywide concerts, raffles, competitions, discounts and special offers and celebrity appearances. It is a high-end shopping event that draws attention to gold, expensive cars and other extravagances. This festival has been pivotal for the Emirate in branding itself one of the world's premier shopping destinations (Dubai Corporation of Tourism and Commerce, 2015).

Souvenir consumption and meaning

A discussion about shopping would be remiss without alluding to the ubiquitous souvenir. Souvenirs are crucibles of meaning. From the destination's perspective, they reveal much about a region and its values. The French word *souvenir* means a memory, or a remembrance, and thus has been adopted over the centuries to denote items brought home from a trip to help travellers remember their journey. Souvenirs have received considerable research attention since the 1990s, with the primary focus being twofold: souvenirs as meaning makers and descriptions of souvenir merchandise available in various destinations (Timothy, 2005; Swanson and Timothy, 2012).

Globalised shopping

Globalisation entails the world becoming smaller and more accessible to increasing numbers of people. Countries, regions and societies are now better connected economically, socially and politically than at any other time, with salient implications for shopping. One such manifestation is merchandise availability and product diversity, which have improved as a result of reduced trade barriers and multilateral trade agreements.

Internet-based shopping is routine in the developed world for household goods, clothing, electronics, food and even souvenirs. For some people, it has replaced the in-store shopping experience almost entirely with some reasons being tax savings, no need to leave home, not having to deal with crowds of shoppers, and a greater diversity of products than what can fit in a physical store (Cheng et al., 2009).

From a tourism perspective, 'indirect tourism', according to Swanson and Timothy (2012), may occur when consumers are able to purchase souvenirs and other items that represent a destination without having to visit that place. Mail-order shopping has long been available to the masses, and today web-based souvenir shopping is popular. Artworks and artefacts, traditional clothing from native peoples and even iconic foodstuffs can be purchased online from their original sources without the consumer having to visit the place personally.

Migration is an inevitable part of globalisation. With shifts in global economics and geopolitics, migratory patterns change. This not only affects demand for shopping and tourism, as noted earlier, but it also means that the world is more readily available at the threshold of home. Migrants bring the globe to people of the adopted country through ethnic foods and traditions. The proliferation of ethnic restaurants attests to this (Frost and Laing, 2016), each depicting varying degrees of authenticity from the homeland (Molz, 2004; Chhabra et al., 2013). The explosive popularity of immigrant-oriented supermarkets in Europe, Australasia and North America attests to the important impact of migration and diasporic identity in the context of shopping. In many Asian markets in the USA, for example, shoppers can buy not only imported foodstuffs from Asia, but also souvenirs, jewellery, religious icons, incense, clothing and other items as 'indirect tourists'.

Neoliberalisation of international trade and geopolitics is another sign of globalisation. As supranationalism advances, decreasing the barrier effects of national boundaries, together with an increasingly affluent society, people's cross-border mobility is growing exponentially. Higher numbers of people in developing countries are travelling abroad than ever before in history. New markets are emerging, such as the Chinese, who have more freedom to travel now than any previous period. Countries are clamouring to be included on China's Approved Destination List for the potential to attract this increasingly lucrative market segment that appreciates opportunities to shop (Guo et al., 2007; Xu and McGehee, 2012). In fact, the Chinese are now considered the top shopping nationality (Tourism Review, 2014), and the Chinese government has made efforts to curtail outshopping to other countries by increasing import tariffs and reducing import allowances (Upchurch and Liu, 2014).

Shopping as cultural immersion

Multisensory experiences can derive from shopping in a destination. The scents of spices in an Arab market, the sound of traditional Native American music or the cuisines of Southeast Asia can stimulate the desire to purchase spices, musical instruments or foodstuffs to enjoy later (Guttentag, 2009; Jolliffe, 2014). Smelling, hearing or tasting these items following a trip can trigger positive memories and help the consumer relive part of his/her journey (Swanson and Timothy, 2012).

Timothy (2005) noted that not all shopping entails buying tangible products. Instead, the retail experience can include window-shopping or simply eyeing the available merchandise. By observing product diversity, assembly techniques, construction materials and prices one can learn a great deal about the culture of a destination. An observant shopper can have a deep cultural experience if he or she is willing to look beyond the front-row merchandise and see the meanings that souvenirs and non-souvenir products project to potential buyers.

One important aspect of the shopping experience that has not been well researched is haggling with sellers. In some places, haggling is considered part of the culture of shopping, while in other places it may be offensive. Price negotiation is a normative cultural practice in many locales and is part of the travel experience (Hawkins, 2010). For some tourists, bargaining with sellers is part of the fun of being in the marketplace (Wu et al., 2014). Unfortunately, in some cases, the incessant haggling over prices has resulted in ill feelings towards certain tourists (e.g. backpackers) by local residents, where the tourists are seen as cheap and inflexible. While tourists may use price quibbling to receive the cheapest possible price for souvenirs and other retail items, this parsimony often drives a wedge between the travellers and destination residents (Kontogeorgopoulos, 2003; Muzaini, 2006).

Collins-Kreiner and Zins (2011) found that tourists tend to buy fewer souvenirs the more often they travel. Likewise, Smith and Olson (2001) concluded that a consumer sophistication process might unfold when people travel to the same destination on multiple occasions. On their initial visit, tourists typically purchase commonplace and stereotypical items that represent their destination, even if these are blatantly inauthentic and manufactured elsewhere. During repeat visits, however, tourists begin to purchase items that are more meaningful and more closely connected to the destination. On subsequent visits, the tourist begins to feel more at home, develop an attachment to the destination and demonstrate a deeper interest in things beyond the kitsch. This results in changing consumption patterns that expose a deeper immersion into local cultures through increased exposure and sense of belonging.

Motivations

What motivates people to shop while on vacation? It really depends on whether shopping is the primary or a secondary attraction. When people travel for the main purpose of shopping, they are typically motivated by pleasure, cultural experiences, sensory stimulation, economic savings or a combination of these (Timothy, 2005). Efforts to preserve positive memories stimulate shopping for souvenirs that will help people recollect and share their experiences after arriving home. For other people, saving money on their household budget may be the main driver for a trip abroad (Swanson and Timothy, 2012).

Cross-border shopping has been well studied inside and outside of tourism (Dmitrovic and Vida, 2007; Sullivan *et al.*, 2012; Baruca and Zolfagharian, 2013; Chang, 2014; Michalkó *et al.*, 2014) and is often undertaken for a mix of economic and leisure reasons. Cheaper prices, lower taxes, greater product diversity and the recreational appeal of the other side of the border have been shown to be the main motivations for this phenomenon (Timothy and Butler, 1995; Michalkó and Timothy, 2001). Timothy and Butler (1995) argued that the nearer a consumer lives to the borderline itself, the more often he or she will cross, the more ordinary the purchases will be and the less likely the journey is to be leisure oriented. For people who live far from the border,

however, the crossing will likely have a more 'touristic' element, may involve larger purchases and will occur less often. While this generally entails utilitarian shopping for household items, there is often an underlying leisure element, particularly as cross-border shoppers undertake other activities such as sightseeing, sports, dining or other forms of entertainment (Timothy and Butler, 1995).

As a secondary activity, browsing or buying may be a way of using spare time, waiting out a rainstorm or buying gifts for people at home. Nearly all tourists shop at some point on their journeys even if it is not their main purpose. Nonetheless, ancillary shopping is an important activity for the visitors and the communities they visit (Timothy, 2005).

Online shopping has even reached the world of tourism. Motives for tourism-associated online retail are manifold (Swanson and Timothy, 2012). For some travellers, internet shopping provides opportunities to buy something they might have missed while in the destination. Maybe purchasing souvenirs from faraway, remote or exotic places can function as a substitution for actually travelling there. For instance, few people can travel to exotic and less accessible places such as Pitcairn Island, St Helena, Greenland or the Faroe Islands, yet souvenirs and handicrafts from these places are readily available online. Mementos purchased on the web can also serve as an information source or a tool to help plan an upcoming trip.

Interactions

Because it is such a pervasive element of the travel experience, shopping has a wide range of connections to other forms of special interest tourism. One of the most notable is shopping and cultural heritage. Past research has shown that heritage tourists tend to spend more than many other niche markets, owing to their generally higher standard of living, higher level of education, and their desire to buy memorable and authentic keepsakes (Timothy, 2011). Heritage sites and museums have earnestly begun to capitalise on this notion and see retailing as a crucial supplementary source of income beyond the expected mineral exports at a mine or entrance fees at an archaeological site. Deeper cuts in public funding, global economic instability for exports and volatile market prices have led many establishments to use souvenir merchandising to supplement their incomes, to justify their continued operation and to raise operational revenue (Swanson and Timothy, 2012; Brown, 2013).

Focus Box 1: Cross-border shopping at the French–Spanish border

People crossing national borders to shop is a common phenomenon all over the world. Along the boundary of Spain and France in the Pyrenees Mountains, there has long been a tradition of trans-boundary commerce. In recent decades, the retail movement has primarily been a one-way southward flow of French consumers crossing into Spain to shop. This pattern reflects a diversity of products, lower taxes and cheaper retail prices on the Spanish side of the border on items such as alcohol, tobacco, pharmaceuticals, toys, leather goods and grocery items (Village du Perthus, 2016).

Two of the most popular venues for this borderland retail phenomenon are located on opposite ends of the Spanish–French border. At the western end near the Atlantic Ocean is the shopping village of Ibardin (Fig. 12.1). On the eastern side, near the Mediterranean Sea, is the divided village of Le Perthus/Els Limits. At Ibardin, the border runs through the village's only road. At Le Perthus, the border parallels the main road along its eastern edge. The Spanish sides of the street in both places are densely populated with large supermarkets, butcheries, wine shops, perfumeries, restaurants, tobacconists and souvenir stores (Leizaola, 2006). On the French sides of the streets are sparse clusters of tattoo parlours, hair salons and small-scale coffee shops. The economic well-being of both communities depends entirely on the phenomenon of cross-border shopping.

While utilitarian shopping motivates much of this French trans-frontier mobility, the leisure element of being in Spain for a day or overnight has become more prominent. This is evidenced by increasing numbers of restaurants, souvenir shops and recreational activities opening on the Spanish side, as well as growing numbers of French visits to museums and historic sites near the border in Spain (Markuszewska *et al.*, 2016).

Fig. 12.1. At Ibardin, the border is visible in the pavement just left of the centre. The shops on the left are in Spain, the shops in the right are in France. (Source: Dallen J. Timothy)

Even in the context of dark tourism, which is a form of heritage tourism, souvenirs may also tell important stories about tragic events and lives of the people most affected. Souvenirs are made from the Berlin Wall, New York City's Twin Towers, or spent artillery shells from the 1990s Bosnian war. In this unusual way, shopping thus helps negotiate the war heritage narratives of Mostar and Sarajevo, the communist and divided legacy of Germany and the terror attacks on America.

Transit tourism is the form of tourism that occurs largely between the traveller's home and his or her destination. Several sorts of activities occur in transit times and spaces, but shopping is certainly one of the most universal. Train stations, border crossings, airports and motorway rest areas are all part of the tourism system and provide shopping opportunities for travellers. These 'in-between' transit spaces may be considered uninteresting, unmemorable and ephemeral, which is part of the reason they have been neglected in research (Timothy, 2014). Yet, they also provide many opportunities for retail activities. Some airport and rail station transit areas have become such prominent retail venues that they resemble large-scale shopping centres and mega-malls (Hobson, 2000; Cresswell, 2006; Marciniak, 2012) (see Fig. 12.2).

Shopping also intersects with rural tourism and agritourism in various ways, through fairs, farmers' markets, wineries and farm visits. Another is the emergence of rural communities whose extractive resources have either been depleted or whose economies have declined for a different reason. These former resource-dependent villages often target tourism as an economic mainstay. Many small communities have redefined themselves as significant recreational shopping areas in scenic locations with interesting heritages. Getz (1993) termed these settlements 'tourist shopping villages' (TSVs), and they dot the rural and peri-urban landscapes of

Fig. 12.2. In many ways, the Dubai International Airport resembles a large shopping mall. (Source: Dallen J. Timothy)

D.J. Timothy

most developed countries (Murphy *et al.*, 2011; Timothy, 2014) and manifest as craft villages in many less-developed parts of the world.

There is also a clear crossover between shopping and food tourism. Food tourism is becoming a more recognised subsector of tourism itself (Long, 2004; Timothy and Ron, 2013; Stanley and Stanley, 2015), but in reality all tourists have food experiences. While some eating enthusiasts travel specifically for certain comestibles, whether on 'taste trails' or to famous restaurants, the tourist appeal of food and gastronomy is undeniable, particularly for the growing 'foodie' market. Food and the experience of consuming it are now seen as salient forms of souvenir retailing and shopping (Alonso and Krajsic, 2013; Jolliffe, 2014; Lin and Mao, 2015). Food exhibits heritage values, a sense of place, local tastes and unique flavours (Timothy, 2016). Gastronomic items are becoming an increasingly more valued souvenir than traditional tangible items that simply occupy space on a shelf. Shopping for food is a cultural experience for many visitors, and reliving their experiences by eating something at home that they enjoyed in the destination adds value to their journey and their retail experience (Swanson and Timothy, 2012).

Impacts and Insights

The majority of research into tourism and shopping has heretofore focused on market characteristics, patterns of demand, merchandising, motives for shopping, shopper experiences and satisfaction against intrinsic and extrinsic variables such as demographics, retail environments, expenditures and behavioural intentions. There has until now been an overemphasis on tourists' retail experiences and outcomes to the point of near information saturation. We also know that different nationalities exhibit different shopping patterns owing to cultural variations and social mores associated with valuation and reciprocal gift giving. However, we know very little about how nationality or cultural background affects the goods purchased and choices of shopping destinations. For instance, Russians prefer Milan for shopping, but why? These are crucial concerns as new markets emerge and their retail demands become more pronounced. Similarly, shopping behaviours and demands differ among types of tourists. More studies are needed to confirm hypotheses between 'type of tourist' and shopping patterns and behaviours.

One area of fruitful research is the symbols and meanings associated with souvenirs and how these are transmitted to consumers in the destination or after their return home. Post-trip information related to items bought on holiday is severely lacking in the shopping tourism literature, as is information about mementos as triggers of nostalgia, handicrafts as cauldrons of identity, and the semiotic stories associated with different souvenir authenticities.

Shopping is used successfully as a branding mechanism in many places. It has found considerable success in Dubai, Paris, Singapore and other famous retail destinations. More work is needed, however, to understand how places use retail in different ways to mark themselves as special or unique, where shopping becomes the competitive advantage over other vacation alternatives. This bleeds over into the incipient work on heritage cuisines and gastronomy in general, for comestibles also help brand places for tourism consumption, literally and figuratively. Examples include Tequila, Mexico, source of the famous drink by the same name, or Emmental, Switzerland, home to some of that country's best-known cheeses. In this sense, food is a shopping product that denotes exceptionality and tells interesting heritage stories.

Shopping is one of the most dominant components of transit time and space. That we know so much about destinations and even the home origins of travellers, yet we know almost nothing about the space and time between home and destination is very telling about how academic researchers and the industry prioritise the travel experience. This raises questions such as has a person actually been 'in' a place if he/she has only been in transit at an airport or railway station? What is required in the human psyche for people to consider themselves having been somewhere? Shopping has a critical role to play in how this plays out in the tourism narrative.

Neoliberalism and globalisation will continue with important implications for tourism and shopping. Not least of these implications is the potential decrease in attractiveness of shopping across the border in supranationalist alliances, such as the European Union, as tax rates and price differentials become more standardised between member states. Technological changes and virtual travel will also affect demand for retail experiences, perhaps disadvantaging local, small-scale shops in favour of those that can offer merchandise online. This might also affect the quality and authenticity of so-called 'traditional' arts and crafts.

Migration is an important issue that Europe and North America particularly are dealing with today. Population changes as a result of mass migration will of necessity change the way societies consume products at home but also on holiday. When Anglo-Americans visit Mexico, for instance, they tend to buy frippery that reminds them of their journey to Mexico (e.g. sombreros, piñatas, serapes, liquor, etc.). Mexican-Americans, on the other hand typically bring home items that will help them stay connected to their homeland (e.g. food ingredients, cooking utensils, celebratory clothing).

As noted earlier, shopping can be a cultural experience, a form of cultural immersion that derives from the interaction with sellers and possessing items deemed to be authentic, representative or nostalgic. For some travellers, crowded marketplaces and haggling introduces culture shock, while for others, these comprise an important and memorable part of the journey abroad.

Shopping in all its forms is a crucial part of tourism. Billions of dollars are spent each year on utilitarian and hedonic purchases by tourists at home, in transit and in the destination. Retail tourist activities have many forms, and all should be of interest to retailers, merchandisers, marketers, destination planners and tourism scholars. For shopping and tourism to provide more symbiotic relationships, we need a more holistic understanding of how supply and demand are connected, how venues and destinations influence people's decision making, and the ways shopping manifests beyond in-store transactions. This will require more research into the role of the community in producing tourist shopping experiences and considering shopping tourism and tourist shopping more holistically than before.

Questions

1. What are the main motivations for cross-border shopping?
2. How might culture or nationality determine tourists' shopping behaviour?
3. In what ways do destinations use shopping as a branding tool?

Further Reading and Website Links

1. International Council of Shopping Centers – Available at: https://www.icsc.org/.

2. World Tourism Organization Global Report on Shopping Tourism, 2014 – Available at: http://affiliatemembers.unwto.org/publication/global-report-shopping-tourism.
3. Dubai Shopping Festival – Available at: http://www.visitdubai.com/en/dsf.
4. Andorra Shopping Festival – Available at: http://andorrashoppingfestival.visitandorra.com/CAT/.

References

Alhosani, N. and Zaidan, E. (2014) Shopping tourism and destination development: Dubai as a case study. *Arab World Geographer* 17(1), 66–81.

Alonso, A.D. and Krajsic, V. (2013) Food heritage down under: olive growers as Mediterranean 'food ambassadors'. *Journal of Heritage Tourism* 8(2/3), 158–171.

Baruca, A. and Zolfagharian, M. (2013) Cross-border shopping: Mexican shoppers in the US and American shoppers in Mexico. *International Journal of Consumer Studies* 37(4), 360–366.

Bojanic, D.C. (2011) The impact of age and family life experience on Mexican visitor shopping expenditures. *Tourism Management* 32(2), 406–414.

Brown, J. (2013) Dark tourism shops: selling 'dark' and 'difficult' products. *International Journal of Culture, Tourism and Hospitality Research* 7(3), 272–280.

Butler, R.W. (1991) West Edmonton mall as a tourist attraction. *Canadian Geographer* 35(3), 287–295.

Carr, N. (2002) The tourism-leisure behavioural continuum. *Annals of Tourism Research* 29(4), 972–986.

Chang, J.C. (2014) Selling strategies and shopping behaviour – an example of Taiwanese guided package tourists to mainland China destinations. *Journal of Quality Assurance in Hospitality & Tourism* 15(2), 190–212.

Cheng, J.M., Wang, E.S., Lin, J.Y. and Vivek, S.D. (2009) Why do customers utilize the internet as a retailing platform? A view from consumer perceived value. *Asia Pacific Journal of Marketing and Logistics* 21(1), 144–160.

Chhabra, D., Lee, W., Zhao, S. and Scott, K. (2013) Marketing of ethnic food experiences: authentication analysis of Indian cuisine abroad. *Journal of Heritage Tourism* 8(2/3), 145–157.

Coles, T. (2004) Tourism, shopping, and retailing: an axiomatic relationship? In: Alan, A., Lew, C., Michael, H. and Allan, M.W. (eds) *A Companion to Tourism*. Blackwell, Oxford, UK, pp. 360–373.

Collins-Kreiner, N. and Zins, Y. (2011) Tourists and souvenirs: changes through time, space and meaning. *Journal of Heritage Tourism* 6(1), 17–27.

Cresswell, T. (2006) *On the Move: Mobility in the Modern Western World*. Routledge, New York, USA.

Dmitrovic, T. and Vida, I. (2007) An examination of cross-border shopping behaviour in south-east Europe. *European Journal of Marketing* 41(3/4), 382–395.

Dubai Corporation of Tourism and Commerce (2015) Dubai Shopping Festival. Available at: https://www.visitdubai.com/en/dsf (accessed 1 April 2015).

du Cros, H. (2013) World heritage-themed souvenirs for Asian tourists in Macau. In: Cave, J., Jolliffe, L. and Baum, T. (eds) *Tourism and Souvenirs: Glocal Perspectives from the Margins*. Channel View, Bristol, UK, pp. 176–188.

Frost, W. and Laing, J. (2016) Cuisine, migration, colonialism and diasporic identity. In: Timothy, D.J. (ed.) *Heritage Cuisines: Traditions, Identities and Tourism*. Routledge, Abingdon, UK, pp. 37–52.

Getz, D. (1993) Tourist shopping villages: development and planning strategies. *Tourism Management* 14(1), 15–26.

Goss, J. (1993) 'The magic of the mall': an analysis of form, function, and meaning in the contemporary retail built environment. *Annals of the Association of American Geographers* 83(1), 18–47.

Guo, Y., Kim, S.S. and Timothy, D.J. (2007) Development characteristics and implications of Mainland Chinese outbound tourism. *Asia Pacific Journal of Tourism Research* 12(4), 313–332.

Guttentag, D. (2009) The legal protection of indigenous souvenir products. *Tourism Recreation Research* 34(1), 23–34.

Han, H., Kim, W. and Hyun, S.S. (2014) Overseas travelers' decision formation for airport-shopping behavior. *Journal of Travel and Tourism Marketing* 31(8), 985–1003.

Hawkins, S. (2010) Cosmopolitan hagglers or haggling locals? Salesmen, tourists and cosmopolitan discourses in Tunis. *City & Society* 22(1), 1–24.

Henderson, J.C., Chee, L., Mun, C.N. and Lee, C. (2011) Shopping, tourism and retailing in Singapore. *Managing Leisure* 16(1), 36–48.

Hobson, J.S.P. (2000) Tourist shopping in transit: the case of BAA plc. *Journal of Vacation Marketing* 6(2), 170–183.

Hobson, J.S.P. and Christensen, M. (2001) Cultural and structural issues affecting Japanese tourist shopping behaviour. *Asia Pacific Journal of Tourism Research* 6(1), 37–45.

Howard, E. (ed.) (2010) *The Changing Face of Retailing in the Asia Pacific*. Routledge, London, UK.

Jansen-Verbeke, M. (1991) Leisure shopping: a magic concept for the tourism industry? *Tourism Management* 12(1), 9–14.

Jolliffe, L. (2014) *Spices and Tourism: Destinations, Attractions and Cuisines*. Channel View, Bristol, UK.

Jones, M.A. (1999) Entertaining shopping experiences: an exploratory investigation. *Journal of Retailing and Consumer Services* 6, 129–139.

Kaell, H. (2012) Of gifts and grandchildren: American Holy Land souvenirs. *Journal of Material Culture* 17(2), 133–151.

Kim, S.S., Timothy, D.J. and Huang, J. (2011) Understanding Japanese tourists' shopping preferences using the decision tree analysis method. *Tourism Management* 32(3), 544–554.

Kinley, T.R., Forney, J.A. and Kim, Y.K. (2012) Travel motivation as a determinant of shopping venue. *International Journal of Culture, Tourism and Hospitality Research* 6(3), 266–278.

Kontogeorgopoulos, N. (2003) Keeping up with the Joneses: tourists, travellers and the quest for cultural authenticity in southern Thailand. *Tourist Studies* 3(2), 171–203.

Kwek, A., Wang, Y. and Weaver, D.B. (2014) Retail tours in China for overseas Chinese: soft power or hard sell? *Annals of Tourism Research* 44, 36–52.

LeHew, M.L.A. and Wesley, S.C. (2007) Tourist shoppers' satisfaction with regional shopping mall experiences. *International Journal of Culture, Tourism and Hospitality Research* 1(1), 82–96.

Lehto, X.Y., Chen, S.Y. and Silkes, C. (2013) Tourist shopping style preferences. *Journal of Vacation Marketing* 20(1), 3–15.

Leizaola, A. (2006) Matching national stereotypes? Eating and drinking in the Basque borderland. *Anthropological Notebooks* 12(1), 79–94.

Lin, L. and Mao, P.C. (2015) Food for memories and culture – a content analysis study of food specialties and souvenirs. *Journal of Hospitality and Tourism Management* 22, 19–29.

Long, L.M. (ed.) (2004) *Culinary Tourism*. University Press of Kentucky, Lexington, USA.

Marciniak, R. (2012) Tourist and retail relationship in departure points and travel hubs consumption: The start of the tourist retail relationship. In: McIntyre, C. (ed.) *Tourism and Retail: The Psychogeography of Liminal Consumption*. Routledge, London, UK, pp. 93–110.

Markuszewska, I., Tanskanen, M. and Vila Subirós, J. (2016) Boundaries from borders: cross-border relationships in the context of the mental perception of a borderline – experiences from Spanish–French and Polish–German border twin towns. *Quaestiones Geographicae* 35(1), 105–119.

Mathieson, A. and Wall, G. (1982) *Tourism: Economic, Physical and Social Impacts*. Longman, London, UK.

McIntyre, C. (2012) Retail tourists as co-creators of tourist retail place and space. In: McIntyre, C. (ed.) *Tourism and Retail: The Psychogeography of Liminal Consumption*. Routledge, London, UK, pp. 63–89.

Meyer-Ohle, H. (2014) Japanese retailers in Southeast Asia: strong local partners, shopping malls, and aiming for comprehensive internationalization. *International Review of Retail, Distribution and Consumer Research* 24(5), 500–515.

Michalkó, G. and Timothy, D.J. (2001) Cross-border shopping in Hungary: causes and effects. *Visions in Leisure and Business* 20(1), 4–22.

Michalkó, G., Rátz, T., Mátyás, H. and Tömöri, M. (2014) Shopping tourism in Hungary during the period of the economic crisis. *Tourism Economics* 20(6), 1319–1336.

Molz, J.G. (2004) Tasting an imagined Thailand: authenticity and culinary tourism in Thai restaurants. In: Long, L. (ed.) *Culinary Tourism*. University of Kentucky, Lexington, USA, pp. 53–75.

Murphy, L., Benckendorff, P., Moscardo, G. and Pearce, P.L. (2011) *Tourist Shopping Villages: Forms and Functions*. Routledge, London, UK.

Muzaini, H. (2006) Backpacking Southeast Asia: strategies of 'looking local'. *Annals of Tourism Research* 33(1), 144–161.

Paraskevaidis, P. and Andriotis, K. (2015) Values of souvenirs as commodities. *Tourism Management* 48, 1–10.

Park, M.K. (2000) Social and cultural factors influencing tourists' souvenir-purchasing behavior: a comparative study on Japanese 'omiyage' and Korean 'sunmul'. *Journal of Travel and Tourism Marketing* 9(1), 81–91.

Peter, S. and Anandkumar, V. (2014) Dubai shopping festival: tourists' nationality and travel motives. *International Journal of Event and Festival Management* 5(2), 116–131.

Rabbiosi, C. (2015) Renewing a historical legacy: tourism, leisure shopping and urban branding in Paris. *Cities* 42, 195–203.

Rosenbaum, M.S. and Spears, D.L. (2005) Who buys that? Who does what? Analysis of cross-cultural consumption behaviours among tourists in Hawaii. *Journal of Vacation Marketing* 11(3), 235–247.

Shackley, M. (2006) Empty bottles at sacred sites: religious retailing at Ireland's national shrine. In: Timothy, D.J. and Olsen, D.H. (eds) *Tourism, Religion and Spiritual Journeys*. Routledge, London, UK, pp. 94–118.

Smith, R.K. and Olson, L.S. (2001) Tourist shopping activities and development of travel sophistication. *Visions in Leisure and Business* 20(1), 23–33.

Stanley, J. and Stanley, L. (2015) *Food Tourism: A Practical Marketing Guide*. CAB International, Wallingford, UK.

Sullivan, P., Bonn, M.A., Bhardwaj, V. and DuPont, A. (2012) Mexican national cross-border shopping: exploration of retail tourism. *Journal of Retailing and Consumer Services* 19(6), 596–604.

Swanson, K.K. and Timothy, D.J. (2012) Souvenirs: icons of meaning, commercialization, and commoditization. *Tourism Management* 33(3), 489–499.

Thompson, C. and Cutler, E. (1997) The effect of nationality on tourist arts: the case of the Gambia, West Africa. *International Journal of Hospitality Management* 16(2), 225–229.

Timothy, D.J. (2001) Postage stamps, microstates and tourism. *Tourism Recreation Research* 26(3), 85–88.

Timothy, D.J. (2005) *Shopping Tourism, Retailing and Leisure*. Channel View, Bristol, UK.

Timothy, D.J. (2011) *Cultural Heritage and Tourism: An Introduction*. Channel View, Bristol, UK.

Timothy, D.J. (2014) Trends in tourism, shopping, and retailing. In: Lew, A.A., Hall, C.M. and Williams, A.M. (eds) *The Wiley Blackwell Companion to Tourism*. Wiley Blackwell, Oxford, UK, pp. 378–388.

Timothy, D.J. (ed.) (2016) *Heritage Cuisines: Traditions, Identities and Tourism*. Routledge, Abingdon, UK

Timothy, D.J. and Butler, R.W. (1995) Cross-border shopping: a North American perspective. *Annals of Tourism Research* 22(1), 16–34.

Timothy, D.J. and Ron, A.S. (2013) Understanding heritage cuisines and tourism: identity, image, authenticity and change. *Journal of Heritage Tourism* 8(2/3), 99–104.

Tosun, C., Temizkan, S.P., Timothy, D.J. and Fyall, A. (2007) Tourist shopping experiences and satisfaction. *International Journal of Tourism Research* 9, 87–102.

Tourism Review (2014) Chinese tourists lead global trend in tax-free shopping. *Tourism Review*, May 19. Available at: http://www.tourism-review.com/global-2013-tax-free-shopping-trends-news4136 (accessed 29 March 2015).

Upchurch, R.S. and Liu, D. (2014) Does shopping matter? A research note discussing China's revised tariff policy and resultant outbound shopping behaviors. *Tourism Analysis* 19, 241–247.

Veblen, T. (1934) *The Theory of the Leisure Class: An Economic Study of Institutions*. The Modern Library, New York, USA.

Village du Perthus (2016) Bienvenue au Perthus. Available at: http://www.le-perthus.com/ (accessed 16 December 2016).

Wong, J. and Law, R. (2003) Differences in shopping satisfaction levels: a study of tourists in Hong Kong. *Tourism Management* 24(4), 401–410.

Woods, R.H. (2001) Important issues for a growing timeshare industry. *Cornell Hotel and Restaurant Administration Quarterly* 42(1), 71–81.

Wu, M.Y., Wall, G. and Pearce, P.L. (2014) Shopping experiences: international tourists in Beijing's Silk Market. *Tourism Management* 41, 96–106.

Xu, Y. and McGehee, N.G. (2012) Shopping behavior of Chinese tourists visiting the United States: letting the shoppers do the talking. *Tourism Management* 33(2), 427–430.

Yüksel, A. (2009) Exterior color and perceived retail crowding: effects on tourists' shopping quality inferences and approach behaviors. *Journal of Quality Assurance in Hospitality & Tourism* 10(4), 233–254.

13 Food Tourism

RONG HUANG

Learning Objectives

- To understand key concepts in food tourism
- To learn food tourist motivation and food tourism impacts
- To discover food tourism in China

Introduction

Hjalager and Corigliano (2000) argue that food and drink products can be among the most important cultural expressions of a country. Tourists and researchers are developing an interest in gaining knowledge of local, regional and national cuisines: Hjalager and Richards (2002), Huang (2009) and Busby *et al.* (2013) emphasise that increasing numbers of people are interested in travelling for gastronomic purposes; Frochot (2003, p. 82) illustrates that 'food tourism could be conceptualised as allowing tourists to achieve relaxation, excitement, escapism, status, education and lifestyle'; and Green and Dougherty (2008, p. 157) argue that food tourism provides 'a novel approach to promoting economic development, constructing a local food system, and celebrating regional culture'.

This chapter provides an introduction to food tourism and also gives an insight into food tourism in China. It is divided into seven sections. This first section provides a brief introduction to the chapter. The second section provides key concepts. It does this by analysing the relationship between food and tourism, and reviewing a range of available definitions of food tourism to provide a working definition of food tourism; two popular typologies of food tourism are also introduced. The third section explores major factors influencing the development of food tourism. The motivations of tourists are crucial in deciding whether or not they are food tourists, therefore their motivations are discussed in the fourth section. The development of food tourism is closely linked with the development of other special interest tourism, hence the fifth section explores such close interactions. The sixth section discusses impacts of food tourism and provides an insight into food tourism in China; the emphases of this section are on the diversity of Chinese food and food tourism promotion. The final section draws conclusions from the chapter.

Key Concepts

'Tourism is reported to be the world's largest industry' (Chen, 2015, p. 111) and is composed of many components, for instance, entertainment, sightseeing, food, accommodation, experience, transportation, and more. Quan and Wang (2004) argue that food can act as both a primary or secondary trip motivator and many authors (Boniface, 2003; Boyne *et al.*, 2003; du Rand *et al.*, 2003a; Long, 2004) agree that food adds value to the image of a destination. Okumus *et al.* (2007, p. 253) state that 'food is one of the most enjoyable activities that tourists undertake during their holidays and is the item that they are least likely to consider reducing expenditure to consume'. Meler and Cerovic (2003) claim that food and beverage expenditures make up nearly one-third of all tourist expenditures of global tourism. Hence Kim *et al.* (2011) and Chen (2015) argue that food is regarded as one of the most important components in tourism.

Cohen and Avieli (2004, p. 756) argue that 'the relations between tourism and different aspects of the culture (such as art, religion and sexuality) at the destination were thoroughly studied by researchers of tourism, the interface between tourism and food was, until recently, neglected by scholars of both tourism and food'. The book *Tourism and Gastronomy* by Hjalager and Richards (2002) is one of the first publications dedicated to this subject area, and it endorses the strengths and diversities of the relationships between tourism and food.

The relationships between food and tourism could be assessed from different aspects within tourism studies, among which the approach to food as motivation for a visit could especially explain the relationship between food and tourism (Boyne *et al.*, 2003; Tikkanen, 2007). Hall *et al.* (2003) point out that for many years the common understanding of the food-tourism relationship was the provision of food for tourists in restaurants, resorts or hotels. However, more recently, Huang (2009, p. 291) recognises that 'food has come to be recognised as part of the local culture which tourists consume, as an element of regional tourism promotion, a potential component of local agricultural and economic development, as a differentiated product in a competitive destination market, as an indicator of globalisation, and as something which is in itself affected by the consumption patterns and perceived preferences of tourists.'

In a review of relevant literature sources, Chen (2015) reveals that academics have argued that:

1. Food is regarded as an important tourist attraction in an assortment of forms, such as the fresh seafood in seaside resorts (one example being the new season Hairy Crab in Suzhou as shown in Fig. 13.1), the peculiar ethnic cuisines of exotic peoples, and the renowned restaurants in luxurious resorts (Cohen and Avieli, 2004; Hashimoto and Telfer, 2006; Henderson, 2009).
2. Food, like other factors such as accommodation, transport and entertainment, is a basic and crucial element of the tourist product (Tikkanen, 2007).
3. Food is touristic experience (Quan and Wang, 2004). Beer (2008) and Henderson (2009) note that for many people food consumption is a central component of their tourist experience, as well as being an experience in its own right.
4. Food is a part of the local culture which tourists consume (du Rand *et al.*, 2003a; Quan and Wang, 2004; Tikkanen, 2007). Food could be viewed as a manifestation of the tourist destination's culture (Westering, 1999; Hjalager and Corigliano, 2000; Chang *et al.*, 2010; Lee and Acroia, 2011).

As food experience is a part of the whole travelling experience, many authors (Telfer and Wall, 1996; Hjalager and Richards, 2002; Quan and Wang, 2004) argue that it is difficult to differentiate between food tourism (or culinary tourism) and food consumption, or food and tourism when travelling. The latter can be seen as the basic physical needs of tourists (McIntosh *et al.*, 1995; Quan and Wang, 2004); food consumption is considered as a 'side'

dish of travelling, supporting the tourists daily needs whilst they experience exotic scenery and heritage. Thus, food is not the main purpose of travelling.

To define food tourism, some relevant academic definitions are consulted (Hall *et al.*, 2003; Smith and Xiao, 2008; Kim *et al.*, 2009; Chen and Huang, 2016). Based on the analysis of definitions of food tourism, for this chapter, food tourism is conceptualised as tourists tasting or experiencing a particular type of food, the specific production region, learning local culture, and having food feature as their primary motivation. Furthermore it also includes travel in which food experience occurs but is not the primary motivation for the trip. Based on the degree of interest in food, further categories suggested by Hall *et al.* (2003) such as gourmet tourism, gastronomic tourism and culinary tourism are also used in a range of academic literature.

The typology of food tourism

With the popularity and importance of food tourism, du Rand *et al.* (2003b) suggest that food tourism enjoys a range of forms. Hjalager and Richards (2002) discuss the development of food tourism in a hierarchical model which illustrates the main elements of typology of food tourism in Table 13.1. The examples of initiatives under each order could lead to a better understanding of the typology.

Six types of food tourism were proposed by Busby *et al.* (2013) based on studies of film tourism and literature-related food/gastronomy tourism. They are: (1) 'homage to an actual location because of restaurants/cafe/eating places with good reviews/ ratings'; (2) 'appeal of areas, as they are on special cuisine/food routes'; (3) 'homage to an actual location because of celebrity chefs'; (4) 'local food gains popularity in a sense that the area becomes a tourist destination in its own right'; (5) 'travel writing/ cookery books induced tourism'; and (6) 'film-induced food tourism' (Busby *et al.*, 2013, p. 574).

Major Factors

A range of factors contributes to the growing interest in food tourism. Gartner (1993) pointed out a wide variety of forces that act separately or jointly to form a destination image in the eyes of the potential/actual tourist. These are included in Table 13.2.

Research has shown that recommendations from friends or families and the public media, such as

R. Huang

Fig. 13.1. New season Hairy Crab (Source: the author)

advertisements or broadcasts about food or food programmes (Fields, 2002; Everett and Aitchison, 2008), become important reasons for tourists to visit certain destinations. Growing evidence indicates that autonomous sources enjoy a higher degree of reliability among potential tourists, and Beerli and Martín (2004) argue that autonomous sources are typically more significant than more formal types of information in forming a destination image. Govers *et al.* (2007) agree and further state that autonomous and covert-induced agents (such as television, magazines, internet, books and movies) are more popular information sources than overt-induced agents such as advertising. Although the popularity of social media (e.g. Tripadvisor, Facebook, Wechat, etc.) and its influence in tourist decision-making processes are well documented by Leung *et al.* (2013), studies into the close relationship between social media and food tourism seem scarce.

Table 13.1. Typology of value added in gastronomy tourism. (Adapted from Hjalager and Richards (2002))

	First order: Indigenous development	Second order: Horizontal development	Third order: Vertical development	Fourth order: Diagonal development
Main input resource	Food production resources	Resources in the service sector	Entrepreneurial resources	Knowledge
Expected tourist behaviour	Enjoy the food	Understand the food	Experience the food	Exchange knowledge about the food
Examples of initiatives to enhance value added	Culinary aspects in regional promotion Campaigns for particular products Regional food trademarks Marketing food fairs and food events	Quality standards Certification and branding Reinventing and commodification of historical food traditions	Opening production plants and sites Routes and trails Visitor centres and museums Cooking classes and holidays	Research and development Media centres Demonstration projects

Table 13.2. Influential sources. (Adapted from Gartner (1993) and Vuckovic (2014))

Sources	Explanation
Induced sources	Traditional forms of advertising generated by the destination or intermediary on its behalf
Autonomous sources	Independently produced image agents such as books, movies, documentaries, news and social networks on the internet
Organic sources	Information gained from word of mouth communication and/or previous travel to the destination

Motivations

Tasting exotic and authentic foods and wine is one essential component of culinary tourism (Frochot, 2003). Fields (2002) summarises that 'motivators for consumption of food and beverages in a tourist destination can be theoretically conceptualized within four categories provided by McIntosh et al. (1995): 'physical motivators', 'cultural motivators', 'interpersonal motivators', and 'status and prestige motivators'.' (Kim, Eves and Scarles, 2009, p. 423). Table 13.3 provides detailed explanation of these four motivators.

Interactions

Food tourism is becoming a real player in the tourism market, and services and events related to food and beverages (wine, tea, coffee etc.) attract large numbers of tourists each year. By a detailed analysis of food tourism's development, one might recognise that this is closely linked with development of other types of special interest tourism (Busby et al., 2013; Fullagar et al., 2012). In reality, among six types of food tourists proposed by Busby et al. (2013), two types of food tourism are directly related to literary tourism and also film tourism.

1. Travel writing/cookery books-induced food tourism. This is 'a vehicle through which places and their food have been re-interpreted and communicated to wide audiences'. For instance, 'the books of Elizabeth David (1999) and Elizabeth de Stroumillo (1979, 1980) opened up European countries' (Busby et al., 2013, p. 574).

2. Film-induced food tourism: tourism resulting from enhanced interest in a destination through watching cookery programmes or films. Focus Box 1 provides a brief introduction to 'A Bite of China'; a Chinese television series that received huge attention from Chinese audiences after being broadcast. In a survey of 302 Chinese people who watched the series, Dai (2013) confirms that 'A Bite of China' has certainly stirred up the curiosity of Chinese people to travel and taste the exotic foods in their own country. According to her research, some respondents had already visited destinations portrayed in the programmes. Dai (2013) also provides strong evidence of an increasing desire for authentic and traditional food and food manners among Chinese people.

Table 13.3. Motivators for consumption of food and beverages in a destination. (Adapted from McIntosh *et al.* (1995) and Fields (2002))

McIntosh *et al.*, (1995) motivators	Explanation	Fields (2002) application
Physical motivators	Refreshment of a person's body and mind, physical rest, desire for recreation, participation in sports. These motivators are associated with reducing physical tension.	The opportunity to taste new and exotic foods. It was also emphasised that food in a destination is a physical experience through people's sensory perceptions, such as sight, taste and smell.
Cultural motivators	The need to not only experience different cultures, such as lifestyle, music, food and dance but also to gain knowledge about other countries in terms of cultural activities.	When experiencing new local cuisines, tourists are also experiencing a new culture.
Interpersonal motivators	A desire to meet new people, spend time with family and friends, visit friends or relatives, and/or get away from routine relationships.	Having a meal during a holiday can be regarded as a means of reproducing social relations.
Status and prestige motivators	Associated with self-esteem, recognition and the desire to attract attention from others.	Eating nice food in a nice place can be recognised as a means to be distinguished from others in terms of social status.

Focus Box 1: A Bite of China

'A Bite of China' is a 2012 Chinese documentary television series on the history of food, eating and cooking in Mainland China. It consisted of seven episodes (Gifts from the Nature, The Story of Staple Food, The Inspiration of Transformation, The Taste of Time, Secret of the Kitchen, A Perfect Blend of Five Flavours, and Our Farm) and presents sophisticated high-definition images of delicious Chinese cuisine. It attracted 30% more viewers than other programmes run in the same time slot and has also been viewed more than 20 million times online (Jia, 2012). It has beaten many TV series in China and become extremely popular on microblogs.

'A Bite of China' brings rich visual, emotional, spiritual and cultural enjoyment. The content of the programme could be divided into two parts, 'the taste on the tongue' and 'the changes in China' (*Global Times*, 2012). The audience learn about the love that Chinese people have for food, but also about the fast development of Chinese social economy (*Global Times*, 2012). There has been much praise for this documentary due to its innovative approach towards the discussion of Chinese food, which typically revolves around the different styles of food, rather than what goes into the making of specific dishes, and the people involved in making them, thus adding a human touch to Chinese food.

Many authors argue that mass media has a great influence upon tourists' destination decision-making behaviours, therefore the popularity of 'A Bite of China' has great potential in motivating audiences to travel to the places that were shown, or to buy the gourmet products discussed in the programme (Chen, 2015). After the programme was widely shown in China, many travel agencies launched tour routes based on the theme of 'A Bite of China', and some travel agencies have increased the proportion of gourmet foods in popular tour routes, both of which attracted many bookings from the tourists. In addition, there have been surging sales of the gourmet products shown in 'A Bite of China' on the Chinese e-commerce hub Taobao and the businesses of the related restaurants have been doing well (Chou, 2012).

The slow food movement founded in 1989 tries to prevent the disappearance of local food cultures and traditions, counteract the rise of fast life and combat people's dwindling interest in the food they eat (Slow food, 2016). Such movement is directly related to a form of slow tourism which embraces 'this emphasis on the local consumption of food that draws upon culinary heritage of organic principles, as well as the sensory embodiment of the journey (taste becomes as important as sights)'

(Fullagar *et al.*, 2012, p. 4). Therefore, food tourism has a clear overlap with slow tourism.

Impacts and Insights

Impacts of food tourism

Many authors recognise food as being expressive of identity and culture (Hall and Macionis, 1998; Scarpato, 2002; Richards, 2002; Hall and Sharples, 2003; Tellstrom *et al.*, 2006; Hall and Mitchell, 2005), which may be a reason why food has become a popular promotional tool amongst destination marketers (Jones and Jenkins, 2002; Fields, 2002; Cohen and Avieli, 2004; Everett and Aitchison, 2008). It is also assumed that destinations can gain a competitive advantage through differentiating themselves from other destinations by promoting their local cuisine (Hall and Mitchell, 2001; Richards, 2002; Sims, 2009). However, Boyne and Hall (2003) argue that there is a lack of empirical data relating to the role of food in consumers' destination decision-making process, and Jones and Jenkins (2002) warn that there is often disparity between the promotion and actual delivery of the food product, which can be counterproductive in terms of the tourist experience.

The economic benefits which food tourism can bring to a destination are commonly present throughout academic literature (Boyne and Hall, 2003; Hall and Mitchell, 2001; Hjalager and Richards, 2002; Bertella, 2006; Henderson, 2009). The increase in tourism will certainly lead to increased sales for some tourism businesses present at the destination (Hall and Mitchell, 2005), and can also lead to the stimulation of local fishing and agricultural industries (Boyne and Hall, 2003; Richards, 2002). Bertella (2006) adds that food tourism can lead to the extension of the tourist season, and that it has substantial potential in terms of regional development. Additionally, Hall and Mitchell (2005) state that food tourism is effective in visitor retention, as memories of a region can be revisited by tasting a product whilst at home. Hjalager and Richards (2002) interestingly add that food tourism can lead to mutual benefits for the food and tourism industries, as tourism offers opportunities for food producers to add value to their products, and gastronomic experiences can add value to tourism by providing the tourist with a link to local culture, landscape and food (Chen, 2015). Evidently there are a wealth of economic benefits that food tourism

can bring to a destination, but Henderson (2009) states that there are also social benefits.

These benefits include the strengthening of local image and identity (Richards, 2002), the sustainment of cultural heritage (Bertella, 2006) and the preservation of values (Everett and Aitchison, 2008). However, in terms of the social impacts of food tourism there are also several negative impacts. These range from tourists having a negative impact on local culture (du Rand *et al.*, 2003a), the dilution of identity (Everett and Aitchison, 2008) and the damage of the cultural heritage of a destination (Bertella, 2006). Everett and Aitchison (2008) state that there are few empirical studies into food-related tourism, particularly from a socio-cultural perspective. Chen (2015) argues a need for future research.

In contrast to the aforementioned benefits of food tourism, which appear to be more common in tourism literature than negative impacts, Jones and Jenkins (2002) assert that there is a debate over the extent of benefits which food tourism can bring to a destination. It is apparent that although food tourism has been recognised as an important topic in the tourism industry, there are still uncertainties amongst academics about the full extent of the impacts (both positive and negative) it can bring to a destination (Chen, 2015).

Insights to food tourism in China

Food has a special meaning to the Chinese people. Huang (2009, p. 293) emphasises that 'food consumption has always played a prominent role in defining Chinese culture. Not only is Chinese cuisine very advanced, but beliefs in the interconnection between medical and nutritional use of food have a long history and are widely held.' She further points out that 'traditional Chinese food and cuisine exhibit Chinese culture, art and reality, and play an essential role in Chinese people's everyday life'. (Huang, 2009, p. 293)

China features a vast geographical area, numerous ethnic groups, different climates and differentiated physical environments. The 'waste not, want not' ethos means that a surprising range and variety of plants and animals, and every part of plants or animals, are used. This has given rise to a remarkable diversity in regional cuisine. There are eight main cuisines (or Eight Great Traditions) listed in Fig. 13.2 and they refer mainly to the Han nationality.

In spite of the often-quoted synergy and complementary nature of the food (Torres, 2002) and tourism sectors, and the increasing recognition of the role of food to attract visitors, relatively little English

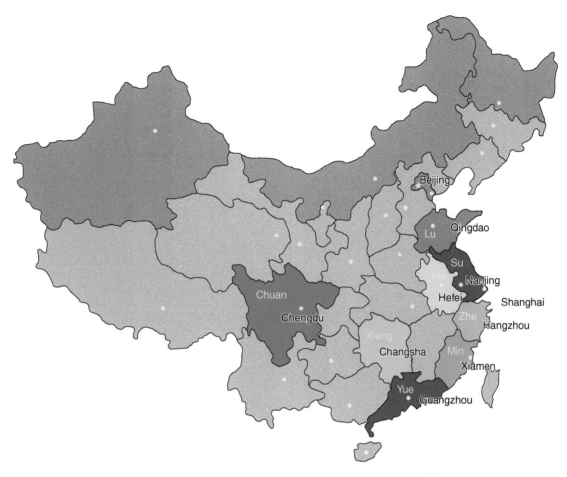

Fig. 13.2. China's Eight Great Regional Cuisines map. (Source: Chen (2015)

research has been published specifically focusing on food tourism linkages in the Chinese context, although some exceptions do exist. A group of researchers show a keen interest in the linkage between Chinese tea and tourism. Huang and Hall (2007) research the nature and regional context of tea festivals developed in the central Chinese province of Hunan from the later 1990s. Fujian's tea culture was reviewed by Xiao (2007); and she identifies the current state of tea tourism in Fujian and recommends ways in which the tea and tourism industries might work together towards sustainable development. By profiling a local tea company, Jolliffe and Zhuang (2007) highlight tea-related tourism in Fuding, insights are gained into the potential role of small tea enterprises in facilitating tea tourism and implementing related pro-poor tourism projects. Focus Box 2 gives an insight into tea tourism in China.

With the quick development and popularity of food tourism, China has already found the potential of developing food tourism. There are many examples, such as in 2003 when China made a tourism promotion theme of 'Chinese cooking Kingdom Tour'. Based on her analysis of industrial practice and relevant Chinese literature sources, Chen (2015) summarises different ways to promote food tourism in China:

1. Develop interesting and attractive food routes, which combine together related food stories, famous people and good restaurants.
2. Base tourism on special local foods, the building of food courts or designated street food areas to bring together noted local foods.
3. Create unique dining environments, and deliver the local culture through restaurant decoration, tableware, services or flavour characteristics.

Focus Box 2: Tea tourism in China

It is widely acknowledged that China is the homeland of tea, and is where tea was first cultivated, processed and consumed (Jolliffe, 2007). Chinese tea may be classified into five categories (as set out in the ddavid.com website (David, 2017)) according to the different methods by which it is processed:

- **Green tea** (the variety which keeps the original colour of the tea leaves and is not fermented during processing).
- **Black tea**, (known as 'red tea' (hong cha) in China, is the category which is fermented before baking; it is a more recent variety developed on the basis of green tea).
- **Wulong tea** (a variety half way between green and black teas, being made after partial fermentation).
- **Compressed tea** (the kind of tea which is compressed and hardened into a certain shape. It is good for transport and storage and is mainly supplied to the ethnic minorities living in the border areas of the country).
- **Scented tea** (made by mixing fragrant flowers in the tea leaves in the course of processing. The flowers commonly used for this purpose are, amongst others, jasmine and magnolia).

Chinese tea has been promoted internationally as one of the top eight culturally loaded souvenirs or goods for tourists. According to Xiao (2007), the dimensions in the art of culture of tea have been associated with, and exploited for, tourism: The growing and processing of tea leaves (as in agri-tourism development that includes tea); the brewing of fine teas for a maximum extraction of flavour and aroma (as in tea ceremonies, demonstrations and festivals for tourists); the cultivation of a taste for all kinds of delightful ceramics and other tea accessories (as in the touristic purchase of tea-related souvenirs, gifts and goods); the collecting of old poems, songs and stories about tea for the enrichment of an attraction or destination; leisurely enjoyment, with extraordinary brewing of kung-fu tea in pleasant surroundings for a short retreat from the stresses and strains of modern life.

The Tea and Horse Trade Route in southwest China links the province of Sichuan and Yunnan with Tibet. The Tea and Horse Trade Route is a cultural landscape full of linkages and features, which indicates it is a culturally significant transport and communication network (Li, 2005). This route has its market appeal for the mass tourism market domestically and internationally to experience tea culture and trade in China. It offers a rich opportunity for tourists to learn more about historic tea production and trade in China through its tangible and intangible heritage. The official Yunnan Tourist website listed 'The Tea and Horse Trade Route' as an important asset and some tour operators are also trying to incorporate it into cultural package tours (du Cros, 2007).

---

4. Take advantage of multimedia tools by using magazines, newspapers, websites and television, or hold food festivals and events.

5. Design local souvenirs like crafts, food specialties, and food related books or videos.

As China is poised to gain a greater market share of the global tourism market, Li and Wang (2010) argue that the effective use of websites as a marketing tool to attract and retain customers will affect the levels of competitiveness within the Chinese tourism industry. The China National Tourism Administration (CNTA) and its regional tourism administrations (CRTAs) who are active Destination Management Organisations for different regions within China, have developed websites and are using them as an important element within their marketing strategies (Ma *et al.*, 2003; Chen, 2015).

Because of interest in food tourism in China, Huang (2009) assesses how well the CNTA and its regional tourism administrations have done to market their destinations through food tourism on the internet. It is apparent from her assessment that Chinese food plays a role in tourism. She argues that Chinese food is 'primarily considered as being a supportive attraction rather than a key attraction in China'; given the importance of food and dining out in tourist experience and sheer economic contribution, 'CRTAs need more aggressive marketing tactics for their local food' (Huang, 2009, p. 300). Based on her assessment, Huang (2009) provides some strategies for future online food tourism in China:

1. An attractive/unknown cuisine can be regarded as a resource of a region and needs to be developed as a regional branding item.

2. Gastronomy routes can promote a region and can contribute to sustainable tourism projects.
3. Speciality restaurants can be developed to assist with the promotion of the special cuisine of a region.

Conclusion

Owing to local or regional food specialities, more and more people seem to be drawn to travel to particular destinations. In a review of relevant research, it is clear that more and more researchers are exploring the relationship between food and tourism. Food plays a significant role in tourism and hence marketing professionals of destinations have gradually increased the promotional emphasis placed upon the important role of food. The motivations as to why food tourists visit particular destinations can be varied. Different types of food tourism proposed by academia reflect a wide range of interests in food. Such typologies should be used as a starting point to segment food tourists and thus assist in the development of highly nuanced food promotion plans for destinations that are interested in promoting food tourism (Chen, 2015).

The story of food in China is full of history and culture, thus it provides a solid foundation for the future development of food tourism. The regional diversity within food in China means that there is great marketing potential for food tourism in China. The recent success of the television series 'A Bite of China' has certainly impacted upon the tourism industry. Such a creative approach could be developed further so as to promote local food and culture and subsequently promote associated destinations (Dai, 2013). What has been shown to work in China, and in other destinations, could possibly be extended to other countries and regions which are looking to expand their tourism offerings and thus increase revenues from tourists without the requirement for large state investments in infrastructure.

Questions

1. Busby *et al.* (2013) proposed six types of food tourism. Identify three popular types of food tourism with supporting examples.
2. Critically evaluate a wide range of food tourism resources in China and develop some potential food tourism routes for international tourists.

Further Reading and Website Links

Hjalager, A.M. and Richards, G. (eds.) (2002) *Tourism and Gastronomy*. Routledge, London, UK. [One of the first publications dedicated to this subject area, and it endorses the strengths and diversities of the relationships between tourism and food. The book draws together a group of international experts in order to develop a better understanding of the role, development and future of gastronomy and culinary heritage in tourism.]

Busby, G., Huang, R. and Jarman, R. (2013) The Stein effect: an alternative film-induced tourism perspective. *International Journal of Tourism Research* 15(6), 570–582. [This research considers the Stein Effect in Padstow. More specifically it determines visitors' motivation for visiting Padstow and the importance of Rick Stein in terms of tourism to the town. It provides categories of food tourism. CHAID method was used to analyse different types of tourists to Padstow.]

The World Food Travel Association (WFTA) (http://worldfoodtravel.org/). [This is a non-profit and non-governmental organisation (NGO) and the world's leading authority on food travel. The Association is at the forefront of food travel development and promotion with cutting-edge resources for today's food, drink, travel, hospitality and media professionals.]

References

Beer, S. (2008) Authenticity and food experience – commercial and academic perspectives. *Journal of Foodservice* 19, 153–163.

Beerli, A. and Martin, J.D. (2004) Factors influencing destination image. *Annals of Tourism Research* 31(3), 657–681.

Bertella, G. (2011) Knowledge in food tourism: the case of Lofoten and Maremma Toscana. *Current Issues in Tourism* 14(4), 355–371.

Boniface, P. (2003) *Tasting Tourism: Traveling for Food and Drink*. Ashgate Publishing, Burlington, USA.

Boyne, S. and Hall, D. (2003) Managing food and tourism development: issues for planning and opportunities to add value. In: Hall, C.M., Sharples, L., Mitchell, R., Macionis, N. and Cambourne, B. (eds) *Food Tourism Around the World: Development, Management and Markets*. Elsevier, Oxford, pp.285–295.

Boyne, S., Hall, D. and Williams, F. (2003) Policy, support and promotion for food-related tourism initiatives: a marketing approach to regional development. In: Hall, C.M. (eds) *Wine, Food and Tourism Marketing*. Haworth Press, Binghampton, USA, pp. 131–153.

Busby, G., Huang, R. and Jarman, R. (2013) The Stein effect: an alternative film-induced tourism perspective. *International Journal of Tourism Research* 15(6), 570–582.

Chang, R.C.Y. and Kivela, J. *et al.* (2010) 'Food preferences of Chinese tourists.' *Annals of Tourism Research* 37(4), 989–1011.

Chen, Q. (2015) *An Investigation of the Role of Food Tourism in Promoting Chinese Regions*. PhD thesis, Plymouth University, Plymouth, UK.

Chen, Q. and Huang, R. (2016) Understanding the importance of food tourism to Chongqing, China. *Journal of Vacation Marketing* 22(1), 42–54. DOI: 10.1177/1356766715589427.

Chou, J. (2012) CCTV Finds the Way to Viewers' Hearts is Through Gorgeous Food Documentary. *The Wall Street Journal*. [Online]. Available from: http://blogs.wsj.com/chinarealtime/2012/06/11/cctv-finds-the-way-to-viewers-hearts-is-through-gorgeous-food-documentary (accessed 20 December 2012).

Cohen, E. and Avieli, N. (2004) Food in tourism: attraction and impediment. *Annals of Tourism Research* 31(4), 755–778.

Dai, Y. (2013) *The Impact of 'A Bite of China'*. Unpublished honours project, Plymouth University, Plymouth, UK.

David, D. (2017) A Long Desire: China, Available at http://ddavid.com/alongdesire/china3.htm (accessed on March 2015).

David, E. (1999) *Italian Food*. Penguin, London, UK.

de Stroumillo, E. (1979) *The Tastes of Travel: Normandy, Brittany*. Harvill Press, London, UK.

de Stroumillo, E. (1980) *The Tastes of Travel: Western Loire, Aquitaine*. Collins, London, UK.

du Cros, H. (2007) China's tea and horse trade route and its potential for tourism. *Tea and Tourism: Tourists, Traditions and Transformations* 11, 167.

du Rand, G.E., Heath, E. and Alberts, N. (2003a) 'The role of local and regional food in destination marketing.' *Journal of Travel & Tourism Marketing* 14(3/4), 97–112.

du Rand, G.E., Heath, E. and Alberts, N. (2003b) The role of local and regional food in destination marketing: a South African Situation Analysis. Available at: http://repository.up.ac.za/bitstream/handle/2263/6080/DuRand_Role(2003).pdf?sequence=1 (accessed 10 November 2010).

Everett, S. and Aitchison, C. (2008) The role of food tourism in sustaining regional identity: a case study of Cornwall, south west England. *Journal of Sustainable Tourism* 16(2), 150–167.

Fields, K. (2002) Demand for the gastronomy tourism product: motivational factors. In: Hjalager, A.M. and Richards, G. (eds) *Tourism and Gastronomy*. Routledge, London, UK, pp. 36–50.

Frochot, I. (2003) An analysis of regional positioning and its associated food images in French tourism regional brochures. In: Hall, C.M. (ed.) *Wine, Food and Tourism Marketing*. Haworth Press, Binghampton, USA, pp. 77–96.

Fullagar, S., Markwell, K. and Wilson, E. (eds) (2012) *Slow Tourism: Experiences and Mobilities* (Vol. 54). Channel View Publications, Bristol, UK.

Gartner, W.C. (1993) Image formation process. In: Uysal, M. and Fesenmaier, D.R. (eds) *Communication and Channel Systems in Tourism Marketing*. Haworth Press, Binghampton, USA, pp. 191–215.

Global Times (2012) Taking a bite of China. [Online]. Available from: http://www.globaltimes.cn/NEWS/tabid/99/ID/713406/Taking-a-bite-of-China.aspx (accessed 20 December 2012).

Govers, R., Frank M.G. and Kumar, K. (2007) Promoting tourism destination image. *Journal of Travel Research* 46(1), 15–23.

Green, G.P. and Dougherty, M.L. (2008) 'Localizing linkages for food and tourism: culinary tourism as a community development strategy.' *Community Development* 39(3), 148–158.

Hall, C.M. and Macionis, N. (1998) Wine tourism in Australia and New Zealand. In: Butler, R., Hall, C.M. and Jenkins, J. (eds) *Tourism and Recreation in Rural Areas*. Wiley, Chichester, UK, pp. 197–224.

Hall, C.M. and Mitchell, R. (2001) Wine and food tourism. In: Douglas, N. and Derret, R. (eds) *Special Interest Tourism: Context and Cases*. John Wiley & Sons, Brisbane, Australia, pp. 307–329.

Hall, C.M. and Sharples, L. (2003) The consumption of experiences or the experience of consumption? An introduction to the tourism of taste. In: Hall, C.M., Sharples, L., Mitchell, R., Macionis, N. and Cambourne, B. (eds) *Food Tourism Around the World: Development, Management and Markets*. Butterworth-Heinemann, Oxford, UK, pp. 1–24.

Hall, C.M. and Mitchell, R. (2005) Gastronomic tourism: comparing food and wine tourism experiences. In: Novelli, M. (ed.) *Niche Tourism, Contemporary Issues, Trends and Cases*. Butterworth Heinemann, Oxford, UK, pp. 89–100.

Hall, C.M., Sharples, L., Mitchell, R., Macionis, N. and Cambourne, B. (eds) (2003) *Food Tourism around the World: Development, Management and Markets*. Butterworth Heinemann, Oxford, UK.

Hashimoto, A. and Telfer, D.J. (2006) Selling Canadian culinary tourism: branding the global and the regional product. *Tourism Geographies* 8(1), 31–55.

Henderson, J.C. (2009) Food tourism reviewed. *British Food Journal* 111(4), 317–332.

Hjalager, A.M. and Corigliano, M.A. (2000) Food for tourists – determinants of an image. *International Journal of Tourism Research* 2(4), 281–293.

Hjalager, A.M. and Richards, G. (eds) (2002) *Tourism and Gastronomy*. Routledge, London, UK.

Huang, R. (2009) The role of food in promoting Chinese regions on the web. *International Journal of Tourism Policy* 2(4), 289–305.

Huang, R. and Hall, D. (2007) The new tea appreciation festival. In: Joliffe, L. (ed.) *Tea Tourism: Global Trends and Developments*. Channel View Publications, Bristol, UK, pp. 98–114.

Jia, M. (2012) Readers sink their teeth into a bite of China. *China Daily*. 26 June 2012. Available from: http://www.chinadaily.com.cn/cndy/2012-06/26/content_15522345.htm (accessed 20 December 2012).

Jolliffe, J. (ed.) (2007) *Tea Tourism: Global Trends and Developments*. Channel View Publications, Bristol, UK, pp. 98–114.

Jolliffe, J. and Zhuang, P. (2007) Tourism development and the tea gardens of Fuding, China. In: Kim, Y.G., Eves, A. and Scarles, C. (2009) Building a model of local food consumption on trips and holidays: a grounded theory approach. *International Journal of Hospitality Management* 28, 423–431.

Jones, A. and Jenkins, I. (2002) 'A taste of wales—Blas Ar Gymru': Institutional malaise in promoting welsh food tourism products. In: Hjalager, A.M. and Richards, G. (eds) *Tourism and Gastronomy*. Routledge, London, pp.113–115.

Kim, Y.G., Eves, A. and Scarles, C. (2009) Building a model of local food consumption on trips and holidays: a grounded theory approach. *International Journal of Hospitality Management* 28, 423–431

Kim, Y.H., Kim, M., Goh, B.K. and Antun, J.M. (2009) A comparison between first-timers and repeaters at a food event. *Journal of Culinary Science & Technology* 7(4), 239–249.

Kim, Y.H., Kim, M., Goh, B. and Antun, J.M. (2011) The role of money: the impact on food tourists' satisfaction and intention to revisit food events. *Journal of Culinary Science & Technology* 9(2), 85–98.

Lee, I. and Acroia, C. (2011) The role of regional food festivals for destination branding. *International Journal of Tourism Research* 13, 355–367.

Leung, D., Law, R., van Hoof, H. and Buhalis, D. (2013) Social media in tourism and hospitality: a literature review. *Journal of Travel & Tourism Marketing* 30, 3–22.

Li, X. (2005) *The Tea and Horse Trade Route*. New Star Press, Beijing, China.

Li, X. and Wang, Y. (2010) Evaluating the effectiveness of destination marketing organisations' websites: evidence from China. *International Journal of Tourism Research* 12(5), 536–549.

Long, L.M. (ed.) (2004) *Culinary Tourism*. University Press of Kentucky, Lexington, USA.

Ma, J.X., Buhalis, D. and Song, H. (2003) 'ICTs and internet adoption in China's tourism industry'. *International Journal of Information Management* 23, 451–467.

McIntosh, R.W., Goeldner, C.R. and Ritchie, J.R. (1995) *Tourism Principles, Practices, Philosophies*, 7th edn. Wiley, New York, USA.

Meler, M. and Cerovic, Z. (2003) Food marketing in the function of tourist product development. *British Food Journal* 105(3), 175–192.

Okumus, B., Okumus, F. and McKercher, B. (2007) Incorporating local and international cuisines in the marketing of tourism destinations: the cases of Hong Kong and Turkey. *Tourism Management* 28, 253–261.

Quan, S. and Wang, N. (2004) Towards a structural model of the tourist experience: An illustration from food experiences in tourism. *Tourism Management* 25, 297–305.

Richards, G. (2002) Gastronomy: An essential ingredient in tourism production and consumption? In: Hjalager, A. and Richards, G. (eds) *Tourism and Gastronomy*. Routledge, London, pp. 3–20.

Scarpato, R. (2002) Gastonomy as a tourist product: the perspective of gastronomy studies. In: Hjalager, A. and Richards, G. (eds) *Tourism and Gastronomy*. Routledge, London, pp. 51–70.

Sims, R. (2009) Food, place and authenticity: local food and the sustainable tourism experience. *Journal of Sustainable Tourism* 17(3), 321–336.

Slow food (2016) About us. Available at: http://www.slow-food.com/about-us/ (accessed 22 December 2016)

Smith, S.L. and Xiao, H. (2008) Culinary tourism supply chains: a preliminary examination. *Journal of Travel Research* 46, 289–299.

Telfer, D. and Wall, G. (1996) Linkages between tourism and food production. *Annals of Tourism Research* 23(3), 635–665.

Tellstrom, R., Gustafsson, I. and Mossberg, L. (2006) Consuming heritage: the use of local food culture in branding. *Place Branding* 2(2), 130–143.

Tikkanen, I. (2007) Maslow's hierarchy and food tourism in Finland: five cases. *British Food Journal* 109(9), 721–734.

Torres, R. (2002) Toward a better understanding of tourism and agriculture linkages in the Yucatan: Tourist food consumption and preferences. *Tourism Geographies* 4(3), 282–306.

Vuckovic, V. (2014) *Destination Image of Serbia among Italian Travellers*. Published thesis, Universita Degli Studi Di Pisa.

Westering, J. (1999) Heritage and gastronomy: the pursuits of 'new tourists'. *International Journal of Heritage Studies* 5(2), 75–81.

Xiao, H. (2007) Tea culture and tourism in Fujian province, China: towards a partnership for sustainable development. In: Joliffe, L. (ed.) *Tea Tourism: Global Trends and Developments*. Channel View Publications, Bristol, UK, pp. 98–114.

14 Garden Tourism

Richard Benfield

Learning Objectives

- To understand the place and dimensions of garden tourism within the tourism industry
- To learn what demographic and psychographic segment undertakes garden tourism
- To learn what motivates a person to undertake a garden tourism experience
- To discover contemporary approaches to marketing garden tourism

Key Concepts

On the basis of garden history, garden motivations (see below) and garden tourism locations, it would appear that garden tourism is a distinct sub-set of cultural tourism. The act of visiting a garden or visiting other garden tourism activities (such as flower shows) is probably based on the second most popular outdoor leisure activity of gardening,[1] undertaken by 83% of US households and 86% of the UK population (Benfield, 2013).

However it is not only gardeners that visit gardens: sedentary visitors, often senior citizens that no longer garden, population cohorts without a garden such as young millennials beginning household formation and inner city populations, often ethnic minorities, without access to large green open spaces such as parks, have all been identified as garden visitors. Thus garden visitors span the spectrum of the tourist population. Having said that, most garden audience data suggest the typical visitor is over 60 years of age, female and with higher incomes leading most garden managers to worry that audience in the future may decline or even disappear. This worry is exacerbated by the recent decline in housing starts (thus resulting in a decline in gardeners), the reduction in lot sizes mitigating the need for a large garden and the apparent move in popular culture away from leisure activities like gardening to a more technologically based leisure industry. In contrast, a number of garden managers have pointed out that while there may

certainly be a demographic shift in potential visitors, this will not occur for a number of years. It is argued that while the baby boomer generation in the USA, Canada and the UK is ageing, and that the percentage of gardeners will drop as this cohort becomes increasingly less able to undertake the strenuous work required by gardening, this does not preclude, indeed it may encourage, (former) gardeners to visit gardens and view gardens in lieu of undertaking gardening itself. If one assumes that, even with that occurrence, the large cohort of baby boomers will stop at age 75 even garden visiting, then one might assume that this fall off in boomer visits will start to become apparent around the year 2025 and when those born at or after the US peak birth rate of 1957,[2] then those persons will be 75 in 2032. Thus in garden management circles, the desire has been to get ahead of the trend and to start attracting both the so-called Gen X – the lost generation – and Gen Y – the Millennials – and this has now become the major marketing challenge and thrust for garden managers. Much of this thrust has come in the form of embracing social media as a vehicle for attracting this audience. As a result a significant segment of this chapter (see below) will be devoted to social media marketing and the garden.

While the major marketing emphasis is on attracting a younger demographic to the garden, there may be signs that this is already happening. Connell found that gardening enjoys significant interest from young people in their twenties and, by their thirties, gardening enjoys a strong following (Connell, 2004) (Fig. 14.1).

Data from tourism destinations like VisitBritain show a median age of 39 for international garden visitors, comparable to that of the population as a whole (VisitBritain, 2011). In 2014, *The Telegraph* (Goldhill, 2014) also announced that gardening was more popular amongst 25–35 year olds than going to the cinema. This was partially attributable to a rise in concern by this cohort over climate warming, plant sustainability and conservation, and the

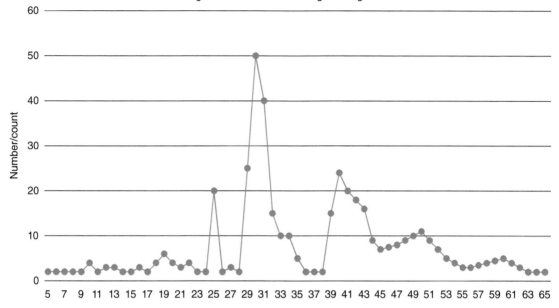

Fig. 14.1. Age respondent first became interested in garden visiting. (Connell, 2005)

Major Factors

associated rise by this group of organic gardening and urban greening which might make garden visiting even more popular and necessary.

If we define special interest tourism as being tourism with low numbers, or a niche market for the commercial tourist industry or an interest that is defined by a low total number of participants, then this chapter, dedicated to garden tourism, does not belong in this book. If we define special interest tourism as being generally unrecognised as a major contributor to leisure activity with a paucity of academic enquiry, then this chapter on garden tourism should take centre stage. At a general level, the importance of garden tourism to the tourist industry is staggering. Wyse Jackson estimated in 2000 that 150 million people visited the world's botanic gardens (Wyse Jackson and Sutherland, 2000). Assuming an average annual growth rate of tourism arrivals of 3% since 2000, it is not inconceivable that by 2017 over 225 million people may have visited botanic gardens worldwide,[3] a figure that would rank garden visiting as amongst the most popular tourism activities in the world.

Individual gardens also post some impressive numbers when compared with other tourist attractions worldwide. Singapore Botanic Garden regularly exceeds four million visitors, Beijing Botanic Garden over two million and all of the botanic gardens in Australia's major cities exceed 1.5 million visitors yearly,[4] often making them the most popular tourist attraction for the city. In the UK the Royal Botanic Garden at Kew regularly attracts over 1.1 million visitors and in some years has exceeded 1.8 million visits, the RHS at Wisley and the Eden Project in Cornwall experience over one million visitors annually and most other gardens attract over 250,000 visitors on a regular basis. In the USA, visitation to Longwood Garden in Pennsylvania now exceeds one million visitors, making it the most popular garden in the USA, though Montreal Botanic Garden in 2013 with the Blockbuster Moseiculture show exceeded 1.4 million visitors that year. Many gardens in the USA (Chicago, New York, Atlanta and Brooklyn) are approaching the one million mark and Brooklyn Botanic Garden has accommodated over 35,000 visitors in one day – a figure that ranks with some of the most popular attractions by day visitors in America. In the United States more people go to gardens (100 million, est. APGA, 2015) than go to Disneyland and Disneyworld combined (38 million); more people go to gardens than to the top urban destinations of

Orlando (62 million), New York City (55 million) or Las Vegas (42 million).

In the United Kingdom it is estimated that there are between 300 million and 400 million garden visits (English Heritage, 2002; cited in Fox and Edwards, 2008)[5] and that almost one-third of all international visitors to the UK desire to visit a garden, the third most popular activity of international visitors and ahead of visiting museums, historic sites and amusement parks! (VisitBritain, 2011). These industry data are borne out by data from VisitScotland that found in 2011 that 56% of overseas visitors to Scotland have a propensity to visit gardens (six percentage points higher than the UK as a whole) ahead of churches and historic homes and only slightly behind castles and monuments, attractions that are often considered synonymous with Scotland. If special interest tourism is defined by the number of sites at which garden tourism is undertaken[6] then garden tourism becomes an easily documented product. In France there are 784 gardens, in the USA 503 public gardens and in the UK it is estimated there are over 2000 public gardens[7] and over 3000 private gardens open to the public. In short,

garden tourism is not only underappreciated but it is large and apparently a major draw for local, regional, national and even international destinations.

Interactions within Tourism

The nature and significance of garden tourism is rooted in the history of tourism both as a leisure pursuit and as an academic discipline. Regarding historic garden tourism, both Western and Eastern literature is replete with the journeys of writers and artists to see, appreciate and understand the significance of gardens. For academic enquiry, the literature is much more recent and can best be seen in the light of the evolution of mass tourism and the psychological attributes of the participants.

The earliest literature on the sociology of travel and tourism originates with Boorstin (1964) who places the tourist within an environment of inauthentic, contrived group travel, enjoying what he called 'pseudo events'. Turner and Ash (1975) were the first to recognise this as a mass phenomenon and derived the term 'mass tourism' to describe staged authenticity for a mass of gullible and vacuous

---

International Case Study: Using multimedia at Butchart Gardens, Victoria, BC, Canada

As an example of the power of Facebook, Butchart Gardens in Victoria, Canada created a post in 2013 that unexpectedly went viral. Initially people, and then radio and TV stations, were asking for photos of a rare snowfall that had fallen on 5 December 2013 and the garden promised them they would get back to them once a photographer had been out to take pictures. Butchart subsequently posted a photo of snow in the garden. The reach on this single photo was 75,000 people, almost 7000 likes, comments and shares and 6500 actual post clicks. It is apparent that in rare instances, a fledgling brand, such as a garden can really rise up above the noise and chatter on social media. To give perspective, the largest local paper in Victoria, BC, has a circulation of 58,000. Myriad conversations came out of this single post, keeping Butchart Gardens top of mind for the day and the weeks after.

Butchart Gardens use hashtags extensively, mostly to index posts and to get noticed by people outside their social media channels. They use three 'branded' tags: #butchartgardens, #butchartchristmas and also #butcharttraffic (to give real-time traffic

updates to people waiting in line for special events and high-volume days) among many others. This gets like-minded individuals into a conversation together so in the gardening world, #gardens, #gardening and #gardenchat are very popular hashtags.

Finally it should be noted that Facebook, like other social media, has the ability to share content with other tourist and business organisations in a collaborative fashion for post-exposure to a wider potential market. Thus Chambers of Commerce and Destination Marketing/Management organisations become natural partners using social media. For example, outside of organic search, Facebook is the second most important driver to Butchart Gardens' website after their local DMO, Tourism Victoria.

It should be noted that many Facebook users gauge success on the number of likes or followers, but that does not equate to return on investment: it is engaged followers that counts. Again Butchart noted that in one week those who were actually engaging in terms of liking and commenting and sharing were the older demographic – in fact older and more female on average than their fan base suggests.

---

individuals being shown a restricted, scripted and thus sanitised version of what was reality. Thus it was MacCannell, with the publication of *The Tourist* in 1976, who moved away from the explanation of a mass of gullible individuals but rather suggested individuals were motivated by what resembled a sacred journey or pilgrimage looking for authenticity (which was a reaction to what he identified as 'staged authenticity') in their tourist travels and rejecting staged authenticity. John Urry (1990) indicated that the major feature of this viewing of 'the other' was the visual and hence termed the phenomena *The Tourist Gaze*. Both must be seen, therefore, as the earliest and most impactful publications on tourist psychographics or what has come to be known as *semiotics*. Since 1990, Urry's work has been reissued as a third edition (2011). Some of the findings are new (especially in the area of globalisation and performance – see below) and some of the old bear repetition. First and foremost, Urry (2011) ties the tourist gaze into the search for pleasure and happiness when people leave their normal abode and travel. Furthermore Urry notes 'The notion of the tourist gaze is not meant to account for why specific individuals are motivated to travel' (Urry, 2011, p. 17), rather gazes are related to building, design, content and social practices and discourses. Finally, rather than the static gaze of viewing or visualising, Urry (2011) now suggests there is a less static gaze called the 'performance turn' where 'Tourism demands new metaphors based more on being, *doing, touching, and seeing* rather than just "seeing" ' (author's italics) (Urry, 2011, p. 190). Thus in the context of garden tourism as a special activity with special unique psychological drivers, it is suggested, sequentially, that:

- individuals come to gardens – tourism;
- according to Urry, tourist gazes are structured according to class, gender, age, and ethnicity; thus in any investigation of semiotics, demographic variables become important to frame the discussion that ensues;
- tourists travel to find pleasure and happiness;
- tourists come to gardens for pleasure and happiness (as opposed, one would think, to tourist attractions like casinos, theme parks, etc.);
- tourists come with differing motivations;
- what they participate in, in the garden, is related to garden building, design, content;
- the researcher might expect to encounter social practices and discourses in the garden;

- gazing is a set of practices that can be seen, probed and displayed; and
- the tourist gaze in gardening and garden viewing is all about the 'being, doing, touching, and seeing' (Urry, 2011).

In 2014 Cengage Learning, a college educational company, applied Connell's findings (see Motivations sections below) to Urry's classification of tourist gazes as a case study. The results are reproduced herein. Table 14.1 shows the marriage between garden visiting and the semiotics of tourist experiences, and can thus be tested by probing motivations and charting tourist patterns and activities in a garden.

Motivations for Visiting Gardens – the UK Experience

The pioneering work on garden tourism motivations was conducted by Joanne Connell (Connell, 2004) who wrote what must be considered the first and seminal work on garden visitors. While her initial objective was to provide baseline data on the previously completely ignored activity of garden visiting, she also focused not only on the characteristics of garden visitors, but also on their motivations.

At the most simplistic level, when asked to *describe why they visit gardens*, most visitors to gardens in the

Table 14.1. The tourist gaze and reasons for garden visiting. (After Page and Connell, 2014)

Reason for visit	Form of tourist gaze	Type of visit
For a day out	Spectatorial	Casual
To enjoy a garden	Romantic	Casual
For interest/curiosity	Spectatorial/ romantic	Casual
To see something specific	Spectatorial	Purposive
Been before	Anthropological	Casual
Group visit	Collective/ spectatorial	Purposive
To show someone else	Collective	Purposive
To get ideas	Spectatorial/ romantic	Purposive
To see progress	Anthropological/ environmental	Purposive
Magazine/TV feature	Spectatorial	Purposive
Yellow book	Spectatorial	Purposive
Saw leaflet	Spectatorial	Purposive

UK describe themselves as 'visitors with an interest in gardening'. A minority had a 'specialized horticultural interest' and even fewer are in a garden for 'a pleasant day out'. Thus the frequent garden visitor has strong garden(ing) links, while those who visit for just a pleasant day out visit less frequently.

However Connell goes on to indicate that motivations for visiting gardens are often a mixture of the three options above, and probably more complex (Table 14.2). Thus when directly asked what *motivated them* to come to a garden, Connell found, by means of using an open question, that 'for day out' (15.1%), 'to enjoy a garden' (14.9 %), and 'for interest' (13.4%) to be the most popular stated reasons. Thus the stated *reasons* for garden visitation seem quite general, but underlying motivations behind those reasons (values and emotions) were not apparent.

To further explain motivation Connell undertook a factor analysis and remarkably she found that three components explain 67% of the variation in the data. The three dimensions of garden visitor motivation are:

● social (28%) – enjoying the company of others (family, group);

● horticultural (21%) – related to their own garden; and

● setting (16%) – sensual immersion, peace, tranquillity.

Clearly 'social' and 'setting', at almost two-thirds of the components identified, suggest that semiotics is a vital and fruitful area of research in understanding garden tourist visitation. Connell also provided cross-tabulation of the visitor's age, occupational class and typology of the visitor in reference to their *activities* whilst in the garden. The results are shown in Table 14.3.

What Table 14.3 clearly indicates is that those more sedentary activities, or what Urry might identify as social discourse (sitting and chatting), are undertaken by all age groups, while active activities such as picnicking and painting are weighted towards the younger age cohorts. Older visitors are more likely to take notes (perhaps for educational purposes?) and undertake photography. Occupational groups appeared to show little difference in their activities in the garden except chatting, which was more important in more manual labour groups, a group that had less interest also in nature study.

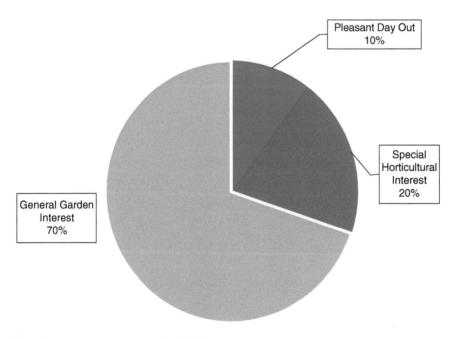

Fig. 14.2. Visitor description. (Source: Connell, 2004)

R. Benfield

Table 14.2. Motivation for visiting gardens (percentage of visitors). (Source: Connell, 2004)

Motivation	Tranquillity	Horticultural aspects	Somewhere to go	Nice environment to visit	Be with others like me	Visit as part of a group	To get ideas for own garden
Age							
18–39	97.6	78.0	65.9	93.9	11.4	12.5	65.5
40–60	95.8	93.0	59.1	94.9	29.6	10.6	87.5
Over 60	93.3	93.4	58.9	96.1	46.5	27.4	88.4
p-value	0.192	0.000	0.162	0.615	0.000	0.000	0.000
Occupational grading							
A,B	94.4	91.1	60.2	95.1	27.1	12.0	80.9
C1,C2	95.4	90.1	62.7	89.7	37.8	19.7	89.1
D,E	100	100	47.1	95.0	43.8	31.3	100
p-value	0.968	0.228	0.814	0.752	0.020	0.007	0.132
Garden owner	94.5	91.4	59.4	95.0	31.7	16.3	87.5
p-value	0.788	0.004	0.476	0.948	0.953	0.576	0.000
Type of visitor							
Special horticultural interest	92.4	98.1	28.5	84.0	21.5	25.5	92.1
General gardening interest	94.3	95.1	57.4	95.2	34.6	15.9	92.1
Just seeking pleasant day out	97.0	70.1	83.1	98.9	23.4	12.9	51.5
p-value	0.248	0.000	0.000	0.012	0.017	0.091	0.000

Note: Percentages indicate strongly agree and agree responses for each factor.

Table 14.3. UK garden visit activities – percentage of visitors participating by category. (Source: Connell, 2004)

	Photography	Nature study	Painting	Picnicking	Sitting	Chatting	Taking notes
Age							
18–39	43.4	27.7	4.8	44.6	73.5	59.0	25.3
40–60	51.3	43.7	8.0	28.7	76.6	49.0	49.4
Over 60	47.7	34.4	3.6	27.2	72.8	47.2	56.4
p-value	0.417	0.015	0.123	0.10	0.624	0.180	0.000
Occupational grading							
A,B	44.7	39.6	5.8	28.7	74.5	48.0	48.7
Cl,C2	55.3	40.2	6.7	30.7	76.5	49.7	47.5
D,E	43.9	23.8	9.5	38.1	76.2	71.4	42.9
p-value	0.076	0.335	0.769	0.634	0.887	0.117	0.861
Type of visitor							
Special horticultural interest	48.1	51.9	7.4	14.8	61.1	37.0	75.9
General gardening interest	51.2	35.9	5.5	27.1	74.8	47.9	51.2
Just seeking pleasant day out	35.9	35.0	6.8	48.5	83.5	64.1	17.5
p-value	0.023	0.066	0.786	0.000	0.008	0.002	0.000

Note: Percentages indicate strongly agree and agree responses for each factor.

Motivations for Visiting Gardens – the USA Experience

Connell's work was confined exclusively to gardens and garden visiting in the UK. In the United States the only study on motivations was conducted on visitors to Olbrich Botanic Garden in Madison, Wisconsin. Here the choice or reason as to why tourists visited gardens was much wider. The stated reasons (Olbrich Botanic Garden, 2003, unpublished results) were:

- enjoy outdoor beauty (73%)
- butterflies and other special events (55%)
- to enjoy a day outside (49%)
- visit conservatory (39%)
- bring out-of-town guests (30%)
- learn about plants and gardening (28%)
- celebrate special occasions (24%)
- learn about rainforests (12%)
- attend meeting (7%)
- take a class (4%)
- train show (1.5%)
- music/concerts (1.5%)
- plant show to buy plants (1%).

The Olbrich survey also probed what would happen if more events were offered;[8] 45% said they would visit if this scenario occurred (and still come at other times). Again in the USA, the Atlanta Botanic Garden probed, by means of a touch screen survey, what motivated visitors to come to their garden and the results were: (i) to see the garden in general; and (ii) see specific exhibitions and events. Furthermore the garden notes that exhibitions and events specifically create visitation as they are held during certain given time frames that add a sense of urgency to the reason to visit.

In a US survey undertaken by the author, over 85% found the educational value of the garden they visited positive or very positive, suggesting that education is a very important outcome, but not necessarily a motivator, for garden visitation in the United States.

Motivations of Garden Visitors – the Australian Experience

What is of particular interest to garden managers and educators is that rarely do garden visitors suggest they come to the garden to learn about specific plants or biological conservation. Specifically Ballantyne *et al.* (2008) found much the same motivations for visitation as Connell in the UK (see Tables 14.4 and 14.5) but what was conspicuously absent was any reference to conservation or environmental education.

When motivations were probed by Ballantyne, respondents indicated they were even less interested in education and conservation than other environmental areas and activities. Perhaps motivations for garden visitors are best summed up by Ballantyne *et al.* (2008), who state:

- Botanic garden visitors report having a relatively low level of interest in and commitment to conservation issues.

Table 14.4. Conservation interests and commitment by site, measured on a 7-point scale. (Source: Ballantyne *et al.*, 2008)

	Botanic gardens	Whale watching	Turtle hatching	Aquarium	Marine park
I am interested in learning about environmental issues	4.41	4.85	5.01	4.86	5.10
I often think about whether my actions harm the natural world	4.74	4.66	4.93	4.83	5.13
I actively search for information about environmental conservation	2.77	3.39	3.61	3.46	3.70

Table 14.5. Personal goal subscales by site. (Source: Ballantyne *et al.*, 2008)

	MU	AG	WC	AQ	HS	NP	MP	EC	BG
Enjoyment	4.28	4.33	4.80	4.41	4.60	4.23	4.82	4.37	4.42
Learning and discovery	4.69	4.46	4.31	4.24	4.38	3.89	3.98	4.21	3.23
Restoration	3.08	3.29	3.94	3.86	3.85	4.10	3.87	3.74	3.94
Social contact	1.99	2.04	3.03	2.73	3.44	3.12	2.79	2.37	2.47
Self-fulfilment	2.56	2.73		2.46	2.33	3.27			2.04
Learning about plants/gardens									2.51
Enjoyment of plants/gardens									4.74

Legend: MU = museum; AG = art gallery; WC = wildlife centre; AQ = aquarium; HS = heritage site; NP = national park; MP = marine park; EC = ecotourism experience; BG = botanic gardens. Blank cells were not measured. Items were rated on a 7-point scale from 0 = 'not important' to 6 = 'extremely important'.

R. Benfield

- The most important reasons given for visiting the botanic gardens were to enjoy oneself; to admire the gardens' scenery; to spend quality time with family or friends; and to enjoy being outdoors in nature.
- Botanic garden visitors were similar to national park visitors in that they rated restoration as more important, and learning and discovery as less important, motivations for visiting. Frequent visitors, in particular, were more likely to be motivated by restorative factors.

As a result it is clear there is a need for further research into visitor characteristics in terms of their attitudes, opinions, values and lifestyle habits, and that might lead to further insight or possibly even to defining the visitor in a more complex yet meaningful fashion. With this enhanced definition not only will academics be more adept at understanding garden tourism but it will also allow practitioners and managers to more accurately target existing and potential audiences. This is the realm of market segmentation which to date has been somewhat unrefined and almost entirely based on demographics rather than the psychological values which seem to be seen as the driving force behind motivation to visit gardens

Market Segmentation and Gardens

Most gardens, on the basis of the kinds of visitor data they collect, seem to have segmented their market into:

Primary markets

1. An elderly demographic (often loosely referred to as the Baby Boomers).
2. Often or predominantly female.
3. Higher (disposable) incomes and education.
4. All age groups with an interest in gardens and gardening.
5. Usually house owners.
6. Educational groups; K-12/ kindergarten to sixth-form.
7. Tourists, both domestic and international, and day visitors.

Secondary or emerging markets

1. Millennials (those born between 1980 and 2005).
2. Those with a propensity to visit gardens as sedentary leisure-time outdoor activity.

3. New house owners usually 25 years of age and older.
4. Generation X born 1964–1980. A smaller demographic, often with a garden and in need of upgrading landscape.

Psychographic segmentation for gardens

As one can see, the foregoing segments are primarily demographic in nature. However an alternative segmentation method has increasingly become popular in tourism and other business circles, as many believe it is a much better base from which to market a (tourism) product. The method is called psychographics (Dembey, 1994)[9] and uses values, beliefs, attitudes and behaviours as the base from which to differentiate visitors. The technique was first used as far back as World War One by differentiating people by looks. For much of the 20th century, demographic segmentation was favoured over or preferred to psychographics but psychographics was effectively used to describe tourist segments by Plog as early as 1974 (Plog, 1974, 1991). The Stanford Research Institute (SRI) in 1978 in the groundbreaking VALS typology (https://www.sri.com/sites/default/timeline/timeline.php?timeline=business-entertainment#!&innovation=vals-market-research) provided further use of the technique but it was the advent of the computer and its ability to handle large and complex data, especially using cluster analysis that permitted wider application of the technique. In garden tourism research, the motivations described by Connell are clearly psychographic in nature. A more recent (2015) and promising use of psychographic segmentation has been undertaken by bdrc continental for the Royal Botanic Garden at Kew in London. It identified eight clusters all of which, to some degree, have a propensity to visit Kew Gardens. While the study is too exhaustive to detail herein,[10] the characteristics of one segment are repeated below to describe how psychographic segments are characterised and to indicate the kind of visitor the garden might wish to solicit:

> This active, outgoing segment likes to live life to the full. They are always on the lookout for new experiences – unconventional ideas or combinations really appeal to them. Having fun with others is important to them but they want more than a social experience – they enjoy the intellectual and emotional benefits that days out can offer…they are prolific social networkers…

The Kew study also indicates how a garden tourism marketer might wish to communicate with the eight segments both in message and channel – in the case of the segment described above social media would clearly be a major vehicle to market to this group if it was assigned a high priority within the eight segments. Thus in the following the importance of social media to gardens in the application of motivations and segmentation is explored.

Examples of Application

Historically, the results of research into gardens' major visitor markets have been applied in the form of paid and unpaid advertising (news and press releases). However paid advertising has been the prerogative of the larger, more wealthy gardens, whereas the majority of gardens are smaller, often not-for-profit or governed by a trust, and thus without large amounts of money to dedicate to paid advertising. When paid advertising (or the output of garden writers) is sought, placement in gardening and lifestyle magazines seems to provide the best return on investment. This choice is invariably borne out by consumer research. In the case of small gardens, local community advertising may be used, but more often the garden uses a steady diet of press and news releases to impart their information. Furthermore a major presence in advertising campaigns, often coordinated by the local, regional or national tourist offices, has been a major source of awareness and marketing. This is now changing with the advent and undoubted success of social media and this new phenomenon is explored in subsequent sections.

Impacts and Insight: the Economic and Social Role of Botanic Gardens

Economic benefits of a garden

For a tourism sector with such a large number of participants and thus a large economic impact there is a paucity of data on the economic impacts of gardens. The Royal Botanic Garden in Edinburgh, one of Britain's largest gardens, estimated a total economic output of £23 million and a direct visitor impact of £3 million. In the United States the State Botanic Garden of Georgia in Athens, Georgia, estimated their total economic impact at $25 million. Finally, in terms of direct employment, by their very nature gardens need significant manual labour. The Morton Arboretum in Chicago employs 135 full-time and 90 part-time and 1000 seasonal workers; in comparison a regional theme park in the US typically has 41 full-time and 1300 part-time/seasonal employees.

Social benefits of a garden[11]

Again, much like economic impacts, the social impacts of botanic gardens have been little researched and established. Botanic Gardens Conservation International funded and piloted a study in 2011 that asked 'How socially relevant are botanic gardens?' The study came up with four findings. These are:

- Botanic gardens are well placed to educate the public on conservation issues and the human role in environmental change.
- Botanic gardens are enhancing their relevance by broadening their audiences and undertaking such projects as Community gardening, greening communities and education.
- Botanic gardens around the world are taking action by demonstrating their social worth.
- Future developments should include redefining their mission, active consideration of their social roles, communicating and advocating for the environment, and modelling themselves on places like the Eden Project, Cornwall, which has at its core social responsibility and relevance.

The Australian Bureau of Statistics (www.abs.gov.au) has been a world leader in the definition of what constitutes social capital and their Social Capital Framework breaks down what is commonly called social or civic participation into three types of participation: social participation, civic participation and community support. Numerous examples exist of gardens actively involved in all three.

Impacts and Insight: the Role of Social Media and Botanic Gardens

Since the mid-1990s and the boom in the internet,[12] there has been an explosion of the phenomena of social media as primarily a part of the mix in marketing of gardens for visitation development. Thus it seems mandatory that an examination of what gardens are doing in the realm of social media would be included in an assessment of gardens as part of special interest (special marketing?) tourism and especially in garden management for tourist visitation.

The first thing that has to be said about social media in general, and certainly for gardens, is that it is very important to garden tourism because there is so much 'noise' out there, and social media allows individual gardens to get noticed. In short, social media levels the playing field a bit – if a garden has great content, it can compete with the likes of top brands to rise above the marketing noise. For example, *USA Today* held a contest on the Top 10 Gardens in North America. The Butchart Garden was the only Canadian venue nominated out of the 20 gardens that were initially nominated. Then *USA Today* invited readers to vote on their favourite garden over a period of a month.

The results were:

1. Longwood Garden
2. Lewis Ginter Botanic Garden
3. The Butchart Gardens

Apparently Longwood Garden did very little social media promotion in this contest, but Lewis Ginter, without a lot of marketing budget, was able to race to the top, helped by a very loyal online following both locally and regionally, and a decent-sized population centre. At points, all three gardens were in the running for the top spot. At one point Butchart was even out of the top ten. In general, none of the gardens put marketing dollars into the campaign – but all were engaged relentlessly on social media and got noticed. According to *USA Today*, it was the second most-voted-on contest in their history – that's garden tourism and social media in action.

Secondly, one can say that social media is the first medium available to gardens that can connect hundreds of thousands of people in real time. Standard print or electronic advertising has never had that ability. In the 21st century, close, immediate, personal links are desired by all people and furthermore, considering that sense of personal values, attitudes and lifestyles (psychographics) may be the hallmark of defining visitors and their motivation, social media has the potential to be a major force in garden visitation.

Thirdly, social media lends itself well to garden tourism and vice versa. Why?

1. It doesn't require a huge investment and a lot of gardens don't have a lot of marketing dollars and those that do have already ear-marked them.
2. Gardens are visual and much of social media is all about the visual, which is why Tumblr and Instagram are the fastest-growing social platforms and Instagram has the highest rate of engagement.
3. Social media is about telling a story (or it should be) through the use of great content – and gardens are replete with deep, varied stories. Anyone can use a smartphone to take a photo or video, edit it within the phone or social platform, and publish it.

4. With social media gardens can 'brand listen' using free tools like Hootsuite, and follow hashtags to 'hear' what the public is saying (or not saying) about their garden – and then join in! One garden is even using social media (obliquely) to decide on which photos to put into the calendars that will be sold in their gift shop – an important profit centre that was noted in the book *Garden Tourism* (Benfield, 2013), essentially looking at what people on social media liked and then compiling that with other data to make informed decisions.

Having said that, the use and efficacy of social media in gardens has yet to be fully defined, owing to its infancy and a lack of academic studies on this topic. Indeed this chapter represents the first delineation of social media in gardens known to the author, although the American Public Garden Association compiled a list of best practices of 12 gardens in North America and Australia using social media; it may be consulted at: http://publicgardens.org/resources. The suggestions below come from a sample of North American gardens and certainly do not represent any prevailing patterns of use but it certainly provides an initial assessment of gardens and social media.

Gardens that use social media (and a cursory survey of Western gardens shows all gardens have some social media presence, usually a Facebook page) use different social media channels for different reasons:

- The main reason is that each targets a different demographic with respect to garden tourism – who are they after and what social media channels are they using? It is generally the case that gardens use different social platforms to target different demographics. The so-called millennials (who will be gardens' future customers) are rabidly using Instagram. Some gardens get more engagement on Instagram than all other social platforms combined! Yet it seems many gardens are late to the game with usually a limited (less than 2000) number of followers – but those that follow, love gardens. One garden went from zero followers on that platform to over 6000 in one year. Facebook is interesting: in one garden, 73% of the garden fans are women but for all of Facebook, women comprise only 46% of Facebook users. Thus 25% of the followers at this same garden are men and 2% have indicated no gender. Furthermore, at this same garden women aged 45–54 are 18% of followers – but they comprise only 4% of all people on Facebook. Clearly this garden has an audience that is interested in gardens and that garden in particular. Most interesting though is that these demographics almost exactly match their Facebook equivalent demographics on Sina Weibo (新浪微博) in China!

- Secondary reasons are the type of content (particularly, gardens desire channels that display visuals quite well, for example), immediacy of the information going out or the activity that is being delivered on the channel (broadcasting 'Hey look at me!' or brand listening, etc.).
- Tertiary reasons might be ease of use, ability to schedule or archival value.

The danger of wholly relying on social media is that the organisation does not own the platform – so if Facebook decided to delete content (for any reason) – the garden would have lost not only the content but all the context around it – often just as important as the content. Obviously to mitigate this, gardens can regularly archive metrics, take screen shots and save content – and/ or share the same content across multiple platforms.

The following is a list of the major social platforms gardens use, in general order of importance. Importance doesn't necessarily mean that the garden likes or endorses the platform, but sometimes a garden must market in areas they find individually less than desirable for their product.

Facebook (FB)

FB is the most popular channel on the planet, with 1.3 billion users in 2014, and hence most gardens use it. It shows visuals (photos and video) incredibly well and has great metrics. It is popular across most age demographics and cultures. It is used in the major tourism markets of Canada, USA, UK, Japan and Australia. It allows for paid targeting of FB users both geographically, demographically and by interest. However, it is a 'closed garden' – a term used on the internet to mean that content is not universally accessible or searchable. It is banned in China (potentially a very large market for outbound tourism in the future) and its organic reach (reach without paying) is declining (2% for brands – which means that only 2% of posted content ever gets to people that are following you).

Facebook is now a public company with shareholders, so gardens now have to pay, but for smaller entities this just may not be effective, feasible or cost-effective.

Most gardens use FB to broadcast events, pretty photos and videos – mostly to great acclaim. In turn gardens get valuable feedback in terms of likes, shares and comments from around the world in real time. Similarly the garden can engage followers in real time and in their own language (translation function embedded). A garden can test ideas and photos for traditional marketing on Facebook, and ask those most interested in the garden experience what they think about ideas or plans that are being considered – all valuable feedback.

What is also of great benefit is one can immediately see what is popular and invariably what people want to see are lovely photos of gardens. However most gardens go beyond that and craft the message with informational posts, posts about non-flower/garden points of interest (such as food or the gift shop). This is why gardens also use other platforms.

Twitter (TW)

There are 221 million Twitter users outside of the USA and 57 million in the USA. For gardens, TW is mainly used for broadcasting important information regarding an event, a change in hours, to engage followers, to brand monitor or to get other information in usually a short time frame by asking followers or other Twitter users. In a typical tweet a garden might have pinned their hours. The next tweet may engage followers with a cute photo taken in the Gift Shop (this lets people know there is one without overtly selling; it should be noted that using social media to sell something specific is frowned upon – it is better to market and give people information and options – so one won't see a garden posting prices or saying things like: 'Buy now at $25.50!'). A third tweet might promote the transportation option of a partner that brings people to the garden; it gives a link for more information and is hashtagged. A fourth tweet is a call to action to look at someone else's photos, engaging them by 'retweeting' their original post which started out on Instagram, was posted to Twitter where the garden was tagged, noticed it and are in effect saying: 'Look at this, someone else besides us thinks this is at least worth looking at, if not visiting!'.

Instagram (IG)

IG is one of the fastest-growing social media platforms. A photo-sharing app, it is highly visual and, not surprisingly, gardens – highly visual places – are seeing great engagement with Instagram. It is almost devoid of ads. It gives few demographic stats but is currently heavily weighted in the 24–34 age range. These are the millennials, the people that are stereotyped as wanting everything yesterday and aren't afraid to say so, and they are mobile (IG only works on a smartphone or tablet). They want choice and they want it their way.[13] Almost all gardens yearn for millennials but they, like McDonalds, are facing the problem of attracting them. Many gardens are trying to start the engagement process now as they are the garden's future customers – and they love engaging, love to love brands, and aren't afraid to tell the world about it For one garden, of the top five photos posted on IG, four were landscapes and only one a close up shot. Interestingly, only one is of flowers.

Garden blogs

A blog (a truncation of the expression 'weblog') is a discussion or informational site published on the World Wide Web and consisting of discrete entries (posts) typically displayed in reverse chronological order (the most recent post appears first). Until 2009 blogs were usually the work of a single individual, occasionally of a small group, and often covered a single subject. More recently 'multi-author blogs' (MABs) have developed, with posts written by large numbers of authors and professionally edited. MABs from individual gardens account for an increasing quantity of blog traffic. The rise of Twitter and other 'microblogging' systems helps integrate MABs and single-author blogs into societal news streams.

The majority are interactive, allowing visitors to leave comments and even message each other via GUI widgets on the blogs, and it is this interactivity that distinguishes them from other static websites. In that sense, blogging can be seen as a form of social networking service. Indeed, bloggers not only produce content to post on their blogs, but also build social relations with their readers and other bloggers.

The top gardening blogs in America (BlogRank http://www.blogmetrics.org/gardening) are:

1. GardenRant – primarily written by Elizabeth Licata, Amy Steward and Susan Brown and covering not only the art of gardening but garden tourism in general
2. Cold Climate gardening
3. Veggie gardening Tips
4. Backyard gardening blog
5. Busy-at-Home.

In the UK the top blogs are:

1. Alternative Eden
2. Fennel & Fern
3. The Galloping Gardener
4. Wellywoman
5. Two Thirsty Gardeners.

GardenRant averages 80,000 page views per month and has 11,000 dedicated followers. The site also has a profile of its viewers http://gardenrant.com/2008/01/who-are-you-p-1.html. It unfortunately does not indicate how many of the readers are driven to gardens as tourists by the blog, but Ms Licata indicates that because she has such a loyal following, she knows most go to gardens that have been featured or mentioned in GardenRant (Elizabeth Licata, personal communication).

Google+

G+ is used by gardens primarily for archival purposes and to get Google to notice that a garden has made an important blog post, so it is useful for search engine optimisation. Some gardens may find their fans on Google+ but for the most part it is believed they are not, so it is often only used in this limited format. A garden's blog is key to getting noticed by Google, because Google is looking for good new content. At the beginning of last year one garden got 200 views a day on their blog – today they are getting upwards of 1500 views of their blog per day.

YouTube (YT)

YT is something that gardens have not done a lot with, though one North American garden has almost half a million views. It is not a key component of social media marketing but it will become so because gardens and garden activities are uniquely suited to video, whether it be a 6 s clip or a 15 min YT video.

Pinterest (PN)

PN is new for most gardens. In the past PN used to highlight important branded accounts or regionally significant accounts. Lewis Ginter Botanic Garden in Richmond, Virginia, does Pinterest well – they have over 2.5 million followers – partly due to the way Pinterest is used to highlight accounts. As Pinterest is highly visual with a predominately female audience,[14] Pinterest is a great fit for a garden.

TripAdvisor (TA)

TA is a consumer review site, not a social medium. While it is not a social media site that the garden can control or post to,[15] it is (and should be) integral to the marketing of many gardens. Essentially, TA is used as a kind of third-party confirmation of social authority/licence – 'See what people are saying about us, organically, without our involvement (and by the way, they LOVE us)!'

Ranking social media

In an informal research project, a number of the gardens most heavily using social media were asked: 'if they had to give up all their social media except one, what would they keep?' Instagram appeared to be the most popular social medium, and most desired to keep TA as it wasn't social media.

Questions

1. The most basic question to be answered, much like other areas of special interest tourism, is the magnitude of garden tourism visitation. There are a limited number of gardens collecting this information[16] and yet with it garden tourism may be able to be recognised for its importance and move into the realm of a major tourism activity. This would appear to be the most important, albeit baseline, data needed.

2. From this most basic level, it is clear there is a need for further research into garden visitor characteristics in terms of their attitudes, opinions, values and lifestyle habits and that might lead to further insight and possibly even to defining the visitor in a more complex yet meaningful fashion. This may lead to a more meaningful segmentation of the garden visitor. Furthermore as applied tourism research, for garden tourism managers, this type of segmentation is fundamental for, from this information, media habits can be ascertained and the role and importance of social media would appear to be a question that is begging to be addressed.

3. Should restorative factors, as suggested by Ballantyne, be a major motivator to garden visitation and furthermore as the sensual attraction of gardens seems, according to Connell, to be a major motivator to gardens, it might be instructive to explore the tourism research pertaining to the sensual in garden tourism.

Conclusions

It seems evident from the research that tourism to gardens was for many years both unappreciated and unnoticed. This began to change around the turn of the millennium as gardens became more relevant, probably owing to the desire for conservation, sustainability and a realisation of the sociocultural value of gardens and gardening. It might be expected in the coming years that the research agenda suggested in the three questions above will be the most pressing and lucrative areas for research by both garden managers and academics, although the baseline data will probably be easier to obtain than conclusions about the sensual benefits of gardens.

More recently, the academic world, governments and the tourism industry have begun to investigate garden visiting and gardening as actual and potential tourist attractions. Three case studies in the upcoming Botanic Gardens Conservation International update of the *Darwin Technical Manual for Botanic Gardens* for garden managers (Gratzfeld, 2016) bear testament to that view. Thus it might be concluded that garden tourism is on the threshold of becoming a major component of 21st-century tourism and that much of this growth may revolve around the unique therapeutic nature of plants. This growth might easily be enabled by the linkage of social media and gardens. Once this threshold has been reached, garden management decisions can be made on how gardens might go to the next level and what new paradigm they must embrace.

Further Reading

As a starting point for understanding garden tourism in the context of tourism theory, the reader can do no better than Urry's groundbreaking work in

1990 and subsequent update in 2011. Interspersed with the Urry framework is the work by Connell, specific to garden tourism, both in 2004 and 2005.

Fox's *Understanding Garden Visitors: The Affordances of a Leisure Environment* (2007), subsequently in refined form as Fox and Edwards (2008), must be considered a seminal work on garden tourism management, albeit specific to the UK.

Benfield (2013) provides a summary of all work written to date on garden tourism. Today, perhaps tellingly, much of the work on the importance of gardens for tourism is coming from government and other not-for-profit agencies as they realise that garden tourism is an area ripe for product development.

Notes

[1] Walking is usually identified by participants as their most popular outdoor leisure activity

[2] In the USA, this rate peaked somewhat later than in Canada and the UK.

[3] This compares with some 313 million who visited theme parks worldwide in 2012 and 100 million who visited the top 20 museums worldwide in 2012 – worldwide museum visitation being somewhat inflated by the large visitation numbers to Chinese museums.

[4] Thus for example in the cities of Adelaide, Perth and Brisbane, the botanic gardens are the most popular tourist attractions in the city.

[5] The figure cited above from Wyse Jackson is one of visitors to public botanic gardens alone. The UK figure is on visits to all gardens, public and private, and to which multiple visits primarily by members or locals is a common occurrence.

[6] Much of special interest tourism is difficult to quantify as spatial locations and definitions are often vague and ephemeral. Ecotourism is a prime example of this difficulty.

[7] This includes National Trust properties, botanic gardens and English Heritage properties.

[8] In the USA specific events are used to draw visitors much more than in other gardens around the world, though this is certainly changing in UK and European gardens.

[9] Significantly, it was in the tourist magazine *Holiday* that Demby first used the term 'psychographics'.

[10] For a comprehensive analysis of the Kew studies see: Benfield, *Garden Tourism* 2nd Edn (in press).

[11] The World Bank defines social capital as the institutions, relationships and norms that shape the quality and quantity of a society's social interactions. Increasing evidence shows that social cohesion is critical for societies to prosper economically and for development to be sustainable. Social capital is not just the sum of the institutions which underpin a society – it is the glue that holds them together.

[12] The sharing of information began as early as the seventies (with bulletin board systems) and Compuserve in the eighties. AOL first began the widespread sharing of personal information but it was Friendster (2002), Myspace (2003) and finally Facebook in 2004–06 that heralded the boom in social media as a marketing tool.

[13] Google 'McDonalds Millennial Problem' to show the problems a major corporation like McDonalds is having attracting millennials.

[14] In contrast, in Britain the audience is about 50/50 male to female, while in Japan and N. America the female audience predominates.

[15] Trip Advisor is the second most visited travel site in the world (after booking.com which is part of the Priceline group) with an average of 260 million unique visitors per month. Unfortunately, many recipients of TripAdvisor reports, especially it seems hoteliers, resort to TripAdvisor fraud – posting fake positive reviews themselves or encouraging their personal network to do so – in an effort to boost the hotel's TripAdvisor reputation.

[16] A major development in this area will be the conducting of a benchmarking study of all US gardens by the APGA in 2015 and the work of the International Garden Tourism Network http://www.internationalgardentourism.com

References

American Public Garden Association (2015) Available at: http://www.publicgardens.org/ (accessed 10 January 2017).

Ballantyne, R., Packer, J. and Hughes, K. (2008) Environmental awareness, interests and motives of botanic garden visitors: implications for interpretive practice. *Tourism Management* 29(3), 439–444.

Benfield, R.W. (2013) *Garden Tourism*. CAB International, Wallingford, UK.

Boorstin, D. (1964) *The Image : A Guide to Pseudo-events in America*. Harper & Row, New York.

Connell, J. (2004) The purest of human pleasures; the characteristics and motivations of garden visitors in Great Britain. *Tourism Management* 25, 229–247.

Connell, J. (2005) Managing gardens for visitors in Great Britain: a story of continuity and change. *Tourism Management* 26, 185–201.

Demby, E.W. (1994) Psychographics revisited: the rebirth of a technique. *Marketing Research* 26(2) pp. 26–29.

Fox, D. (2007) *Understanding Garden Visitors: The Affordances of a Leisure Environment*. PhD Thesis, University of Bournemouth, UK.

Fox, D. and Edwards, J. (2008) Managing gardens. In: Fyall, A., *et al.* (eds) *Managing Visitor Attractions*. Elsevier, Oxford, UK, pp. 217–236.

Goldhill, O. (2014) Why Young People Find Gardening Cooler than the Movies. *The Telegraph*, 19 August.

Available at: http://www.telegraph.co.uk/gardening/11041376/Why-young-people-find-gardening-cooler-than-the-movies.html (accessed 23 November 2017).

Gratzfeld, J. (ed.), (2016). *From Idea to Realisation – BGCI's Manual on Planning, Developing and Managing Botanic Gardens*. Botanic Gardens Conservation International, Richmond, UK.

MacCannell, D. (1976) *The Tourist: A New Theory of the Leisure Class*. Schocken, New York, USA.

Page, S.J. and Connell, J. (2014) *Tourism: A Modern Synthesis* Table 4.1W (CourseMate). Available at: http://www.cengagebrain.com/shop/isbn/1408088436 (accessed 6 January 2017).

Plog, S.C. (1974) Why destination areas arise and fall in popularity. *Cornell Hotel and Restaurant Administration Quarterly* 14(4), 55–58

Plog, S.C. (1991) *Leisure Travel: Making it a Growth Market... Again!* Wiley, New York, USA.

Turner, L. and Ash, J. (1975) *The Golden Hordes: International Tourism and the Pleasure Periphery*. Constable and Company, London.

Urry, J. (1990) *The Tourist Gaze: Leisure and Travel in Contemporary Societies*. Sage, London, UK.

Urry, J. and Larsen, J. (2011) *The Tourist Gaze 3.0. Theory, Culture and Society*, 3rd edn. Sage, London, UK.

VisitBritain (2011) Activities undertaken in Britain. Available at: http://www.visitbritain.org/activities-undertaken-britain (accessed 22 December 2016).

VisitScotland Insight Department Available at: http://www.visitscotland.org/pdf/Visitor%20Survey%202011-2112%20Scotland%20National%20Summary%20V1_pptx%20[Read-Only].pdf (accessed 22 December 2016).

Wyse Jackson, P.S. and Sutherland, L.A. (2000) *International Agenda for Botanic Gardens in Conservation*. Botanic Gardens Conservation International, London.

15 Transport and Special Interest Tourism

Derek Robbins

Learning Objectives

- To understand the dependency of special interest tourism on transport provision and infrastructure
- To appreciate the specific challenges to provide transport access for special events
- To investigate transport planning and operating strategies designed to reduce the transport impacts of special events
- To understand transport as a leisure-based special interest activity

Introduction: Key Concepts

Transport as transit

The role of transport in special interest tourism cannot be overstated. Without adequate transport links special interest events simply cannot take place. The relationship between transport and tourism has been traditionally outlined in the Tourism System model (Leiper, 1990; Page, 2009) and is illustrated here in an adapted version (see Fig. 15.1). Clearly tourists or visitors need to be able to travel from their home area, traditionally termed the tourist generating region, to the location of the special interest activity or event. In the case of events there are additional complexities (see Robbins et al., 2007). Whilst travel for tourism purposes will produce uneven patterns of demand, with peak periods generated by factors ranging from seasonal changes in weather through to the dates of school and public holidays, the transport demands for events are much more constrained. In addition to the very specific time constraints, they are spatially constrained as well. Large numbers of participants and or spectators are required to be in the same location at the same time over the duration of the event which therefore concentrates the demand for transport services.

Many traditional texts on tourism transport distinguish between the role of transport as transit to the destination and transport in the destination area (Lumsdon and Page, 2004; Fletcher et al., 2013). This chapter will not focus on this distinction as these components of tourism transport are not mutually exclusive, they have become increasingly blurred. In the case of day visits there is no clear divide between the transit journey to and travel in the destination area. Likewise some holiday options such as coach tourism can incorporate both the transit journey and the travel within the destination area into a single tourism product. Special interest locations and events will attract a mix of day visitors and staying tourists and the transport issues posed by the time and spatial constraints are the same for both groups.

Transport to destinations is essentially a derived demand. It is rarely undertaken for its own sake but serves the transit function of getting the tourist from their home area to the location of the special interest activity (Fig. 15.1). The traditional view of transport is as a disutility which assumes that the quicker and easier it can be undertaken the better. Indeed much of the study of transport economics revolves around the value of time and many transport infrastructure projects, particularly road construction, have been largely justified using cost benefit analysis on the time savings achieved. Traditionally, 80% of the measured economic benefits of a road scheme are time savings (Wardman, 2004). This approach makes sound economic sense when measuring the time savings of people in the course of their work, ranging from businessmen travelling to meetings, to salesmen and through to professional drivers. In theory, the time savings accrue to the employers who can then benefit by gaining greater productivity from their

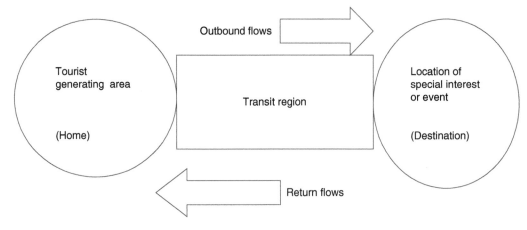

Fig. 15.1. The tourism system for special interest tourism.

employees, although in the case of small time savings re-investing the time saved in alternative productive output may prove more difficult than the theory suggests.

However what is perhaps more difficult and more questionable is how to value non-work time that is saved. Some non-work trips such as commuter journeys to and from work would not appear to be pleasurable or desirable and therefore would appear to be a disutility with benefits from time saving. Likewise special interest journeys can be challenging, time-consuming and unpleasurable experiences for which time saving has a value. Focus Box 1 outlines the very difficult journey faced by those attending the Isle of Wight Festival in June 2012 and similar difficulties were experienced prior to the Glastonbury Festival in June 2016 when queues of up to 12 hours developed (BBC, 2016). Time savings are given a monetary value; traditionally non-work savings are valued at a much lower figure than the average wage rate used to value 'in work' time savings (25% of the wage rate) because the benefits accrue to the traveller who is prepared to pay somewhat less for this additional personal time. In the case of special interest tourism linked to events, the pressure placed on the transport infrastructure is of such a short-term temporary nature that solutions to reduce the travelling time are limited and largely exclude permanent infrastructure development such as additional roads, as these would not be utilised for the remainder of the year. Policies predominantly focus on travel planning and influencing travel behaviour.

Transport as a leisure or a special interest activity

Time spent on many leisure journeys forms a component of the leisure activity and may be seen as enjoyable with a value placed on the journey itself by the consumer. It is not clear that such time savings should be given a monetary value at all. Furthermore some transport is being undertaken as a leisure activity consumed and enjoyed for its intrinsic qualities. This chapter will explore examples where transport is the special interest activity in its own right rather than merely providing access to the special interest activity.

Major Factors

Transit travel to special interest events

The derived nature of transport creates uneven patterns of demand for all tourism transport providers and special interest travel is no exception. Special interest activities will have a peak season which may be influenced by a range of factors such as climatic or meteorological considerations. For example, winter sports will produce high transport flows to the Alpine region of Europe over the winter months, although within the peak season there will be fluctuations in demand created by other factors such as school holidays. Likewise the Aurora Borealis (Northern Lights) generates peak demand for travel to Nordic countries between December and March. There is relatively little that transport providers can do to influence or change the patterns of demand, as the special interests dictate when the tourists want or need to travel. However the derived nature of the demand for transport services is at its most inflexible for special interest events. Demand is constrained to the duration of the event, often just three or four days in the case of a major music festival, with the vast majority wishing to arrive immediately prior to the event and to leave immediately afterwards. This very specific demand for travel to a specific location at a specific time creates unique problems.

Robbins *et al.* (2007) argued that responsibility for transport problems generated by events was not easily attributed. Event organisers tended to focus their attention on the event itself, arguing that access issues were the responsibility of public transport providers, local authorities and highway authorities. However this is now much improved with event organisers having to develop and implement coordinated transport plans in conjunction with transport operators and local authorities, in part controlled in the UK by the need for event organisers to acquire a licence to hold their events. However the need for events to continue to develop a robust transport strategy and improve performance has been amply demonstrated by examples of poor planning, inadequate provision and a failure to have alternative contingency plans in place as demonstrated by the Isle of Wight music festival in June 2012 (see Focus Box 1).

There are several factors which influence the transport impacts that events have on the local environment and the local population. First and foremost is the location of the event itself. There has been a tendency for many major popular music festivals, for example, to be located in rural locations. The initial reason for using rural locations is unclear but dates back to the Woodstock festival staged in upstate New York in 1969, or the original Isle of Wight Festival, held for the first time in 1970. The largest and most iconic UK music festival is at Glastonbury. The location of many of these festivals and special events are now so established historically and culturally they are very unlikely to close or be relocated and yet the choice of a remote or rural location is not ideal from a transport access point of view as discussed in the Impacts and Insights section.

Special interest events in urban locations with good public transport access are more manageable. However, even here policies of appropriate best practice are required to effectively integrate the event with the appropriate transport infrastructure. For example, historically the early report time for participants in the London marathon made it difficult (sometimes impossible) for participants to use bus and in particular tube services, even though of course most spectators lining the route who arrived later were able to use public transport. This has been resolved over time.

A second factor influencing the transport impact is the frequency of the event. There are advantages of holding an annual or recurring event over a one-off event in a temporary location. The Glastonbury festival transport plan briefly outlined in Focus Box 2 has been developed over years of experience, although there are limits on the degree to which one can alleviate road congestion when transporting such large numbers of people to a remote location. Likewise, the Isle of Wight festival organisers have developed a more robust travel plan with greater contingency planning following the events of 2012. On the other hand one-off events in new locations are more likely to throw up unforeseen consequences due to inexperience or underestimated demand. For example, The Mutiny festival was required to relocate from Portsmouth to Fontwell Park racecourse in July 2015. The new location generated a large range of complaints from residents, many related to parking and congestion. It returned to a new Portsmouth venue for 2016 and again in 2017.

The role of prior experience is well demonstrated in much smaller events. The author attended a relatively small local food festival (Dorset Food & Drink Christmas Fair) hosted by Attlehampton House, a stately home in Dorset in November 2013. The organisers had significantly underestimated demand and failed to supply additional car parking; when the visitors' car park was full, queuing cars quickly generated large-scale local traffic congestion on the surrounding rural road network (West Dorset Foodie, 2013). In contrast, the annual Sturminster Newton Cheese Festival held every September, for which the vast majority of arrivals are by car, has over the years developed ample temporary car parking, a park and ride service and a one-way system to aid traffic flow on the narrow country roads (Sturminster Newton Cheese Festival, 2015). The Athlehampton venue quickly learned from experience and when the same venue hosted the Dorset Food & Drink Christmas Fair in November 2015, there were free park and ride services operating from Dorchester and the transport plan worked far more effectively.

A third factor influencing transport to special events is the weather. Special events held outdoors are vulnerable to weather disruption. For example the annual Hogmanay street party in Edinburgh, which attracts around 100,000 visitors, was cancelled in 2006 and again in 2013 on safety grounds due to heavy rain and gale-force winds. Although the vast majority of open air special events, in particular musical festivals, are held over the summer months, they are still vulnerable to weather disruption. The widespread use of rural locations for many events further decreases their resilience to severe adverse weather, which was a clear contributory factor to the transport-related issues at the Isle of Wight Festival in 2012 (Focus Box 1) and also the congestion at Glastonbury in 2016 (BBC, 2016).

Focus Box 1: Gridlock at the Isle of Wight Festival 2012

The three-day Isle of Wight music festival in June 2012 created traffic chaos. Heavy rain caused access problems to the festival site at Seaclose Park, Newport from the Thursday night, with festival goers taking up to 10 hours to access the site on day one. Over the weekend the position deteriorated as roads on the Isle of Wight gridlocked resulting in over 600 passengers becoming stranded on ferries as cars could not disembark and subsequent ferries were unable to dock.

In addition to the gridlock causing major disruption to residents on the Isle of Wight, who were unable to undertake routine journeys such as commuting to work and travel to school, it also impacted on road networks in Portsmouth and Southampton as festival goers were unable to board ferry services.

Whilst clearly the major cause was the extreme weather conditions, it is clear that a combination of poor planning, in particular the failure to develop alternative access routes onto the site, combined with poor contingency planning and the lack of emergency response strategies contributed significantly to the resulting chaos.

Improved road access strategies onto the festival site were required by the Local Authority prior to the granting of the licence to hold the 2013 event.

Source: *Daily Mail* On-line (2012).

Fig. 15.2. Isle of Wight Festival June 2012.

D. Robbins

Transport provision and mega-events

Despite the obvious inter-dependency between transport and special interest tourism including events, there is a relatively sparse research literature exploring the topic, although as already outlined in Focus Boxes 1 and 2, event organisers are beginning to develop best practice. However one area that has attracted research attention is planning transport access for mega-events, specifically the Olympic Games (Hensher and Brewer, 2002; Kassens-Noor, 2012, 2013) and FIFA World Cups (Malhado· and Rothfuss, 2013).

Actually the transport requirements for the two types of event vary significantly. The summer Olympic Games are a multiple-sports event predominantly held in a single city location, and whilst some components of the 2012 Olympics were dispersed from London (for example football at Cardiff and Glasgow, sailing at Weymouth and rowing at Eton) the bulk of the transport network planning and enhancement was on the urban transport systems required for the main venues in London. In the case of a FIFA World Cup the games are dispersed around the whole country, requiring both teams and fans to travel long distances between matches.

Mega-events generate significant transport demand both from the games family and most particularly from spectators. The Olympics traditionally take place in major urban areas and although they are a one-off three-week event, in contrast to the special events held in rural areas, they justify the construction of additional transport infrastructure such as a new tram system in Athens (2004) or rail lines to Stratford in London (2012). A number of studies focus on the transport legacies of hosting mega-events (Kassens-Noor, 2013; Malhado·and Rothfuss, 2013). The hosting city also becomes an attractive location for hosting future major sporting events, for example London hosted the IAAF World Athletics Championships in 2017, making use of the stadia developed for the Olympics; the improved transport infrastructure is an additional attraction.

However, in addition to new infrastructure, significant planning is required to ensure sufficient transport capacity for mega-events. Transport for London modelled expected demand by time of day as well as by day of event. Some capacity is generated by displacement. In the case of Athens in 2004, ridership levels on the metro system are traditionally at their lowest in August, as Athenians head away from the city to holiday islands for their summer break, and this created some of the capacity required for Olympic traffic. In London, the local demand falls somewhat less in the peak summer months, and here perhaps a greater contribution to displacement was created by tourists not wishing to attend the Olympics staying away from London during the Olympic period to avoid perceived overcrowding as well as high accommodation prices. Nevertheless, in an attempt to create the required capacity and reduce overcrowding, Transport for London introduced a number of additional strategies. In the first instance they encouraged the local population to amend their travel behaviour to avoid travelling in the peak Olympic times using an imaginative and humorous poster campaign. They attempted to stress the advantage of travelling at less crowded times.

The second strategy was to introduce on-line travel planning information for those attending games events, including a mobile app. This produced real-time travel information and identified congested elements of the network, including stations. The most significant pinch point on the network was the Jubilee Line south of Waterloo which served two key locations (the South Greenwich Arena hosting the gymnastics and the Olympic Park itself). As a consequence of overcrowding, the travel advice often encouraged visitors to travel to West Ham (the second closest station to the Olympic Park) as an alternative to Stratford.

Motivations

Transport as transit

The motivation for much special interest related transport is the transit journey to a special event and as previously discussed such demand is derived and dependent on the timing and location of the event. As such, both transport operators and planners have little opportunity to influence either the desired time of travel or the volume of demand. The impacts that such a concentrated pattern of demand have on local communities, transport operators and transport planners is discussed in more detail in impacts and insights.

However a second motivation for some special interest related transport is its enjoyment as a leisure activity consumed and enjoyed for its own sake.

Transport as a special interest tourist activity

Some authors have argued that a different theoretical approach is required for leisure travel, which as a pleasurable activity is valued as a utility rather than as a disutility, and have developed the concept of a tourism transport continuum (Fig. 15.3) (Robbins, 1995; Lumsdon and Page, 2004; Page, 2009) where different transport experiences have different intrinsic values for the tourists.

The concept is straightforward. At one end of the continuum, transport services act as tourist attractions and the transport vehicle itself forms a significant part of the tourist activity. For example there are heritage railway lines all over the world including over 100 in the UK attracting visitors, often using steam locomotives. The key mass tourism example is the rapidly expanding ocean cruise market, although river cruises are also developing from a low base.

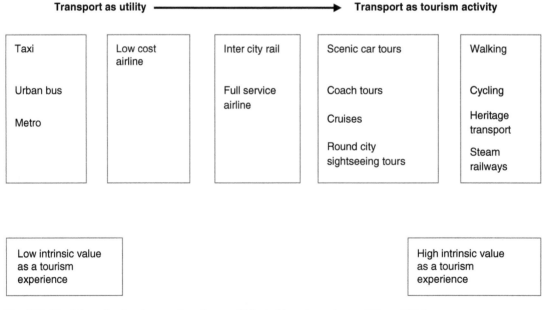

Fig. 15.3. The leisure tourism transport continuum. (Adapted from Lumsdon and Page, 2004)

D. Robbins

Other examples range from specialist rail services, such as the Orient Express, to specialised sightseeing bus services in the destination (Robbins, 2003). Occasionally, vintage vehicles may form part of the regular transport service also used by the local population, often as a result of under-investment over time, and yet such networks can become a tourist attraction. For example, there is a significant literature on the impact of the vintage bus fleet which served the island destination of Malta until recently (Robbins, 1996; Attard and Hall, 2003; Attard, 2005; Childs, 2008; Page, 2009).

However whilst the continuum is a valuable concept, its application needs to be supported by a great deal more empirical data. For example, the continuum shown in Fig. 15.3 has been categorised in terms of mode of transport. Taxi, urban bus and metro have all been categorised as of low intrinsic value and yet this will surely vary between different visitors. Black taxis and red double-decker buses in London or yellow taxis in New York have an iconic status, perhaps developed from media portrayal and may well attract tourists to ride in them who will place a high intrinsic value on the experience. These transport modes act as a symbol of the destination as evidenced by the volume of model taxis and buses offered for sale in gift shops. On the other hand frequent visitors to the destination are likely to place a much lower intrinsic value on these journeys. Therefore mode of transport alone cannot be the sole arbiter of whether a transport journey has a low or high intrinsic value to the user.

The characteristics, personality and interests of the user are key components to the value placed on a journey. Occasional or even first-time flyers potentially may place a higher intrinsic value on a flight compared to frequent travellers, thus novelty is a positive influence on the value placed on a journey. Other positive factors for a minority of travellers will be personal interest, so a rail enthusiast will value a long rail journey more highly than other consumers. On the other hand negative factors may include fear (perhaps of flying), motion sickness and even travelling with young children, which has been shown to increase stress levels.

This alternative theoretical paradigm, that time spent on travel is not a disutility, is being more widely adopted in transport studies (Holley et al., 2008; Metz, 2008; Germann-Molz, 2010; Banister, 2011). There are widespread calls to re-appraise the paradigm that travel time needs to be minimised for other journey purposes. For instance

Salomon and Mokhtarian (1998) identify 'excess travel' where people deliberately travel further than they need to in their everyday lives and 'undirected travel' where the destination rather than the journey is ancillary (Mokhtarian and Salomon, 2001). Relatively short periods of personal travel, identified at around 30 minutes per day commute time for example, are seen as desirable and enjoyable by consumers offering a natural respite and a clear distinctive barrier between 'home' and 'work' (Mokhtarian and Salomon, 2001), and therefore transport becomes a disutility only for journeys exceeding this.

A further argument to re-appraise the paradigm that travel time needs to be minimised is the sudden discovery that not all travel time is wasted time. The productive use of travel time on some modes of transport, especially rail (Lyons et al., 2007; Holley et al., 2008; Banister, 2011), is beginning to influence policy appraisal with opponents of the proposed UK high-speed rail link, HS2, questioning whether the value of economic benefits attributed to the rail link from journey time savings are overestimated because there is scope to use time on the existing journeys productively (Aizleiwood and Wellings, 2011). These changing interpretations of time in wider transport studies perhaps question whether tourism transport is characteristically different to transport for other journey purposes.

Slow travel

Although many transit journeys may be seen as enjoyable and as forming part of the holiday or leisure experience, in reality they are still being undertaken as a derived demand. Even if the holiday is perceived to begin as the journey begins rather than as the journey ends, nevertheless it is only being undertaken as a means to an end, with the destination being the principal motive for the journey. However for some niche consumers there is a natural progression to 'the journey itself becoming the main reason for going somewhere... to free oneself from the mind-set of modern holidaying... by immersing oneself in the life-changing experience of real travel' (Kieran, 2012). Slow travel or slow tourism (the phrase appears interchangeable) has attracted much research interest and forms a case study in Chapter 16. However it is problematic in that the phrase is widely used by a range of authors but with differing meanings and concepts, particularly between European and North Americans commentators.

Most authors concur that slow travel is about the quality of holiday experiences (Caffyn, 2009). In a European context most definitions of slow travel have three components:

- the pleasure of the journey as an important dimension of the holiday experience;
- travel conducted at a slow pace to enjoy more fully the places visited and engage with the local population and culture to produce a more rewarding tourist experience; and
- using modes of transport with a low carbon intensity (Dickinson *et al.*, 2010; Dickinson and Lumsdon, 2010).

However this definition is not universally accepted and specific conflicts and ambiguities emerge for holiday trips which do not meet all of the components. One area of debate is drive tourism. *Macquarie Dictionary* (2009) and Mintel (2009) specifically include car touring holidays as a form of slow tourism, whereas Speakman (2005) and Dickinson and Lumsdon (2010) exclude it on grounds of high carbon intensity. Whilst it can be argued that car tourism can include driving at a slow pace and taking a circuitous route to include a wide range of experiences and engagement with local people and culture, some slow tourists argue that car tourists occupy their own small bubble and miss out on engagement with the local area.

However a bigger conflict emerges between the USA and Europe on the inclusion of the transit journey as slow travel (Cho and Robbins, 2012). Whilst the European definition incorporates both the transit journey from the tourist origin to the destination and travel at the destination, the US interpretation dismisses this view arguing:

...it is overlapping green travel with slow travel. The concept of slow travel in the US is not that you travel slowly to your destination, but that once there you take the time to become familiar with it, to explore it up close. Don't spend your precious time in transit. (slowtraveltalk, 2012)

Other contributors to the slowtalk blog further explain how geography has shaped these different interpretations:

For many of us (Americans), we are very envious that, in Europe, it is vastly easier (and more affordable) to travel on public transportation. Also, you are able to experience different cultures, languages, and food within a few hours' or a day's travel. (slowtraveltalk, 2012)

Europeans can, by virtue of the smaller size of our continent and the sheer diversity of cultures and languages that it encompasses, 'afford' to take a greener view of slow travel; that does not mean that approach should be prescribed for everyone. (slowtraveltalk, 2012)

Whilst much credence is given to slow travel, as it has the potential to improve the sustainability of tourism travel, two key conclusions emerge. First, that the main motivation for slow travellers in Europe is to slow down, engage with the local population and gain authentic experiences (which is also the main motivation of the North American market once in the destination area). Therefore whilst sustainability and a low-carbon journey may be a fortunate benefit for European slow tourists, it is not a major motivation for most of them. Second, that whilst slow travel has also gained a wide following in North America, the understanding of the concept is completely different from the European market and the US interpretation has significant negative implications for carbon reduction.

River cruises

One interesting special interest market is the strong and rapidly growing demand for river cruises. The UK market for cruises in Europe has risen rapidly, by 59% between 2009 and 2013 (Mintel, 2014), with a concentration on itineraries along central Europe rivers (Rhine, Moselle, Danube), French trips on the Rhone and Seine, and Portuguese on the Douro (Table 15.1).

This increase has been fuelled by the introduction of new vessels in European waters in the past few years (Table 15.2) which are larger than their predecessors, enabling a greater variety of meal choices, spa facilities and balconies, all enhancing the product. In contrast river cruises taken in long-haul destinations have declined, although political instability has been a factor in the dramatic decline of cruises on the Nile.

Viking River Cruises is the leader in this niche sector which is aggressively expanding, having increased the number of berths by 47% in 2013 and 29% in 2014, and added 12 new vessels in 2015 (Mintel, 2014; Cruise Critic, 2015).

Initial investigation into the river cruise market suggests that the attractions are somewhat different to the ocean cruise market. Whilst many river cruise passengers have previously undertaken ocean cruises,

Table 15.1. UK river cruise market – passenger volume by destination. (Source: Mintel, 2014)

Destinations	2009 ('000)	2010 ('000)	2011 ('000)	2012 ('000)	2013 ('000)	% change, 2009–2013
Rhine/Moselle & tributaries	21.2	23.6	20.0	26.9	35.5	+67.5
Danube	11.3	12.5	12.9	15.0	17.3	+53.1
Rhine/Danube	1.8	4.1	8.3	4.6	5.1	+183.3
Rhone/Seine	8.6	8.0	10.1	10.2	14.1	+64
Russian	3.8	4.4	4.9	5.2	6.4	+68.4
Italian (Po)	3.9	2.0	2.9	3.0	3.1	−20.5
Elbe	2.1	2.5	2.2	2.4	3.6	+71.4
Douro	5.0	8.7	9.4	9.3	10.7	114.0
Other European	11.3	9.1	9.6	13.4	14.2	25.7
Total European	**60.0**	**74.9**	**80.3**	**90.0**	**109.9**	**59.3**
Nile	57.4	59.0	25.2	28.3	12.2	−78.7
Far East China	5.5	4.7	5.0	6.9	4.3	−21.8
Other Non-Europe	4.9	4.6	3.3	4.6	5.2	+6.1
Total Non-Europe	**67.8**	**67.3**	**33.5**	**39.8**	**21.7**	**−68.0**
Total	**136.8**	**142.2**	**113.8**	**129.8**	**131.6**	**3.8**

Table 15.2. Numbers of new vessels added within the river cruise sector. (Source: Mintel, 2014; Cruise Critic, 2015)

Year	Number of new vessels
2012/2013	27 vessels launched
2014	24 vessels introduced
2015	30 vessels scheduled for launch

the overall impression conveyed by feedback posted on The River Cruise Enthusiast special-interest Facebook communities indicates that river cruises are a much more intimate experience. Customer satisfaction appears very high even though it is a premium-priced product. Overall the attractions identified by the Facebook respondents are a high degree of immersion in the culture of the destination, meaningful contact with the local population, and an authentic experience. Indeed the following four quotes imply strong links between the motivations of slow travellers and river cruisers. The motivations of the river cruise market is an area worthy of significant future research.

I love how close you are to the towns, and can just watch the world go by.

Watching the farms and towns go by while having exquisite food and drink. Docking in the heart of and exploring historic cities on foot and bicycle. Chatting with people on land through the open doors of our cabin. Love it!!!

It's real life happening in the places where the cruises stop and you have time to experience it.

River cruising is more intimate, you're closer to land and able to get a better view of your surroundings from your private balcony, meet locals and immerse yourself in the culture. The best part, you won't get sea sick, rivers are calm and you won't be getting off with thousands of people at the same time to visit the different ports.

River Cruise Enthusiasts (2015)

Impacts and Insights

Transport as transit

Transit journeys to special events inevitably produce significant impacts on the local community for the duration of the event. This is particularly true for large-scale events held in rural locations. For example, in 2012 the Isle of Wight site was licensed to accommodate 90,000 visitors, although only 55,000 were expected and the resident population is only 140,000. The impact of such a large temporary population descending on the region for around four days, with many arriving by car, places a considerable strain on the local infrastructure. In the first instance public transport provision in such areas is much less comprehensive than in urban areas, so the location choice contributes to the event being car dominant. Whilst additional public transport capacity can be offered, as evidenced by the provision of both express coach services and also a shuttle bus service from the closest railhead to the Glastonbury festival site, public transport providers have to find additional vehicles for this short-term increase in capacity. Clearly some vehicles can be redeployed from areas where there is low demand over the festival period and possibly temporarily hired from other operators, but there is a finite source of spare capacity that can be temporarily used to accommodate the festival and thus increase the public transport share over car arrivals. The incentive of offering much lower fares during periods of lower demand to try and reduce the level of peak demand is totally ineffective as event consumers cannot travel at alternative times.

Rural areas are served predominantly by a single-carriageway road network with finite capacity and little opportunity to increase capacity. Significant additional road construction would be neither economically viable, as it would be under-utilised for the remainder of the year, nor appropriate as it would destroy the character of the destination. The available strategies therefore are limited to a well planned and coordinated travel plan (see Focus Box 2). Whilst there is some scope to reduce congestion by dispersing arrival times with early opening of the festival site and also dispersing traffic over alternative routes with careful signposting, there are limits to how effective these can be and it is even more difficult to disperse traffic on departure. Even small events can generate significant traffic congestion if poorly planned as evidence by the earlier analysis of the Dorset Food & Drink Christmas Fair, although significantly lower volumes of traffic can be accommodated much more easily with appropriate strategies.

Urban areas, particularly large cities, are much more resilient to temporary increases in visitor arrivals for special interest events, as they have a much more comprehensive public transport network. The peak period of travel for many leisure journeys does not clash with peak periods of demand from commuting and therefore occurs when the network has spare capacity offering public transport operators important opportunities to increase revenue at very low additional cost. Nevertheless those destinations hosting mega-events may suffer overcrowding at peak times of demand, although even here there is scope with careful planning to release some capacity with the displacement of other passengers. Furthermore the largest events usually benefit from a legacy of improved and increased transport infrastructure.

Transport as a special interest tourist activity

Tourists who undertake transport journeys as a leisure activity also offer revenue earning opportunities to the transport operator. In some instances they may also offer a low-carbon alternative to the rapidly growing international tourism market by air, although this is largely an incidental benefit.

Conclusions

There is relatively little research on the transport requirements of special events, although there is now a growing literature on both the planning for and also the legacy from mega-events such as the Olympic Games.

This chapter has identified two key roles for transport in special interest tourism. In the first instance transport is required to transit tourists from their home area to the location of their special interest activity in the destination area. However, where special interest activities take place in remote or rural locations, transporting tourists to these activities needs careful specialist planning. Even then the basic transport infrastructure, especially the road network, means that transporting large numbers to such locations will have significant environmental and social impacts.

In the second instance the journey becomes the principal special interest activity or at least a very important component of the overall trip such as in the case of slow travel.

Questions

1. Outline the main reasons why large special events located in rural areas create a more significant transport impact than those held in urban areas.
2. What do you understand by the term slow travel? Using examples, identify the key motivations for slow travellers.
3. Transport is a derived demand. Explain what this means and investigate the implications for providing transport services and infrastructure for special interest events.

Further Reading and Website Links

Robbins, D.K., Dickinson, J.E. and Calver, S. (2007) Planning transport for special events: a conceptual framework. *International Journal of Tourism Research* 9, 303–314.

Kassens-Noor, E. (2013) Transport legacy of the Olympic Games, 1992–2012. *Journal of Urban Affairs* 35(4), 393–416.

Glastonbury Festival (2016) Getting here. Available at: http://www.glastonburyfestivals.co.uk/information/getting-here/.

References

Aizleiwood, K. and Wellings, R. (2011) *High Speed 2: The Next Government Project Disaster? (IEA Discussion Paper 36)*. Institute of Economic Affairs, London, UK.

Attard, M. (2005) Land transport policy in a small island state – the case of Malta. *Transport Policy* 12(1), 23–33.

Attard, M. and Hall, D. (2003) Public transport modernisation and adjustment to EU accession requirements: the case of Malta's buses. *Journal of Transport Geography* 11(1), 13–24.

Banister, D. (2011) The trilogy of distance, speed and time. *Journal of Transport Geography* 19(4), 950–959.

BBC (2016) Glastonbury festival-goers caught up in traffic chaos, Available at: http://www.bbc.co.uk/news/uk-england-somerset-36594006 (accessed 6 January 2017).

Caffyn, A. (2009) The slow route to new markets. *Tourism Insights*. VisitBritain, London, UK. Available at: http://www.cabdirect.org/abstracts/20103307661.html;jsessionid=49AC41399C52C7AE3FC1801C58AF4F7A (accessed 27 July 2015).

Childs, R. (2008) *Bus Regulation, Network Planning and Bus Service Procurement – The Malta Experience*, European Transport Conference, Leiden, The Netherlands. Available at: http://abstracts.aetransport.org/paper/index/id/2917/confid/14 (accessed 27 July 2015).

Cho, J. and Robbins, D.K. (2012) Slow travellers. Who are they and what motivates them? BEST EN Think Tank XII: Mobilities and Sustainable Tourism, Le Château de Laval in Gréoux les Bains, Provence, France. June. Available at: http://www.besteducationnetwork.org/Papers_Presentations/4043 (accessed 27 July 2015).

Cruise Critic (2015) New River Cruise Ships in 2015. Available at: https://www.cruisecritic.co.uk/articles.cfm?ID=1713 (accessed 14 October 2017).

Daily Mail On-line (2012) Swamped in a sea of mud: Traffic jams and soggy tents as downpours hit Isle of Wight festival. Available at: http://www.dailymail.co.uk/news/article-2163073/Isle-Wight-festival-2012-Music-fans-arrive-mudbath-UK-faces-months-rain-24-hours.html (accessed 27 July 2015).

Dickinson, J.E. and Lumsdon, L. (2010) *Slow Travel and Tourism*. Earthscan, London, UK.

Dickinson, J.E., Lumsdon, L.M. and Robbins, D. (2010) Slow travel: issues for tourism and climate change. *Journal of Sustainable Tourism* 19(3), 281–300.

Fletcher, J., Fyall, A., Gilbert, D. and Wanhill, S. (2013) *Tourism Principles & Practice*, 5th edn. Pearson, Harlow, UK.

Germann-Molz, J. (2010) Performing global geographies: time, space, place, and pace in narratives of round-the-world travel. *Tourism Geographies* 12(3), 329–348.

Glastonbury Festival (2016) Getting here, Available at: http://www.glastonburyfestivals.co.uk/information/getting-here/ (accessed 14 April 2016).

Hensher, D.A. and Brewer, A.M. (2002) Going for gold at the Sydney Olympics: how did transport perform? *Transport Reviews* 22(4), 381–399.

Holley, D., Jain, J. and Lyons, G. (2008) Understanding business travel time and its place in the working day. *Time and Society* 17(1), 27–46.

Kassens-Noor, E. (2012) *Planning Olympic Legacies – Transport Dreams and Urban Realities*. Routledge, London, UK.

Kassens-Noor, E. (2013) Transport legacy of the Olympic Games, 1992–2012. *Journal of Urban Affairs* 35(4), 393–416.

Kieran, D. (2012) *The Idle Traveller – The Art of Slow Travel*. AA, Basingstoke, UK.

Leiper, N. (1990) *Tourism Systems: An Interdisciplinary Perspective (Occasional Papers No 2)*. Massey University, Palmerston North, New Zealand.

Lumsdon, L. and Page, S.J. (2004) Progress in transport and tourism research: reformulating the transport-tourism interface and future research agendas. In: Lumsdon, L. and Page, S.J. (eds) *Tourism and Transport: Issues and Agenda for the New Millennium*. Elsevier, Oxford, UK, pp. 1–27.

Lyons, G., Jain, J. and Holley, D. (2007) The use of travel time by rail passengers in Great Britain. *Transportation Research Part A: Policy and Practice* 41(1), 107–120.

Macquarie Dictionary (2009) Slow tourism. *Macquarie Dictionary: Australia's National Dictionary Online*. Available at: http://www.macquariedictionary.com.au (accessed 27 July 2015).

Malhado, A.C.M. and Rothfuss, R. (2013) Transporting 2014 FIFA World Cup to sustainability: exploring residents' and tourists' attitudes and behaviours. *Journal of Policy Research in Tourism, Leisure and Events* 5(3), 252–269.

Metz, D. (2008) The myth of travel time saving. *Transport Reviews* 28(3), 321–336.

Mintel (2009) *Slow Travel Special Report*. Mintel, London, UK.

Mintel (2014) *Cruises – UK – October 2014*. Mintel, London, UK.

Mokhtarian, P. and Salomon, I. (2001) How derived is the demand for travel? Some conceptual and measurement considerations, *Transportation Research: Part A* 35(8), 695–719.

Page, S.J. (2009) *Transport and Tourism: Global Perspectives*, 3rd edn. Pearson, Harlow, UK.

River Cruise Enthusiasts (2015) Closed Facebook Group. Available at: https://www.facebook.com/groups/RiverCruiseEnthusiasts/ (accessed on 1 June 2015).

Robbins, D.K. (1995) The Leisure Transport Continuum. Universities' Transport Study Group Annual Conference, Cranfield, January.

Robbins, D.K. (1996) A sustainable transport policy for tourism on small islands: a case study of Malta. In: Briguglio, L., Butler, R., Harrison, D. and Leal Filho, W. (eds) *Sustainable Tourism in Islands and Small States*. Pinter, London, UK, pp. 180–198.

Robbins, D.K. (2003) Transport as a tourist attraction. In: Fyall, A., Garrod, B. and Leask, A. (eds) *Managing Visitor Attractions: New Directions*. Butterworth Heinemann, Oxford, UK, pp. 86–102.

Robbins, D.K., Dickinson, J.E. and Calver, S. (2007) Planning transport for special events: a conceptual framework. *International Journal of Tourism Research* 9, 303–314.

Salomon, I. and Mokhtarian, P. (1998) What happens when mobility-inclined market segments face accessibility-enhancing policies? *Transportation Research Part D: Transport and Environment* 3(3), 129–140.

slowtraveltalk (2012) Forum for the Slow Travel Community. Available at: http://slowtalk.com/ (accessed on 16 May 2012).

Speakman, C. (2005) Tourism and transport – future prospects. *Tourism and Hospitality, Planning & Development* 2(2), 129–135.

Sturminster Newton Cheese Festival (2015) Travel and Parking. Available at: http://www.cheesefestival.co.uk/map.html (accessed 27 July 2015).

Visit Dorset (2015) Dorset Food and Drink Christmas Fair. Available at: http://www.visit-dorset.com/whats-on/dorset-food-and-drink-christmas-fair-2015-p1788743 (accessed 27 July 2015).

Wardman, M. (2004) Public Transport values of time. *Transport Policy* 11, 363–377.

West Dorset Foodie (2013) Dorset Food and Drink Christmas Fair 2013, Available at: http://www.westdorsetfoodie.co.uk/dorset-food-drink-christmas-fair-2013 (accessed 27 July 2015).

16 Slow Tourism

Alison Caffyn

Learning Objectives

- To understand the key elements of slow tourism
- To learn what motivates people to want to slow down on holiday
- To discover ways in which destinations, travel and tourism businesses are beginning to include slow elements in their products and services

Introduction

Holidays have traditionally involved an escape from our everyday lives. Now that life has speeded up to such an extent with busy schedules, rolling news and smart phones meaning friends and work can get in contact at any time, is it any wonder that many people are seeking to escape the incessant speed of modern life and take a slow holiday?

Slow is, for a simple word, a complicated concept, and slow tourism has been understood in a variety of ways while attracting increasing attention over recent years. This chapter gives a brief overview of the background to slow tourism and considers the key dimensions of speed, time and distance. It explores the main factors involved in slow holidays from both the supply side – the types of slow holiday currently being developed and promoted – and the demand side – the types of experiences which increasing numbers of people are seeking. The final section will consider the implications for the tourism industry and destinations of more people desiring slow holidays.

The question which underlies the whole chapter is whether slow tourism is in fact a form of special interest tourism or whether it represents a more fundamental potential shift across the whole industry. Can the key elements and concepts of slow tourism be applied to other forms of tourism, to the benefit of the global environment, local communities and indeed tourists themselves?

Key Concepts

Slow relates to both speed and time. In terms of speed, slow approaches have been developed as the antithesis to all things fast; the increasing speed of modern life, high speed forms of travel and the way that value is given to fast productivity and that speed is seen as a measure of success and fulfilment.

The slow movement started with Slow Food and Cittaslow in Italy (1989 and 1999 respectively) largely in response to the negative aspects of fast food and the increasing speed of life in towns and cities. Slow Food (www.slowfood.com) now has over 100,000 members in 150 countries. Slow Food's principles for food are that it should be:

- **good:** a fresh and flavoursome seasonal diet that satisfies the senses and is part of the local culture;
- **clean:** food production and consumption that does not harm the environment, animal welfare or health;
- **fair:** accessible prices for consumers and fair conditions and pay for small-scale producers.

Carlo Petrini (Slow Food's founder) states: 'Slow Food unites the pleasure of food with responsibility, sustainability and harmony with nature.'

Cittaslow now has a network of about 150 slow towns in over 20 countries (www.cittaslow.org). Cittaslow, or slow towns, apply slow principles to a range of aspects of government and management of the town. There are a list of goals that they must prove they meet to qualify as a slow town which include:

- the environment and pollution;
- infrastructure and information;
- urban fabric and conservation;
- local produce and products;
- hospitality and community; and
- promoting Cittaslow itself.

In time 'slow' began to be applied to more aspects of life. A landmark book was Carl Honoré's

In Praise of Slow (2004) in which he discussed how slow can also be applied to health, education, raising children, leisure and even slow sex. Interestingly there is almost no mention of tourism, transport or holidays. Honoré recommends a balance – choosing the *tempo giusto* or right speed for each activity and circumstances. He describes the slow approach as making real and meaningful connections – with people, culture, work, food, everything. Caffyn (2009) applied this to tourism saying slow tourism can be defined as 'that which involves making real and meaningful connections with people, places, culture, food, heritage and environment'. She added that people included local people in the holiday destination, but also one's holiday companions and reconnecting with oneself.

Slow also relates to time. Several authors (Kieran, 2012; Howard, 2012) have identified that modern society tends to conceive of time as a linear concept – referencing the Greek god of time, *Chronos*. We tend to think of time as a linear resource looking back into the past and forward into the future, every hour having the same length and value. However they point out that there was also a second Greek god of time *Kairos* – the god of divine time – of important moments in one's life. By seizing such moments and opportunities one can savour key times and experiences. This is similar to the current trend for mindfulness – living in the moment and paying attention to the here and now. Similar are calls to be more idle (https://www.idler.co.uk; Kieran, 2012), to relish not doing very much and make the most of it.

So slow holidays need to involve some slowing down of speed and also some change in perception of time. The thinking is that by doing both, the tourist will have a more satisfying, enjoyable and beneficial holiday. Too many people race through their holiday, trying to pack too much in, travelling long distances, ticking off must-do sights, posting on social media all the while and often arrive back home more exhausted than when they left and with only a fleeting impression or superficial understanding of the places they visited.

Distance is the other relevant dimension. By travelling fewer miles during your holiday and travelling at a slower speed you are more likely to engage successfully with the places you visit and feel more relaxed. You are also likely to have a much reduced carbon footprint which is the other essential element of slow tourism – although as we shall see later slow is often applied to tourism products without including the environmental aspects.

Dickinson and Lumsdon (2010) have come closest to defining slow tourism unequivocally. They insist on two key elements:

1. Experiential – having an authentic, deep and slow experience. Other authors refer to 'embodied experiences' – real, grounded holiday experiences as opposed to virtual and superficial ones. Hodgkinson (2012) represents this as rather than an escape, a choice to actively engage with a place, people and local culture – having time to explore, experience and think about where you are. This includes detaching oneself from technology.

2. Environmental – consuming less carbon during the holiday, including the travel to reach the holiday destination. Much modern tourism is dependent on motorised transport. Dickinson and Lumsdon state that slow travel excludes use of car, ship or aeroplane. Certainly it is vital to consider the distance travelled, the means of transport, how many people are sharing the means of transport (four or five people sharing a car is less fuel inefficient) and the length of time stayed at the destination (staying a month or more at a long haul destination could be considered less damaging than a one week holiday). In essence, slow holidays are more sustainable and tend to involve doing less, consuming less, using fewer resources and generating fewer impacts.

It is interesting to note that today's slow forms of transport include the train which can obviously travel at considerable speed and much faster than cars. However as a shared form of transport, like buses and coaches, trains consume relatively little carbon *per passenger*. In fact when railways were built there was much concern about the excessive speed and mechanisation of transport. Today slow forms of transport are generally considered to include walking and cycling, riding and horse/animal-drawn transport, shared forms of surface travel and canal boats. But it can get complicated as obviously canal boats tend to use high levels of diesel, while electric boats are much greener (Fallon, 2012). Also walking, mountain biking and canoeing trips sound very environmentally friendly but tend to involve car trips to get to the locations and possibly baggage transfer by car.

Some authors distinguish between slow tourism and slow travel. Lumsdon, in particular, feels slow travel is more about the whole experience of travelling – the places you travel through, pause at and

A. Caffyn

people you meet en route – 'the journey is the thing' (Lumsdon and McGrath, 2010). Obviously some holidays involve the tourists being on the move throughout, such as cycling breaks, canal trips or a journey on a famous railway. However the majority of holidays tend to include a short period of travel to a destination and then a longer period of time in and near the destination itself before travelling home again.

Geography is important. It is easy enough for Europeans to visit other countries by train but for Australians, New Zealanders or Japanese the slow travel choices are largely limited to domestic holidays. Similarly there are some destinations which can only easily be reached by air such as small island states. Conway and Timms (2010, 2012) take objection to European perceptions of slow travel. They emphasize slow tourism's bottom-up community-led approach and how it can contribute to sustainable development even when, inevitably in a Caribbean context, most tourists arrive by air.

For the purposes of this chapter the importance of the travel phase to and from the destination is acknowledged as fundamental but the focus is largely on the activities people engage in once they have arrived. Also the term slow tourism is preferred; some people will take journeys they consider slow travel but most people think in terms of going on holiday or taking a short break and slow tourism seems more appropriate for holiday products or the aspects of a holiday experience which could be slowed down, as long as the travel element is not ignored.

It is already clear that slow tourism is a much broader concept than sustainable tourism or green/eco-tourism which has attracted so much focus in the tourism literature in recent decades. The environmental aspects are crucial but so is the experiential. In addition to these two key elements there are further aspects which are often part of slow tourism and some would consider to be essential:

1. Ethical – as Slow Food is defined as good, clean and *fair*, so slow tourism should take into account where the tourism product is sourced and who benefits from the economic and social transactions involved. Slow tourism should in principle involve paying fair wages, fair terms of employment, largely locally sourced goods and services, and promoting maximum benefits for the local communities. Bottom-up, community-led and co-operative approaches complement slow tourism, with minimal economic leakages outside the local area. Wearing *et al.* (2012, p. 47) also argue that slow ecotourism should 'help decommodify and de-objectify the host communities' experiences of tourism and tourists'.

2. Mindful/healthy – in addition to a slow holiday being an authentic and deep experience, it can also include a major element of well-being for the tourist themselves. Slow tourists are more mindful and attentive to what is around them – taking pleasure in simple things – going for a walk, a delicious meal, people-watching, revisiting simple childhood pleasures. Slowness should allow time and space for an intensity of experience. For some this will have spiritual elements. Having a restful and thoughtful holiday will be beneficial for someone's mental health, de-stressing and unwinding from a busy everyday life. Physical well-being is also often an aspect – outdoor activities, yoga and spa type breaks all benefit the health of the tourist.

3. Non-conformist – just as Slow Food started as a backlash to fast food chains, slow tourism often includes an element of contestation or resistance to the mainstream – and as such to the most popular forms of tourism, mass tourism and globalisation (Dickinson and Lumsdon, 2010). Parkins and Craig (2006) call slow living a conscious negotiation of life in the present – challenging contemporary modernity and global orthodoxies. Again much has been written on the subject of mass tourism, the tourism system and alternative forms of tourism. Here it is just important to note that people consciously choosing slow holidays may be motivated by wanting to spend their money with smaller operators and local businesses, rather than large global companies or brands. They may also relish 'alternative hedonisim' (Soper, 2008; quoted in Markwell *et al.*, 2012) choosing an unusual experience to differentiate themselves from friends and relatives. The decline of travel agencies and rise of independent booking online hasn't changed the fact that big companies dominate the new forms of holiday booking (Dickinson and Lumsdon), so slow tourists will be more likely to use routes such as AirBnB or owners abroad – staying in locally owned properties and avoiding chains and big companies.

Before moving on to focus on the main factors of slow tourism it is worth considering briefly what is *not* slow tourism. Firstly the obvious point needs to be made that for many people in the world travelling by slow forms of transport is not a choice but the only option – where incomes are very low and few forms of transport exist. At the other end of the spectrum there are people who travel professionally – travel writers for example who may document their slow travels. Other people travel on a long-term basis (over a year) – as a gap year or major career break – and can scarcely be said to be taking part in slow tourism (although their choices of means of travelling round could be slow).

The opportunities for people to travel abroad to volunteer or participate in a work exchange programme (for example WWOOFing – World Wide Opportunities on Organic Farms, (Lipman and Murphy, 2012)) are increasing. Also, an increasing number of people are taking extended or unpaid leave, sabbaticals and career breaks as more companies are seeing the advantages of such flexibility. Are these in a different category? Again there is no hard and fast rule – slow tourism as we shall see encourages people to take their time and spend longer periods away, especially in more distant locations. However our main focus here is on holidays and ways of applying slow to more mainstream holiday experiences.

Taking a historical perspective, slow tourism bears many similarities to ancient forms of tourism – pilgrimages – slow journeys to find oneself (or one's god); the Grand Tour to engage with different places and cultures using (of necessity) slow forms of transport; or spa tourism whereby unwinding and seeking health benefits were the prime motivators.

Murayama and Parker (2012) have assembled a comparative list of the features of fast and slow tourism. In addition to the elements discussed above they point out that slow tourism is usually smaller in scale than conventional tourism. Scale here applies both to the groups of tourists and to the facilities at the destination. So, while it is conceivably possible to have a large group all going on a slow holiday together, the experiential element of their trip will be less slow the larger the group as the dynamics of the group are likely to dominate. Similarly it is less likely that slow holidays will be hosted in large hotels or holiday complexes, as ownership of these is usually through large corporations, and few will have a major commitment to local sourcing, etc.

There is then no one definition of slow travel but a number of elements or principles (Caffyn, 2012) which most slow holidays should include. However there are also many grey areas and it is perhaps better to think of slower choices people can make about many elements of their holiday.

Two of the most important choices are about how far to travel to take the holiday and how to travel to reach the destination. No holiday that involves long-haul air travel for just a fortnight can ever be very slow, however slow the activities are which are enjoyed whilst at the destination. There is a danger that this type of 'faux slow' holiday may increasingly be promoted as the concept of slow tourism is commercialised by tourism companies. There are also many journalists who focus more on the lack of mobile phone signal (digital detoxing) than any environmental or ethical aspects in the increasingly common articles about slow travel in weekend travel supplements. It is not enough to just focus on the experiential aspects of the holiday – they should also be environmental and ideally ethical, mindful and non-conformist as well.

This brings us back to the question of whether slow tourism is just another form of 'adjectival tourism'; a special interest for a minority of holiday makers; or whether it has the potential to help transform mainstream tourism more fundamentally. Dickinson and Lumsdon (2010) see slow travel as a form of 'new tourism' – a new pathway for tourism development and innovation with a focus on low carbon economies.

In the next section the major factors of the supply side are examined to see how slow tourism has begun to manifest itself in a relatively limited way within the tourism industry and destinations; the types of slow holidays and products currently being developed and promoted.

Major Factors

Guide books were one of the first manifestations of slow tourism. Sawdays started the trend with their *Go Slow England* in 2008, followed by *Go Slow Italy* and *Go Slow France* (2009, 2010). The books include a collection of 'special places to stay, slow travel and slow food' – selected from the mainstream Sawday guide books as places that were particularly 'beautiful, slow and inspiring', run by people who have chosen a slower and better quality of life. Sawday (2008, p. 21) says that 'slowness is, fundamentally, about happiness. ....the faster and more materialistic society is, the less happy are its members'.

More recently Bradt Guides have published a series of 15 *Slow Guides to England* (and parts of Scotland), e.g. Locke (2011). The company says 'Bradt has always preferred a "slow" pace of travel.

Ours is a sedate, measured approach which is all about getting under the skin of a place so that you leave feeling as if you really know it and haven't just scratched the surface.' (www.bradtguides.com/series/slow-travel-guides). In Australia, Affirm Press have published *Slow Guides to Melbourne, Sydney, London* and *Dublin*.

In the UK Lumsdon has published *A Guide to Slow Travel in the Marches* (2011) which has a more specific format focusing on eight towns in the English–Welsh borderlands. He makes suggestions for interesting itineraries from each on foot, bicycle or public transport, alongside information on food, drink, festivals, farmers markets and activities.

There is a good match between slow tourism and the markets for this type of guidebook. People who are curious about where they are visiting, travelling independently and prepared to make some effort to do their research. Some of the guides (Bradt in particular) are similar to standard guidebooks, with good sections on local heritage, wildlife, food specialities and slightly more information on local walks and public transport options. Ironically, some advocates of slow tourism specifically suggest you throw away your guidebook and just explore, allowing serendipity to rule your experiences and encounters.

One of the first slow travel websites was www.slowtrav.com. An American site, it promotes travelling slowly, mainly in Europe, staying in vacation rentals (villas, farms, cottages, apartments), rather than hotels. Slowtrav recommends 'see what is near you: Use the "concentric circles" theory for day trips. Think of your touring area as a series of concentric circles around your base. See what is close to you instead of dashing about on long day trips to see the "must-sees".'

There are online visitor guides which use the term slow such as www.slowtravelberlin.com. Other online resources and apps take a slow approach – encouraging visitors to engage with a destination like a local person. Examples include www.spottedbylocals.com which has city guides for 58 cities worldwide and www.withlocals.com – linking with 'local guides' across Asia. Dotmaker Tours (www.dotmakertours.co.uk) offer a 'London in Slow Motion' guided walk.

An online search reveals that a relatively limited number of tourism operators and destinations are using the word 'slow' in their promotions. Amongst operators Inntravel (Focus Box 1) have taken up the 'slow' label most obviously, calling themselves 'the slow holiday people' and using the tagline 'enjoy life in the slow lane'. Other operators use the word slow in a less direct way – for example Butterfield and Robinson's 'slow down to see the world' in

---

Focus Box 1: Inntravel

Inntravel (established in 1984) is a UK-based company offering mainly walking, cycling and snow holidays throughout most of Europe, plus Morocco, India and Nepal. It promotes its holidays as: 'holidays which reveal the lesser-taken path and which offer a truly individual holiday experience' (https://www.inntravel.co.uk/). Inntravel's snow holidays are given a different emphasis from most winter ski holidays. They are based in smaller more traditional towns and villages which offer cross-country as well as downhill skiing and a mix of other snow activities such as tobogganing and snow shoeing. It also offers family holidays, community tourism holidays in India and Nepal and 'journey' holidays – train, fly–drive and boat journeys.

While most customers probably use the air and self-drive options to reach their holiday, the website encourages UK tourists travelling to nearby countries to travel by train. They offer to book the rail tickets and stress the advantages of travelling by train, including overnight sleepers and the opportunity to stay an extra day or two on a city break en route. They even offer train travel to their Morocco holidays.

The website has a page which explains Inntravel's slow philosophy – this emphasises experiential and not environmental aspects. 'Slow is a position. A state of mind. Slow is looking differently at the world. Slow is where time doesn't stand still, it expands. Slowly. Where you see more by slowing down. Immersing yourself into local life. Meeting local people. Eating local food. Enjoying local hospitality. Exploring beautiful countryside. And feeling energised. Revitalised. Refreshed.' They claim to take 'the social, economic and environmental responsibilities of tour operating very seriously', and state their holidays, particularly the walking and cycling itineraries, are by their nature 'green'. They highlight the AITO sustainable tourism guidelines.

Fig. 16.1. Inntravel tour operator website.

promoting their cycling and walking holidays. Slow Travel Tours (www.slowtraveltours.com) – is a group of small operators from several countries working together to promote themselves under the slow travel label.

There are some examples of individual small accommodation businesses branding themselves as slow holidays including a self-catering business in the Auvergne (http://www.slowholidays-auvergne. com/) and apartments in Kefalonia (www.agnantia. com/slow-holidays-offer.html). Groenendaal (2012) researched such 'cultural creative entrepreneurs' who set up lifestyle tourism businesses of a slow nature. She focused on Dutch nationals who have set up small tourism businesses in France and found they generate demand directly from those who want such slow experiences. These micro-businesses have modest economic motives them-selves – they are motivated more by conscious

personal values and this encourages visitors to stay in the locality, rather than touring around.

Destinations which have used 'slow' in some form on promotional websites are relatively few and far between. Matos (2004), in one of the earli-est academic articles on slow tourism, recommends slow tourism be developed in Alpine and other mountainous areas – based on a high-quality and low-environmental impacts model. However since then few places have used the word slow in their promotions. Examples include:

- Slovenian Tourist Board (slow tourism packages – see Focus Box 2);
- Sardinia (slow and chic);
- Austria (slow travel featured under green tourism);
- Aosta Valley (slow holidays);
- Yukon, Canada (de la Barre, 2012) (slow as a way of marketing a wild and remote area);

A. Caffyn

- Japan (Slow Japan movement – see Case Study 1);
- Several places in the UK have used slow in occasional webpages such as Vale of Glamorgan (slow coastal activities); Yorkshire (food finder); West Wales (a greener destination); Sussex (encouraging residents to take local holidays).

There is reluctance amongst visitor destinations to using the term slow. It appears they feel it is not well enough understood, or possibly could be perceived as too elitist or niche. It is more likely that destinations have invested in slow actions within their visitor management strategies than in their marketing strategies. Many destinations have invested in slowing down traffic and giving higher priority to pedestrians, introducing car free days or encouraging the greater use of rented bicycles. It will be interesting to monitor over coming years whether more destinations use the term slow and how they choose to apply it.

While there are an increasing number of slow travel and tourism products, and the label is being used in more contexts, it is much less common than many types of special interest tourism products. Only a few operators have decided to promote slow holidays – mostly those where they see a close fit between their existing/potential markets and the sector of the population who are interested in or receptive to slow messages. Many operators feel the message is not clear or attractive enough, it is expensive, or that the ethics (particularly the sustainable travel elements) are counter to the company's activities.

It appears that slow tourism is much more a consumer led market than industry led (Murayama and Parker, 2012). It is more often the tourist who decides they want a slow holiday and chooses something which seems to meet their aspirations. The next section explores tourist motivations in choosing slow holiday options and the range of push and pull factors which make slow tourism an attractive choice.

Focus Box 2: Italy – Slovenia

The European Union has supported at least two slow tourism initiatives. In 2007–8 a Slow Tourism project between Italy, Croatia and Bosnia-Hercegovina called Rural Fairs, was funded through the PHARE programme. The focus was improving the promotion of rural events by engaging the local community, promoting traditional rural products and new services. It included setting up a Slow Tourism Club, using a hedgehog as a logo, 'a guide through traditional lifestyle and culture, offering unique ways of knowing some destination and taking special care about ecology'. It proposed setting up Slow Tourism Embassies – local groupings of organisations all working to promote the slow tourism ethos (https://www.slowtourismclub.eu).

A second project ran from 2007–13 between Italy and Slovenia, from Trieste to Ravenna (www.slow-tourism.net). The project aimed to 'valorize and to promote slow tourism forms in Italian and Slovenian areas, characterized by naturalistic and environmental elements and wetlands, through joint and integrated actions.' It worked to introduce a slow tourism philosophy whilst strengthening tourist resources, particularly focusing on cycling routes, river tourism, canoeing, birdwatching and nature tourism. A slow tourism network was developed, with a joint marketing strategy, integrating sustainable forms of transport and new opportunities for local people to work in nature tourism; 125 tourism

operators joined the network and a large number of itineraries were developed.

The slow philosophy that they encouraged operators to sign up to included six elements:

- Contamination – generating fruitful exchange between guests and local people;
- Authenticity – offering distinctive and non-artificial experiences rooted in local culture and traditions;
- Sustainability – minimising environmental and social impacts, involving a long-term approach, ethically and socially fair toward the guest and the local community;
- Tempo – allowing time for businesses to plan and deliver improvements in quality and services to offer guests comfortable and well paced experiences;
- Length – the capability to organise and deliver "slow" tourism products, involving the guest in the destination and focusing on the quality of the stay;
- Emotion – generating memorable moments for the guest, that marks him/her by a true involving and gratifying experience.

It published a comprehensive document with guidelines for slow tourism (Zago, 2011) – aimed at tourism operators with examples of best practice on marketing, ICT, transport, accommodation, food etc. There was also an app promoting 40 routes and itineraries across the area.

Case Study 1: Japan

Murayama and Parker (2012) discuss how Japan has been labelled the 'fastest nation in the world'. They describe how the *Kaizen* mentality, which stresses speed, efficiency, continuous improvement and convenience, became more dominant in the post-war reconstruction period when traditional philosophies linked to Buddhism and Shintoism were overtaken by the focus on economic development and materialism. As with other Western societies work-life has been prioritised over leisure with limited annual leave entitlements. Holidays are of necessity shorter and faster, often trying to cram in a quantity of experiences rather than a more limited number of quality experiences. In the 1980s the phenomenon of *Karoshi* or death by overwork and high levels of suicide were recognised. This is the period which spawned stereotypes of US and Japanese tourists racing round 'doing' countries within a few days, capturing major landmarks with cameras.

More recently attitudes in Japan have begun to change and younger generations are said to be more concerned with their mental well-being and quality of life. Murayama and Parker highlight the 'U turners', people returning to live in the countryside and 'J turners' who move from urban areas to rural. In tourism terms rural holidays and working holidays on the land have become more popular with Japanese urban audiences.

The Slow Japan movement or 'Sloth Club' was established in 1999 (slowjapan.wordpress.com). It is an environmental NGO and promotes the concept of 'slow' as a prescription against the ever accelerating 'fast' world, by holding events, running campaigns and encouraging a network of 'slow cafes' to develop. In tourism terms Slow Japan seeks to 'create a form of "engaged tourism" where participants are not just "looking at" a new country or environment or culture but actually become involved and immersed in their experience.' They spell out a slow tourism manifesto:

- Slow tourism means reconnecting: Feel nature, then study, protect and enjoy it. Our goal is to reconnect people, and provide a trip that rediscovers connections between people and nature.
- Slow tourism is a cultural trip: Experience and appreciate local cultures in all their diversity
- Slow tourism is ecological: Airplanes, automobiles … we understand these travel necessities have a big impact on the ecosystem. So, we do something small to make the world a better place, like planting a tree, or picking up trash instead of creating trash.
- Slow tourism is fair trade: We visit and support indigenous people and producers who engage in organic agriculture and are building a sustainable economy and society.
- Slow tourism changes you: What can you bring back to your life? Everything starts from the moment you come home from a slow tour.

It is interesting to note from a Japanese perspective it is much more difficult to avoid using airplanes to travel to other countries and their ecological objectives are limited to mitigating the environmental impacts of this. Muruyama and Parker surmise that slow tourism is only slowly gaining ground in Japan. The term is used by some tourism authorities but usually only in policy contexts not as a marketing label. They see the concept as a great opportunity and as a good match with Japan's traditional culture. However they also identify the danger that the label could simply be applied piecemeal to certain niche products.

Motivations

Limited research has been undertaken into slow tourists or their motivations. One of few studies was undertaken in Turkey's first Cittaslow (Seferihisar) and identified what were called 'dedicated slow tourists'. These are tourists who are:

- open to slow experiences and discover new and different cultures and identities;
- are educated, and have a good cultural knowledge and slow philosophy;
- are independent travellers;
- have high expectations with regard to the region they are visiting; and
- enjoy eco-gastronomy (Yurtseven and Kaya, 2011)

Accounts of slow tourism in the literature identify a range of push and pull motivations. Many people seek out slow holidays because they are dissatisfied or disillusioned with previous experiences. Those people who have downshifted or chosen to avoid commodified products in other parts of their lives are more likely to want alternative choices to mainstream tourism operators or mainstream online listings. They may be tired of holidaying at inauthentic resorts with little local character and reject homogeneous holiday accommodation. Other people will be reacting against holidays where they have raced around too much and found themselves exhausted. Woehler (2004, p. 90) refers to time scarcity during holidays and how pressure leads to the 'fast forward consumption of standardized tourism products in destinations'. The escape may not be so much from everyday life as from previous holiday experiences. People desire to do less on holiday – not ticking off must-see sights in guide books but just chilling out and relaxing. Kieran (2012) feels that many major sites have become so commodified that they are largely inauthentic and often offer hollow experiences anyway.

Having said that, the escape from busy lives is still a motivation for slow holidays – escaping an unsatisfactory or hectic everyday to slow down, take a breath, chill out and enjoy a more meaningful experience. Some people may choose a slow holiday to escape their increasingly digital life. They may want a break from their dependence on social media and new technology and want to switch off for a period (Harris, 2014).

There are many 'pull' factors which motivate people to choose slow holidays or to slow down whilst on holiday. They seek a range of perceived benefits. These include the experiential, environmental, ethical, mindful and non-conformist elements discussed already. But there are additional components which attract tourists:

- Interactions with nature – walking, cycling, canoeing etc. all allow you to get closer to nature so you see more – wildlife, views, etc. Hodgkinson (2012) talks about the need to reconnect with wild places. The National Trust's campaign 50 Things to do before you're 11¾ (www.50things.org.uk) aims to tackle the modern phenomenon of Nature Deficit Disorder (Moss, 2012) and encourage children to enjoy the outdoors through simple activities like climbing a tree or making mud pies.
- Well-being – physical and mental health, leading to increased happiness. Axt and Axt-Gadermann (2005) present an interesting argument for how laziness is good for your health – and how stress harms an individual's immune system. Woehler (2004) points out that wellness can't be rushed.
- Sensory – using all one's senses. Memorable experiences and heightened sensations – from special meals, music, gardens etc.

- Peaceful – allowing time to chill out, avoid digital life, think and relax. Some people may meditate or go on a retreat.
- Active participation – some people will seek out participatory experiences – engaging with the destination and local people rather than a passive experience.
- Self-awareness – Kieran (2012) speculates that travel activates people's brains neurologically leading to more positive conscious thought processes. So people away from home become more aware of what's around them and more self-aware.
- Meaning – choices of holiday which give one's life more meaning – this could include volunteering, learning a new skill or some form of personal development.
- Challenge – personal challenges as a form of holiday, such as doing the UK's Land's End to John O'Groats cycle route, often for charity. Such endurance events help people affirm themselves, their lives and improve their fitness. However whether these can really be called slow holidays is questionable – while the transport may be low carbon there is minimal engagement with the places travelled through – the focus is usually on the activity and mileage covered each day.
- Social connections, conviviality and hospitality – meeting and enjoying time spent with people, often over food. This links to Slow Food's ethos of conviviality.
- Caring – respectful and caring for and about other people, places, culture and environment
- Authentic – discovering a sense of place, *terroir*, and contact with local producers and local markets. The defence of local cultural identity and regional landscapes. Anti-homogenisation, e.g. supermarkets and hotel rooms. Appreciating artisan products and practices – food, craft, art, music etc.
- Traditional – Some suggest that slow holidays are a significant way of linking back in time to our heritage or the local heritage of the destination – its *terroir* (Parkins and Craig, 2006). So canal holidays allow people to experience something of the time when it was a major form of transport (Fallon, 2012). Riding holidays might be similar – giving you an appreciation for the time and effort travelling by horse took.

None of these factors is essential – for example slow holidays don't have to involve wild or rural places but are perfectly possible in urban locations.

They would normally involve meeting people but actually could be solitary experiences such as a solo long distance walk.

Slow doesn't have to mean traditional (it could be modern and urban), and some might argue that it does not hark back to earlier, simpler times – that in fact it is a new paradigm, and that 'fast' is now old fashioned.

Do slow tourists have to leave their smart phones behind at home then? While it might be advisable to detach from digital technology while on a slow holiday if you really want to unwind and engage, slow is not by definition anti-technology. Online information or interpretation might be helpful and enhance an experience, putting you in touch with local people or finding out about events going on. However the focus would be on keeping the use of phones, tablets and laptops to a minimum and focusing on the real world and physicality of the place and the people.

Harris (2014) mourns the loss of 'absence', of day dreaming of doing nothing in particular, of being open to 'real life' that many people now experience being permanently connected digitally. However, he says that while technology is likely to alienate people from some part of their lives the important thing is to notice this and choose how much to use the technology. To find the right balance for the situation and the individual; which sounds very similar to Honoré's right speed.

Impacts and Insights

There are potential benefits for destinations from promoting slow tourism. Visitors will want to travel around the area less – reducing congestion – and be happy with fewer experiences, as long as they are satisfying, quality activities. They may be willing to stay longer, generating more spend. Slow holidays should offer more enjoyable, distinctive and fulfilling experiences and thus generate more satisfied visitors, repeat visits and recommendations (Caffyn, 2009). Given that few destinations have chosen to brand themselves slow, the early adopters may also have a considerable market advantage and increased PR coverage. Some rural and remote areas have seen the potential in turning a negative (lack of mobile phone reception) into a positive selling point, such as the Yukon (de la Barre, 2012).

The types of action which destinations could implement to improve their offer for slow visitors include providing places where visitors can relax; such as outdoor cafes, picnic sites, outdoor seating, viewpoints, gardens, car free areas and peaceful oases. Slow activities should be easily available, including walking routes, guided walks, cycle hire, rowing boats, natural play areas, spa facilities, trips on local buses/trains and opportunities to participate in arts and crafts. Slow transport options and easy information and interchanges are vital. Local markets, good eating places, specialist food shops, local crafts available to buy and related festivals and events would all be of interest to slow visitors, as would a well-cared-for historic environment.

Many small tourism businesses have chosen to 'go slow' already – such as the accommodation featured in Sawday's *Go Slow* guidebooks. Some of these businesses are lifestyle businesses or those who have developed their slow tourism product on the back of a personal interest (e.g. raising pigs, pottery, fishing, cycling) and ethical standpoint. There are a range of actions which any tourism business could take to make their offer slower or to develop specific slow products. These include encouraging visitors to travel by public transport, giving good information, transfer options and perhaps a discount or incentive for those arriving without a car. It would also include encouraging people to travel around the area by walking, cycling, offering bike hire, electric bikes or cars to hire, highlighting boat trips, guided walks, riding etc.

Another option is to give visitors more choice and flexibility about the pace and speed of their holiday, for example by encouraging longer breaks and extension options, perhaps with incentives. Restaurants and other similar businesses could train their staff to better recognise body language – serving people in a hurry promptly, whilst allowing those who want to relax more time for their meal, additional nibbles and drinks, etc. A similar approach at museums and attractions might entail a fast-track option for those in a hurry and more in-depth interpretation for people wanting to take their time.

Again businesses can offer slow places, tranquil areas, mobile-phone-free zones, and also bring out the local distinctiveness of the locality, landscape, heritage, food etc. Some may choose to develop specifically slow products – off-grid log cabins, special menus, tours, activities and breaks which emphasise various aspects of slow tourism. Transport companies such as train operators could offer frequent user benefits (like frequent flyers) to

Fig. 16.2. Ludlow; one of the UK's first Cittaslow towns which markets its heritage, landscape and local food culture.

incentivise passengers – such as the Thalys TheCard which earns users train miles. The guidelines developed in the Italy–Slovenia project (Focus Box 2) include a long list of actions operators could implement.

People can choose to slow down while on holiday or in their choice of holiday. One option is to holiday closer to home. The recent growth in staycations (usually attributed to the economic recession) is interpreted either as holidaying in one's own country or even holidaying while staying at home – by exploring one's local area more deeply and visiting all the places you don't normally have time to. Choosing a lower carbon form of transport would be an obvious choice. Dickinson *et al.* (2010) found that slow travellers conceptualise tourism differently from other people. Instead of deciding on a destination and then working out the best way to travel there, slow travellers are more likely to choose a mode of transport for the holiday and then decide where to go using that transport. Travelling more slowly involves being open to other cultures, people and ways of life and a certain degree of humility. Individuals can choose a holiday which includes a large number of the factors outlined earlier in this article; 'Slow travel is about making conscious choices' (Gardner, 2009).

Several sets of guidelines or principles for slow tourists have been published (for example Carpinelli in Nitti, 2013). The way of slow travel (http://www.thewayofslowtravel.com/) gives ten principles:

1. Slow down
2. Stretch your comfort zone
3. Simplify
4. Let go of the plan
5. Spend less
6. Take root
7. Blend in
8. Rely on strangers
9. Practice gratitude
10. Celebrate the ordinary

Slowing down is more likely to be an approach to one's whole life – not only to choice of holiday. Slow tourists are likely to be people who are willing to think about their choices, care about the impact they have on the planet and their locality and want to have more meaningful, authentic experiences.

Slow tourism appears to promise much. A relatively sustainable form of tourism, celebrating what is special about a place, keeping more economic benefits within the local community and delivering meaningful and satisfying experiences. A potential 'win-win-win' (Caffyn, 2012). One of the main challenges thus far has been how to market it and make it an attractive proposition. But increasingly operators and destinations are finding ways of using 'slow' to appeal to customers and no doubt the more it is used, the better it will be recognised and the more it will spread.

The more important challenge is how to prevent the environmental and low-carbon elements of slow tourism being lost in the process. There is a danger that people – journalists, tourism businesses and marketers – will use the slow label purely in terms of the experiential elements. Slow could become increasingly commodified into slow products, PR angles and meaningless labels applied to mainstream offers. It could be shunted into a side alley as simply a special interest niche to be applied to holidays anywhere on the globe, regardless of distance travelled. If mis-applied and discredited it is less likely to lead to any beneficial changes.

There has been hope in the slow tourism and travel literature that slow could represent a potential longer-term shift in tourism. As the reality of climate change sets in, fossil fuels become scarcer and more expensive there could be a considerable decline in long-haul tourism. Dickinson and Lumsdon (2010) foresee a possible new tourism paradigm – that the adaptation of destinations could lead to more ubiquitous slower forms of tourism, mainly around domestic tourism. They remind us that globally domestic tourism is already currently five times larger in volume than international tourism and only 2% of tourists take international flights. It's an exciting prospect that by adopting slow tourism, destinations and companies could offer visitors rich experiences that benefit the individual as well as the local community, economy and environment.

But then as discussed above, there is no one meaning or model, so perhaps even faux slow tourism is to be welcomed. The emphasis should be placed upon facilitating those people who care, to choose slower holidays which benefit them and the local area and hopefully do relatively little damage to the planet. The concept of individual carbon allowances, sometime proposed, might address issues around distance travelled. People could choose to take long-haul flights very occasionally, balancing them out with many low carbon trips. Or they could purchase additional carbon allowances from people who are happy not to use their allowance.

It would be counter-productive to get drawn into too detailed a debate about definitions or accusations of elitism and hypocrisy (something that seemed to hinder discussion about ecotourism for many years). Better to accept that slow has much to offer and can be applied to a greater or lesser extent in many contexts. As Honoré said initially about the concept of slow – it's about being slow when it matters and consciously choosing the right speed for the situation; trying to find the balance.

Questions

1. Why have so few destinations adopted the terminology slow in their marketing and promotions – how can the word and the concept be better communicated?

2. Is it inevitable that slow tourism products will be commodified and lose their slow integrity? Does this matter?

3. How could slow principles be best integrated into mainstream tourism business practice and destination management?

Further Reading and Website Links

Dickinson, J. and Lumsdon, L. (2010) *Slow Travel and Tourism*. Earthscan, London, UK.
Fullagar, S., Markwell, K. and Wilson, E. (eds) *Slow Tourism; Experiences and Mobilities*. Channel View, Bristol, UK.
www.Slowfood.com
www.cittaslow.org
www.slowtrav.com
www.thewayofslowtravel.com/
www.idler.co.uk/
www.bradtguides.com/series/slow-travel-guides
www.inntravel.co.uk/
www.slow-tourism.net
www.slowjapan.wordpress.com/

References

Axt, P. and Axt-Gadermann, M. (2005) *The Joy of Laziness; How to Slow Down and Live Longer*. Bloomsbury, London, UK.
Caffyn, A. (2009) The slow route to new markets. *Tourism Insights* September 2009, VisitBritain, London. Available at: http://www.cabdirect.org/abstracts/20103307661.html; jsessionid=49AC41399C52C7AE3FC1801C58AF4F7A (accessed 27 July 2015).

Caffyn, A. (2012) Advocating and implementing slow tourism. *Tourism Recreation Research* 37, 77–80.

Conway, D. and Timms, B.F. (2010) Rebranding alternative tourism in the Caribbean: the case for slow tourism. *Tourism and Hospitality Research* 10, 329–344.

Conway, D. and Timms, B.F. (2012) Are slow travel and slow tourism misfits, compadres or different genres? *Tourism Recreation Research* 37, 71–76.

de la Barre, S. (2012) Travellin' around *on Yukon time* in Canada's north. In: Fullagar, S., Markwell, K. and Wilson, E. (eds) *Slow Tourism; Experiences and Mobilities*. Channel View, Bristol, UK.

Dickinson, J. and Lumsdon, L. (2010) *Slow Travel and Tourism*. Earthscan, London, UK.

Dickinson, J.E., Robbins, D. and Lumsdon, L. (2010) Holiday travel discourses and climate change. *Journal of Transport Geography* 18, 482–489.

Fallon, J. (2012) 'If you're making waves then you have to slow down': slow tourism and canals. In: Fullagar, S., Markwell, K. and Wilson, E. (eds) *Slow Tourism; Experiences and Mobilities*. Channel View, Bristol, UK.

Gardner, N. (2009) A manifesto for slow travel. *Hidden Europe* 25, 10–14.

Groenendaal, E. (2012) Slow tourism initiatives; an exploratory study of Dutch lifestyles entrepreneurs in France. In: Fullagar, S., Markwell, K. and Wilson, E. (eds) *Slow Tourism; Experiences and Mobilities*. Channel View, Bristol, UK.

Harris, M. (2014) *The End of Absence; Reclaiming What We've Lost in a World of Constant Connection*. Penguin, New York, USA.

Hodgkinson, T. (2012) Introduction to Kieran, D. *The Idle Traveller*. AA Publishing, Basingstoke, UK.

Honoré, C. (2004) *In Praise of Slow*. Orion, London, UK.

Howard, C. (2012) Speeding up and slowing down: pilgrimage and slow travel through time. In: Fullagar, S., Markwell, K. and Wilson, E. (eds) *Slow Tourism; Experiences and Mobilities*. Channel View, Bristol, UK.

Kieran, D. (2012) *The Idle Traveller; the Art of Slow Travel*. AA Publishing, Basingstoke, UK.

Lipman, M.B. and Murphy, L. (2012) 'Make haste slowly': environmental sustainability and willing workers on organic farms. In: Fullagar, S., Markwell, K. and Wilson, E. (eds) *Slow Tourism; Experiences and Mobilities*. Channel View, Bristol, UK.

Locke, T. (2011) *Slow Sussex and South Downs National Park*. Bradt, Chalfont St Peter, UK.

Lumsdon, L. (2011) *A Guide to Slow Travel in the Marches*. Logaston Press, Herefordshire, UK.

Lumsdon, L. and McGrath, P. (2010) Developing a conceptual framework for slow travel: a grounded theory approach. In *Journal of Sustainable Tourism* 19, 265–279.

Markwell, K., Fullager, S. and Wilson, E. (2012) Reflecting upon slow travel and tourism experiences. In: Fullagar, S., Markwell, K. and Wilson, E. (eds) *Slow Tourism; Experiences and Mobilities*. Channel View, Bristol, UK.

Matos, R. (2004) Can slow tourism bring new life to alpine regions? In: Weiermair, K. and Mathies, C. (eds) *The Tourism and Leisure Industry: Shaping the Future*. Haworth Press, Binghampton, New York, USA.

Moss, S. (2012) *Natural Childhood*. National Trust, Swindon, UK.

Murayama, M. and Parker, G. (2012) 'Fast Japan, Slow Japan': shifting to slow tourism as a rural regeneration tool in Japan. In: Fullagar, S., Markwell, K. and Wilson, E. (eds) *Slow Tourism; Experiences and Mobilities*. Channel View, Bristol, UK.

Nitti, G. (2013) Slow tourism: the new frontier of the conscious traveller. *The Italian Insider* 23 November. Available at: www.italianinsider.it/?q=node/1910 (accessed 25 October 2017).

Parkins, W. and Craig, G. (2006) *Slow Living*. Berg, Oxford, UK.

Sawday, A. and McKenzie, G. (2008) *Go Slow England*. Sawday Publishing, Bristol, UK.

Sawday, A. and King, J. (2009) *Go Slow Italy*. Sawday Publishing, Bristol, UK.

Sawday, A. and Cooke Yarborough, A. (2010) *Go Slow France*. Sawday Publishing, Bristol, UK.

Wearing, S. Wearing, M. and McDonald, M. (2012) Slow'n down the town to let nature grow: ecotourism, social justice and sustainability. In: Fullagar, S., Markwell, K. and Wilson, E. (eds) *Slow Tourism; Experiences and Mobilities*. Channel View, Bristol, UK.

Woehler, K. (2004) The rediscovery of slowness, or leisure time as one's own and as self-aggrandizement? In: Weiermair, K. and Mathies, C. (eds) *The Tourism and Leisure Industry: Shaping the Future*. Haworth Press, Binghampton, New York, USA.

Yurtseven, H.R. and Kaya, O. (2011) Slow tourists: a comparative research based on Cittaslow principles. *American International Journal of Contemporary Research* 1, 91–95.

Zago, M. (2011) Guidelines for the slow tourism. *Italia Slovenia Programme*, Trieste, Italy.

17 Conclusion

SHEELA AGARWAL, GRAHAM BUSBY AND RONG HUANG

Introduction

As the well known Maslow's Hierarchy of Needs model (1943) suggests, once the essential requirements of existence are met, individuals go in search of self-actualisation. For many, this involves participation in the experience economy as tourists seek to co-create and suppliers co-produce memorable, individualised, focused activity and interest based tourism moments, or in other words special interest tourism (SIT). As one of the most dynamic and creative segments of tourism, special interest tourists shy away from mass-produced products and instead seek exciting and authentic experiences. Indeed, this edited volume provides plentiful examples of such participation, involving a stay away from home for more than 24 hours and enjoyment of some forms of special interest. Consequently, SIT as an area of academic inquiry is concerned with the features and characteristics of tourist demand and in particular the categorisation of tourist types according to specific motivations and behaviour, and their consumption of uniquely differentiated tourism products and experiences.

In terms of origin and evolution, then, SIT has developed as a result of both increased leisure time and disposable incomes. This edited text again details plentiful examples of the growth and development of different interest based forms of tourism. It is clear that SIT will have different impacts, marketing challenges and contributions to destination development as it evolves over time (Ali-Knight, 2011). Moreover it provides some insights into how they may evolve in the future, with each being impacted differentially by a range of social, economic, political and environmental drivers within the contexts that they occur. What should not be forgotten is that technology also plays a part, whether it relates to improvements in bicycle design affecting cycle tourism or better lenses for binoculars for wildlife tourism. Additionally, there is also the increase in awareness of available activities resulting from social media, besides television. Indeed, it is argued that broadcast media has made many activities that might once have appeared specialist much more accessible, if not yet mainstream. The rise of special interest tourism parallels the growth of the experience economy and it is technology, in many cases, that permits customisation for the individual. Augmented Reality (AR) and Virtual Reality (VR) are recent applications of technology, yet other forms have had a significant influence.

The complexities of defining special interest tourism also can be seen from the chapters in this book; some activities will not appear as 'special' as others and there is no doubt that greater participation, axiomatically, encourages perceptions of a mass leisure market rather than a niche one. Furthermore this textbook provides examples of how several approaches may be operationalised to conceptualise and understand SIT, with product- and market-based underpinnings being the most prevalent. Additionally, this textbook provides numerous illustrations of the SIT market and the many types of SIT consumers which exist. With this comes enhanced knowledge of the challenges destinations face combined with a greater understanding of niche tourist behaviour which can aid the industry in positioning and targeting their products.

The purpose of this concluding chapter is to provide a succinct summary of the book's chapters, and to highlight some further observations associated with the origins and evolution of SIT, the complexities of defining SIT, and the markets and types of SIT which exist. Thus, in the first part of this chapter, a detailed chapter overview is provided along with insights into future developments. This is followed in the second part by consideration of how the SIT market might evolve in the future. Given that many special interest tourists are concerned about the potential consequences of their consumption decisions for host environments and communities (see Chapter 1), particular attention is drawn to the notion of ethical consumption in framing future product and marketing developments from both consumer and supplier perspectives.

Chapter Overview and Future Developments

Chapter 1 provides a very detailed overview of the key concepts and theoretical approaches to the study of SIT. In particular, it refers to earlier notions of SIT and draws the example of cultural tourism to demonstrate how a form of SIT may evolve over time to become a product that is perhaps now more associated with mainstream mass tourism. On reflection however, it is possible to view this particular activity as still being a SIT form although, interestingly, and as with other forms, one which has become segmented. This is primarily because cultural tourism has been conceptually categorised by both product and person; in the former scenario, there is tourism based around traditional dance, for example, resulting in notions of intangible cultural heritage (ICH), whereas, from the person perspective, possession of personal cultural capital can also be seen to influence forms of special interest tourism. In the case of visitors to Newstead Abbey, for example, because of the strong connection with the poet Byron, they tend to be educated to a higher level, as Chapter 6 (Literary Tourism) indicated.

A particular drive that is perhaps contributing to the super-segmentation of SIT generally is the cult of celebrity worship, or at least fashion, which is much more apparent now than it was fifty years ago. This is manifest in tourism terms by those who visit film or television locations as Chapter 8

showed. Furthermore, it may not be the location *per se* that is important. Instead, it may be the fact that the individual has put their imprimatur on a destination; this is particularly the case with locations in Turkey associated with Kıvanç Tatlıtuğ (Busby *et al.*, 2013). In essence, the super-segmentation of SIT is best viewed as a consequence of post-Fordist tourism consumption, involving the creation of more individual, specialised niche markets (see Table 17.1). According to Poon (1993) and Urry (1995), tourists have more control created through heightened purchasing power, resulting in the co-creation and co-production of special interest forms of tourism defined by tourists' tastes and preferences. The nature of such demand is likely to remain critically important in the future as the power of consumerism becomes more entrenched.

Following Chapter 1's introduction to SIT, the first part of this textbook is structured around 'family and faith', and it is in this context that the second chapter is couched, addressing a specific form of SIT, this being social tourism. In particular, it illustrates how the origins of the concept evolved from different backgrounds. Social tourism is about the provision of tourism for those on lower incomes or with disabilities; as Minnaert *et al.* (2009) point out, there is an added moral value with this form of tourism because there is the distinct aim of benefit to the visitor or host. Minnaert's chapter identifies how social tourism has evolved from the golden years which spanned three decades 1950–1980, when it was in its heyday, to a period of transformation in the last three decades, when social tourism is seen as a right for all, according to the European Economic and Social Committee

Table 17.1. Characteristics of post-Fordist tourism consumption. (Source: adapted from Urry (1995), p. 151)

Characteristics of post-Fordist consumption	Characteristics of special interest tourism
Consumers seek value creation through co-creation and co-production	Increasing demand for diversity of tailor-made, personalised experiences
Increased market segmentation	Emergence of a huge array of different forms of special interest tourism around interests and activity preferences
Growth of a consumers' purchasing power	Social media, and in particular user-generated have revolutionised the ways in which tourists make purchasing decisions.
Development of many new products, each of which has a shorter life	Tourists' preferences and desires drive the demand and supply of tourism, heavily influenced by changes in fashion
Increased preferences expressed for non-mass forms of production/consumption	Growth of the special interest tourist market
Consumption as less and less 'functional' and increasingly aestheticised	The super-segmentation of interest-based and activity-focused preferences into de-differentiated forms of special interest tourism

(Campos and Avila, 2006). Social tourism overlaps with other forms of SIT, not least community-based, thereby demonstrating some of the complexities of defining SIT. Moreover, by definition, there is also a link with the next form of SIT to be summarised, this being family tourism.

Here, in Chapter 3, it is demonstrated that, axiomatically, there is a parallel in its development with changes in society at large. In the United Kingdom, entrepreneurs such as Billy Butlin and Fred Pontin catered for the family market by establishing holiday camps in the 1930s. As the cost of overseas holidays fell, in real terms, family tourism switched from being predominantly a domestic product to much more of an international one. Alongside this, the development of VFR (Visiting Friends and Relatives) can be seen as one category of family tourism which has emerged more recently. As the chapter illustrates, a range of demographic factors are important in the context of family tourism, and some may influence interaction with other forms of SIT. For example, children are influential in the holiday decision-making process and this can lead to the motivation and demand to see film-induced locations, such as those used in the making of the Harry Potter movies or those featured on children's television (Connell and Meyer, 2009).

Following the 'family and faith' theme, the fourth chapter focuses on cathedral tourism. It demonstrates how the motivations underpinning this form of tourism have evolved over time from once being just a religious activity, to today, whereby tourists are motivated by a wish to see cultural elements and high-quality architecture. A good illustration of such a phenomenon is the attraction of Barcelona's Sagrada Familia or St Peter's Basilica in Rome. Other motivations include the wish to see sites associated with historic and cultural figures such as Jane Austen's tomb at Winchester Cathedral. The evolution of this form of SIT is also demonstrated by one aspect of popular culture, namely links to Harry Potter and, thereby, film-induced tourism for Gloucester Cathedral, featured in the films, and tourists are motivated to visit by this (Busby and George, 2004). Importantly, the ecclesiastical built heritage may be a key destination component, being the primary motivation for the visit or a subsidiary one (Busby, 2002, 2004). Indeed, by definition, cathedrals attract greater numbers of tourists than churches. In the 21st century, the marketing of this form of tourism is significant; cathedrals require large amounts of finance in order to maintain their fabric and that means enticing visitors.

Chapter 5, Islamic tourism, emphasises the symbolic relationship between tourism and Islam in terms of the influence of religion upon tourism development and the decision to travel to religiously and culturally significant destinations. Although the relationship between religion and tourism is well established and has been considered in many secular and non-secular contexts, there are a range of definitions of Islamic tourism given including various references to Muslims as participators, Islamic countries as tourist locations, activities with cultural, economic and religious dimensions, products consumed, and service encounter management (Duman, 2011). The author, Ali, explores how Islamic ways of life, Islamic identity, safety and security influence this form of special interest tourism to develop in Muslim and non-Muslim countries. The author argues that marketing Islamic tourism and terrorism might impact tourist behaviour and experience in Islamic destinations, and future development of Islamic tourism.

The second part of this textbook focuses on the 'performing arts' and thus Chapter 6, literary tourism, details its origins as a form of SIT, which in the UK, can be traced back three hundred years, evidenced by small numbers of visitors to Shakespeare's Stratford-upon-Avon. Today, literary tourism encompasses much more than locations associated with playwrights and authors of fiction; natural scientist Charles Darwin, author of 'The Origin of Species' wrote much at Down House in Kent and his study can be visited. However, the evolution of this form of tourism has been significantly bolstered by developments in technology, particularly the rise of the World Wide Web. As with other forms of SIT, its marketing is undertaken on small and large scales, the determinant usually being the amount of finance available.

Like literary tourism, the level of participation in music tourism (Chapter 7) is influenced by popular culture and overlaps with other forms of tourism such as film tourism (Chapter 8) and carnival tourism (Chapter 9). Watson discusses how the emergence of the Buena Vista Social Club stimulated cultural tourism to Cuba although it is the 1999 documentary film, of the same name, that brought awareness to a wider audience. Watson considers that for many participants, music tourism is a type of pilgrimage and clearly, there is overlap with dark tourism, if visiting the grave of a composer or artist, such as Jim Morrison, or religious tourism. The

S. Agarwal, G. Busby and R. Huang

practice is a sub-component of cultural tourism and in activities such as carnivals it is a form of intangible cultural heritage (ICH). In terms of destination marketing, music can represent a form of destination-based cultural capital (Busby and Meethan, 2008), from figures involved with high culture, such as Wagner and the museum at his home (Tribschen, near Lucerne), to Elvis Presley's home at Graceland (Memphis) which has been reviewed by Alderman (2002). Even destinations such as Sheffield have drawn on links with musicians, past and present, to encourage visitors (Long, 2014).

Chapter 8 explores film tourism in which Croy discusses the film tourism experience, something that has evolved over the last five decades. The movement of individuals to sites as a response to celluloid creations is certainly not new: *The Sound of Music* was released in 1965 and American visitor numbers to Austria doubled in the first few years after. More pertinently, the effect is ongoing for 'Even today, three out of four tourists still give this film – which is frequently shown on TV in the USA … as the main reason for their trip' (East and Luger, 2002, p. 230). In the evolution of this form of special interest, Croy points out that movie tours are participated in by both fans and non-fans – one of the various ways in which film tourists can be categorised. In terms of how this form will evolve, rapid technological development is argued to impact on film-induced tourism; individuals can already receive television via their PC but IPTV (internet protocol television) has led to a real convergence of the two technologies. For example, view *Captain Corelli's Mandolin*, then search the Internet Movie Database (IMDb) and Amazon websites for further information, amounting to over 200 reviews (Hudson and Ritchie, 2006). This has a range of implications for Destination Management Organisations' (DMO) marketing with some of them being clearly much more pro-active than others (Semley and Busby, 2014; Pike, 2016).

Turning to carnival tourism (Chapter 9), it can be seen that there are links with other forms of special interest reviewed in this book; significantly, there are connections with forms not featured in or as a specific chapter in this textbook, such as diaspora tourism. As the author Cuffy suggests, carnivals have evolved in a number of ways, from the celebration of identity to urban regeneration. The Notting Hill Carnival is outlined in detail and illustrates the economic importance, forming one component of the London destination mix. As with other forms of SIT, carnival tourism has been brought to a wider audience by way of social media marketing, undertaken both by DMOs and by private individuals. In fact, Cuffy points out that corporate sponsorship has taken over from creativity in some cases, thereby providing a good example of commodification.

It is at this juncture that this textbook shifts its attention away from the 'performing arts' and towards the theme of 'active' forms of SIT which frame section three of this textbook. Chapter 10 shows that golf tourism is a form of special interest that has fewer links with others despite having a long pedigree. In the United Kingdom, the origins of golf are associated with the Royal and Ancient Golf Club of St Andrews, founded on 14 May 1754 (http://www.randa.org/Heritage/The-Royal-Ancient/The-Royal-Ancient-Golf-Club, 2017) and the desire of overseas visitors to play in Scotland has driven golf tourism by 30 per cent in the last decade, such that it is worth £286 million a year (Bradley, 2017). As Humphreys indicates in this chapter, this special interest is a form of sport tourism and is three-dimensional in the sense that those interested individuals may travel to play, to watch or to participate in sports attractions. Internationally, golf tourism has increased dramatically in the last fifty years and is now a key part of the tourist offer for many destinations. Humphreys reflects on the New Zealand international golf tourism strategy and identifies the lack of world-class tournaments as a barrier to expansion. The marketing to address this includes familiarisation tours and online provision of information.

Adventure tourism (Chapter 11) encompasses a range of activities and the author, Buckley, identifies four major motivational categories, usually divided into external or internal psychological motivations for individuals. The cultural contexts for adventure tourism vary from one country to another with concomitant implications for clothing and supervision. The author also points out that emotional outcomes may be the most significant motivation for specialised tours and participants.

Having summarised the chapters falling within the theme 'active', the fourth part of this textbook concentrates on exploring forms of SIT which fall under the 'therapeutic and leisure' topic area. Chapter 12 on shopping tourism emphasises that travel and shopping activities are complementary and relate in several ways. These multiple relationships result in the existence of numerous complexities which make it difficult to define shopping tourism. However, this chapter also reinforces a clear need to differentiate shopping tourism from tourist shopping (Timothy, 2014). Timothy, the author, argues and explains that emerging trends influence the development of shopping tourism, including for example demand characteristics, retail as a branding mechanism, unconventional retail spaces, the importance of souvenirs, effects of globalisation, and shopping as a cultural experience. Additionally, he summarises several research gaps in knowledge, highlighting in particular that little is known about how nationality or cultural background affects the goods purchased and the choices of shopping destinations, post-trip information related to items bought on holiday, how places use retail in different ways to mark themselves as special or unique, where shopping becomes the competitive advantage over other vacation alternatives, and how globalisation and technological changes impact upon shopping tourism.

Chapter 13 provides a working definition of food tourism to address the origin and evolution of this form of SIT. As different types of food tourism proposed by academia reflect a wide range of interests in food, such typologies should be used as a starting point to segment food tourists (Robinson and Getz, 2014) and thus assist in the development of highly nuanced food promotion plans for destinations that are interested in promoting food tourism (Sánchez-Cañizares and López-Guzmán, 2011). The author, Huang, provides some insights into Chinese food and tourism development in mainland China. The regional diversity within food in China means that there is great marketing potential for food tourism in China, as evidenced by the recent success of the TV series 'A Bite of China'. Such a creative approach could be developed further so as to promote local food and culture and subsequently promote associated destinations. What has been shown to work in China could possibly be extended to other countries and regions which are looking to expand their tourism offerings and thus increase revenues from tourists without the requirement for large state investments in infrastructure (Chen and Huang, 2016).

Meanwhile, Chapter 14, on garden tourism, argues that it is a distinct sub-set of cultural tourism on the basis of garden history, garden motivations and locations. However the author is consciously aware of various perspectives for understanding special interest tourism and clearly puts forward his argument as to how garden tourism could be defined as a form of special interest tourism. Motivations of garden visitors in the UK, USA and Australia are closely analysed based on some key literature sources. The author, Benfield, gives his insights into marketing and garden tourism segments. Given that one of the 'mega-trends' that has significantly impacted the tourism system is the role and use of social media in tourists' decision making and in tourism operations and management (see Leung *et al.*, 2013), this chapter details how botanic gardens used or could use a range of social media tools to promote and manage the gardens and garden tourists. The author argues that the growth of garden tourism might easily be enabled by the linkage of social media and gardens and garden tourism is on the threshold of becoming a major component of 21st-century tourism.

Following this, this textbook shifts its focus away from 'therapeutic leisure' and towards the theme 'travelling along' which comprises the fifth and final part. Chapter 15, transport tourism, identifies two key roles for transport in SIT: transport as transit and transport as a leisure or a special interest activity. Because of such different understandings, transport tourism is defined and discussed separately. Between these sub-categories of transport tourism, the author shows a clear interest in transport as transit to the location of their special interest activity in the destination area. Where special interest activities take place in urban areas, these activities are more manageable; however when they take place at remote or rural locations, transporting tourists to these activities needs careful specialist planning due to potential significant environmental and social impacts. As far as the journey becomes the principle special interest activity such as in the cases of river cruise, ocean cruise and scenic train travel, less attention is received. However as tourists are eagerly searching for meaningful and memorable experiences (LCEEI, 2009), creativity in the provision of tourist experience is critical to their future development, as acknowledged in the extant tourism literature (Richards and Wilson, 2007; Richards, 2011).

Chapter 16, slow tourism, defines slow tourism by considering its background based upon three key dimensions (speed, time and distance). The author, Caffyn, agrees with Honoré's (2004) concept of slow – reinforcing the notion that it is about being slow when it matters, and consciously choosing the right speed for the situation. Closely examining the main factors involved in slow holidays from both the supply side – the types of slow holiday currently being developed and promoted – and from a demand perspective – the types of experiences which increasing numbers of peoples are seeking (Markwell *et al.*, 2012) – Caffyn questions whether slow tourism is a form of special interest tourism or instead represents a more fundamental potential shift for such experiences across the whole industry. She argues that the emphasis for slow tourism should be placed upon facilitating those people who care about environmental issues to choose slower holidays which benefit them and the local areas. In other words, slow tourists are perhaps better viewed as conscious travellers (Nittin, 2013) and there is much value in accepting that slow has much to offer and can be applied to a greater or lesser extent to many tourism contexts.

Selected chapters included in this textbook, such as slow tourism (and of course those that haven't appeared in this particular edited collection, including volunteer tourism, pro-poor tourism and wildlife tourism), appeal to those special interest tourists who are concerned about the potential consequences of their consumption decisions for host environments and communities and who desire to deliver a more sustainable form of tourism (see Chapter 1 for further details). Indeed ethical consumption is a term that is increasingly being used in wealthy capitalist nations around the world to describe an approach which highlights the broader implications of current consumption practices which largely involve unsustainable life-styles and over-consumption (Lewis, 2016). Such reference reflects the alleged rise of the ethical consumer, a finding revealed in research undertaken by Global Market Insite (2005) across 17 countries including the USA, Australia, Japan, China, India and various European countries, which found that 54% of online consumers would be prepared to pay more for organic, environmentally friendly or Fair Trade products. Furthermore, a survey of 1003 Americans published in *Time* magazine in 2009 demonstrated that 'nearly 40% said they purchased a product in 2009 because they liked the social or political values of the company that produced it' (Stengle, 2009, p. 24).

Ethical Consumers: the Future for SIT?

Ethical consumption is thus a term that now has mainstream appeal to describe a set of everyday decisions and practices of consumers relating to a wide range of concerns including for instance, child labour, working conditions, human rights abuses, carbon footprints, and environmental and social sustainability (Lewis, 2016). It marks the politicisation of life-style practices (Lewis, 2016) and has legitimised the pervasiveness of more radical forms of intervention into free market capitalism. In a tourism context, the prime example is the Fair Trade Federation and Fair Trade Tourism, which encompasses the antithesis of an individualist, consumer-driven approach as it links purchase behaviour from the global North to a broader global fair trade movement, and to the political and economic rights of destinations in the South.

As a consequence, SIT products designed to meet the needs and demands of ethical consumption and consumers are likely to become increasingly more important in the drive to create and capture new and untapped markets. It may also mean re-thinking, re-branding and the reconfiguration of traditional mass market products such as all-inclusive holidays known for their negative impacts on host economies, environments and communities, particularly if subject to negative modes of campaigning such as that advocated by Tourism Concern. This organisation has long since been running a high-profile public campaign which highlights the numerous serious issues being experienced by employees, local businesses, local economies, and which negatively impact on the tourist experience. These include the failure to recognise workers' rights to join a trade union, lack of training, being pressurised into working a considerable amount of unpaid overtime, and not earning a living wage (Tourism Concern, 2015). In addition, Tourism Concern (2015) state that a high dependency on tourism means power relations between local entrepreneurs, residents and international tour operators are hugely unequal citing several examples of its negative impacts. For instance, in Majorca, all-inclusive holidays are blamed for a loss of local business, whilst in Turkey, only 10% of tourist spend from all-inclusive holidays found its way into the regional economy, with even less reaching the immediate local area, and in the Dominican Republic, all-inclusive holidays are blamed for restaurant closures and increased negative local attitudes towards tourists (Tourism Concern, 2015).

Of course such political activism around consumerism is not a new phenomenon. Early examples include the US White Label Campaign of 1988 in which activists attached positive 'white' labels to the products of factories with good working conditions

(Lewis, 2016). Undoubtedly, the media have played a prominent role in focusing consumer attention on global environmental issues. For instance the film *An Inconvenient Truth* (2006) and 'Live Earth', a green entertainment spectacle, have highlighted the impacts and consequences of global warming. Meanwhile, critical commentaries of modern living and the 'affluenza' in wealthy developed nations (De Graaf *et al.*, 2005) portrayed within films such as *They Live* (1988), *Fight Club* (1999), *Super Size Me* (2004) and *Into the Wild* (2007) have incited anti-consumerism activism around over-consumption and corporate practices. Given the increasing popularity of ethical consumption, the marketing of SIT products is likely to focus on highlighting the benefits to the consumer of positive ethical purchase behaviour, or in other words, buying holidays and travel experiences that are associated with ethical characteristics. However, as recent experiences of three popular forms of ethically oriented SIT – backpacker, volunteer and slum tourism – demonstrate, often more harm than good is incurred.

Ethical consumption: backpacker tourism

In the case of backpacker tourism, traditionally, the governments of developing countries have ignored,

sometimes actively discouraged or even banned backpackers instead preferring to attract higher-value luxury tourists primarily because of the economic benefits it is assumed they bring. In the Maldives for example, up until recently backpackers have not been welcome and in Bhutan, they are prohibited. Despite the fact that backpackers can facilitate local development in numerous ways (Scheyvens, 2002; Kain and King, 2004; see Table 17.2) this special interest form of tourism can also have a number of extremely undesirable impacts.

First, even though one of the primary aims of backpacking is to seek the authentic, the majority of backpackers spend most of their time interacting with other backpackers (Cohen, 2003). Moreover, in an attempt to live off limited funds for an extended period of time, some become excessively concerned with bargain hunting and haggling, resulting in local people, desperate for a sale, accepting unreasonably low prices due to the poverty they live in (Goodwin *et al.*, 1998). Second, in the search for authentic experiences, backpackers are increasingly invasive (Scheyvens, 2002), behaviour reflected in Mowforth and Munt's (1998, p. 135) relabelling of such as 'ego-tourists'. Third, some backpackers have been accused of adopting socially inappropriate behaviour particularly in

Table 17.2. The ways in which backpacker tourism contributes to development. (Source: adapted from Scheyvens (2002) p. 152)

Economic development criteria	Non-economic development criteria
Spend more money than other tourists because of the longer duration of visit	Enterprises catering for backpackers are generally small and thus ownership and control is in local hands
Adventuresome nature and longer duration of visit means money spent is spread over a wider geographical area, including remote, economically depressed or isolated regions	Local people gain self-fulfilment through running own tourism enterprises rather than filling in menial positions in enterprises run by outside operators
Do not demand luxury therefore will spend more money on locally produced goods (such as food) and services (transport, homestay accommodation)	Because they operate their own businesses local people can form organisations which promote local tourism, giving the community power in upholding their interests and negotiating with outside bodies
Economic benefits can be spread widely within a community or even individuals with little capital or training can provide desired services or products. Formal qualifications are not needed to run small enterprises; skills can be learned on the job	The interest of backpackers in meeting and learning from local people can lead to a revitalisation of traditional culture, respect for the knowledge of elders, and pride in traditional aspects of one's culture
Basic infrastructure is required therefore ensuring low overhead costs and minimising the need for imported goods	Backpackers use fewer resources (like cold showers and fans rather than hot baths and air conditioning), therefore are kinder to the environment
Significant multiplier effects from drawing on local skills and resources	Local servicing of the tourism market challenges foreign domination of tourism enterprises

ghettos or backpacker enclaves such as those which exist in Khatmandu, Bangkok and Pushkar (Noronha, 1999). Fourth, some see backpacking as a variant of global tourism which reinforces the inequitable links between the West and the developing world and that this sort of development does not improve the lives of those living in these countries (Roxborough, 1979). Based on such characteristics, it is not surprising that some authors have questioned the right of backpackers to take the moral high ground when comparing their tourism experiences to those of conventional tourists (Scheyvens, 2002). Indeed Aziz (1999), commenting on backpackers in the Egyptian resort of Dahab, suggests that far from being a more sustainable and ethical form of tourism, backpacking has turned into another strand of mass institutionalised tourism, a contention reinforced by Westerhausen (2002), Welk (2004), and Ooi and Laing (2010). According to Scheyvens (2002, pp. 149–150), 'This backpacker culture includes particular forms of dress (tie-dyed T-shirts), music (rap and hip-hop) and behaviour (moving from coffee shop to coffee shop, consuming endless pancakes, pizzas and milkshakes, engaging in sexual liaisons and consuming drugs)'. It is clear from this evidence that some backpackers are engaging in a self-centred form of poverty tourism, with self-gratification and indulgence being the primary motivations.

Ethical consumption: volunteer tourism

Volunteer tourism or 'voluntourism' is another form of special interest tourism that is often viewed to incorporate ethical characteristics as tourists have altruistic motives for participating voluntarily in goodwill activities (Bussell and Forbes, 2002, p. 246). Indeed according to Wearing (2001, p. 1), volunteer tourists are those 'who for various reasons, volunteer in an organised way to undertake holidays that might involve aiding or alleviating the material poverty of some groups in society, the restoration of certain environments or research into aspects of society or environment'. Moreover Wearing (2001) contends that the volunteer experience offers an opportunity to examine the potential of travel to develop oneself. Given the importance of altruistic desires, volunteer tourism has thus also been linked to the serious leisure tourist (Stebbins, 1992; see Chapter 1).

Since the 1990s, volunteer tourism has grown relatively rapidly, into what is arguably now a mass niche market (Brown, 2005; Gray and Campbell, 2007; Herbutt, 2012; Lupoli et al., 2014; Bargeman et al., 2016). An estimated 1.6 million people worldwide participated annually in volunteer tourism in the 1990s, increasing more recently to 10 million. It is estimated that spending within this market sector is between £832 million and £1.3 billion per year (Wearing and McGehee, 2013; McGehee, 2014). One factor influencing such growth is the increased availability of opportunities to participate in a wide range of volunteer projects which seek to conserve landscapes or cultural heritage, which encourage economic development through the construction of new schools or health-centres, which involve working within the community, and which nurture social development through the teaching of language, reading and writing. Other factors are the variety of destinations, including developing countries, in which volunteer tourism may take place, and the range of target markets which exist, spanning professionals and those self-employed embarking on career breaks, senior travellers and school or university gap students. Additionally, the growth of volunteer tourism has also been aided significantly by the establishment of travel companies specialising in this form of tourism. Indeed, the commercialisation of this form of SIT is reflected by the existence of websites such as 'Go Abroad' which offer over 2000 volunteer programmes (GoAbroad.com, 2016).

Until relatively recently, volunteer tourism has widely been applauded for the benefits it can bring the developing world. This is because it encapsulates the notion of ethical consumption through the 'good will' (Sin, 2009, p. 480) and altruistic motivations of the participants, combined with the positive impacts it can potentially bring to local people in host destinations. These include poverty alleviation, environmental conservation, the generation of revenue within communities which would not normally profit from tourism, and more meaningful and beneficial tourist–host interaction (Corti et al., 2010; Bargeman et al., 2016). However, increasingly, the real value of volunteer tourism has been questioned as it has been linked with some possible negative impacts. For instance, given the immersion of volunteer tourists amongst the community, some have argued that it is socially and culturally invasive and may as a result instigate cultural changes through the demonstration effect (Guttentag, 2009; Richter and Norman, 2010; McGehee, 2012; Tuovinen, 2014). Furthermore, volunteer tourism may also be responsible for strengthening cultural differences between 'them' and 'us' (Guttentag, 2009; McGehee, 2012).

Additionally, some volunteer tourism neglects the desires of the local community for development, particularly if they conflict with environmental objectives of projects (Guttentag, 2009; McGehee, 2012), whilst the presence of volunteers may take jobs away from local people and disrupt local economies by promoting a cycle of dependency on overseas aid and charity (Simpson, 2004; McGehee, 2012). Moreover, given also that there are no requirements of specific skills sets, some volunteer tourism may also hinder work progress and result in unsatisfactory or inappropriate work being undertaken. In particular, attention has been drawn to the inappropriateness of volunteers working with children generally and in orphanages specifically. The volunteers who apply to work with the children from orphanages, schools or youth groups often do not have to have any training or experience in the education system. Yet, companies offering the volunteer experiences charge up to '£1500' for three weeks of teaching abroad (Projects Abroad, 2016).

Indeed, the dangers of sending untrained volunteers who repeatedly teach children the same thing at a low level, to work in schools and orphanages was highlighted in a 2011 UNICEF report. Other serious concerns regarding this specific form of volunteer tourism include the objectification of children in their own homes (Pitrelli, 2012; Reas, 2013) and the vulnerability of children to sexual abuse, malnutrition, poor hygiene and unsanitary and/or poor living conditions (Ruhfus and Haan, 2012; Tuovinen, 2014). Such occurs primarily because volunteer or facility background checks are not exercised and orphanages are unregulated (Guiney, 2012; Tuovinen, 2014; Carpenter, 2015a). In fact, Pitrelli (2012) and Ruhfus and Haan (2012) both suggest that some organisations are purposefully keeping children in poor conditions to encourage donations as a form of income generation. Furthermore, with the continuous in-flow and out-flow of volunteers, children, many of whom have already experienced abandonment, neglect and abuse, are prone to attachment disorders (Carpenter, 2015a), which can lead to problems in their social, psychological and physical development ultimately damaging their health and well-being in the future (Emond, 2009; Richter and Norman, 2010; Guiney, 2012). Evidence shows that after care in orphanages, young adults suffer with trafficking, drugs, homelessness and broken family ties (Tuovinen, 2014).

Although prevalent in many developing countries, Cambodia in particular has witnessed one of the largest 'booms' in orphanages and orphanage tourism (Carpenter, 2015b), with the former increasing by 75% since 2005 (UNICEF, 2011). However, although difficult to establish precisely due to a lack of data, studies suggest that between 70 and 90% of children in Cambodia's orphanages are not in fact orphans (UNICEF, 2011; Ruhfus and Haan, 2012; Tuovinen, 2014; Hartman, 2014; Lumos, 2016), and 70% of the orphanages have been opened by individuals without official registration (UNICEF, 2011). Volunteer tourism is the influential factor in this rapid increase, where institutions are growing faster than the rate of orphans (Hartman, 2014; Tuovinen, 2014). This rapid growth has led to concerns over the commodification of orphans (Conran, 2011; Reas, 2013; Carpenter, 2015a) and the exploitation of Cambodia's local culture where 'parents believe that by selling their children [...] they will get a better life' (Tuovinen, 2014, p. 38) in institutionalised care (Carpenter, 2015a, b; Friends-International, 2015). Buyers target fragile communities to find children to supply to orphanages in countries such as Cambodia, China and South Africa. According to Smolin (2007, p. 17), 'Birth parents accept a little food and cash, but are told some kind of inducing lie. Perhaps they are told that the child is only going to the orphanage for temporary care and can be retrieved at will'.

In light of these potential negative impacts, it is hardly surprising that the worthiness of this form of SIT has been questioned. Instead of grooming a generation of youths who are passionate about volunteer work, this form of tourism is perhaps instead catering for those who are passionate about travelling overseas. This situation is exacerbated when a volunteer project is organised by a private business that may be primarily interested in earning a profit and as the commercial segment of volunteer tourism grows, more and more communities who are supposedly benefiting from it, will be neglected. In response to concern around orphanage tourism, J.K. Rowling, author of the 'Harry Potter' book series established a foundation, Lumos, which is working towards aiding children 'worldwide to regain their right to a family life and to end the institutionalisation of children' (Lumos, 2016, no page). Reaching a million viewers during a Facebook live broadcast (Lumos, 2016), 60 thousand likes on Facebook (Facebook, 2016) and over 30 thousand shares on various news platforms (Oppenheim, 2016), issues concerning this mass

S. Agarwal, G. Busby and R. Huang

niche market (Reas, 2013; Burrai *et al.*, 2015) have reached a global audience. Of course, whilst many instances of volunteer tourism do very little to help the communities visited (Simpson, 2004; Lyons *et al.*, 2012; McGehee, 2014; Guiney and Mostafanezhad, 2015; Tourism Concern, 2016a) and exploit the good intentions of many volunteers (Tourism Concern, 2016b), not all volunteer organisations are bad (Tourism Concern, 2016a). Therefore it is imperative that information and advice regarding ethical volunteer tourism opportunities is provided, such as that which is provided by Tourism Concern.

Ethical consumption: slum tourism?

The ethics of consuming slum tourism, another form of SIT that is alleged to have sustainability as one of its core principles, have additionally been questioned (Freire-Medeiros, 2008; Ma, 2010). Slum tourism involves visiting impoverished areas or slums which according to the United Nations (2003), are generally understood to be heavily populated areas characterised by sub-standard housing and squalor. Whilst its origins may be traced back to the early 19th century, with Victorian tourists visiting the slums of Whitechapel and Shoreditch in London and Manhattan in New York, since the turn of the Millennium, it has become increasingly prominent in developing nations including India, Brazil, Kenya and Indonesia. Today, slum tours are sold as a more realistic form of experiencing a country and it is estimated that 40,000 tourists annually visit the favelas in Rio De Janeiro, Brazil and around 300,000 visit the townships in Cape Town, South Africa (Tourism Concern, 2014). In terms of who visits, an overwhelming majority of visitors to slum destinations are deemed 'curious, rich Westerners' (Freire-Medeiros, 2008, p. 584), with a study by Ma (2010) undertaken within Mumbai's Dharavi slum revealing that Americans and Australians with an average annual income of $100,000 made up the largest proportion of visitors.

Inevitably, this form of SIT is having a negative impact on the slum communities and their culture, and because of this the ethics of visiting these environments is hotly debated (Steinbrink *et al.*, 2012). A primary accusation against slum tourism is that it turns poverty into entertainment (Tourism Concern, 2014; Diekmann and Chowdhary, 2015), it is voyeuristic (Monroe and Bishop, 2016), and it represents a form of 'reality tourism' which can be experienced momentarily and then escaped from. As a result, local communities have become part of the tourist gaze transforming them into human zoos (Tourism Concern, 2014), thereby infringing their basic human rights to privacy and dignity. Indeed, Monroe and Bishop (2016) state that some companies run safari-style tours that allow tourists to stay on the bus but at the same time experience the living conditions of the slum. Moreover, slum tourism lacks consent as it does not involve collaboration with residents to 'shape the way in which the tourism activities are envisioned and carried out' (Whyte *et al.*, 2010, p. 5) and little consideration is given as to whether it conflicts or not with the residents' daily lives (Freitas, 2011).

The authenticity of the representations of slums provided by tour companies has also been criticised (Meschkank, 2010; Dyson, 2012; Steinbrink *et al.*, 2012). Many companies promise to provide an accurate, truthful account of reality (Tourism Concern, 2014), however, according to Cejas (2006, p. 225) 'tour operators, like television producers, can essentially write a script for tour guides on what is said – who is the hero, who is the villain, and what areas should be highlighted'. Some of the township tours in South Africa for instance capitalise on tourists seeking 'the African spectacle' whereby they include exotic and 'tribal' aspects that aren't necessarily authentic or traditional and this is sometimes done so that the tourists can experience the exotic tribes and poverty of Africa all in one place and on a tour (Monroe and Bishop, 2016).

Special Interest Tourists as Ethical Consumers: the Way Forward

What these examples demonstrate is the tendency for ethical consumption to be more celebrated than practised as clearly there is a divergence between the desire to be a green and ethical consumer and reality (Tallontire *et al.*, 2001). According to Arnold (2013), it's also important to remember that the ethical consumer can change their purchase behaviour, with factors such as the time of day, the context and recession influencing their decisions. As a result, tourists can be choosy about buying an ethical holiday or travel experience one minute and purchase those that are known to incur negative impacts such as all-inclusive holidays with no conscience, the next. It is therefore dangerous to place too much emphasis on individual ethical purchases as a panacea for over-consumption at the expense of ignoring the social responsibility of tourism businesses and corporations. Such inconsistent consumer behaviour can thus be explained by the multitude of personal, social and political factors underpinning the reasons why people make ethical choices (Arnold, 2013), and because of this complexity, a number of different types of green consumers have been identified.

Typologies of green consumers

One of the earliest typologies of green consumers was proposed by the Roper organisation for the consumer goods company Johnson and Son in 1990 which identified five key groups consisting of the 'true blue greens', the 'green back greens', 'sprouts', 'grousers' and 'apathetics' (see Table 17.3). Since then a plethora of green consumer typologies have been suggested, all of which are based upon a range of social, economic, demographic and psychological variables. Newholm (1999) for instance divides the behaviour of ethical consumers into three groups: distancers, integrators and rationalisers (see Table 17.4). Such research demonstrates that there are similarities and differences in the ways in which ethical consumers behave although it is important to note that whilst most tend to fall into one group type, an individual's behaviour may exhibit traits of all three categories depending upon the factors and circumstances influencing the ethical decision-making process. These typologies also highlight the fact that since not all ethical consumers are the same, by implication it is likely that they respond differently to the messages that are disseminated by ethical product providers (Arnold, 2013).

This contention is reinforced by a study of a Danish fair-trade business, Max Havelaar, and its marketing and communication by Langland (1998).

Table 17.3. Categories of green consumers. (Source: adapted from Peattie (1992))

Categories of green consumers

True blue greens: These are environmental leaders and activists and are more likely to do the green walk not just the green talk. This group represents almost one-third of the population. (Nearly half turn to environmental groups as their main source of green information.)

Green back greens: These busy people do not have time to be completely green and not likely to give up comfort and convenience for the environment, but willing to buy green products. Like offsetting, makes for easy green. This group represents 10% of the population. (Nearly half get information on green issues from newspapers.)

Sprouts: These are your environmental 'fence sitters' who buy green only if it meets their needs. This group represents just over one-quarter of the population. (One-third cite newspapers as their main source of green information.)

Grousers: Generally unmotivated, uninvolved and disinterested in green issues. They think individual behaviour cannot improve the environment, so why bother. This group represents 15% of the population. (Newspapers again serve as their major information source on green issues.)

Apathetics: Don't really care at all. Little concern for the environment so take little action and believe environmental indifference is the mainstream. This group represents about a fifth of the population. (TV programmes are their main source of environmental information.)

Table 17.4. Typology of green consumers. (Source: adapted from Newholm (1999))

Typology of green consumers

Distancers: aim to avoid consuming goods and services they consider unethical, sometimes to the extent of limiting their overall consumption. Involves life-style change, separating them from the bulk of consumer society. Some require considerable information to enable them to implement their holistic philosophy whilst for others minimising their consumption is sufficient.

Integrators: attempt to implement their ethical views in all aspects of their life from work, to consumer goods to financial products. Because they spend much time working and campaigning on these ethical issues they may have to limit their engagement in ethical consumption.

Rationalisers: Tend to act on their ethical values in certain limited ways, for example, consuming particular products with ethical attributes. They accept consumer society and enjoy its pleasures and conveniences. However, they believe they should act in those (few) cases where consumerism creates real problems.

S. Agarwal, G. Busby and R. Huang

It found that those who were more aware of fair-trade issues respond to messages highlighting the problems that the product and trading relationship seek to address (i.e. 'sick baby messages'). In contrast, those who are less aware of fair trade respond better to messages highlighting the positive impact of their purchase (e.g. 'well-baby messages'). Based on these differing responses and reactions, a plethora of green consumer typologies have been proposed. One example of such is proffered by Cone Communications and Echo Global (2013) which divides green consumers into four distinct profiles; each are motivated by slightly different ideals and respond to different types of communication. The four groups are:

1. **Old Guard:** this group usually comprises over 55-year-old male consumers who don't believe they play much of a role in solving social or environmental issues. Thus, they rarely buy green products and if they do it is primarily due to chance rather than by design. Producers and suppliers can reach this group by keeping ethical messages simple and traditional.

2. **Happy-Go-Lucky:** this category consists of consumers who are typically on the younger side (between 18 and 34 years old), and who are motivated by the desire to feel good about buying responsibly. Companies can reach this group by emphasising the benefits of responsible purchasing for both consumers and society.

3. **Bleeding Hearts:** this type usually comprise young, female consumers who go out of their way to buy responsibly so they can fulfil their goal of positively impacting society. Companies need to go beyond merely communicating their ethical practices in order to effectively reach and keep these consumers.

4. **Ringleaders:** are usually middle-aged men and women (typically over 35 years old), who go out of their way to not only buy responsibly themselves, but encourage others to do the same. Companies can reach this group by offering transparent and consistent information about their ethical practice, and by providing opportunities for these individuals to advocate on the companies' behalf.

Whilst this research is valuable in identifying different types and characteristics of ethical consumers, it also reveals that those who are willing to make considerable changes to their usual consumer habits in order to practice ethical behaviour are relatively small in number, and typically have low spending power (Arnold, 2013). This finding is reinforced by a European Commission study (2013) which showed that as educational level increases and by implication, income, the proportion of consumers who act on awareness and actually purchase fair-trade products also increases (Arnold, 2013). Moreover, ethical products, including SIT tend to be more expensive as a percentage of the price is set aside for development projects in the producer community as in the case of fair trade, or may be due to the higher costs of production or to the costs of certification (Tallontire et al., 2001). The costs therefore attached to ethical SIT may outweigh concerns about its impact on the environment and communities or affect consumers' willingness to pay a premium. However, clearly the extent to which this occurs depends on consumer perception of whether the experience bought is a luxury or whether it is considered to be essential (Tallontire et al., 2001).

Furthermore, often it is difficult for consumers to identify ethical products for a number of reasons, a difficulty which has obvious implications for the future marketing of SIT. This is because according to Tallontire et al. (2001, p. 23), 'not all consumers have access to the symbolic and economic resources required to shop virtuously'. Moreover, forms of SIT that are sold as being ethical may be subject to cleverly designed product packaging and marketing ploys that hide any unsustainable attributes or which camouflage the mass tourism nature of the product. They bring just as many tourists to a destination but are marketed in such a way that because it appeals to individual and more adventurous tourists, this type of holiday implies a more personalised service that is only possible with limited numbers of tourists (Mowforth and Munt, 2009). A good example here of course is wildlife tourism, specifically safari holidays in Kenya which are mass produced and marketed and yet often are sold on the basis of providing intimate and small group experiences (Mowforth and Munt, 2009). Another illustration occurs when special interest tourists are encouraged to buy local products or use public transport to help developing economies and communities. Yet SIT often involves international travel, and it is the airline component of travel which is the most polluting and harmful. Thus, SIT sold on an ethical basis is open to superficial platitudes of ethical consumption and manipulation which either encourages people to continue consuming while simply replacing less 'caring' products with others, or falsely leading them to believe they are behaving in an ethical manner.

Concluding Remarks

Overall, this chapter has sought to summarise the contribution of each form of SIT that has been outlined in this textbook and in doing so, has explored issues relating to its origins and evolution, definitional complexities, approaches to its conceptualisation, and its markets and types of special interest tourists. This chapter ends by taking a holistic perspective and considers the future of SIT in its entirety by exploring the implications of a shift towards ethical consumerism for SIT. What and who are ethical consumers, what is meant by ethical consumption, and the possibility of ever having a sustainable consumer culture in a market-driven society, are important questions that SIT companies wishing to project an ethical dimension to their business operations must grapple with. Understanding how consumers become aware of ethical issues in tourism and the ways in which they translate this into ethical purchase behaviour is critical for developing strategies for not only raising the awareness of consumers in general but also in encouraging the production of a generation of special interest tourists with a conscience.

References

Alderman, D. (2002) Writing on the Graceland wall: on the importance of authorship in pilgrimage landscapes, *Tourism Recreation Research* 27(2), 27–33.

Ali-Knight, J.M. (2011) *The Role of Niche Tourism Products in Destination Development*. Unpublished PhD by Published Works. Napier University, Edinburgh, UK.

Arnold, C. (2013) *Understanding the Different Types of Ethical Consumer*. Available at: http://www.creativeorchestra.com/insights/assets/understanding-the-different-types-of-ethical-consumer.pdf (accessed 24 April 2017).

Aziz, H. (1999) Whose culture is it anyway? *In Focus* (Spring), 31, 14–15.

Bargeman, B., Richards, G. and Govers, E. (2016) Volunteer tourism impacts in Ghana: a practice approach. *Current Issues in Tourism* 1–16, doi:10.1080/13683500.2015.1137277.

Bradley, J. (2017) Value of golf tourism to Scotland soars by thirty per cent, *The Scotsman*, 21 April, Available at: http://www.scotsman.com/business/companies/media-leisure/value-of-golf-tourism-to-scotland-soars-by-30-per-cent-1-4425244 (accessed 15 October 2017).

Brown, S. (2005) Travelling with a purpose: understanding the motives and benefits of volunteer vacationers. *Current Issues in Tourism* 8(6), 479–496.

Burrai, E., Font X. and Cochrane, J. (2015) Destination stakeholders' perceptions of volunteer tourism: an equity theory approach. *International Journal of Tourism Research* 17, 451–459.

Busby, G. (2002) The Cornish church heritage as destination component. *Tourism* 50(4), 371–381.

Busby, G. (2004) The contested Cornish church heritage. In: Payton, P. (ed.) *Cornish Studies Twelve*. University of Exeter Press, Exeter, UK, 166–183.

Busby, G. and George, J. (2004) *The Tailor of Gloucester: Potter meets Potter – literary tourism in a cathedral city, Conference Proceedings – Tourism and Literature,* Harrogate, UK, 22–26 July, ISBN 1843870853.

Busby, G.D. and Meethan, K. (2008) Cultural capital in Cornwall: heritage and the visitor. *Cornish Studies* 16(1), 146–166.

Busby, G., Ergul, M. and Eng, J. (2013) Film tourism and the lead actor: an exploratory study of the influence on destination image and branding. *Anatolia* 24(3), 395–404, DOI: 10.1080/13032917.2013.783874.

Bussell, H. and Forbes, D. (2002) Understanding the volunteer market: the what, where, who and why of volunteering. *International Journal of Nonprofit and Voluntary Sector Marketing* 7(3), 244–257.

Campos, J.L.M. and Avila, R.C. (2006) *The Social Economy in the European Union*. European Economic and Social Committee, International Centre of Research and Information on the Public, Social and Cooperative Economy, Brussels.

Carpenter, K. (2015a) Childhood studies and orphanage tourism in Cambodia'. *Annals of Tourism Research* 55(November), 15–27.

Carpenter, K. (2015b) Continuity, complexity and reciprocity in a Cambodian orphanage. *Children and Society* 29, 85–94.

Cejas, M. (2006) Tourism in shantytowns and slums: a new 'contact zone' in the era of globalization. *Intercultural Communication Studies* 15(3), 224–230.

Cohen, E. (2003) Backpacking: diversity and change. *Journal of Tourism and Cultural Change* 1(2), 95–110.

Chen, Q. and Huang, R. (2016) Understanding the importance of food tourism to Chongqing, China. *Journal of Vacation Marketing* 22(1), 42–54.

Cone Communications and Echo Global (2013) *Corporate Social Responsibility Study*. Cone Communications, Boston.

Connell, J. and Meyer, D. (2009) Balamory revisited: an evaluation of the screen tourism destination-tourist nexus. *Tourism Management* 30(2), 194–207.

Conran, M. (2011) They Really Love Me!: Intimacy in Volunteer Tourism. *Annals of Tourism Research* 38(4), 1454–73.

Corti, I.N., Marola, P.N. and Castro, M.B. (2010) Social inclusion and local development through European voluntourism: a case study of the project realized in a neighbourhood of Morocco. *American Journal of Economics and Business Administration* 2(3), 221–231.

S. Agarwal, G. Busby and R. Huang

De Graaf, J., Naylor, T.H. and Wann, D. (2005) *Affluenza: The All-Consuming Epidemic*. Berrett-Koehler, San Francisco, USA.

Diekmann, A. and Chowdhary, N. (2015) Slum dwellers perceptions of tourism in Dharavi, Mumbai. In: Diekmann, A. and Smith, M.K. (eds) *Ethnic and Minority Cultures as Tourism Attractions*. Channel View, Bristol, UK, pp. 113–136.

Duman, T. (2011) Value of Islamic Tourism Offering: Perspectives from the Turkish Experience (online), paper presented at the World Islamic Tourism Forum (WITF), Kuala Lumpur: Malaysia, 12-13 July. Available at:http://www.iais.org.my/e/attach/ppts/12-13JUL2011-WITF/ppts/Dr%20Teoman%20Duman.pdf (accessed 15 February 2015).

Dyson, P. (2012) Slum tourism: representing and interpreting 'reality' in Dharavi, Mumbai. *Tourism Geographies* 14(2), 254–274.

East, P. and Luger, K. (2002) Living in paradise: youth culture and tourism development in the mountains of Austria. In: Voase, R. (ed.) *Tourism in Western Europe – A Collection of Case Histories*. CAB International Publishing, Wallingford, UK, pp. 227–242.

Emond, R. (2009) I am all about the future world: Cambodian children's views on their status as orphans. *Children and Society* 23, 407–417.

Facebook (2016) Lumos Page. Available at: https://www.facebook.com/lumos.at.work/ (accessed 21 April 2017).

Freire-Medeiros, B. (2008) The favela and its touristic transits. *Geoforum* 40(2), 580–588.

Freitas, E. (2011) Slum Tourism. Available at: https://www.tourismconcern.org.uk/slum-tourism/ (accessed 15 October 2017).

Friends-International (2015) Think Child Safe. Available at: http://www.thinkchildsafe.org/thinkbeforevisiting/ (accessed 21 April 2017).

Global Market Insite (2005) GMI poll finds doing good is good for business. Available at: http://www.csrwire.com/press_releases/18938-GMI-Poll-Finds-Doing-Good-Is-Good-For-Business (accessed 24 April, 2017).

GoAbroad.com (2016) Volunteer Abroad for 1-2 Weeks. Available at: http://www.goabroad.com/volunteer-abroad/search/1-2-week/volunteer-abroad-1 (accessed 21 April 2017).

Goodwin, H., Kent, I., Parker, K. and Walpole, M. (1998) Tourism, conservation and sustainable development: case studies from Asia and Africa. *IIED Wildlife and Development Series* No. 12. International Institute for Environment and Development, London, UK.

Gray, N.J. and Campbell, L.M. (2007) A decommodified experience? Exploring aesthetic, economic and ethical values for volunteer ecotourism in Costa Rica. *Journal of Sustainable Tourism* 15(5), 463–482.

Guiney, T. (2012) 'Orphanage tourism' in Cambodia: when residential care centres become tourist attractions. *Pacific News* 38, 9–14.

Guiney, T. and Mostafanezhad, M. (2015) The political economy of orphanage tourism in Cambodia. *Tourist Studies* 15(2), 132–155.

Guttentag, D. (2009) The possible negative impacts of volunteer tourism. *International Journal of Tourism* 11(5), 537–551.

Hartman, E. (2014) Why UNICEF and Save the Children are Against Your Short-Term Service in Orphanages. Available at: http://globalsl.org/why-unicef-and-save-the-children-are-against-you-caring-for-orphans/ (accessed 21 April 2017).

Herbutt, T. (2012) *Volunteer Tourism: Challenges and Opportunities; Attitudes and Perception*, Master's Thesis, Technische Universität München, Germany.

Honoré, C. (2004) *In Praise of Slow*. Orion, London, UK.

Hudson, S. and Ritchie, J.R.B. (2006) Film tourism and destination marketing: the case of Captain Corelli's Mandolin. *Journal of Vacation Marketing* 12(3), 256–268.

Kain, D. and King, B. (2004) Destination-based product selections by international backpackers in Australia". In: Richards, G. and Wilson, J. (eds) *The Global Nomad: Backpacker Travel in Theory and Practice*. Channel View Publications, Clevedon, UK, pp. 196–216.

Langland, L. (1998) On communicating the complexity of a green message. Part 1: the Max Havelaar case. *Greener Management International*, Summer 1998.

LCEEI (2009) Handbook for experience stagers. In: Tarssanen, S. (ed.) *Lapland Centre of Expertise for the Experience Industry*. Rovaniemi, Finland.

Leung, D., Law, R., van Hoof, H. and Buhalis, D. (2013) Social media in tourism and hospitality: a literature review. *Journal of Travel and Tourism Marketing* 30(1–2), 3–22.

Lewis, T. (2016) Ethical consumers and sustainability citizenship. In: Horne, R., Fien, J., Beza, B. and Nelson, A. (eds) *Sustainability Citizenship in Cities: Theory and Practice*. Earthscan, London, UK.

Long, P. (2014) Popular music, psychogeography, place identity and tourism: the case of Sheffield. *Tourist Studies* 14(1), 48–65.

Lumos, J.K. (2016) Rowling Shines a Light on the Eight Million Forgotten Children in Orphanages in Global Facebook Live Broadcast. Available at: https://wearelumos.org/news/jk-rowling-shines-light-eight-million-forgotten-children-orphanages-global-facebook-live (accessed 21 April 2017).

Lupoli, C.A., Morse, W.C., Bailey, C. and Schelhas, J. (2014) Assessing the impacts of international volunteer tourism in host communities: a new approach to organizing and prioritizing indicators. *Journal of Sustainable Tourism* 22(6), 898–921.

Lyons, K., Hanley, J., Wearing, S. and Neil, J. (2012) Gap year volunteer tourism: myths of global citizenship? *Annals of Tourism Research* 39(1), 361–378.

Ma, B. (2010) A trip into the controversy: a study of slum tourism travel motivations. *Penn Humanities Forum* on Connections. University of Pennsylvania Scholarly Commons, pp. 1–51.

Markwell, K., Fullager, S. and Wilson, E. (2012) Reflecting upon slow travel and tourism experiences. In: Fullagar, S., Markwell, K. and Wilson, E. (eds) *Slow Tourism; Experiences and Mobilities*. Channel View, Clevedon, UK.

Maslow, A. (1943) A theory of human motivation. *Psychological Review* 50(4), 370–396.

McGehee, N.G. (2012) Oppression, emancipation, and volunteer tourism. *Annals of Tourism Research* 39(1), 84–107.

McGehee, N.G. (2014) Volunteer tourism: evolution, issues and futures. *Journal of Sustainable Tourism* 22(6), 847–854.

Meschkank, J. (2010) 'Investigations into slum tourism in Mumbai: poverty tourism and the tensions between different constructions of reality. *GeoJournal* 76(1), 47–62.

Minnaert, L., Maitland, R. and Miller, G. (2009) Tourism and social policy. *Annals of Tourism Research* 36(2), 316–334.

Monroe, E. and Bishop, P. (2016) Slum tourism: helping to fight poverty...or voyeuristic exploitation. *Tourism Concern Research Briefing*. Available at: https://www.tourismconcern.org.uk/wp-content/uploads/2016/02/Slum-Tourism-Report-print-web.pdf (accessed 24 April 2017).

Mowforth, M. and Munt, I. (1998) *Tourism and Sustainability: New Tourism in the Third World,* First Edition. Routledge, London.

Mowforth, M. and Munt, I. (2009) *Tourism and Sustainability: New Tourism in the Third World*, Third Edition. Routledge, London, UK.

Newholm, T. (1999) *Considering the Ethical Consumer and Summing Up the Case Studies*. PhD thesis. Open University, UK.

Nittin, G. (2013) Slow tourism: the new frontier of the conscious traveller. *The Italian Insider* 23 November.

Noronha, F. (1999) Culture shocks. *In Focus* (Spring), 4–5.

Ooi, N. and Laing, J.H. (2010) Backpacker tourism: sustainable and purposeful? Investigating the overlap between backpacker tourism and volunteer tourism motivations. *Journal of Sustainable Tourism* 18(2), 191–206.

Oppenheim, M. (2016) JK Rowling condemns 'voluntourism' and highlights dangers of volunteering in orphanages overseas. *Independent* (23 August 2016). Available at: http://www.independent.co.uk/news/people/jk-rowling-twitter-voluntourism-volunteering-in-orphanages-risks-a7204801.html (accessed 21 April 2017).

Peattie, K. (1992) *Green Marketing*. The M&E Handbook Series. Pitman Publishing, London, UK.

Pike, S. (2016) *Destination Marketing – Essentials*, 2nd edn. Routledge, Abingdon, UK.

Pitrelli, M. (2012) Orphanage tourism: help or hindrance? Monica Pitrelli investigates the impact of tourists visiting orphanages in Cambodia. *The Telegraph*, 3 February 2012. Available at: http://www.telegraph.co.uk/expat/expatlife/9055213/Orphanage-tourism-help-or-hindrance.html (accessed 21 April 2017).

Poon, A. (1993) *Tourism, Technology and Competitive Strategies*. CAB International, Wallingford, UK.

Projects Abroad (2016) Volunteer abroad, gap years and Internships with projects abroad. Available at: http://www.projectsabroad.co.uk/?utm_source=bing&utm_medium=cpc&utm_campaign=UK_Generics%3EVolunteer%20Abroad&utm_term=volunteer%20tourism&utm_content=Voluntourism%3EExact (accessed 21 April 2017).

Reas, P.J. (2013) Boy, have we got a vacation for you: orphan tourism in Cambodia and the commodification and objectification of the orphan child. *Thammasat Review* 16, 121–140.

Richards, G. (2011) Creativity and tourism: the state of the art. *Annals of Tourism Research* 38(4), 1225–1253.

Richards, G. and Wilson, J. (2007) *Tourism, Creativity and Development*. Routledge, London, UK.

Richter, L.M. and Norman, A. (2010) AIDS orphan tourism: a threat to young children in residential care. *Vulnerable Children and Youth Studies* 5(3), 217–229.

Robinson, R.N.S. and Getz, D. (2014) Profiling potential food tourists: and Australian study. *British Food Journal* 116(4), 690–706.

Roxborough, T. (1979) *Theories of Underdevelopment*. Macmillan, London, UK.

Ruhfus, J. and Haan, M. (2012) Cambodia's Orphan Business. Available at: http://www.aljazeera.com/programmes/peopleandpower/2012/05/201252243030438171.html (accessed 21 April 2017).

Sánchez-Cañizares, S.M. and López-Guzmán, T. (2011) Gastronomy as a tourism resource: profile of the culinary tourist. *Current Issues in Tourism* 15(3), 229–245.

Scheyvens, R. (2002) Backpacker tourism and third world development. *Annals of Tourism Research* 29(1), 144–164.

Semley, N. and Busby, G. (2014) Film tourism: the pre-production perspective. a case study of VisitSomerset and the Hollywood story of Glastonbury. *Journal of Tourism Consumption and Practice* 6(2), 23–53.

Simpson, K. (2004) Doing development: the gap year, volunteer-tourists and a popular practice of development. *Journal of International Development* 16(5), 681–692.

Sin, H.L. (2009) Volunteer tourism – involve me and I will learn? *Annals of Tourism Research* 36(3), 480–501.

Smolin, D.M. (2007) Child laundering as exploitation: applying anti-trafficking norms to intercountry adoption under the coming Hague regime. *Vermont Law Review* 32(1), 1–55.

Stebbins, R. (1992) *Amateurs, Professionals, and Serious Leisure*. McGill-Queen's University Press, Montreal, Canada.

Steinbrink, M., Frenzel, F. and Koens, K. (2012) Development and globalization of a new trend in tourism. In: Frenzel, F., Koens, K. and Steinbrink, M. (eds) *Slum Tourism Poverty, Power and Ethics*. Routledge, London, UK, pp. 1–18.

Stengle, R. (2009) The responsibility revolution. *Time* 174, 24–27.

Tallontire, A., Rentsendorj, E. and Blowfield, M. (2001) *Ethical Consumers and Ethical Trade: A Review of Current Literature. (Policy Series Number 12)*. Natural Resources Institute, University of Greenwich, London, UK.

Timothy, D.J. (2014) Trends in tourism, shopping, and retailing. In: Lew, A.A., Hall, C.M. and Williams, A.M. (eds) *The Wiley Blackwell Companion to Tourism*. Wiley Blackwell, Oxford, UK, pp. 378–388.

Tourism Concern (2014) *Slum Tourism*. Available at: https://www.tourismconcern.org.uk/slum-tourism/ (accessed 21 April 2017).

Tourism Concern (2015) *The Perceived impact of All-Inclusive Package Holidays on Host Destinations*. Tourism Concern, London.

Tourism Concern (2016a) *The Child-Centred Model of International Volunteering*. Tourism Concern. Available at: https://www.tourismconcern.org.uk/the-child-centred-model-of-international-volunteering/ (accessed 21 April 2017).

Tourism Concern (2016b) *Child Rights Impacts in Travel and Tourism*. Available at: https://www.tourismconcern.org.uk/child-rights-impacts-in-travel-and-tourism/ (accessed 21 April 2017).

Tuovinen, H. (2014) *Shadows of Voluntourism and the Connection to Orphanage Business in Asia and Cambodia*. Experience and Wellness Management Thesis, Haaga-Helia, University of Applied Sciences, Helsinki, Finland.

UNICEF (2011) With the best intentions. A study of attitudes towards residential care in Cambodia. UNICEF, Phnom Penh, Cambodia.

UN (United Nations) (2003) *The Challenge of Slums: Global Report on Human Settlements*. Earthscan, London, UK.

Urry, J. (1995) *Consuming Places*. Routledge, London, UK.

Wearing, S. (2001) *Volunteer Tourism: Experiences That Make a Difference*. CAB International, Wallingford, UK.

Wearing, S. and McGehee, N.G. (2013) Volunteer tourism: a review. *Tourism Management* 38, 120–130.

Welk, P. (2004) "The beaten track: Anti-tourism as an element of backpacker identity construction". In: Richards, G. and Wilson, J. (eds) *The Global Nomad: Backpacker Travel in Theory and Practice*. Channel View Publications, Clevedon, UK, pp. 77–91.

Westerhausen, K. (2002) *Beyond the Beach: An Ethnography of Modern Travellers in Asia*. White Lotus, Bangkok, Thailand.

Whyte, K., Selinger, E. and Outterson, K. (2010) Poverty tourism and the problem of consent. *Journal of Global Ethics*, 7 (3), pp. 337–348

www.randa.org (2017) Available at: http://www.randa.org/Heritage/The-Royal-Ancient/The-Royal-Ancient-Golf-Club (accessed 20 April 2017).

Index

Page numbers in **bold** type refer to figures, tables and boxed text.

voluntary sector
    social tourism provision 23, 33
    volunteer tourism development 203–205
    volunteering travellers 186
voucher schemes, holiday 23, **24**

walking holidays 184, 191, 192
weather, disruption of events 174, **174**
well-being 185, 191
Westminster Abbey, London 41, 43, 63
Whitby, Yorkshire 67
White Label campaign (US) 201–202
wildlife tourism 123, **125**, **189**, 207
window-shopping 137

workers
    issues raised by Tourism Concern 201
    rights to paid holidays 20
    seasonal, for peak holiday periods **36**
World Bank, social capital definition
        32, 169
World Food Travel Association (WFTA) 153
WWOOFing 186

youth tourism 78, **79**
YouTube 167

Ziarat (visits to Islamic holy sites) 52, 57